59552

Published by Charles E. Merrill Publishing Company
A Bell & Howell Company
Columbus, Ohio 43216
Cover Designer: Cathy Watterson
Production Coordinator: Molly Kyle

PHOTO CREDITS: Cover—top, Herbann, Inc.; bottom, Jean Greenwald. Pages xii, 76, 134, 147, 157, 187, 397—Strix Pix; pages 32, 302, 331, 360—Jean Greenwald; page 45 —© Harvey R. Phillips/Phillips Photo Illustrators; pages 73, 235, 318—© C. Quinlan; page 110—Rohn Engh; page 193, Heather Nelson; page 314—Paul Conklin.

Library of Congress Catalog Number: 84-71914
International Standard Book Number: 0-675-20131-4
Printed in the United States of America
1   2   3   4   5 --- 90 89 88 87 86 85

Teaching Gifted Children and Adolescents

Raymond H. Swassing
The Ohio State University

Charles E. Merrill Publishing Company
A Bell & Howell Company
Columbus   Toronto   London   Sydney

To Bob

Preface

The purpose of this textbook is to facilitate learning for a special and valuable population—our gifted and talented children. The emphasis is on content, the "what" rather than the "how," although we also describe methods that are appropriate for enhancing these children's education. We stress content because gifted and talented children have abilities that demand more knowledge than that usually offered in standard graded courses and commercial textbooks.

When we study gifted education, we must address not isolated aspects of giftedness but the interactions of a variety of elements that combine into giftedness, as well as the foundations of today's practice, and current theories and processes.

Part One, therefore, concerns the background we need for educating gifted and talented children. Chapter 1 summarizes key issues and provides a historical perspective; Chapter 2 concerns identification, assessment, and programming. In Chapter 3 we examine the social and emotional growth of gifted children and adolescents, and in Chapter 4 we address the preschool years.

Part Two covers four major content areas: mathematics, science, social studies, and language arts, including reading and writing. Each chapter emphasizes the essential concepts of its content area and describes how to differentiate for the gifted with examples of instructional strategies and adaptation of materials.

In Part Three, we deal with educational considerations that must be integrated into kindergarten through secondary school experiences—the use of computers, career development, and creativity. Chapter 12 discusses critical issues in administration, implementation, and evaluation.

The contributors to this text have demonstrated expertise in their areas as well as an understanding of education for the gifted and talented. I thank them for their participation, along with all the others who have helped me complete this project. I have had many respected mentors; W. B. Barbe and T. M. Stephens are among those who have been instrumental in this project. Thanks are due to Marianne Taflinger for initiating the project and to Vicki Knight for her persistence in seeing it to conclusion. I also wish to thank the reviewers—Carol Takacs, Cleveland State University; Jo Breiter, Iowa State University; C. June Maker, University of Arizona; Kenneth Seeley, University of Denver; Margaret Carmean, Mississippi College; Carolyn Callahan, University of Virginia; and Tom Lough, Piedmont Community College and editor for *The National Logo Exchange*—for their interest in the profession as well as in this particular project. I appreciate, as well, those authors and editors who have given permission to reproduce their material. To Cabrini and Maria: thank you—another project completed.

Ray Swassing

Contents

Part One

Foundations

Since 1970, we have seen many important changes in American education. Equal educational opportunities for the handicapped, minorities, and women have been focal points of court discussions, federal and state legislation, policy decisions of state and local school boards, and of national, state, and local professional education organizations. The movement for equal education stresses the right of individuals to fulfill their potential. Equal educational opportunities for the gifted and talented requires that for them to live a life consistent with their abilities and to share in the rewards of society, their education must go beyond the standard curriculum and delivery of instruction consistent with their ability to learn. This approach to equal education for the gifted and talented does not address the rewards society will receive when the gifted are effectively educated.

Gifted and talented children today can assume effective roles in continuing our nation's heritage of an ever-increasing quality of life. Society cannot afford to lose talent. We can look to an exciting future if talent is nurtured and developed.

The four chapters of Part One consider historical, educational and sociological foundations of current practice. Of the several themes running through Part One, the most obvious is the traditional view of the field. Chapters 3 and 4 discuss the sociological aspects of giftedness. Chapter 4 recognizes giftedness prior to kindergarten or first grade.

A third, less obvious, theme is that giftedness is a lifelong phenomenon. Each person has a unique past, present, and future, but is gifted throughout it all. The schools play a 12-year role in that life, but need to respond to the individual's lifelong personal history.

The last theme is that of individual differences. The four chapters emphasize the need for differential education of the gifted and talented, with differentiated experiences building on the special skills and abilities of the learners. By definition, gifted children cannot maximize their potential from the usual curriculum; they require unique opportunities. Unique experiences are developed from a solid knowledge of the learner, the content to be learned, and the techniques for facilitating that learning.

Chapter 1 provides a review of the field; chapter 2 describes educational assessment and implementation; chapter 3 presents the social aspects; and chapter 4 is an introduction to preschool practice. Part One provides the backdrop for effective instructional responses to unique and exciting learners.

1

Overview

Raymond H. Swassing

Gifted education is not the study of isolated aspects of giftedness, but the study of interactions of a variety of elements that combine into giftedness and gifted education. It is the study of the foundations of today's practice as well as an investigation of current theories and processes. There are many such interacting elements: history, research, theory, practices, ability, creativity, and curriculum, to name a few. Interacting factors in the delivery of instruction include history, definition, characteristics, educational approaches, and curriculum approaches. Definition and characteristics go hand-in-hand; education must respond to the characteristics of the learners, while curriculum is the specification of the knowledge, skills, attitudes, and values the learners will acquire.

An Historical Perspective

Much of today's practice with the gifted and talented can be traced to four major figures: Louis M. Terman, Paul A. Witty, S. L. Pressey, and Leta S. Hollingworth. Their careers overlapped in time as well as professional interests. All agreed on the need for appropriate experiences for the gifted and talented, but who the gifted were, what the appropriate experiences were, and how they should be delivered have been the substance of 50 years of dialogue and discourse.

Louis M. Terman (1877–1956) is the first American mentioned in the history of the gifted child movement in the United States, based on his longitudinal study of 1500 gifted children, *Genetic Studies of Genius*. The first volume was published in 1925, and four later volumes in 1926, 1930, 1947, and 1959. Terman began publishing on the topic in 1906 (Seagoe, 1975), and shared with Maud Merrill the most successful translation of Binet's intelligence scale, The Stanford-Binet.

Terman published on several topics: leadership, sex differences (Terman & Miles, 1936), race differences (1922), and mental measurements. He considered his contributions in mental measurements more important, but realized that his efforts in the field of gifted children would be the contribution most remembered (Seagoe, 1975). Indeed, the characteristics of gifted children as reported in the literature can be traced to Terman's longitudinal study, and current identification procedures reflect those instituted by Terman.

Terman's study has been critically examined over the years; Witty (1930) questioned the use of the word "genius" and the absence of racial minorities in the population (1934), and selection procedures (Jacobs, 1970) and sampling (Keating, 1975) have formed the major points of discourse. Witty (1951) pointed out that Terman's procedures encouraged the search for the gifted and talented to concentrate on the higher middle income groups, with little attention to locating gifted and talented among racial and ethnic minorities and lower socioeconomic groups.

Paul A. Witty (1898–1976) was Terman's contemporary. Their professional lives overlapped from the middle of the 1920s to the middle 1950s. Witty published on a variety of topics in the field of the gifted over a 50-year period. He was among the first to critically examine the *Genetic Studies of Genius* by conducting research of his own on Terman's findings. He questioned sex differences, the absence of blacks (Witty & Jenkins, 1934; 1936), the role of drive in giftedness (Witty & Lehman, 1927)

3

and the term "genius" (Witty & Lehman, 1930). Over the years, he continued to question narrow definitions of giftedness, or those based only on IQ, in favor of broader constructs (1940; 1951; 1962), and was among the first to refer to the gifted as our "greatest resource" (1955). The Yearbook of the National Association for the Gifted (1951), his 50-year commitment to the field, and the quality of the professionals he trained are major factors in the field today.

Leta S. Hollingworth (1886–1939) began work with the very highly gifted in 1916 (Hollingworth, 1975), and began publishing her findings in 1926; her *Children Above 180 IQ* was originally published in 1942. Hollingworth wrote on curriculum instruction and the emotional development of the gifted, and about the long-term histories of her students. Her longitudinal studies with the very highly intelligent emphasized their special needs as well as their similarities to more average children.

S. L. Pressey (1888–1979) was the first to address the question of acceleration for the gifted from the end result rather than from the starting point of education. He contended that if the gifted progressed rapidly through school, they would have more years of productive life. Building in part on Lehman's *Age and Achievement* (1953), he maintained that longer periods of productivity could substantially improve the contributions of the gifted for both themselves and society, and acceleration would lead to the longer productive period. Pressey brought a strong research orientation toward service delivery to the field of the gifted and talented. He offered an alternative to Witty's position of extending the curriculum (Pressey, 1962, 1965).

Terman, Witty, Hollingworth, and Pressey each approached the topic of education of the gifted and talented from a different perspective, yet each believed firmly in the need to foster giftedness. Terman brought measurement strategies to the study of giftedness; Witty is notable for his insistence on a definition that exceeded IQ limitations. Hollingworth contributed to the field of the very highly gifted, and Pressey added the perspective of acceleration. Each contributed to the study of individual differences. Pressey, for example, initiated the use of the first teaching machine, and Witty made numerous contributions to the teaching of reading.

Our historical perspective must also include mention of J. P. Guilford and his Structure of Intellect model (SI). Guilford (1950) also challenged us to view intelligent behavior as something more than IQ scores. His SI model emphasizes the dimensions of Operations, Content, and Products. The operations component led to much of the understanding we have today of the concept of creativity (Frierson, 1969). Since publication of the model in 1956, it has dominated American thinking and research on intelligence and creativity.

Definition of Gifted and Talented

There are currently two definitions for the gifted and talented. The more popular definition is that of the United States Office of Education:

> The term gifted and talented children means children, and, where applicable, youth, who are identified at the preschool, elementary or secondary school level as possessing demonstrated or potential abilities that give evidence of high performance responsibility in areas such as intellectual, creative, specific academic, or leadership ability, or in the

performing and visual arts, and who by reason thereof, require services or activities not ordinarily provided by the school. (P.L. 94-561, 1978; Zettel, 1979, p. 21).

The other frequently used definition is Renzulli's "three ring" definition:

Giftedness consists of an interaction among three basic clusters of human traits—these clusters being above-average general abilities, high levels of task commitment, and high levels of creativity. Gifted and talented children are those possessing or capable of developing this composite set of traits and applying them to any potentially valuable area of human performance. Children who manifest or are capable of developing an interaction among the three clusters require a wide variety of educational opportunities and services that are not ordinarily provided through regular instructional programs. (Renzulli, 1978, p. 184.

Clearly, either definition is a move away from the narrow concept of giftedness as an IQ score. The first definition stresses areas of giftedness, while the "three ring" definition emphasizes three important clusters of traits. When these clusters of traits overlap within an individual, special opportunities are required. Both definitions stress the need for experiences "not ordinarily provided" by schools, and both emphasize achievement or the potential to achieve. The important similarity is that achievement, realized or potential, requires educational opportunities beyond the curriculum and instructional practices of regular education.

After defining the gifted and talented, we can derive the characteristics of the learners, and from these characteristics, we can begin to develop our educational plans.

Characteristics of the Gifted

What are gifted children like? Are they social isolates? Are they well adjusted and well liked? Are they always "lost in books"? We need to remember that gifted and talented children are first children. Some will be energetic, verbal, and popular; others will be less social and energetic. Some will be taller than average, others will be shorter than average. There will be wide differences in social, academic, and personal skills; growth patterns and motor abilities; and socioeconomic class, creed, and race. The common denominator that emerges, however, is an outstanding ability in one or more areas of human endeavor—an ability so noteworthy that special provisions are necessary to facilitate development of the child's potential. Let us consider three such children.

Fred is a white, fifth-grade boy from a middle income family who attends school in a middle income neighborhood. His teachers, principal, and parents were quite surprised when the school psychologist reported Fred's IQ to be 165. Fred was considered a "C" student; his achievement test data supported this. As it happened, Fred had figured out the system. He could read when he entered first grade, and tried to get the teacher to let him read books he was interested in. The teacher insisted that Fred stay with the books designed for first-grade reading. When the teacher asked questions, Fred knew the answers, but he quickly noticed that the other children did not appreciate his answering. He learned not to answer questions. As he went through school, he learned to calculate how many questions, problems, or spelling words he needed to miss to earn an "average" grade, then decided which ones to answer incorrectly. Fred became "average" and remained so until he was "caught" by his fifth-grade teacher, who became suspicious when she noted the quality of his creative writing, the poetry he wrote in his free time, and the vocabulary he used when talking privately with her. She brought him to the attention of the school psychologist, who brought Fred's secret into the open.

Hugh's case is another instance where giftedness might have remained hidden. Hugh was in the eighth grade when he was discovered. He lived in the center of the city and had gone to the same school since first grade. He came from a family with a history of hard work and long hours; both parents worked for minimum wages. He was the second of four children. His performance during his previous years in school was average, and he had to apply himself to maintain his standing. Luckily, his English teacher discovered him—not, as in Fred's case, by the richness of vocabulary, but by Hugh's colorful, descriptive expressions, his combinations of everyday words into rich metaphors and similes, and his astute observations of people, animals, and events. Hugh was a novelist, journalist, or playwright in the rough. As the English teacher worked with Hugh, giving him a diet of literature, plays, museums, journals, grammar, vocabulary, and encouragement, Hugh found an important key to learning and his school work steadily improved.

Not all gifted children are as difficult to identify as were Fred and Hugh. Sometimes it seems that one has to be looking the other way to miss seeing some gifted and talented children, as with Jennie.

Jennie was in the fourth grade. She attended a suburban school in an upper-middle income neighborhood. She liked to study, play, talk, and read; she enjoyed vacations, museums, art shows, writing, and animals—she liked everything, and did everything well. The one thing she did better than anything else was arithmetic. Arithmetic and anything associated with mathematics could keep her busy for hours, sometimes right through meals. Achievement test data revealed that in most subjects she was performing at the sixth- and seventh-grade levels; in mathematics, she was at the ninth-grade level. Jennie was gifted, not in an offensive or ostentatious way, but as a known and accepted fact.

The stories of Fred, Hugh, and Jennie demonstrate that gifted and talented children may differ greatly from the list of characteristics we expect to find. We offer the following list of characteristics with the understanding that the items are generalizations and that some children may demonstrate other characteristics not listed. Gifted and talented children:

- Typically learn to read earlier, with a better comprehension of the nuances of language. As many as half of the gifted and talented population have learned to read before entering school. They read widely, quickly, and intensely, and have large vocabularies.
- Commonly learn basic skills better, more quickly, and with less practice.
- Are better able to construct and handle abstractions than their age mates.
- Are frequently able to pick up and interpret nonverbal cues and draw inferences that other children have to have spelled out for them.
- Take less for granted, seeking the "hows" and "whys."

- Display a better ability to work independently at an earlier age and for longer periods of time than other children.
- Can sustain longer periods of concentration and attention.
- Have interests that are often both wildly eclectic and intensely focused.
- Frequently have seemingly boundless energy, sometimes leading to a misdiagnosis of "hyperactive."
- Are usually able to respond and relate well to parents teachers and adults. They may prefer the company of older children and adults to that of their peers (Boston, 1978).

Most lists of characteristics present only the positive aspects of giftedness. Teachers need to be aware, however, that while it can be exciting to work with a highly verbal child on an activity he is enjoying, it can also be difficult to work with a child who is expert at talking his or her way out of things; exciting to have a highly curious child in science and exasperating to try to keep the curious out of other students' activities. Table 1–1 presents the two sides of behavior that gifted and talented children may exhibit.

Table 1–1   TWO SIDES TO THE BEHAVIOR OF THE GIFTED

Positive Behaviors	Negative Behaviors
1. Expresses ideas and feelings well	1. May be glib, making fluent statements based on little or no knowledge or understanding
2. Can move at a rapid pace	2. May dominate discussions
3. Works conscientiously	3. May be impatient to proceed to next level or task
4. Wants to learn, explore, and seek more information	4. May be considered nosey
5. Develops broad knowledge and an extensive store of vicarious experiences	5. May choose reading at the expense of active participation in social, creative, or physical activities
6. Is sensitive to the feelings and rights of others	6. May struggle against rules, regulations, and standardized procedures
7. Makes steady progress	7. May lead discussions "off the track"
8. Makes original and stimulating contributions to discussions	8. May be frustrated by the apparent absence of logic in activities and daily events
9. Sees relationships easily	9. May become bored by repetitions
10. Learns material quickly	10. May use humor to manipulate
11. Is able to use reading skills to obtain new information	11. May resist a schedule based on time rather than task
12. Contributes to enjoyment of life for self and others	12. May lose interest quickly
13. Completes assigned tasks	
14. Requires little drill for learning	

From Raymond H. Swassing, Gifted and talented children, in *Exceptional Children*, ed. W. L. Heward and M. D. Orlansky (Columbus, Ohio: Charles E. Merrill, 1980), p. 310. Developed with the assistance of graduate students at The Ohio State University.

Language

The stories of Fred, Hugh, and Jennie and the lists of gifted characteristics show that gifted children do tend to acquire and manipulate symbols and symbol systems earlier and more effectively than their more average age mates—as Gallagher (1975a) states, "the *sine qua non* of giftedness" (p. 12). Thoughts are communicated through symbols, whether the symbols are verbal (language), mathematical, musical, artistic, or physical (dance). Gifted and talented children acquire the symbols more readily, use them effectively, are aware of subtle nuances between similar symbols and symbol systems, and use symbols and symbol systems in complex and unique ways.

The literature does not tell us much about gifted children's styles of language usage, although Jensen (1973) raises the provocative question of whether gifted children perhaps speak a sort of dialect. A study of the language of 80 fifth-grade students, 40 gifted and 40 average, with 20 boys and 20 girls in each group, concentrated on fluency and grammatical control in both casual and "careful" language situations. The superior students had larger, more diversified vocabularies, made more tentative, rather than dogmatic, statements, issued fewer commands, and emphasized general, scientific, or practical concerns. "Language style most frequently differentiated performance on a given variable" (Jensen, 1973, p. 338).

Language modification according to context, referred to as "situational shift" (Fishman, 1973), is of interest to the sociolinguist. A situation is "the co-occurrence of two (or more) people related to each other in a particular way, communicating about a particular topic in a particular setting" (Fishman, 1973, p. 272). The situation "shifts" according to the people, the style of communication, the topic, and the setting. A shift in language style takes place when a situation has been perceived as altered; for example, another may join the group, the topic may change, the style of relating may vary, or the purposes of the communication shift. Ability to perceive the changes is known as "context sensitivity" (Fishman, 1973). Fishman suggests that gifted children's language acquisition and usage depends on sociological as well as psychological factors.

Merely because gifted children have advanced vocabularies and can use language accurately, however, does not mean they have learned when or when not to use what they have learned. They must also learn to make conscious choices about substituting a more common but less accurate word for a higher level, more precise word, for the sake of facilitating communication and relationships with more average peers. They need not always make this choice, but must be aware of the need to choose. They must know their options and the consequences of choosing.

If the gifted child chooses to use higher level, more precise language, she runs the risk of "turning others off," acquiring a derogatory label, or ostracism. On the other hand, two youngsters who are involved in a conversation may automatically shift into the language style that best accommodates their communication and thought processes. If theirs is a higher order of discussion with many lower level thoughts automatically presumed, the conversation may be abbreviated, or punctuated by short phrases and nonverbal cues. An observer may feel left out of the dialogue, and think the other two are arrogant, or that they are talking in a dialect or "isolect" (Ornstein-Galicia, 1981, p. 22). Whether the gifted use a "true" dialect is open to both research and discussion, but often their communication behavior is at least a shorthand version of long thought chains known to be held by both parties, although not necessarily by others overhearing the exchange. Gifted children must know the impact this conversational style has on others, and must be helped to choose whether to adjust.

Intelligence Testing

The most common way to measure children's acquisition of symbol systems is through language and intelligence testing (Gallagher, 1975a). Figure 1–1 presents a graph of mental age changes for various chronological ages and IQs across school ages, as determined by the Stanford-Binet (Terman & Merrill, 1973). Analysis of the data reveals some interesting insights into the growth of IQ among gifted children. The IQ scores are deviation IQs (statistically derived) rather than ratio IQs (IQ equals MA/CA × 100), so that a youngster with a CA of six and an MA of six does not necessarily have an IQ of 100 (the deviation IQ is six years, four months, or 6–4).

Note that six first-grade youngsters, with IQs ranging from 100 to 160, have different MAs (from 6–4 to 9–10, approximately) at the start of grade one (an approximate range of 3–6). As CA increases, the differences in MA increase as IQ increases until CA 14, where the MA difference for IQs of 100 and 160 is 8–8. (The

Figure 1-1 MENTAL AGE CHANGE AS A FUNCTION OF BOTH IQ AND CHRONOLOGICAL AGE

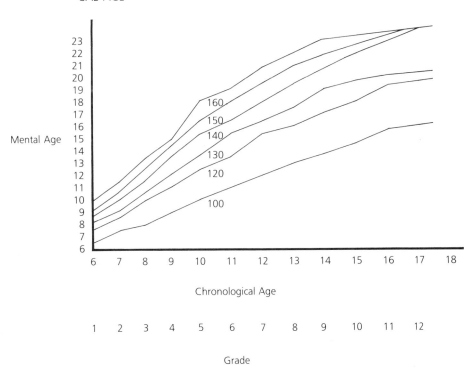

test does not measure any higher than CA 14, the "ceiling" or "ceiling effect.") The same is true for IQ 150 at CA 15 and IQ 140 at CA 16. The MA change over the 10 years, from CA 6 to 16 for the child with an IQ of 100, is 9–10. For the child with an IQ of 160, the MA change is 13–1 at CA 14, or three years, three months (3–3), *more* growth in two *fewer* years.

The information about the differing rates of MA growth for differing IQ levels demonstrates Stanley's position that

> High mental abilities, well beyond one's chronological age, imply higher final levels of ability—*higher*, not just earlier. High test scores at an early age do not, then, merely indicate "developmental" differences of rate or sequence. They presage long-range, lasting differences in ultimate ability. (Stanley, 1976, pp. 5–6).

Descriptions of the gifted that emphasize scores, IQ, achievement, and grades are examples of numerical or *quantitative differences.* Quantitative differences are easier to present because it is easier to obtain the information. Measurement and testing are the processes of assigning numerical values to attributes or traits; however, qualitative differences are also important.

Qualitative differences refer to the level of the thought processes or the product, and to the degree of abstractness, generalization, or transformation that takes place. For example, for average learners or for children with learning problems, it is common to isolate skills and teach them specifically. After the children master two or more skills, the skills are combined into a concept, and concepts are connected by instruction in relationships. From relationships, we teach generalizations and, finally, transformations.

For many children, acquiring nine months' worth of skills in the nine-month school year is a major undertaking. Many children do not reach that level of success; for those who do, upward movement through the hierarchy is appropriate. Few reach the transformation level.

Instruction

Instruction for gifted children should begin with generalizations and move down the hierarchy to specific skills. After they master generalization, relationships, concepts, and specific skills, they can begin to work at experiences for acquiring transformations.

Table 1–2 is a rather common device for teaching multiplication facts (and division as well). For many children, the task begins with the table of "ones" (1 times 1, 1 times 2, etc.), then moves on to the "twos," "threes," and so on up to the "tens." Table 1–2 helps them if their memory slips. For gifted children, however, the table is an overview of the base 10 number system. The teacher can ask questions about the relationships of the numbers to each other, or about the relationships of the numbers in the upper right half of the table to the numbers in the lower left half, and explore reasons for the various relationships. The students can play games with the table or develop a code system; they thus learn the multiplication facts, and

Table 1-2   MULTIPLICATION

	0	1	2	3	4	5	6	7	8	9	10
0	0	0	0	0	0	0	0	0	0	0	0
1	0	1	2	3	4	5	6	7	8	9	10
2	0	2	4	6	8	10	12	14	16	18	20
3	0	3	6	9	12	15	18	21	24	27	30
4	0	4	8	12	16	20	24	28	32	36	40
5	0	5	10	15	20	25	30	35	40	45	50
6	0	6	12	18	24	30	36	42	48	54	60
7	0	7	14	21	28	35	42	49	56	63	70
8	0	8	16	24	32	40	48	56	64	72	80
9	0	9	18	27	36	45	54	63	72	81	90
10	0	10	20	30	40	50	60	70	80	90	100

everything that follows is practice and retention building. This is an example of "compacting" (Renzulli & Smith, 1980).

Planning

Gallagher (1981) points out that three skills the gifted have in abundance are:
- The ability to relate one idea to another.
- The ability to make sound judgments.
- The ability to see the operation of larger systems of knowledge than is seen by the ordinary citizen (p. 137).

These skills are important in educational planning, which involves both the approaches and the curriculum. The approach determines how the curriculum will be delivered.

Educational Approaches

Educational approaches fall into two general categories: enrichment and acceleration. *Enrichment* provides educational experiences that are "appropriate and adequate" to each learner's nature and abilities (Passow, 1981) and relate to both past and future learnings. After children master basic skills, they may take part in field trips, library work, art projects, history projects, science experiments, music activities, producing a journal, and creative writing. Time during the day or week is devoted to enrichment activities. Administratively, enrichment is usually managed by a combination of approaches, such as special experiences within the regular classroom, special classes, grouping within the classroom, resource rooms, field trips, special camps, hobby clubs, Saturday and evening programs, guest lecturers, and individual mentors.

Acceleration means to advance children through skills and/or content at their own pace, moving through the basic educational sequence at a rate suitable to their abilities. Acceleration approaches include: early admission to school, grade skipping, concurrent enrollment in both high school and college, Advanced Placement tests, early admission to college, and content acceleration, such as reading with fifth graders while remaining in fourth grade, or advancing the content while keeping the child with her classmates.

Both enrichment and acceleration have their advocates and detractors. Enrichment has been criticized as random, haphazard, and lacking an adequate research base. Acceleration has been encouraged as a means of reducing the time children stay in school and adding time for productivity (Pressey, 1962). Its detractors cite increasing problems of social and emotional adjustment, although research indicates that when appropriately implemented, adjustment problems do not arise (Gallagher, 1975b). The study of Mathematically Precocious Youth (Stanley, Keating and Fox, 1974) substantiates the value of acceleration in mathematics.

The choice of acceleration or enrichment really depends on the child. Two children with the same abilities but different social skills might require different placement. Vivian, a socially immature sixth grader, might have trouble adjusting in seventh grade, but Tim, a socially precocious sixth grader, may do very well in seventh grade. Some children may be able to complete most of the work at an advanced level except in one or two subjects. Acceleration has a solid research base (Gallagher, 1975b), but it must be implemented wisely.

Figure 1–2 presents a different way to examine the issue. The horizontal line *A-B* represents some period of time—day, week, month, or year—available for instruction. The period between *C* and *G* is the time typical children spend on basic skills; the period between *E* and *F* is the time gifted children spend on basic skills. All children need some enrichment; therefore, arrow 1 is the time available for enrichment for typical children and arrow 2 is the enrichment time available for gifted children. The vertical line *C-D* is the acceleration line. Effective enrichment will provide accelerating experiences, and acceleration will provide some expansion or enrichment of the curriculum. The choice is not between enrichment or acceleration, but is rather a matter of emphasis.

Regardless of whether one emphasizes enrichment or acceleration, the major issue is the needs of the children who are receiving special experiences. Feldhusen and Wyman (1980) identify 12 special needs that regular education does not address:

Figure 1–2 AN ACCELERATION/ENRICHMENT COMPARISON

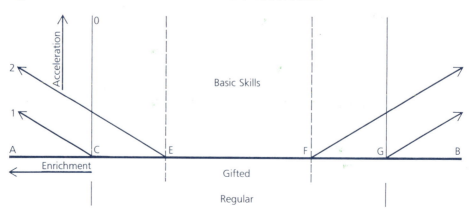

1 Maximum achievement of basic skills and concepts
2 Learning activities at appropriate level and pace
3 Experience in creative thinking and problem solving
4 Development of convergent abilities, especially in logical deduction and convergent problem solving
5 Stimulation of imagery, imagination and spatial abilities
6 Development of self-awareness and acceptance of own capacities, interests, and needs
7 Stimulation to pursue higher level goals and aspirations (models, pressure, standards)
8 Exposure to a variety of fields of study, art, professions, and occupations
9 Development of independence, self-direction, and discipline in learning
10 Experience in relating intellectually, artistically, and affectively with other gifted and talented students
11 A large fund of information about diverse topics
12 Access and stimulation to reading (Feldhusen & Wyman 1980, p. 15)

Of these 12 needs, Feldhusen and Wyman considered the first two of major importance.

The gifted require the same basic skills all children need, but the teacher can spend less time on their instruction, and can help the children with skills not offered to most of the school population, such as: research/library skills, foreign languages, note taking, speedreading, computer literacy, and typing.

Approaches to Curriculum and Instruction

A curriculum is a sequentially arranged set of experiences designed for particular learners. The curriculum should be carefully arranged to involve content and process geared to specified purposes and identified target audiences (Saylor, Alexander, & Lewis, 1981). The curriculum may be made up of several small or "partial" plans ranging in size from a domain to a single learning activity package. Each of these plans combines to identify the complete set of goals and objectives the learners will receive.

Tyler (1949) identifies four questions that must be answered when developing such a plan.

1 What educational purposes are sought?
2 What educational experiences will facilitate attainment of the purposes?
3 How can the experiences be effectively organized?
4 How can we tell if the purposes have been attained?

We can probably agree that the target audience is gifted and talented children, but from that point on agreement becomes less likely. Purposes, facilitating, and organization comprise a substantial body of literature and dialogue, although there are some general guidelines regarding educational purposes that are appropriate for all education. Saylor, Alexander, and Lewis (1981) suggest four domains of educational goals and objectives:

- Personal development
- Social competence

- Continued learning skills
- Specialization

Differentiation   Differentiation should occur at all levels and components of the curriculum, and involves components, modes of differentiation, and content adjustment. Passow (1981) identifies these componens of a plan: (1) goals, (2) content, (3) instructional strategies, (4) resources, and (5) evaluation, and the modes of curricular differentiation as breadth and/or depth, tempo and/or pacing, and nature and kind.

We can differentiate curriculum for the gifted and talented by providing expanded or more detailed study of a topic and increasing the rate of presentation, depending on the discipline. There are at least five ways to adjust content:

1   Telescoped common core
2   Expansion of basic skills and concepts
3   Programmatic augmentation
4   Provisional augmentation
5   Out-of-school augmentation (Tannenbaum, 1981, pp. 160–63)

Programmatic augmentation is directed, sequential, and an ongoing part of the curriculum, giving new dimensions to the curriculum for those students who may benefit from them. Provisional augmentation refers to the unique learning experiences each teacher brings to the classroom according to the teacher's particular strengths and interests. Capitalizing on the teacher's special interests and abilities extends the learner's opportunities in special ways.

Out-of-school augmentation takes education outside the schoolhouse walls and moves it into the community. Children can work either during or outside normal school hours, with scientists, artists, businessmen, and industrialists to acquire the background, attitudes, and skills appropriate for specialized fields of study and endeavor.

Much of the programming for the gifted and talented noticeably lacks "scope and sequence" (Passow, 1981, p. 4), where scope refers to what will be covered and sequence defines the order in which the material will be presented. Experiences for the gifted and talented based on the fields under study and their logical organization and structure will provide a program of consistent knowledge, attitude, and skill acquisition.

Curriculum Development   Developing a curriculum for the gifted requires attention to the domains of goals and objectives, curricular components, modes of differentiation, content adjustments, and scope and sequence. Ehrlich (1981) offers eight principles for developing curriculum:

1   The gifted need to be exposed to a differentiated and enriched curriculum suited to their ability levels and their special needs, a curriculum that considers affective needs an integral part of the cognitive process.
2   The curriculum should be broad in scope and touching on all aspects of learning as an integrated experience rather than a piecemeal doling out of information in a manner that makes all fields of knowledge seem to be unrelated.
3   The curriculum should be goal-oriented, and these goals should involve an awareness of student needs in a future that will be far different from the present.

4   The program should have continuity and be involved with growth processes.
5   The curriculum should explore moral, ethical, and spiritual values that are universally acceptable.
6   A major goal of a curriculum for the gifted should be the teaching and practice of the thinking skills at all levels of the hierarchy.
7   A curriculum for the gifted should attempt to develop the basic skills required in reading and the language arts, mathematics, the social and physical sciences, and other curriculum areas as early as possible and to the greatest extent possible.
8   Verbal skills are a necessary adjunct of intellectual capacity and should form a major component of the curriculum for the gifted. (p. 220)

Even with well established educational goals, it is difficult to develop enough instructional activities for all the children in a classroom. Curriculum guides and graded courses of study offer suggestions and guidelines for instructional activities that are appropriate for most learners, but teachers of the gifted and talented have had to look elsewhere for instructional suggestions and curricular guidance. The usual models are Bloom's *Taxonomy of Educational Objectives* (1956), Guilford's *Structure of Intellect* (1956), Renzulli's *Enrichment Triad* model (1977), and Williams's *Cognitive-Affective* model (1970). Less frequently used models are those of Suchman (1961), Taba (1963), Treffinger (1975), and Bruner (1966).

Bloom's Taxonomy began as part of an effort to establish a framework for developing test material and examining relationships between tests and education. The taxonomy classifies educational objectives into three domains: cognitive, affective, and psychomotor. The cognitive and affective classifications have frequently been used in developing programs and instruction for the gifted and talented.

The taxonomy is considered hierarchical; that is, each level presumes that the previous level has been mastered. For example, to interpret (comprehend) some fact about the American Civil War, the student must first have knowledge of the fact. Knowledge is the lowest element in the classification, evaluation the highest.

The most common application of the taxonomy is through its six major classifications: knowledge, comprehension, application, analysis, synthesis, and evaluation. Curriculum is "differentiated" for the gifted by having them perform activities at the analysis, synthesis, and evaluation levels. Of course, *all* children should learn to make evaluative judgments, but gifted children should make judgments with more complex internal and external criteria derived from differential knowledge bases. Also, because a task is evaluative does not make it automatically appropriate for the gifted.

On the other hand, the taxonomy has been most beneficial in moving classroom activities beyond the knowledge level. Color-coded learning centers are an example of use of the taxonomy in differentiating for the gifted. A different color is assigned to each taxonomic level, tasks are designed for each level, and the task cards are color-coded to the level. All children may do tasks at the knowledge level, but different cards represent tasks of varying difficulty and task cards are assigned individually. The average child may be assigned tasks 1–6 in the red cards, 1–3 in the yellow, and so forth; while gifted children may be assigned tasks 3–7 in the red and 4–6 in the yellow. The *Action Words Chart* (VORT, 1979) and *Action Words Dictionary* (VORT, 1979) are helpful sources of words for developing objectives and activities within the taxonomy framework, as are Gronlund's (1970) illustrative objectives and behavioral terms.

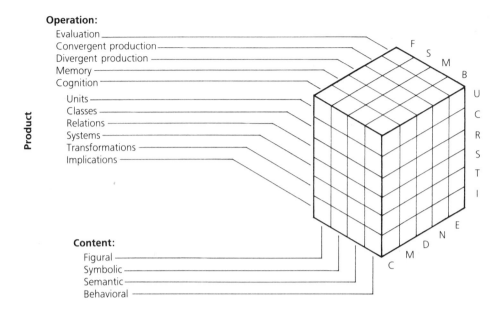

Operation:
Evaluation
Convergent production
Divergent production
Memory
Cognition

Units
Classes
Relations
Systems
Transformations
Implications

Product

Content:
Figural
Symbolic
Semantic
Behavioral

Figure 1-3   GUILFORD'S STRUCTURE OF INTELLECT MODEL

Guilford's Structure of Intellect

Guilford's Structure of Intellect (SI) Model (1956) has had substantial impact on the entire educational and psychological field (Wolf, 1981). The major components of Guilford's model are operations, contents, and products. The operations or abilities are cognitive, memory, divergent thinking, convergent production, and evaluative abilities. The four broad classes of information or "contents" are figural, symbolic, semantic, and behavioral, and the organization or "products" are units, classes, relations, systems, transformations, and implications.

Meeker (1969), Maker (1977), Kester (1982), and Navarre (1983) all suggest using the model as a diagnostic-prescriptive approach. Based on the Structure of Intellect Learning Abilities Test, instructional activities are developed for strengthening identified areas and to utilize strengths to develop weaknesses (Kester, 1982). Navarre (1983) points out the uses of the model for career guidance; for example, strength in *Cognition of Symbolic Relations* (CSR) relates to possible careers in computer sciences, while strength in *Cognition of Semantic Units* (CMU) can indicate ability for conceptual work. Each of the 120 abilities within the three major dimensions of the model can be identified with tests and addressed with instructional materials.

Enrichment Triad

Renzulli (1977) developed the Enrichment Triad Model (ETM) in response to the need for differential experiences for the gifted. ETM is based on three levels, or "types" of enrichment. Type I Enrichment, General Exploratory Activities, lets students survey a variety of topics and gives them ideas for further study. Type II Enrichment, Group Training Activities, involves students in "training exercises" designed to provide the skills, knowledge, and attitudes necessary for future in-depth study, to learn how to learn within a subject or content area. Type III Enrichment, Individual and Small Group Investigations of Real Problems, emphasizes real problems and investigations. Children are to act as real investigators in adding to the knowledge base in some area, and as real investigators, they must address real problems. Real problems are not imposed by the teacher, but have meaning in light of the subject matter and circumstances.

It is the Type III activities that differentiate the instructional experience. The "laboratory environment" is particularly important because it highlights the attitudes of scientists and authors as well as the processes used by professionals. Essentially, a laboratory environment establishes a lifelike and reality-based setting for the tasks at hand. For example, if children wish to study the use of playground equipment and space and recommend changes to the principal, they will make a "laboratory environment" of the playground, studying equipment use, traffic patterns, times of the day, and weather conditions. With the data, they can create a scale-model playground, complete with drawings and diagrams, present their findings and plans to the principal, and pursue whatever courses of action open to them to implement the plan. Thus, in Type III Enrichment activities, the problems must be real; processes should reflect real processes; activities should lead to products; and there should be an audience for the products.

Cognitive-Affective Model

The Cognitive-Affective model (Williams, 1970) emphasizes classroom behaviors along three dimensions—Curriculum, Teacher Behavior (strategies), and Pupil Behavior (processes). Although developed for the elementary curriculum, the model can be applied to any grade level. The Pupil Behavior dimension is divided into cognitive and affective behaviors, to show that learning involves both types of processes and to encourage instruction that integrates the two processes, and, in addition, to relate creativity to regular instruction. Williams offers an extensive list of objectives that demonstrate the model, suggest meaningful activities, and help teachers prepare to use the model.

Of these four models for differentiating instruction for the gifted and talented, The Enrichment Triad Model is the only one designed especially for implementation with gifted learners, but all have been helpful in guiding instructional activities for the gifted.

Instruction has generally emphasized the "discovery" (Taba, 1962) or "inquiry" (Suchman, 1961) approach. The purpose of the discovery approach was to teach children to think while the inquiry model was intended to teach learners the processes of formulating concepts and generalizations through information gathering and organizing. Both Suchman and Taba developed their models from Piaget's developmental theory and Bruner's instructional theory.

Piaget's Principles

The four important concepts of Piaget's system are equilibrium, assimilation, accommodation, and schemes. *Equilibrium* is achieved when the child is in harmony with the environment. Assimilation takes place when the child adjusts the environment to

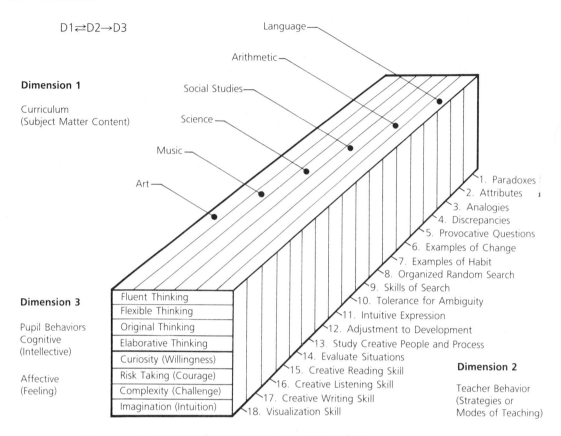

Figure 1-4 WILLIAMS'S COGNITIVE-AFFECTIVE MODEL

fit the biological or intellectual systems in place. Accommodation refers to the individual's adjusting the biological or intellectual systems to fit the environment and equilibrium is achieved when assimilation and accommodation are in balance. Schemes are patterns of behavioral or intellectual (cognitive) structures arranged hierarchically, which also combine into more complex or higher order schemes (Robinson & Robinson, 1976, pp. 243–45).

Piaget postulates four important periods in the development of intelligence:

1   Sensorimotor intelligence (birth to two years)
2   Preoperational thought (two to seven years)
3   Concrete operations (seven to eleven years)
4   Formal operations (eleven years onward)

During the period of Preoperational Thought (two to seven years), children become efficient with the use of internal symbol systems. They can distinguish between the word and what it represents, and develop schema that help organize time and space. The period of Concrete Operations (seven to eleven years) is the time when children develop well organized systems for dealing with their environment. They now have the ability to develop and comprehend hierarchical structures and their interrelationships, and class inclusion. Children at this level are able to combine

Lehman, H. C. *Age and Achievement*. Princeton, N. J.: Princeton University, 1953.

Maker, C. J. *Teaching Models in the Education of the Gifted*. Rockville, Md.: Aspen, 1982.

Maker, C. J. *Providing Programs for the Gifted Handicapped*. Reston, Va.: Council for Exceptional Children, 1977.

Meeker, M. N. *The Structure of Intellect: Its Interpretation and Uses*. Columbus, Ohio: Charles E. Merrill, 1969.

Navarre, J. "How the Teacher of the Gifted Can Use the SOI." *G/C/T* 26 (1983): 17–18.

Newland, T. E. *The Gifted in Socioeducational Perspective*. Englewood Cliffs, N. J.: Prentice-Hall, 1976.

Ornstein-Galicia, J. "Varieties of Southwest Spanish: Some Neglected Basic Considerations." In *Latino Language and Communication Behavior*. Edited by R. P. Duran. Norwood, N. J.: Ablex, 1981.

Passow, A. H. "Nurturing Giftedness: Ways and Means." In *Gifted Children: Challenging Their Potential, New Perspectives and Alternatives*. Edited by A. H. Kramer, D. Bitan, N. Butler-Por, A. Evyator, and E. Landau. New York: World Council for Gifted and Talented Children, 1981.

Pressey, S. L. "Two Basic Neglected Psychoeducational Problems." *The American Psychologist* 20 (1965): 391–95.

Pressey, S. L. "Educational Acceleration: Occasional Procedure or Major Issue?" *Personnel and Guidance Journal* (1962): 12–17.

Pritchard, M. C. "The Contributions of Leta S. Hollingworth to the Study of Gifted Children." In *The Gifted Child*. Edited by P. Witty. Boston: D. C. Heath, 1951.

Renzulli, J. S. "What Makes Giftedness? Reexamining a Definition." *Phi Delta Kappan* (1978): 180–84.

Renzulli, J. S. *The Enrichment ... d Model: A Guide for Developing Defensible Programs for the Gifted and Talented*. Wethersti. Conn.: Creative Learning Press, 1971.

Renzulli, J. S., and L. H. Smith. "An Alternative Approach to Identifying and Programming for Gifted and Talented Students." *Gifted/Creative/Talented* 15 (1980): 4–11.

Robinson, N. M., and H. B. Robinson. *The Mentally Retarded Child: A Psychological Approach*. 2nd ed. New York: McGraw-Hill, 1976.

Saylor, J. G., W. M. Alexander, and A. J. Lewis. *Curriculum Planning for Better Teaching and Learning*. 4th ed. New York: Holt, Rinehart, and Winston, 1981.

Seagoe, M. V. *Terman and the Gifted*. Los Altos, Calif.: William Kaufman, 1975.

Shane, H. G. "The Silicon Age and Education." *Phi Delta Kappan* 63 (1982): 303–8.

Sisk, D. "Unusual Gifts and Talents." In *Children with Exceptional Needs: A Survey of Special Education*. Edited by M. S. Lilly. New York: Holt, Rinehart, and Winston, 1979.

Stanley, J. C. "Uses of Tests to Discover Talent." In *Intellectual Talent: Research and Development*. Edited by D. P. Keating. Baltimore, Md.: Johns Hopkins University Press, 1976.

Stephens, T. M., and J. S. Wolf. "The Gifted Child." In *Behavior of Exceptional Children: An Introduction to Special Education*. 2nd ed. Edited by N. G. Haring. Columbus, Ohio: Charles E. Merrill, 1978.

Suchman, J. R. "Inquiry Training: Building Skills for Autonomous Discovery." *Merrill Palmer Quarterly* 7 (1961): 147–69.

Swassing, R. H. "Gifted and Talented Children." In *Exceptional Children*. 2nd ed. Edited by W. L. Heward and M. D. Orlansky. Columbus, Ohio: Charles E. Merrill, 1984.

Taba, H., and F. Elzey. "Teaching Strategies and Thought Processes." *Teachers College Record* 65 (1964): 524–34.

Taba, H. "Learning by Discovery: Psychological and Educational Rationale." *Elementary School Journal* 63 (1963): 308–16.

Tannenbaum, A. "A Curriculum Framework for Differentiated Education for the Gifted." In *Gifted Childen: Challenging Their Potential, New Perspectives and Alternatives.* Edited by A. H. Kramer, D. Bitan, N. Butler-Por, A. Evyator, and E. Landau. New York: World Council for Gifted and Talented Children, 1981.

Terman, L. M., and M. A. Merrill. *Stanford-Binet Intelligence Scale: Manual for the Third Revision Form L-M.* Boston: Houghton Mifflin, 1973 (1982 Norms Edition).

Terman, L. M., and C. C. Miles. *Sex and Personality-Studies in Masculinity and Femininity.* New York: McGraw-Hill, 1936.

Terman, L. M. "Were We Born That Way?" *The World's Work*, 1922.

Terman, L. M. "Genius and Stupidity—A Study of Some of the Intellectual Processes of Seven 'Bright' and Seven 'Dull' Boys." *Pedagogical Seminar* 13 (September 1906): 307–73.

Treffinger, D. J. "Teaching for Self-Directed Learning: A Priority for the Gifted and Talented." *Gifted Child Quarterly* 19 (1975): 46–59.

Trezise, R. L. "The Hilda Taba Teaching Strategies in English and Reading Classes." *English Journal* 61 (1972): 577–80, 593.

Tyler, R. W. *Basic Principles of Curriculum and Instruction.* Chicago: The University of Chicago Press, 1949.

VORT. *Action Words Chart.* Palo Alto, Calif.: VORT, 1979.

VORT. *Action Words Dictionary: An Index to Verbs for Setting Objectives.* Palo Alto, Calif.: VORT, 1979.

Whitmore, J. R. *Giftedness, Conflict and Underachievement.* Boston: Allyn and Bacon, 1980.

Williams, F. E. *Classroom Ideas for Encouraging Thinking and Feeling.* Buffalo, N. Y.: D. O. K., 1970.

Witty, P. A. "A Decade of Progress in the Study of the Gifted and Creative Pupil." In *Attention to the Gifted a Decade Later.* Edited by W. B. Barbe and T. M. Stephens. Columbus, Ohio: Ohio Department of Education, 1962.

Witty, P. A. "Gifted Children—Our Natural Resource." *Nursing Education.* (1955): 498–500.

Witty, P. A., ed. *The Gifted Child.* Boston: D. C. Heath, 1951.

Witty, P. A. "Contributions to the IQ Controversy from the Study of Superior Deviates." *School and Society* 51 (1940) 502–8.

Witty, P. A. "The Relative Frequency of Gifted Boys and Girls in the Secondary School." *Educational Administration and Supervision* 20 (1943): 606–12.

Witty, P. A. "A Study of One Hundred Gifted Children." *Bulletin of Education,* University of Kansas 2 (1930).

Witty, P. A., and M. Jenkins. "Intra-race Testing and Negro Intelligence." *Journal of Psychology* I (1936): 179–92.

Witty, P. A., and H. C. Lehman. "Nervous Instability and Genius: Some Conflicting Opinions." *Journal of Abnormal and Social Psychology* 24 (1930): 486–97.

Witty, P. A., and H. C. Lehman. "Drive—A Neglected Trait in the Study of the Gifted." *Psychological Review* 34 (1927): 364–76.

Witty, P. A., and M. D. Jenkins. "The Educational Achievement of a Group of Gifted Negro Children." *Journal of Educational Psychology* 45 (1934): 585–97.

Witty, P. A., and W. L. Wilkins. "The Status of Acceleration or Grade Skipping as an Administrative Device." *Educational Administration* 19 (1933).

Wolf, J. S. "An Interview with James J. Gallagher." *The Directive Teacher* 3 (1981): 25–27.

2

Identification, Assessment, and Individualization

Raymond H. Swassing

The task of selecting those who are gifted and talented from among millions of school age children is a commanding one. Compounding the enormity of the job is the need to avoid, where possible, the "false positives", those who seem gifted but later prove not to be. Avoiding the "false negatives," those who are gifted but do not appear to be, is even more of a problem. Since current identification procedures are not 100 percent accurate, it is better to overidentify than to under-identify. Both the rights of the children and the potential loss of human resources demand that we find as many gifted and talented as possible.

Identifying children for special experiences has a long and difficult history. "Few practices in modern education and psychology have received as much criticism as have testing and decision making based on test scores. Few practices are so deserving of criticism" (Salvia and Ysseldyke, 1981, p. 529). Our purpose here is to examine the conditions that will improve the decisions we make from test data. Dubious practices need not continue. Careful examination of issues such as test selection, administration, and interpretation will bring informed judgment to decision making.

Identification

The first step leading to appropriate education for the gifted and talented is identification. Identification is a two-part process: screening and actual identification. Screening is an initial sorting of all students into two groups: those who are likely to be candidates for the specialized experiences and those who will not be served by the program. Identification is an in-depth examination of the pool of candidates to decide who will enter the program.

Procedures

The first step in the identification process is the formation of a placement committee to develop and monitor procedures. The receiving teacher, the principal, the coordinator, one or more recommending teachers, and a school psychologist should make up the committee. Its functions include:

- Developing a definition of the gifted and talented
- Specifying grade levels and numbers of children to be served
- Developing procedures to assure that special needs populations are included
- Deciding on assessment procedures and tests to be used
- Making placement decisions

The placement committee must first develop a definition of the gifted and talented. The definition sets limits and guidelines for both instrument and student selection. The definition also contributes to the screening process because it tells those outside the committee what characteristics children should have to be considered for the programs. (Chapter 1 presents two current definitions.)

Screening

After the definition has been established, screening activities are initiated, including selecting the instruments and conducting the screening. Frazier (1980) suggests these guidelines:

1   Screening should allow every child in the target population to be evaluated

2   The process should limit those evaluated during screening

3   Screening data can provide helpful information for later planning

The purposes of screening are to give every child an opportunity to participate, if appropriate, and to institute a procedure that effectively reduces the number of candidates to a group that can reasonably be evaluated. The process should be both efficient and effective, but if a choice must be made, effectiveness is more important (Pegnato and Birch, 1959). Include as many as possible of the children suspected of being gifted, even if it means including a group that will not, during final selection, prove to be gifted.

No single instrument or procedure serves the cause of screening and identification; rather, we must use multifactored procedures. Several sources of data are required for sound placement decisions, including: (1) teacher nomination, (2) group achievement tests, (3) group intelligence tests, (4) parent interviews, (5) peer identification, and (6) pupils' work and achievements (Clark, 1979).

Test Selection

Selection of achievement and intelligence tests should be based on measurement and statistical concepts, particularly:

- Are the tests valid for the group to be tested?
- Do the test questions reflect the content presented to the students?
- Do the tests measure achievement or intelligence?
- Are the tests reliable?
- How do the achievement tests reflect the goals of the program in which the selected students will be placed?
- Can we interpret the results of the testing in terms of the statistical properties of the tests?
- Are the statistical properties of the tests meaningful to the intended program?

Affirmative answers to these questions help assure that screening will be based on meaningful criteria and that we find what we are looking for.

Checklists

Teacher, parent, and peer nominations are commonly made on some type of form or checklist. The forms are almost always locally developed, frequently from forms obtained from other gifted and talented programs. The checklists may, at best, have face validity; that is, items on the checklists "look like" they would be appropriate for locating gifted and talented children since they were developed from lists of characteristics of gifted and talented children. Any statistical properties, however, are not examined. These procedures are understandable at the beginning of a program, but to continue year after year without examining the checklists is hard to justify; it would not be difficult to compare checklist items to success in the program.

There are two notable exceptions to the lack of statistical information on checklists. The *Scales for Rating the Behavioral Characteristics of Superior Students* (SRBCSS; Renzulli et al., 1976) has had some statistical examination (Renzulli et al.,

1976; Renzulli & Smith, 1980). The 10 scales currently available have been analyzed for internal consistency, that is, whether or not the items contribute to the total score. Factor anayltic studies have been performed to identify which factors are identified by the scale items and the total scales. The tests were conducted mainly with fourth, fifth, and sixth graders; in some instances, the sample sizes were smaller than might be desirable.

The more recent *G.I.F.T.S. Identification Instrument* (Male & Perrone, 1979a, b; 1980) has not been used as much as the SRBCSS. G.I.F.T.S. has six categories: Convergent Thinking and Behavior, Divergent/Creative Thinking and Behavior, Goal Related Thinking and Behavior, Social Skills and Behavior, Physical Skills and Behavior, and Affective Thinking and Behavior. Instruments are administered to the student, teacher, and parents. Correlation coefficients calculated to determine the overlap among categories showed no more than 25 percent overlap, suggesting that for the 57 ninth graders in the sample, the six categories were different but somewhat related.

The question remains as to whether the SRBCSS and G.I.F.T.S. help locate gifted and talented children for particular programs. That answer depends on the particular program, but when used as the authors suggest, in conjunction with other information sources, they augment the identification process.

Selecting Candidates

After screening has produced a pool of possible candidates, actual selection must take place. This is best done by a team representing various disciplines (Clark, 1979), and the team will need a great deal of information about each child. Tongue and Sperling present a matrix for organizing the data that includes areas of giftedness, test data, performance data, and developmental data. The areas of giftedness are academic/intellectual, artistic/expressive, leadership/psychosocial, divergent production/process, and kinesthetic. Test data includes that which measures intelligence, achievement, creativity/divergent thinking, aptitude, and divergent feeling; it may also include a biographical inventory, and all measures must be culture free. Performance data comes from grades, demonstration of skills, and nominations, checklists, and scales made by teacher/school personnel, peers, parents, and the student. Developmental data is put together from case studies, anecdotes, biographical data, and interviews (Tongue & Sperling, 1976, p. 14).

The Baldwin Identification Matrix, or BIM (Baldwin & Wooster, 1977) uses similar pieces of information but provides a system for weighting scores based on the interaction of locally derived information and scoring procedures for the various instruments. The outcome is a student profile of weighted scores derived from several sources, both standardized and of the checklist type.

Standardized Tests

Identification involves both standardized or norm-referenced testing and derives sources of information locally. Individualized intelligence tests remain good predictors of general academic ability. Stanley (1976) and the Study of Mathematically Precocious Youth (SMPY) make a strong case for the use of achievement tests for specific academic abilities:

1 Tests are a prime way—probably the prime way—for the preliminary identification of high-level developed aptitude or achievement.

2 It is even more important than generally realized for tests to have enough "ceiling" (and "floor," too) for each individual tested. This means bold use of tests designed for much older persons, as Hollingsworth (1942) illustrated long ago.

3 The higher an examinee's scores are, the greater his or her potential tends to be. For *appropriate criterion*, validity does not drop at the upper part of the score range of a test *that is difficult enough* for the persons tested. (p. 5)

Stanley's second point may cause the most discussion. "Ceiling" refers to how difficult the test items must be before the child misses all the items. Difficulty is associated with age or grade level; older ages and higher grades imply more difficult items. A fifth-grade youngster capable of ninth-grade math will not be "tested" by a fifth-grade math test. The test items and the grade equivalent data do not reflect the child's abilities, but only that the child exceeded the fifth-grade norms. Stanley's point applies here: intellectual giftedness is manifest not only in the increased rate of learning but also in that the peak (or asymtote) of learning is at a higher, much more complex level. In other words, the gifted acquire learning more rapidly, the learning rate continues for a longer period of time (over the growth period), and is at a higher cognition level. Use of advanced achievement tests for a highly selected group would be consistent with their abilities, but not necessarily consistent with school and/or testing abilities, and using such tests would be "bold" (Stanley, 1976, p. 5). If we wish to determine the extent of a youngster's knowledge in a certain subject area, however, testing the youngster's limits can be achieved only through advanced instrumentation (Keating, 1976).

The Study of Verbally Gifted Youth (SVGY: McGinn, 1976) was modeled after the SMPY. Both used the Scholastic Aptitude Test (SAT) as the initial selection device. The SAT is commonly administered to high school juniors and seniors intent on college entry (McGinn, 1976). SVGY was interested in the location and development of verbal precocity at the seventh and eighth grade levels. The children selected for the SAT–Verbal section had scored at or above the 98th percentile on grade-appropriate tests. The 287 twelve- and thirteen-year-olds earned scores ranging from 230 to 680 on the SAT–V; the average score was 445, while the norm group (juniors and seniors in high school) average was 443. SVGY results clearly show that grade-appropriate tests simply do not examine gifted children's upper limits of abilities.

Since 1980, the SMPY Talent Search model has expanded across the country. Talent search centers are located at Duke, Northwestern, and Arizona State Universities, with additional summer programs at Franklin and Marshall and Dickinson Colleges in Pennsylvania (Durden, 1983).

Creativity

There appears to be no direct equivalent of either SMPY or SVGY in the area of creativity. Khatena (1976) identified the major problems of locating creative children as the complexity of the concept and the lack of agreement over definitions of creativity. In addition, the many ways in which people can be creative and the theoretical framework from which creativity is viewed are reflected in the development of measurement devices. Thus far, the *Torrance Tests of Creative Thinking* (Torrance, 1974) are the most frequently used for both identification and validation of other instruments.

Clark (1979) presents an integrated model of creativity and describes creativity as a rational thinking function (p. 246). From this point of view, creativity can be defined as a high score on a creativity test. Most instruments for identification originate from this point of view (Clark, 1979).

Special Groups

Identifying the majority of the gifted and talented is a complex problem, while special group status compounds the task even more. Special populations present unique issues. For the handicapped, minorities, and women, the processes of identification must be cautious enough to be effective and bold enough to encompass appropriate strategies. Maker (1977) discusses the problems of searching for the gifted among the handicapped, beginning with the problem of explaining the seeming dichotomy between "handicapped" and "gifted." The dichotomy is artificial, arising from administrative and/or service delivery systems that require strict adherence to rules and regulations. For identifying the gifted handicapped, Maker supports the use of the procedures developed by Meeker (1969) and of the *Checklist of Creative Positives* developed by Torrance (1974), among other items. Maker also points out the need for a thorough understanding of the intellectual characteristics of those with various handicapping conditions. She suggests three approaches for identifying the gifted handicapped:

1 Search for potential rather than demonstrated ability.
2 Compare the performance of the handicapped with that of members of his or her own subgroup.
3 Give more weight to those characterisics that enable a handicapped person to more effectively compensate for his handicap (p. 30).

Bias The search for the gifted and talented among the culturally different presents special concerns as to the use of standardized testing. First we must consider the issue of bias, the extent to which tests, materials, and procedures are either racially or culturally discriminatory (Ysseldyke, 1979). The difference between cultural loading and cultural bias is important. An item or test is culturally loaded to the extent that success on the items varies with the background and experience of those taking the test. An item or test is biased if opportunities to learn the content of the items are not common to all environments (Reschly, 1979). "The degree of cultural loading of an item, however, depends upon the characteristics of the persons taking the test, not the item per se" (Reschly, 1979, p.231).

Categories of bias include:
- Content bias—if opportunities to learn the content are not common to all environments

Cultural bias presents concerns in identifying gifted and talented.

- Bias in use, or predictive validity—"tests cannot be regarded as fair unless they predict with equal accuracy for all groups" (p. 234)
- Atmosphere bias—testing conditions can affect the outcome and therefore the decisions made
- Bias in use, or social consequences—"test use is fair if the results are more effective intervention leading to improved competencies and expanded opportunities for individuals" (Reschly, 1979, 235)

Of all forms of bias, social consequences seem to have most impact on selection of gifted and talented children for two reasons: first, the empirical evidence regarding bias is not as strong as it may seem as first (Reschly, 1979; Sattler, 1974; 1982); second, and more important, the effects of the identification process must be that of "improved competencies and expanded opportunities" (p. 235). We must be aware of and control for bias during all steps of the process from screening to program planning. Scores may be lower, because of lack of opportunity rather than lack of potential, and the social consequences of not being selected for special experiences should be clear, both from the child's point of view and from society's vantage point.

Bruch (1975) identifies four major issues of measurement and cultural differences. First, there is a middle-class, mainstream basis to measurement instruments, resulting in conflict of values between minority and majority cultures; "culturally loaded" content that is irrelevant to the culturally different child's experience; and the need to replace the "deficit" concept with a "difference" model focusing on the development of a particular culture. Second, current assessment devices do not reflect subculture values, abilities, and knowledge. Third, there is a negative motivational impact from culturally loaded or irrelevant questions, negative expectations on the part of examinees, and the effects of teacher's and administrator's attitudes on rapport. Fourth, some concepts of measurement may be fallacious; for example, that objective measurement is the *way* to measure, that culturally different children develop in the same manner, that standardized tests measure adult competence, and that IQ tests measure unitary abilities, or an innate quality known narrowly as intelligence (p. 356).

One approach to overcoming the problems of identification among subcultures is that developed by Mercer and Lewis (1981), *The System of Multicultural Pluralistic Assessment* (SOMPA), although its use, particularly for the gifted and talented, has yet to be well documented (Oakland & Goldwater, 1979) and should be considered experimental (Salvia & Ysseldyke, 1981).

Currently, there is substantial effort to examine intelligence under conditions that do not require certain kinds of language, academic, and environmental experiences. The theoretical work of Sternberg (1981) and the assessment battery developed by Kaufman and Kaufman (1983) emphasize processes rather than products of intelligence. The use of intellectual abilities is measured rather than what has been acquired by intellectual effort. Sternberg (1982a) makes the point that most intelligence tests test for tasks and concepts that are "natural in everyday experience" (p. 63), while creativity tests look for uncommon experiences. Intelligence tests, then, penalize those who have not had opportunities to experience the tasks and concepts considered common.

Theories of Intelligence

Sternberg (1981) characterizes theories of intelligence as either psychometric or information processing. A *factor* is the common element of psychometric theories, while a *component* is the main unit of information processing theories. "A component is an elementary information process that operates upon internal representations of objects or symbols" (Sternberg, 1981, p. 86). The five functions of components are:

- Executive and control processes, called metacomponents
- Processes used in problem solving, called performance components
- Skills involved in learning or acquisition components
- Retrieving information
- Generalization or transfer components (pp. 90–91)

The gifted would be those with "superior access to and implementation of certain kinds of information-processing components" (p. 92), and emphasis should be on the central functions, or those particularly relevant to a discipline. Finally, training must be built on a sound and rich knowledge base.

The *Kaufman Assessment Battery for Children* (K-ABC) (Kaufman & Kaufman, 1983) is an instrument based on intelligence as "mental processing or problem-solving ability." The theories underlying the K-ABC are hemisphericity, neuropsychology, and mental processing, with emphasis on intelligence as mental processing free of language and academic experiences, although achievement is one of the four global scales. The other three global scales are sequential processing, or solving problems in a serial order such as copying hand movements (motor patterns); simultaneous processing, or holistic processing such as visual analogies; and mental processing, a composite of sequential and simultaneous processing or a global estimate of intellectual functioning (Kaufman & Kaufman, 1983, p. 4). Each scale has a mean of 100 and a standard deviation of 15. The K-ABC was developed for use with children from 2½ to 12½ years of age. Both theories offer exciting alternatives to traditional constructs and measures. The emphasis on process rather than product is particularly valuable for minorities; however, caution is still necessary since the appropriateness of these approaches for the gifted and talented have yet to be documented.

Torrance (1977) has formulated the notion of "creative positives" that can be observed among black disadvantaged children when they engage in challenging learning. These creative positives are observable characteristics, without the use of tests, for guiding the structuring of learning experiences.

Gifted Females

Regarding gifted women, Callahan (1979) and Fox (1977) find that the weight of evidence indicates no differences between the sexes in the intellectual processes of perception, learning, and memory.

> It appears that the only areas where boys in the general population seem clearly and consistently superior to girls are visual-spatial ability and achievement in mathematics

and science. Further, these differences are only apparent after the onset of adolescence. (Callahan, 1979, pp. 403-404)

Problems surrounding identification of gifted women rest not so much with instrumentation as with attitudinal and environmental effects and biasing. Fox (1977) points to sex-role stereotyping as one area of needed research, and Reschly's (1979) discussion of bias applies here. Before selecting a test or other instrument for identifying gifted girls, we must answer these questions:

1 Do girls and boys have the same opportunities to learn the content of the test items?
2 Do the tests predict equally well for boys and girls?
3 Will the testing atmosphere be conducive to motivation, language, values, and learning styles?
4 Will the testing result in appropriate educational experiences?

To combat sex-role stereotyping and the four sources of bias, test items should be environmentally equal; testing should be done by women in a flexible atmosphere; inservice information should be provided to counselors and teachers about the needs and characteristics of the gifted before they are asked to make nominations; and screening and identification procedures account for the effects of expectations on motivation and performance, so women (role-models) should perhaps explain such effects to the girls and encourage their fullest performance. Ideally, there should be no need for such steps in identifying gifted women, but we have not reached that point. In the meantime, we are not providing equal educational opportunities as long as stereotyping and expectations control performance.

The Arts

Identification of the gifted and talented in the arts presents yet another set of perplexing problems. Kreitner and Engin (1981) report that "Musical talent . . . must be measured not by its products, but by its symptoms, and there seems to be precious little agreement as to what the symptoms really are" (p. 193). They break musical talent into five categories:

- Perception—the ability to distinguish differences in physical quantities (frequency, amplitude, wave form, duration, etc.)
- Memory—the ability to remember these discriminations over time
- Reproduction—the ability to recreate (by singing, playing an instrument, or whatever) what is remembered
- Taste—the ability to distinguish good sounds from bad, either by culture's definition or one's own
- Artistry—the ability (including creativity) to put one's emotions into music (Kreitner & Engin, 1981, pp. 193–194)

Of the instruments available for identifying musical talent, each seems to measure some components that are not common across the range of tests. Finding reliable tests, then, must rest with the "symptoms," and the validity of tests to measure those symptoms.

Ellison and others (1981) suggest using biographical information to identify artistic talent. Ellison tried to identify three major biographical keys that would offer predictive validity across artistic areas and groups of individuals: performance, academic achievement, and leadership (p. 167).

Identifying artistic talent is complicated by the interactions of definitions, "symptoms," measurement strategies, and the predictive qualities of the instruments. We can make a tentative recommendation for combining test instruments, biographical keys, a checklist of items from the "Correlates of Artistic Talent" (Ellison et al., 1981), and Torrance's (1977) "Checklist of Creative Positives" as a multifactored procedure to cut across cultures and socioeconomic classes; however, the results need empirical validation.

Concepts and Definitions

Correct use of the vocabulary of identification and assessment adds precision to the practice, and increases the accuracy of communication among professionals. Understanding the terms enables the consumer to comprehend the material that accompanies tests and research discussions. The consumer—teacher, parent, or other professional—can then more accurately determine what material is appropriate or inappropriate in a particular situation and what will lead to valid decision making. Standardizing technical terminology assures that one concept or phrase will have the same or similar meaning to all who use it; for example, everyone accepts *mean* as the arithmetical average of a set of scores, their sum divided by the number of scores. Finally, adherence to fundamental concepts of assessment and identification yields meaningful information; ignoring the concepts results in erroneous information and/or results will, at best, be meaningless. At the extreme, the results may be erroneous but receive wide acceptance.

Technical Concepts

Measurement   "In its broadest sense, measurement is the assignment of numerals to objects or events according to rules" (Stevens, 1951, p. 1). Kerlinger (1973) points out that we can replace the word "numerals" (1, 2, 3, . . .*N*) with "symbols" (yes, no, Y, N, etc.). Numerals or symbols can be assigned according to a variety of rules that lead to different scales and different kinds of measurement (Stevens, 1951). We can see how numerals can be assigned to characteristics such as height or weight, or to classify items into two categories, such as tall or short, heavy or light, but intelligence, creativity, or achievement (actual or potential) are more difficult concepts to enumerate, and require complex rule systems.

Reliability   One of the first questions to ask about a measuring instrument is, "Is it reliable?" That is, will it yield the same or similar results each time we use it? How consistent is the scale?

For educational and psychological purposes, we must examine the extent to which the scores of a group of students will be similar over one or more retests with the same instrument. This consistency is usually expressed as a *reliability coefficient* or *coefficient of correlation.* The coefficient may be derived from test-retest data, the use of alternative forms, dividing the test into two equal parts (split-half), and deriving correlation coefficients from the scores obtained.

It is difficult to define a "good" coefficient of reliability. Coefficients of reliability (correlation) range from -1.0 to $+1.0$; thus, the answer depends on the test and what the results will be used for. The test may be the only one of its kind, or the learners' ages may differ. For example, the average coefficient of reliability for the WISC–R (Wechsler, 1974) is .96 for the Full Scale IQ score, and the various subtest averages range from .73 to .94 (split-half correlations). The correlations for the Stanford-Binet 1960 scale (Terman & Merrill, 1973) average .66; for the ages 2 years 6 months to 5 years, the mean correlation was .61; for the years 6 through 14 the mean was .67; at the adult years, the average correlation was .73. Determining "good" reliability, then, depends on the individual's age, the purpose of the testing, and the available options.

Validity   Validity refers to how well a test does what we want it to do. There are several types of validity, each of which plays a part in test selection and utilization and must be considered in light of the purpose for the testing. *Face validity*, a somewhat nontechnical term, means the test "looks" as if it will measure what it is supposed to measure. Face validity is determined by examining the test and its various components, subtests, and test items to see if it "makes sense" in light of the purpose of the test and the reasons for its use.

Content validity, which is particularly important for achievement tests, refers to how well a particular test measures content, skills, and knowledge in terms of adequate sampling of content and balance of items to intended outcomes. We judge content validity by comparing the test to course objectives and instructional materials.

Predictive validity refers to how well test results predict future success. For example, will an achievement test administered in high school predict grade-point average in college? Or, will an IQ obtained in the early grades predict success in high school?

Concurrent validity is a comparison of one measure to another measure of known merit. For example, new IQ tests are checked against known tests, such as the Stanford-Binet or WISC–R, by administering both the new test and the standard and correlating the results or examining them in some other way.

The final form of validity is *construct validity*. A construct is a relatively abstract trait or ability, such as intelligence and creativity. We do not actually measure intelligence, but the manifestation of intelligence, or what the test-maker considers the behavioral manifestations of intelligence. Vocabulary items, for example, frequently appear on intelligence tests. The number of words a child can define is considered evidence of his degree of intelligence; vocabulary acquisition is one component of the construct "intelligence." Construct validity is determined by analyzing the traits and comparisons of the test items to external data. Guilford's (1979) work exemplifies construct definition, identification, and analysis.

Reliability and validity are extremely important in the field of the gifted and talented. The selection and use of instruments for screening and identification, program evaluation, and research improve as measurement moves from discourse to precision. We must first know what we are looking for, then search for it with some confidence that what we find *is* what we were looking for.

Two other concepts of selection and use of test instruments are *effectiveness* and *efficiency* (Pegnato & Birch, 1959). *Effectiveness* refers to the percentage of gifted children located by a screening procedure. The procedure is effective depending on the number of gifted children located compared to the actual number of gifted in the population. If there are 100 gifted children in a population and the procedure locates 50, it is 50 percent effective (Pegnato & Birch, 1959).

Efficiency refers to the percentage of the number of children located by the screening process who are actually gifted. If 10 are referred and nine are (by criteria) gifted, the procedure is 90 percent efficient (Pegnato & Birch, 1959, p. 302). In actual practice, however, Pegnato and Birch recommend that if one must make a choice, one should sacrifice efficiency for effectiveness, that is, choose overnomination rather than miss children who should be selected.

In terms of instrument selection, we seldom discuss effectiveness and efficiency. An assessment or diagnostic tool is effective if it provides more useful information for developing learning experiences than can be obtained some other way. The amount of learner and teacher (or other professional) resources required to obtain the information determines efficiency. If the teacher or other professional can obtain the information in less time or at lower cost by other means, the instrument in question is not the most efficient method.

One must consider efficiency and effectiveness when selecting from among two or more possible tests or instruments. If two instruments provide essentially the same information, decide which requires fewer resources, such as professional and learner time, cost of administration, and scoring. On the other hand, one must also decide which instrument will provide the most useful data. The best selection is obviously the process with the high degree of both effectiveness and efficiency, but a procedure is not efficient if it is not effective.

Sometimes, of course, a test or other assessment tool serves some other purpose. Reliable and valid data add credibility to the identification process, to explanations of the selection process, and to elucidation of program effectiveness (evaluation), so one must always consider the purposes of data collection and what procedures will lead to the best use of resources.

Assessment   Assessment refers to determining the current status of an event or phenomenon—determining an individual's actual performance at a particular time. It does not focus on past events, or causes, nor on future events, or predictive potential.

Assessment procedures include standardized, norm-referenced tests, criterion-referenced tests, teacher-made tests, and observations. Intelligence, achievement, and creativity tests, sociograms, behavioral checklists, questionnaires, and interest surveys are all aspects of assessment. Assessment requires no underlying constructs for interpreting information. One obtains data and does not make inferences (Herson & Barlow, 1976).

Diagnosis   In contrast to assessment, diagnosis determines causes. The process of diagnosis involves gathering data to support or refute a possible underlying cause or set of causes. In educational terms, diagnosis determines the underlying causes of learner behavior. It involves inferred constructs manifested in behavior. Measurement procedures are indirect (Herson & Barlow, 1976); for example, intelligence is inferred by responses to test items.

Norm-Referenced Testing   Standardized tests are norm-referenced; that is, an individual's results are compared to a "normative" group, to show how the individual performed in comparison to those to whom the test was administered for purposes of establishing the "norm." Intelligence and achievement tests represent norm-referenced tests.

Criterion-Referenced Testing   Criterion-referencing compares a student's performance to some criterion to indicate adequate or appropriate task completion (Hambleton, 1982); for example, success, or mastery, may be correct completion of four out of five items, or 80 percent.

Stephens (1975) mentions six differences between criterion-referenced and norm-referenced measures.

1   Normed tests are based on representative sample populations; sampling procedures are not required for criterion measures.
2   Scores of normed tests are based on the mean number of responses of the sample population; scores on criterion measures are based on individual responses.
3   Performances of individuals on normed tests are relative to the group upon which the tests were standardized; criterion measures compare the individual's performances against predetermined criteria.
4   On normed tests, the student's performance is relative to other measures or conditions; on criterion measures, results are specific to tasks contained in the measures.
5   The goal of normed tests is to determine students' relative performances; the goal of criterion measures is to measure absolute performances.
6   Normed tests compare a student's performance to other students; criterion measures compare the individual's performance to a criterion. (Stephens, 1975, p. 56)

Statistical Terms

Mean   The mean is the arithmetical average of a set of numbers, the sum of the numbers divided by N, or the number count (number of numbers).

Standard Deviation   The standard deviation shows how the scores are distributed around the mean, or the average difference of each score from the mean, according to the formula:

$$\text{Standard Deviation} = \pm\sqrt{\frac{\text{Sum of the squared differences from the mean}}{N \text{ (number of scores)}}}$$

The larger the standard deviation in comparison to the mean, the wider the range of scores. There is no "good" or "bad" standard deviation; it depends on how far the scores range from the mean and on the total number of scores.

Percentile   The percentile is "the point (score) in a distribution at or below which fall the percent of cases indicated by the percentile (Mitchell, p. 5)." The 50th percentile would be the score or point below which 50 percent of the scores fall; for example, given nine scores, the 50th percentile would fall at 4.5 scores from the top or bottom score (.50 × 9 = 4.5). With an odd number of scores, one may count the midscore; with an even number of scores, say 16, the 50th percentile would be the eighth score (.50 x 16 = 8).

In the field of gifted education, one becomes accustomed to seeing scores in the 90th, 95th, or 99th percentiles, or above 90, 95, or 99 percent of the population who took that test for norming and standardizing purposes.

Median   The median is the score at the 50th percentile; out of 16 scores, the median is the eighth score.

Mode   The mode is the score achieved by most of the individuals who took the test.

Coefficient of Correlation   The coefficient of correlation shows the extent to which two sets of scores may vary concomitantly. It expresses the relationship, although not cause-effect relationship, between scores, such as reading achievement and intelligence. As intelligence scores increase, so do reading achievement scores. This relationship is expressed statistically as a coefficient ranging from − 1.00 to 0 to + 1.00. A correlation of + 1.00 indicates that high scores on one test will be accompanied by high scores on the second test; those who scored highest on test A will score highest on test B and those who scored lowest on test A will score lowest on test B. A zero (0) correlation indicates there is no relationship between the two tests, and a correlation of − 1.00 indicates that those who scored highest on test A would perform in the lowest extreme on test B.

Coefficients of correlation are frequently used in test construction to compare the results of a new test to the results of testing performed with instruments that are known to have statistical reliability and validity.

Factor Analysis   At its most basic level, factor analysis is a way to reduce large volumes of data into more manageable groups by examining the correlations among several sets of data. With the scores of 30 tests administered to 300 children, or 9000 scores, we may need to examine the interrelationships of the test scores and reduce the findings into usable categories. The new categories become "factors" defined by the positive and negative relationships among the various scores. Five scores may contribute to factor A, six scores to factor B, and so forth, until the scores of the 30 tests are placed into factors with other scores or become factors by themselves. The factors are hypothetical, but are named by both convention and research examination of logical consistency within and among the factors.

The most notable factor analytic work is Guilford's Structure of Intellect Model (1956), which has furthered the work in creativity (Khatena, 1979) and defined categories of intellectual activity as they apply to education (Meeker, 1969) and to educating gifted and talented children.

Regression toward the Mean   We have defined the mean as the average of a set of scores. "Scores of tests change as a statistical fact of life: on retest, on the average, they *regress* toward the mean" (Kerlinger, 1973, p. 320). In other words, if a youngster achieves a very high score on a pretest, there is a statistical probability that she will get a lower score on a second administration—a score closer toward the mean. By statistical chance alone, a student may obtain a lower score the second time. If, for example, IQ scores change, which they do (Sattler, 1974), it is possible that if the same test is given twice, the second score will be lower than the first. The same may be said for achievement tests as well as other types of tests. Regression affects the lower extreme of scores as well, but the second score is, by chance alone, likely to move up toward the mean. Kerlinger (1974) quotes Galton describing this phenomenon as "regression toward mediocrity" (p. 605).

Standard Error of Measurement   The standard error of measurement expresses the range in which the hypothetically "true" score may lie. If one were to administer the same test to the same individual 100 times, one would obtain not one score, but several. We hypothesize that the person's "true" score would lie somewhere within the range of the various scores. Scores vary because of measurement error and chance; the larger the range, the less confidence we can have in obtaining a "true" score. Mitchell says it is "an amount such that in about two-thirds of the cases the obtained score would not differ by more than one [Standard error of measurement] from the true score. The true score is then within the range of plus-or-minus one standard error of measurement two times out of three."

The average standard error of measurement for the WISC–R Full Scale IQ is 3.19; that is, two-thirds of the time an individual's "true" Full Scale IQ is between plus and minus 3.19 [a Full Scale IQ of 130 would be from 126.81 to 133.19]. Standard errors of measurement differ by test, age, and IQ (Sattler, 1974). For the Stanford-Binet (Terman & Merrill, 1973) at ages 2½ to 5½, and IQs between 140–149, the error is 6.8. At the 16–18 range, the error is 2.4 for IQs between 60–69 (Sattler, 1974, p. 441).

To reduce identification errors, the several measurement concepts we have discussed, coupled with awareness of the types of bias and wise use, will help direct the process toward accuracy across cultures, socioeconomic classes, sexes, and handicapping conditions.

Assessment

After the children have been selected for special experiences, our next step is to determine their current levels of performance in relation to program objectives. This process is called *assessment*. Although we can view assessment from many perspectives, our discussion will concentrate on criterion- and norm-referenced assessment and survey information.

The advantage of criterion-referenced assessment (CRA) is its clear and direct relationship to the program's goals and objectives. We can prepare CRAs with particular children in mind, control vocabulary, and adapt the method of presentation to fit a particular child or group of children. CRAs tell us where a child is in relation to established objectives; they do not infer causes nor predict future performance.

To develop CRAs, one must be familiar with and competent in preparing instructional objectives, since objectives serve as the basis for assessment. Minimum requirements for an instructional objective are:

1 The condition under which the behavior will be performed.
2 The behavior to be performed.
3 The criterion or accuracy of performance (Mager, 1975).
These instructional objectives include condition, behavior, and criterion:

Condition: given a list of 50 biology terms
Behavior: the student will accurately define in writing
Criterion: 45 out of 50 of the terms

Condition: given a sheet of 15 Labonnotation symbols
Behavior: the student will perform
Criterion: each of them in sequence

Condition: given a recording of 15 one-minute passages
Behavior: students will name each passage and composer
Criterion: for 12 of the 15 passages

These three items test knowledge through identification or recall process. They do not test higher level processes. The following items are more difficult to compose and judge:

Condition: given a theme, "Winter," the students will
Behavior: write a three- to five-page story
Criterion: with an unusual beginning, inclusion of the reader, and develop the theme

Condition: given a theme, "Winter," the students will
Behavior: write a three- to five-page story,
Criterion: changing the theme from "Winter" to "Summer" through an unusual ending

Condition: given a theme, "Winter," the students will
Behavior: write a three- to five-page paper comparing "Winter" and "Summer" with political philosphies
Criterion: by stating the premises, supporting the premises, and summarizing the positions taken and their support

Although we can state the criteria for judging the last three items, they are more ambiguous than the criteria for the first three items. An additional criterion might be "as stated by two out of three judges," thus allowing for more than one opinion. A second strategy would be to develop a rating scale; for example,

Good—Average—Poor

or

Poor		Neutral		Excellent
1	2	3	4	5

or

Never   Sometimes   Frequently   Always

The criterion may then be stated as "a rating of four or better," or a rating of "Frequently or Always." As items for measurement become more complex, the criteria become more difficult to express precisely. We can, however, develop criteria that are consistent with the program's goals and objectives and gain information about specific instructional content and activities. (Several examples are available in Renzulli, 1975, and TAG, 1979.)

Norm-referenced assessment (NRA) is based on a comparison of the individual's performance with that of a norm group, the *standardization sample*. Norm-referenced testing thus involves some baseline information that has already been obtained through the identification process.

Remember when using NRAs that many tests do not have an adequate ceiling to measure the performance levels of some of the most gifted. A test constructed for an older population is valid if the test is difficult enough (Stanley, 1976, p. 5). Alvino, McDonnell, and Richert (1981) compiled a list of 120 test instruments and techniques by the five identification categories for giftedness, and Laubenfels (1977) lists the 50 most frequently cited instruments from the literature.

The other type of assessment instrument we will consider is the questionnaire. Interest inventories developed locally or obtained elsewhere (for example, Mehrens & Lehman, 1969), sociograms, sentence completion tests, and attitude inventories provide more information about where the child is in relation to program goals and objectives.

Two important issues to keep in mind when planning and conducting assessments are the relevance of the information, by norms and for the learners, and the utility of the information, for planning and in quantity.

When selecting an NRA instrument, it is most important to

- Review the characteristics of the normative sample
- Select instruments that have been normed on populations that represent the youngsters to be assessed as fairly as possible
- Select instruments whose norms will carry meaning for planning

If the instrument does not provide an adequate sampling of the skill or knowledge in question, the norms will convey little meaning. It is also important to realize that the 99th percentile on one test is not directly comparable to the 99th percentile on another instrument. Items on one test may be more difficult, or one may be required to answer more of the items correctly, so the normative data from the two tests will not be interchangeable.

Utility of data refers to whether the information derived from testing actually helps the planning process. If one accrues a mass of data, one must be able to reduce the information to manageable proportions. There is a fine line between collecting enough information and amassing more data than can be useful to the planning process. We may decide to gather all possible information and then select the data we need for planning, or we may first examine the program goals and collect only enough information to guide each child toward those goals. In terms of ideal practice, one may prefer the first approach; in terms of economy of resources, the second approach is more practical. We need as much assessment as is necessary to direct the learners toward the goals.

Sattler lists these steps in the assessment process:

1   Selecting the test

2 Administering the test
3 Scoring the test
4 Observing behavior
5 Writing the report (interpretation)
6 Counseling activities (possibly)
7 Conducting research (possibly) (Sattler, 1974, pp. 4–5)

Guidelines for conducting assessment can be grouped into three categories: (1) preparation for administration; (2) during administration; and (3) following administration.

Preparation

Before actually assessing a child, one can improve the quality of the results and put both student and administrator at ease by first reading the test manual carefully to note particular administration requirements, time limits, sequencing of items, and other related activities. You should practice with the tests, particularly if you must manipulate things—cards, pictures, or actual objects. Develop some ease in moving from item to item and handling and placing test objects, score sheet, stopwatch, and other paraphernalia. A "trial run" sometimes greatly improves the ease and flow of administration.

After preparing for administration, give careful attention to establishing the test environment. Consider noise level and visual distractions, and arrange comfortable seating for both child and administrator. Establish a technique to reduce interruptions; often a closed door is sufficient.

Next, prepare the equipment and materials for testing. Be sure appropriate marking devices (pens, pencils, crayons, and so forth) and the score sheet or booklet are readily available. Conduct an inventory of the test packet or container to be sure the required objects are there and in their proper place or sequence. Have a stopwatch available if it is needed. If items are needed for the testing that are not included in the kit, collect them and put them in place.

Finally, schedule the test at a time that will encourage participation of both child and teacher. Be attentive to when the teacher is most willing to have the student be absent from class, and be sure the student is not missing a favorite activity. Try to schedule the test when the student is most alert. You will probably not be able to meet all of the requirements, but attention to these details will provide optimal test conditions.

Testing

McLoughlin and Lewis (1981) make several recommendations for actual test administration. First, consider the student's physical needs. Hunger, thirst, seating, and other physiological distractions should be attended to. Address the psychological needs of the examinee. This should be initiated by establishing *rapport*, a "working relationship," between student and examiner. First, introduce yourself, and be pleasant and friendly. Second, ask the student questions about age, grade, and favorite subjects. Third, discuss the purpose of the testing session. Fourth, explain to the student what will happen during the session in terms of time involved, the types of

Select a test setting where you will have minimal interruptions.

activities, that the student is not expected to know all the answers, that he will not be told if an answer is right or wrong, and whether the test will be timed (McLoughlin & Lewis, 1981, p. 125).

After testing begins, the examiner must consider several points. If scoring takes place during administration, is the scoring accurate—in the right place with the appropriate markings? One must also observe the student and the approach to problem solving, including:

1   Motor or vocal responses
2   Time between presentation and response (latency)
3   Amount of response—few or many words, use of elaboration
4   Organization of responses, including logical relationships
5   Kinds of responses in situations where the answer is not known—a shrug,

an excuse, verbal "salad," or possibly restating the question and answering the new

6 Responses that are peculiar to the student (idiosyncratic), sometimes incomprehensible, or do not relate to the question (McLoughlin & Lewis, 1981, pp. 132–34).

Finally, the examiner should be alert for signs of frustration and fatigue and judge whether to proceed or terminate the testing. Testing cannot be terminated in some situations, either because of administration requirements or time commitments by examiner or student. Under these circumstances, testing must continue, but the examiner should take careful notes and consider the impact of fatigue when interpreting the results.

At the close of the testing session, the examiner should acknowledge the student's participation, excuse him, or escort him back to the classroom. If the child is accompanied to the classroom, recognize the teacher, if possible, by voice, nod, or wave.

After Testing

Some tasks remain after the testing session. First and foremost is interpreting the results, including scoring the test and writing observations. Next are the follow-up activities or record keeping—recording results in appropriate locations and sharing the results with the appropriate persons, and any communication with the principal or teacher relating to the conduct of the session rather than results, perhaps a thank-you note or a phone call.

Smith, Neisworth, and Greer summarize the testing process in Table 2-1.

Individualization

One outcome of the identification and assessment process is an accumulation of information about the student. We must then use the information to provide "meaningful learning experiences in the most effective and efficient way" (Fox, 1979, p. 105), or differentiated education. We can define differentiated education as learning opportunities designed for the learner's unique behavioral processes, the roles they are likely to assume as adults, and the children's motivational systems. Specially prepared teachers will present a curriculum of higher cognitive concepts and processes using strategies that accommodate individual learning styles. Special grouping arrangements will include administrative procedures such as special classes, honors classes, seminars, resource rooms, and the like. Continuous screening, special materials, transportation, and evaluation will be integral aspects of implementation, coordination, and planning. A differentiated education will emphasize individualized instruction (Renzulli, 1978, 1975; Ward, 1981).

Individualized instruction is another term that means many things to many people, and not all the meanings are positive. For our purposes, we define it as instruction developed for the learner, based on assessment data and the logical next steps in learning. Individualized instruction does not mean that only one learner can

Table 2-1 ASSESSMENT CHECKLIST: CHILD ASSESSMENT

Components	Question	Yes	No	Undecided
A. The Instrument				
1. Reliability	1. Is there evidence that provides a stable score over time?	_____	_____	_____
	2. Are alternate forms available that are shown to be equivalent?	_____	_____	_____
	3. Are data available on acceptable internal consistency (split-half)?	_____	_____	_____
Enter number of questions answered yes ☐				
2. Validity	4. Does the test cover the content it is supposed to?	_____	_____	_____
	5. Are results on this test comparable to results on other tests that purport to assess the same thing?	_____	_____	_____
	6. Does the test have demonstrated high-predictive capability?	_____	_____	_____
Enter number of questions answered yes ☐				
3. Objectivity	7. Are the test instructions and scoring criteria so clear that different administrators will obtain about the same results with the same child?	_____	_____	_____
Enter number of questions answered yes ☐				
4. Norms and Standardization	8. Does the test include information on results across a large number of children similar to the child being tested? Are norms appropriate for comparison purposes?	_____	_____	_____
Enter number of questions answered yes ☐				

Table 2-1 Continued

Components	Question	Yes	No	Undecided
5. Utility	9. Are the effort and time required to administer the test justified relative to the usefulness of the results in helping the child?	____	____	____
Enter number of questions answered yes ☐				
B. The Examiner 1. Test Selection	10. Has the examiner chosen the test with care, considered the child, circumstances, and other available test options?	____	____	____
	11. Is test selection good in the context of other tests in a battery? Could an oral rather than written test be used, if other tests are written?	____	____	____
Enter number of questions answered yes ☐				
2. Use of Standardized Procedures	12. Does the examiner follow standard procedure in administering the test?	____	____	____
	13. Is the scoring computed appropriately? Do you have confidence in the accuracy of the computations?	____	____	____
Enter number of questions answered yes ☐				
3. Establishing Rapport and the Setting	14. Does the tester smile at the child, use a first name, and use other ways to reduce the unfamiliarity of the situation?	____	____	____

48

Table 2-1 Continued

Components	Question	Yes	No	Undecided
	15. Is the testing location comfortable and adequately lighted?	____	____	____
	16. Is the location free of distraction?	____	____	____
	17. Is the testing situation part of or does it at least resemble the child's usual environment?	____	____	____
Enter number of questions answered yes				
C. The Child	18. Does the examiner consider the test-taking skill of the child?	____	____	____
	19. Does the examiner note whether the child evidences any unusual level of anxiety during the testing?	____	____	____
	20. At the time of testing, is the child free of unusual or adverse circumstances in school or at home?	____	____	____
Enter number of questions answered yes				
D. Interpretation	21. Does the examiner report test results in a way that avoids unwarranted interpretation and conjecture?	____	____	____
Enter number of questions answered yes				

participate in an instructional activity at a time. For example, if a class of 25 students needs information about mitosis, it may be most efficient to present the information to all the students at once; individually, each student obtains the information, not in 25 one-hour sessions, but in one one-hour session, or some other length of time.

Occasionally, people confuse individualized instruction with individualized attention. A situation where every student is doing the same task, perhaps a worksheet, and the teacher spends one minute with one child, three minutes with another child, and two minutes with another child, is an example of individualized attention but not of instruction.

Another aspect of individualized instruction is the practice of setting individual time limits for children to complete the same activity; for example, if the task is to complete 20 mathematical calculations, one child may be given 30 minutes, another 10 minutes, and a third, 15 minutes. One might also give assignments of different lengths. The slow learner might receive 15 problems, the average child 20, and another 30 problems, although this approach tends to discourage giftedness (Delisle, 1982).

More important than varying attention times, varying time limits, and different assignment lengths, however, is basing individualized instruction on the learner's current level of performance and the logical sequence of that which is to be learned. Individualized instruction is prescriptive in that learning is based on current status in relation to longer-range goals.

Methods for Individualizing

There are several ways to individualize instruction, beginning with administrative arrangements—among them, special schools, early entrance, grade acceleration, resource rooms, and Saturday classes. Within the classroom, differentiation takes place through the series of educational experiences, or curriculum. Components (goals, content, instructional strategies, resources, and evaluation) and modes of presentation (breadth and/or depth, tempo and/or pacing, or nature and kind) help to modify curriculum (Passow, 1981, p. 96). Maker (1982) focuses on products and environment as well as content and process.

In Parts Two and Three, we will examine the content, process, products, and environment appropriate for the academically gifted. Differentiation through individualization requires content and strategy changes. We modify content by examining the structure of knowledge in a content area. Structure is expressed through the laws, principles, and generalizations of a field; scope and sequence express the order of presentation. Integration, or transformation, is the interaction of various fields of study. Presently, individualization takes place through individual plans of study.

Individualized Education Plan

The individualized education plan (IEP) documents current levels of performance, goals and objectives, and strategies and evaluation procedures for each child who receives special experiences (Council for Exceptional Children, 1978; Pendarvis & Grossi, 1980; Wolf & Stephens, 1979). The IEP is a result of federal legislation for handicapped children, P.L. 94–142, which was intended to ensure a *free, appropriate* public education for *all* handicapped children (Turnbull, Strickland, & Brantley, 1978). IEPs can improve educational practice by specifying
- Sequential curriculum development
- Coordination of programming
- Increased attention to the individual needs of students
- Specification of needed services
- Systematic evaluation

- Increased professional accountability. (Turnbull, Strickland, & Brantley, 1978, p. 12)

The basic components of an IEP include:

1   A written statement of the child's present levels of performance
2   A statement of annual goals to be achieved by the child
3   Short-term objectives to be realized in the achievement of each annual goal
4   A statement of the extent to which the student will be able to benefit from participation in a regular education program and for what purposes
5   A description of all special education and related services required to meet the student's need
6   The projected starting dates for, and duration of, these services. (Council for Exceptional Children, 1978)

IEPs demonstrate both format and content. The IEP puts into writing the actual experiences each child will receive and the criteria by which outcomes will be judged. It serves as both instructional plan and evaluation plan, and results in communication with parents. In conferences, parents learn what to expect from the child's school experiences, and can accept, offer refinements and alternatives, or reject a particular plan.

Renzulli's work is discussed in chapters 6 and 7.

Contracts

Another form of individual study planning is the contract (Kaplan et al., 1973; Wolf & Stephens, 1979). Effective contracts require (1) a clear statement of the terms of the contract; (2) a clear statement of the responsibilities of all concerned; (3) focus on the positive; (4) fairness; (5) honesty; and (6) an emphasis on accomplishment rather than obedience (Stephens, 1975). A contract should be considered a formal agreement between two parties—student and teacher or students and students. There is an understanding of what each party will do to complete the agreement, under what circumstances, and within what time frame. The contract should include possible "checkpoints," particularly for young children or for those using one for the first time. The checkpoints allow the teacher to examine student progress to see whether the project was too ambitious or whether the student needs additional activities. Checkpoints also let the teacher know if the student is working on the project rather than waiting until the last minute.

Self-Directed Learning

At the highest level of idividualized instruction, the learner directs her own learning activities. Lifelong learning will be the way of life for many gifted and talented children, so they need the tools to facilitate their learning. Treffinger (1975) presents the Self-Directed Learning model for helping to move learning from teacher-directed and controlled to learner-directed; rather than the teacher's specifying content, objectives, strategies, and evaluation, the learner manages her behavior in concert with the teacher. The teacher's role in Self-Directed Learning is that of facilitator and resource.

Cognitive Behavioral Processing

An alternative to Treffinger's Self-Directed Learning model is the Cognitive Behavioral Processing (CBP) model developed by Swassing and Stephens (Swassing, 1982). CBP is a problem-solving model based on Landa's (1976) work in algorithms and heuristics.

> CBP is the systematic application of modeling strategies for the sequential acquisition, manipulation and expression of complex, hierarchical problem-solving systems (Swassing, 1982, P. 8).

CBP has no single model of problem-solving; rather, there are many models. The teacher's task is to prepare the learners, as problem solvers, to develop models of problems. Problem models specify the problem and define the process whereby the learner moves from the problem environment to the solution or outcome. In a problem environment, the problem solver is given some information or set of circumstances and asked to define one or more solutions or outcomes.

Problem Environments Problem environments can be formula, branching, or open. Formula problems are of the closed, or algorithmic, type, and present the task in such a way that there is only one way to solve the problem and only one correct answer, for example, 2 + 2 = 4, or "underline the past tense of run in the following sentence." Figure 2-1 is a diagram of Formula problems.

The branching and open problem environments shown in Figure 2-2 depend on the search field. The search field is the area or areas in which a solution may be found. For a branching problem, the search field is limited by the rules or operations set forth by the task statement (for example, "write a sentence using the word *run*"). The search field for an open problem is unlimited; it is possible that answers may be found in several fields or in some combination of fields.

> The specific difficulties posed by many creative problems are due to the fact that the problem suggests that the solution be sought in one field, when in fact it is to be found in a different one (Landa, 1975, p. 119) . . . difficulties in creative thinking often lie, . . . not in limiting the field of choice and the number of alternatives chosen and tested, but in crossing the boundaries of one field into a new field, one not given beforehand and not suggested by the problem, but in which are to be found objects (actual or ideal) from which the solution may be selected (p. 120).

Besides the differences in their search fields, branching and open problems differ from formula problems in their outcomes. Although different problem solvers

Figure 2-1 The Formula Problem Environment

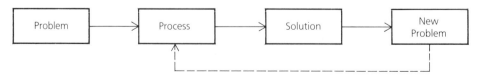

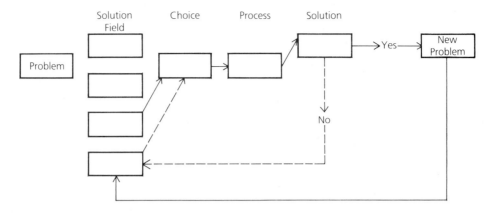

Figure 2-2 Branching and Open Problem Environments

can develop different solutions, branching problems will have conventional or circum-scribed outcomes or solutions. For example, given the task "write as many ex-pressions as you can write for the numeral 9," acceptable answers could include 18 ÷ 2, 3 × 3, 2 × 4 + 1, 3 + 3 + 3, 36 ÷ 4, and so forth. There are many possible answers, but all of them are within the set of mathematical expressions that equal 9 (in base 10).

The outcomes of open problem environments may or may not be conventional. Each problem solver may select different search fields, different paths (actual steps to solve a problem), and therefore different outcomes. Given the state of the art relating to the question, some problem environments may have no solution. There may be a solution in the future, but as of the moment, none is available. In other words, the task statement places few or no limits or rules on the nature of the solution (for example: compose a poem).

The problem environment is initiated when a problem solver is given a task and asked to identify one or more solutions (problem model). The process model is the sequence of events leading from the problem to the solution; for example:

1   Identify the type of problem model—formula, branching, or open—to determine the type of search field and nature of the outcome
2   If it is a formula problem, proceed directly to the process; if a branching or open problem, identify the nature of the search field or fields (limited or unlimited)
3   If it is a branching field, identify the parameters of the field and define the possible paths; if an unlimited field, define as many search fields as possible
4   Select the most likely path from the search field
5   Test the path to see if it will lead to a solution or solutions
6   Confirm or reject the selected path
7   If confirmed, solve the problem
8   If not confirmed, select a new path or define a new search field, and repeat steps 4 to 7 (Swassing, 1982).

The purpose of Cognitive Behavioral Processing is to teach learners (problem solvers) how to prepare problems, identify steps for locating solutions, test possible solutions, then prepare the solution. The problem solvers develop models of the problems and models of the processes for solving these problems. Given a set of procedures, the solver can systematically address many problem models, even problems that do not reveal solutions after systematic efforts.

Learners will need instructional experiences that cross disciplines and arts. Their IEPs will reflect science, art, mathematics, literature, and thought that integrates the range of learning opportunities. The important concepts in the major areas of study will be expressed through overlapping processes and methods common to inquiry in any field. Learning, or problem solving, will set in motion a search for solutions in far-reaching and diverse fields. The integrations, transformations, and solutions will reflect the major concepts of each field, but the solutions will not be anchored in a single discipline.

Summary

Identification, assessment, and programming of gifted and talented children is demanding and difficult. Some children virtually "identify" themselves; on the other hand, some children defy well-guided identification procedures.

The two-part process of identification, screening and identification, should be undertaken by a committee, whose first task will be developing a definition of the gifted. The definition specifies the characteristics of the children sought, and from there the instruments that will be used to measure the characteristics. Identification instruments must meet certain psychometric properties, particularly reliability and validity.

While the overall effects of bias are not as statistically dramatic as previously assumed, bias does play a central role in the use of testing among minority populations, the handicapped, women, and the culturally and racially different. We need to guard against atmosphere bias, or the effects of the testing environment on the child's performance, and bias in use. If testing conditions are distracting, the child may miss the opportunity for the best possible educational experiences.

Appropriate learning or differentiated education is the goal of identification. Specially prepared teachers, with appropriate curriculum, materials, equipment, and environment are key elements to differentiated education. The IEP specifies each child's most appropriate learning opportunities. Self-directed or self-guided instruction is the goal of the educational process for gifted and talented children.

Through the use of problem solving techniques, various disciplines can be integrated into solutions that reflect the disciplines yet differ from any of one or more areas of study. The search for solutions calls for examining many fields and selecting the paths or steps that lead to solutions.

Identification, assessment, and programming represent a triad of processes, each integral to the best possible education for gifted and talented children and emphasizing each child's uniqueness and individuality.

References

Alvino, J., R. C. McDonnel, and S. Richert. National survey of identification practices in gifted and talented education. *Exceptional Children* 48 (1981): 124–32.

Baldwin, A., and J. Wooster. *Baldwin identification matrix inservice kit for the identification of gifted and talented students.* Buffalo, N.Y.: D.O.K. Publishers, 1977.

Boring, E. G. Intelligence as the tests test it. *The New Republic* (1923): 35–37. Reprinted in *Studies in individual differences: The search for intelligence.* Edited by J. J. Jenkins and D. G. Paterson. New York: Appleton-Century-Crofts, 1961.

Bruch, C. B. Assessment of creativity in culturally different children. *The Gifted Child Quarterly* 19 (1975): 164–74.

Callahan, C. M. The Gifted and talented woman. *The gifted and the talented: Their education and development. The seventy-eighth yearbook of the National Society for the Study of Education: Part I.* Edited by A.H. Passow. Chicago: University of Chicago Press, 1979.

Clark, B. *Growing up gifted.* Columbus, Ohio: Charles E. Merrill, 1979.

Council for Exceptional Children. *Developing individualized education programs (IEPs) for the gifted and talented.* Reston, Va.: The Council for Exceptional Children, 1978.

Delisle, J. Learning to underachieve: *Roeper Review* 4 (1982): 16–18.

Delisle, J. R., S. M. Reis, and E. G. Gubbins. The revolving door identification and programming model. *Exceptional Children* 48 (1981): 152–56.

Durden, W. G. Presentation at G/C/T Directions IV: Computers for the gifted at home and school. Mobile, Ala., February 4, 1983.

Ellison, R. L., C. Abe, D. G. Fox, K. E. Coray, and C. W. Taylor. Using biographical information in identifying artistic talent. In *Psychology and Education of the Gifted* 3rd ed. Edited by W. B. Barbe and J. S. Renzulli. New York: Irvington, 1981.

Figueroa, R. A. The system of multicultural pluralistic assessment. *School Psychology Digest* 9 (1979): 28–36.

Fox, L. H. Programs for the gifted and talented: An overview. In *The Gifted and the talented: Their education and development. The seventy-eighth yearbook of the National Society for the Study of Education.* Edited by A. H. Passow. Chicago: University of Chicago Press, 1979.

Fox, L. H. Sex differences: Implications for program planning for the academically gifted. In *The gifted and the creative: A fifty year perspective.* Edited by J. C. Stanley, W. C. George, and C. H. Solano. Baltimore, Md.: Johns Hopkins University, 1977.

Frazier, M. M. Screening and identification of gifted students. In *An administrative handbook on developing programs for the gifted and talented.* Edited by J B. Jordan and J. A. Grossi. Reston, Va.: Council for Exceptional Children, 1980.

Guilford, J. P. *Cognitive psychology with a frame of reference.* San Diego, Calif.: Edits, 1979.

Hambleton, R. K. Advances in criterion-referenced testing technology. In *The handbook of school psychology.* Edited by C. R. Reynolds and T. B. Gutkin. New York: John Wiley, 1982.

Herson, M., and D. H. Barlow. *Single-case experimental designs: Strategies for studying behavior change.* New York: Pergammon Press, 1976.

Kaplan, S. N., J. A. B. Kaplan, S. K. Masden, and B. K. Taylor. *Change for children: Ideas and activities for individualizing instruction.* Pacific Palisades, Calif.: Goodyear, 1973.

Karnes, F. A., and E. C. Collins. *Assessment in gifted education.* Springfield, Ill.: Charles C. Thomas, 1981.

Kaufman, A. S., and N. L. Kaufman. *K–ABC: Kaufman assessment battery for children: Sampler manual.* Circle Pines, Minn.: American Guidance Service, 1983.

Keating, D. P. Discovering quantitative precocitry. In *Intellectual talent: Research and development.* Edited by D. P. Keating. Baltimore, Md.: Johns Hopkins University, 1976.

Kerlinger, F. N. *Foundations of behavior research.* 2nd ed. New York: Holt, Rinehart and Winston, 1973.

Khatena, J. Major directions in creativity research. *The Gifted Child Quarterly* 20 (1976): 336–49.

Kreitner, K., and A. W. Engin. Identifying musical talent. In *Psychology and education of the gifted.* 3rd ed. Edited by W. B. Barbe and J. S. Renzulli. New York: Irvington, 1981.

Landa, L. N. *Instructional regulation and control: Cybernetics, algorithmization and heuristics in education.* Translated by W. Desch. Englewood Cliffs, N.J.: Educational Technology Publications, 1976.

Laubenfels, J. *The gifted student: An annotated bibliography.* Westport, Conn.: Greenwood Press, 1977.

Mager, R. F. *Preparing instructional objectives.* 2nd ed. Belmont, Calif.: Fearon, 1975.

Maker, C. J. *Curriculum development for the gifted.* Rockville, Md.: Aspen, 1982.

Maker, C. J. *Providing programs for the gifted handicapped.* Reston, Va.: The Council for Exceptional Children, 1977.

Male, R. A., and P. Perrone. Identifying talent and giftedness: Part I. *Roeper Review* 2 (1979a): 5–7.

Male, R. A., and P. Perrone. Identifying talent and giftedness: Part III. *Roeper Review* 2 (1980): 9–11.

McGinn, P. V. Verbally gifted youth: Selection and description. In *Intellectual talent: Research and development.* Edited by D. P. Keating. Baltimore, Md.: Johns Hopkins University, 1976.

McLoughlin, J. A., and R. B. Lewis. *Assessing special students.* Columbus, Ohio: Charles E. Merrill, 1981.

Meeker, M. N. *The structure of intellect: Its interpretation and uses.* Columbus, Ohio: Charles E. Merrill, 1969.

Mehrens, W. A., and I. J. Lehman. *Standardized tests in education.* New York: Holt, Rinehart and Winston, 1969.

Mercer, J. R., and J. F. Lewis. Using the system of multicultural pluralistic assessment (SOMPA) to identify the gifted minority child. In *Psychology and education of the gifted.* 3rd ed. Edited by W. B. Barbe and J. S. Renzulli. New York: Irvington, 1981.

Mitchell, B. C. *A glossary of measurement terms.* Test Service Notebook 13. New York: Harcourt Brace Jovanovich, Undated.

Oakland, T., and D. L. Goldwater. Assessment and intervention for mildly retarded and learning disabled children. In *School psychology: Perspectives and issues.* Edited by G. D. Phye and D. J. Reschly. New York: Academic Press, 1979.

Passow, A. H. Nurturing giftedness: Ways and means. Edited by A. H. Kramer, D. Bitan, N. Butler-Por, A. Evyator, and E. Landau. In *Gifted children: Challenging their potential: New perspectives and alternatives.* New York: World Council for Gifted and Talented Children, 1981.

Pegnato, C. W., and J. W. Birch. Locating gifted children in junior high schools: A comparison of methods. *Exceptional Children* 25 (1959): 300-4.

Pendarvis, E. D., and J. A. Grossi. Designing and operating programs for the gifted and talented handicapped. In *An administrative handbook on designing programs for the gifted and talented.* Edited by J. B. Jordan and J. A. Grossi. Reston, Va.: Council for Exceptional Children, 1980.

Popham. W. J. *Educational statistics: Use and interpretation.* New York: Harper and Row, 1967.

Renzulli, J. S. *The enrichment triad model: A guide for developing defensible programs for the gifted and talented.* Wethersfield, Conn.: Creative Learning Press, 1977.

Renzulli, J. S. Identifying key features in programs for the gifted. In *Psychology and education of the gifted.* 2nd ed. Edited by W. B. Barbe and J. S. Renzulli. New York: Irvington, 1975.

Renzulli, J. S., and L. H. Smith. Revolving door: A truer turn for the gifted. *Learning* (1980a): 91-93.

Renzulli, J. S., and L. H. Smith. A practical model for designing individual educational programs (IEPs) for gifted and talented students. *G/C/T,* 11 (1980b): 3-8.

Renzulli, J. S., L. H. Smith, A. J. White, C. M. Callahan, and R. K. Hartman. *Scales for rating the behavioral characteristics of superior students.* Wethersfield, Conn.: Creative Learning Press, 1976.

Reschly, D. J. Nonbiased assessment. In *School psychology: Perspective and issues.* Edited by G. D. Phye and D. J. Reschly. New York: Academic Press, 1979.

Salvia, J., and J. E. Ysseldyke. *Assessment in special and remedial education.* 2nd ed. Boston: Houghton Mifflin, 1981.

Sattler, J. M. *Assessment of children's intelligence and special abilities.* 2nd ed. Boston: Allyn and Bacon, 1982.

Sattler, J. M. *Assessment of children's intelligence.* Rev. ed. Boston: Allyn and Bacon, 1974.

Smith, R. M., J. T. Neisworth, and J. G. Greer. *Evaluating educational environments.* Columbus, Ohio: Charles E. Merrill, 1978.

Stanley, J. C. Use of tests to discover talent. In *Intellectual talent: Research and development.* Edited by D. P. Keating. Baltimore, Md.: Johns Hopkins University, 1976.

Stephens, T. M. *Implementing behavioral approaches in elementary and secondary schools.* Columbus, Ohio: Charles E. Merrill, 1975.

Sternberg, R. J. Nonentrenchment in the assessment of intellectual giftedness. *Gifted Child Quarterly* 26 (1982a):63-67.

Sternberg, R. J. Lies we live by: Misapplication of tests in identifying the gifted. *Gifted Child Quarterly* 26 (1982b): 157-61.

Sternberg, R. J. A componential theory of intellectual giftedness. *Gifted Child Quarterly* 2 (1981): 86-93.

Stevens, S. S. Mathematics, measurement, and psychophysics. In *Handbook of experimental psychology.* Edited by S. S. Stevens. New York: John Wiley, 1966.

Swassing, R. H. Instructional models: Basic skills for the gifted. *The Directive Teacher* 4 (1982): 8.

TAG Evaluation Committee (Eds.) *Sample instruments for the evaluation of programs for the gifted.* Reston, Va.: The Council for Exceptional Children, 1979.

Terman, L. M., and M. A. Merrill. *Stanford-Binet Intelligence Scale: A manual for the third revision for L-M.* Boston: Houghton-Mifflin, 1973.

Tongue, C., and C. Sperling. *Gifted and talented: An identification model.* Raleigh, N.C.: Division for Exceptional Children, State Department of Public Instruction, 1976.

Torrance, E. P. Creatively gifted and disadvantaged gifted students. In *The gifted and the creative: A fifty-year perspective.* Edited by J. C. Stanely, W. C. George, and C. H. Solano. Baltimore, Md.: John Hopkins University, 1977.

Treffinger, D. J. Teaching for self-directed learning: A priority for gifted education. *Gifted Child Quarterly* 19 (1975): 46–59.

Turnbull, A. P., B. B. Strickland, and J. C. Brantley. *Developing and implementing individualized education programs.* Columbus, Ohio: Charles E. Merrill, 1978.

Ward, V. S. Basic concepts. *The gifted student: A manual for program improvement.* Southern Regional Project for the Education of the Gifted, 1962. (Reprinted in *Education and psychology of the gifted.* 3rd ed. Edited by W. B. Barbe and J. S. Renzulli. New York: Irvington, 1981.)

Wechsler, D. *Manual for the Wechsler Intelligence Scale for Children–Revised.* New York: The Psychological Corporation, 1974.

Wilson, M. W. Children with crippling and health disabilities. In *Exceptional children in the schools: Special education in transition.* 2nd ed. Edited by L. M. Dunn. New York: Holt, Rinehart and Winston, 1973.

Wolf, J. S., and T. M. Stephens. Individualized educational planning for the gifted. *Roeper Review 2* (1979): 11–12.

Ysseldyke, J. E. Issues in psychoeducational assessment. In *School psychology: Perspectives and issues.* Edited by G. D. Phye and D. J. Reschly. New York: Academic Press, 1974.

Zettel, J. J. Gifted and talented education over half a decade of change. *Journal for the Education of the Gifted* (1979): 14–37.

3

Social and Emotional Development of Gifted Children and Youth

Joan S. Wolf
Thomas M. Stephens

This chapter discusses the social and emotional development of gifted children and youth and those issues unique to this population. We will also discuss how social behavior is acquired, to identify those issues related to gifted children and their unique characteristics for developing socially and emotionally. The great variability in development of individual gifted children (interindividual differences) will become apparent as we discuss implications for social adjustment and the relationship to cognitive development.

Seven second graders gathered for their reading group. Their task was to respond to a series of questions about The Pony Express. It was Bobby's turn to indicate whether the item was true or false: *the pony express traveled slowly*. He thought a minute, then said, "I can't answer that." "Why not?" asked the teacher, somewhat irritated. "Because slowly is a comparative term," said Bobby. "Does it mean slowly compared to the way mail traveled in earlier days or slowly compared to the way mail travels today?" When the teacher asked what answer he thought was expected, Bobby replied, "I don't know, but I think logically; if you can't, then that's your problem."

"Fact or Fiction" was the title of the worksheet on which Carrie was to mark her answers. *A city without any streets* was one item to test the first graders' knowledge about a unit on the community. Much to the amusement of her classmates, Carrie answered "fact." The children laughed; the teacher was annoyed. Carrie defended her answer. "How about Venice? It has canals instead of streets."

What do these vignettes have to do with the social and emotional development of the gifted? They obviously deal with children's responses to academic material, but is that all? How teachers and peers respond will influence self-concepts and the ability to interact successfully with others. The impact of social experiences during the school years may well set the pattern for children's responses in later years. Erikson describes social development in psychosocial stages involving the child in experiences limited, at first, to home and parents, gradually widening to include the immediate neighborhood, the school, and even expanded environments such as the nation and the globe (Erikson, 1963). While the gifted child's social development may progress sequentially, as Erikson describes, the intellectual disparity between gifted children and their peers may create problems in social relationships. Bobby and Carrie are youngsters whose intellectual capability and performance differ from their peers. An accumulation of incidents in which they are easily misunderstood or unappreciated, as in the situations described, can create feelings of difference, of inadequacy and of reduced self-worth.

According to Erikson (1963), a child's orientation goes through changes according to his needs, as shown in Table 3–1.

Acquiring Social Behavior

Gifted children show great variability in their development. They often advance intellectually years beyond their chronological ages but show behavior in physical, social and emotional areas more typical of their ages. These intra-individual differ-

Table 3-1 A CHILD'S CHANGING SOCIAL/EMOTIONAL ORIENTATION

Approximate Age	Erikson's Psychosocial Stages	Social Radius
0–18 mo.	Trust	Female parent
18 mo.–3 yrs.	Autonomy	Family: parents and other siblings
3–5 yrs.	Initiative	Family, immediate neighborhood, nursery school
6–12 yrs.	Industry	Family, school, neighborhood
13–17 yrs.	Identity	Family, enlarged school, enlarged neighborhood, community

ences are further complicated for a gifted child who may be at one developmental age intellectually, another age chronologically, and still another emotionally. It is difficult, of course, for teachers, parents, and children to deal with these disparities. To understand the problems of variability within gifted children, we must first understand developmental patterns among normal children.

Socially responsible behavior results from experiences children encounter throughout their developmental years. These experiences teach children the values they will apply throughout their lives. Soon after birth, infants learn how to signal their caretakers when they are in need of physical care. In association with physical treatment, they begin to acquire emotional needs that are initially paired with their physical care. As their physical and emotional needs are met, infants begin to discriminate among their various caretakers; they learn to expect certain responses from different people depending upon their earlier experiences.

As they grow, children further differentiate the expectations of others; they soon acquire the values demonstrated by groups and individuals that are important to them. While they may use the *language* they acquire to express their values, they also learn to *behave* in ways that may differ significantly from those verbalized values.

Some behaviors are valued more than others. Those that are highly valued tend to be practiced; those that are not highly valued are practiced or demonstrated less often. But understanding how social behavior is acquired is complicated; consequently, by the time children become students, forces that motivate them towards certain social and emotional behaviors are complicated and not easily known to their teachers.

Explanations of behavior acquisition have been presented in terms of values, motives, attitudes, abilities, intelligence, and traits. Three theorists' work, that of Maslow (1954), Erikson (1963), and Skinner (1953), may help us understand the social and emotional development of gifted students.

Maslow's Theory

Maslow built his ideas of human behavior from studies of highly creative, psychologically healthy adults. He used the phrase *self-actualization* to describe these people's emotional health. Maslow proposed that individuals must satisfy basic needs and physiological drives such as hunger, thirst, and sex, and secondary needs such as affection, security, and self-esteem. In addition to satisfying these needs, other growth factors, such as coping skills, must be fulfilled to attain emotional health.

Maslow identified certain characteristics of self-actualized people:

- Efficient and comfortable perceptions of reality
- Self-acceptance
- Behavior devoid of artificiality
- Desire for privacy, tendency to detachment
- Appreciation of the basic pleasures of life
- Deep feeling of kinship with others
- Deep ties with a few other self-actualized individuals
- Strong ethical sense; definite moral standards
- Sense of humor, related to philosophy, not hostility
- Tendency to be serious and thoughtful
- Original and inventive
- Their own sense of standards rather than those of society, although not necessarily unconventional.

Because it was developed by looking at psychologically healthy adult males, Maslow's theory has limitations for understanding children. Several studies have addressed the unique problems females face in developing psychologically healthy personalities. Broverman et al. (1970) looked at sex-role stereotypes and clinical judgments concerning mental health and found that those behaviors and characteristics judged healthy for adults resembled behaviors judged healthy for men but not for

Figure 3-1 MASLOW'S HIERARCHY OF NEEDS

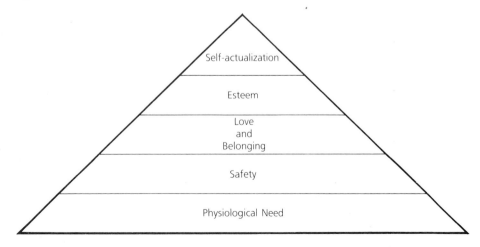

women, indicating that clinicians' concepts of a mature, healthy woman differ from their concepts of healthy adults. Females thus face unique problems of adjustment. Behaviors and personality characteristics valued in men, such as aggressiveness, independence, business skill, self-confidence, and decision making are not equally valued in women. Gifted females may feel conflict between their competence and ability and society's expectations.

Erikson's Theory

Erikson proposed that people progress through various developmental stages on their way to maturity, and that individuals cope with critical problems according to their developmental stage in the hierarchy.

As Table 3–2 shows, Erikson identified eight major conflicts that individuals normally face at different times in their development. In his view, those individuals who are unable to resolve these conflicts satisfactorily will be thwarted in resolving subsequent conflicts. When successful, they gain a sense of achievement and are better able to cope with life experiences. They also incorporate into their self-concepts new qualities that help them face future crises in their development.

Skinner's Theory

Skinner (1953) attributes behavior to the effects of operant conditioning, a process in which the frequency of a response is modified by the consequences of the behavior. Operant conditioning concerns the relationship between behavior and environment. In Skinner's view, we come to understand behavior by gaining knowledge of the factors that modify behavior. He advanced a study of behavior that encompasses only those factors that can be observed, measured, and reproduced.

To Skinner, behavior has two kinds of environmental determinants: contemporary and historical. Thus, behavior is determined not only by the current environment but also by one's previous experience with similar environmental conditions.

Skinner demonstrates a relationship between responses and reinforcing stimuli (rewards) and between responses and punishment. Rewards increase responses, while punishments decrease responses.

Table 3–2 ERICKSON'S EIGHT STAGES OF DEVELOPMENT*

	Stage	Major Goal
	8 Maturity	Ego Integrity
	7 Adulthood	Generativity
	6 Young Adulthood	Intimacy
	5 Adolescence	Identity
	4 Latency	Industry
	3 Locomotor-Genital	Initiative
	2 Muscular-Anal	Autonomy
	1 Oral Sensory	Basic Trust

*Adapted from E. H. Erikson, *Childhood and Society* (New York: Norton, 1963), p. 273.

New social behaviors are often learned through modeling. Bandura (1965) demonstrated that individuals can acquire new responses by observing the behavior of others and noting the consequences of that behavior. A pioneer in learning through imitation, Bandura (1969) makes a distinction between initial learning and using learned responses. He and his associates have demonstrated, through numerous research studies, that social modeling tactics are effective in teaching new behaviors to children through both overt modeling and vicarious modeling. Children learn through social modeling by imitating behaviors they have observed. (Later in the chapter, we will discuss some specific uses of modeling for gifted children.)

Do you know brilliant people who have some extraordinary talent but exhibit social skill deficits? They may be shy, withdrawn, or ill at ease with people, or loud, boisterous, or overbearing. These are often people we tend to avoid. Sometimes their intellectual abilities are not synchronized with their social skill development, as with the youngster who grasps concepts quickly but corrects others, adults and peers, without regard to the social situation and their relationship. This child's social immaturity is one reason for an inability to "read" the environment while simultaneously displaying knowledge. Other gifted children may be intolerant of fellow students' lower performance levels. They show impatience with others' limitations and have the potential to become insufferable and abusive with their peers.

Continuum of Moderately to Highly Gifted

There are conflicting views of the adequacy of social/emotional development among the gifted compared to their nongifted peers. Not only do we find a high degree of variability in development within a gifted child, but gifted children vary greatly from one another. As a group they are heterogeneous and exhibit a wide range of interindividual differences. Intellectual ability, as measured by intelligence tests, follows a continuum of giftedness from moderate to severe (high), and gifted children can deviate from 1 to 4 standard deviations above the mean. Among those youngsters who might be termed moderately gifted, there seem to be some common characteristics that make them vulnerable to conflicts in school experience and to subsequent social and emotional difficulties.

Those youngsters at the far end of the continuum, whom we characterize as highly or severely gifted, are more likely to have social and emotional problems and less peer acceptance than those characterized as moderately gifted (Hollingsworth, 1942; Gallagher, 1958). This fact is understandable when we consider that a highly gifted youngster is less likely to find peers among his age mates and more likely to have widely disparate interests.

Differences Between Social Behavior and Intelligence

Dissonance between social and cognitive development in gifted children comes about partly because of their lack of experience and exposure to various kinds of social situations. Whereas they may have the cognitive ability to generalize and to perceive logical sequences of incidents, their social development may not yet have occurred in a sequential pattern. Thus, although cognitively able, they may behave in socially inappropriate ways. The following incident of social dissonance arose for five-year-old Martin, who reached a conclusion based on data, but, because of his lack of experience, did not perceive its social nuances.

Martin's family was asked to speak to a church Sunday school class about the forthcoming Jewish holiday of Chanukah. On the morning of the program, Martin, his three-year-old brother, Steve, and his mother and father arrived at the Sunday school, set up some materials about which they were to talk, and uncovered a tray of cookies made especially for the occasion. The Sunday school director, Mr. Taylor, introduced Martin's family, who explained some of the customs of the holiday, lit the holiday candles, and answered the children's questions. Then Mr. Taylor told the children, "You are invited now to take a cookie which Mrs. Cole so kindly made. Please limit yourself to one cookie each because we have another class coming in and need to have enough for them." The children did as they were instructed, left the hall, and returned to their classes. The second group entered, took their seats, and participated in the same program. At the end of the question period, Mr. Taylor again invited the children to help themselves to the special cookies. He explained that while the first group was limited to one cookie for each child, since theirs was the last group, he had no need to limit them. Whereupon, Martin spoke up, "But please take just one because we want to take some home." The group laughed and Martin was embarrassed and confused—embarrassed because they had laughed at him and confused because he did not understand why such a logical statement should invite laughter. In fact, he had articulated what the other members of the Cole family were thinking, but were too socialized to express.

When considering the entire area of social adjustment, we must take adult perceptions into account. Teachers consider certain behaviors important when contemplating any measure of social adjustment, such as evaluating exceptional children's potential for interacting with regular children (Gresham, 1981). Teachers often highly value behaviors that facilitate working in groups, such as taking turns, staying on task, and exhibiting compliant behavior. The highly gifted youngster who marches to the tune of a different drummer may create problems for himself and others in a classroom setting. Those who have not followed normal developmental patterns may be concerned with death, world hunger, or fair treatment of the underdog, while their age mates are more concerned with who carries the soccer ball to recess. These youngsters can create negative feelings on the part of other children as well as for teachers who feel they lack the time or ability to deal with these weighty issues. Thus characteristics of gifted children that may be considered positive in theory take on negative features. In Table 3–3, Seagoe (1975) lists positive and negative characteristics of childhood giftedness.

Self-Concept and Social/Emotional Development

Terman's work challenged the stereotypes of the gifted child as a social isolate and emotionally maladjusted. His sample of approximately 1500 subjects, with minimum IQ scores from 132 to 140, revealed superior development socially and emotionally as

Table 3-3 CHARACTERISTICS OF GIFTED CHILDREN

Positive	Negative
Interest in cause-effect relation; ability to see relationships; love of truth	Difficulty in accepting the illogical
Critical thinker; skeptical; self-critical	Critical toward others
Ability to concentrate; long attention span	Resists interruption
Persistent, goal-directed behavior	Stubborn
Sensitive, intuitive, empathy for others; need for emotional support	Needs success and recognition; sensitive to criticism, vulnerable to peer group rejection
High energy, alertness, eagerness	Frustration with inactivity and absence of progress
Need for freedom of movement and action, independence in work and study	Problems of rejection and rebellion; parent, peer group pressure and nonconformity
Friendly and outgoing	Need for peer group relations; problems in developing social leadership

Adapted from M. V. Seagoe, Some learning characteristics of gifted children, in *The Gifted and Talented: A Handbook for Parents,* edited by J. L. Delp and R. A. Martinson. (Ventura, Calif.: Ventura County Superintendent of Schools), pp. 22–23.

well as intellectually. In an early study, Gallagher (1959) reported that the gifted are more emotionally stable than others and better adjusted socially. Other studies report positive self-concepts among the gifted. Lehman and Erdwin (1981) reported that young gifted children score consistently higher on measures of social and emotional adjustment. They reported more positive feelings about themselves, greater maturity in interactions, and better relations with others. These results confirm those of Milgram and Milgram (1976) who found more positive self-concepts in gifted populations of fourth- and eighth-grade Israeli children. Some recent studies, however, point to a higher incidence of emotional problems and poor self-concept among many gifted children. Whitmore (1980) points out that the social environment of the classroom is a key factor in promoting achievement among the gifted. Often our inability, or unwillingness, to deal with the needs of the gifted leads to a high rate of dropouts and deviants in a society that has ignored or even abused them. Schauer (1975) also indicates that, while the majority of gifted children are able to lead well-adjusted lives and have positive self-concepts, there are also gifted children who show social and emotional maladjustment. Maladjustment may be exacerbated when parents, teachers, and the gifted children themselves have unrealistic expectations. Adults may contribute to unrealistic expectations for gifted children by assuming that advanced abilities in one area automatically mean advanced abilities in all areas. They may become frustrated when a five-year-old who talks like an adult still spills her milk or interrupts her elders. They may also become ego-involved with the child's accomplishments and push beyond reasonable limits to higher and higher levels of achievement. Problems sometimes arise because the youngsters set unrealistically high goals for themselves. If significant adults do not recognize this tendency, they may unwittingly exert undue pressure for both achievement and behavior.

Some gifted children deal with pressure by quitting or by refusing to take risks. They do not feel comfortable with anything but the best and develop a fear of failure. Some choose not to compete, opting always for the easier class, or the sure grade. Others develop a negative self-image and play out their perceptions by underachieving, by dropping out of school, or by driving themselves beyond reasonable limits, without allowing themselves to enjoy life and leisure.

Some gifted children, including gifted underachievers, culturally different gifted, and the gifted handicapped, tend to have more than the usual problems with self-concept.

Whitmore (1980) discussed the issues inherent in identifying gifted underachievers and the special problems faced by this population. When using conventional methods of identification, it is easy to overlook the gifted underachiever whose classwork and behavior may not meet the teacher's standards. As a result of teacher and parent perceptions, many gifted underachievers developed low self-esteem and negative attitudes.

Similar problems exist in identifying and meeting the needs of the culturally different gifted. Conventional measures often miss these youngsters and conventional programs may be inappropriate. There are also potential problems in identifying the culturally different because of conflicting values and behaviors. Bernal (1979) recommends that we deal with the culturally different gifted so as to "build on their assets, foster interethnic understanding, and widen the style-of-life options" (p. 400).

Although there are many gifted and talented children among those identified as handicapped, we have not been very successful in attending to the needs of this population in either the cognitive or affective areas. We have tended to focus on areas of disability rather than ability. Some who are handicapped use their high ability to compensate for their disabilities. They appear to be average students and do not receive attention for their giftedness. The student who is both gifted and handicapped faces many frustrations in the regular school system (Wolf and Gygi, 1981). With the emphasis on remediation and placement with other handicapped, nongifted students, opportunities for stimulation are limited. A pattern of failure often emerges that seriously affects the students' self-perceptions, so that they have difficulty understanding what is wrong with them.

Maker (1977) discusses some characteristics of the gifted handicapped population that cause them difficulties. These include their desire for independence, goal directedness, self-criticism, and perceptions of the reactions of others. Their lack of skill promotes dependence rather than independence; they may have trouble setting realistic goals. The learning disabled student may have a long history of failure in academic areas that makes high goals seem out of reach, yet low goals are unacceptable to the student. Gifted students with learning disabilities may be particularly critical of themselves because they are aware of the discrepancy between performance and expectations (Wolf and Gygi, 1981). They may also be subjected to harassment by others who do not understand their problems. These factors contribute to the development of low self-esteem among this population.

In a review of the nature of peer relationships of the academically gifted, Austin and Draper (1981) caution against definitive statements. They suggest that in the preschool and kindergarten years, intellectually gifted students do not necessarily seem to be more popular than their peers of average ability; however, as the child moves into the elementary grades, a positive correlation between IQ and social acceptance appears. This relationship is not linear, in that the highly gifted may have trouble relating to same-age mates. In the adolescent years, there are some differences between boys and girls with relation to social acceptance. While both gifted boys and girls tend to lose status during the adolescent years, boys regain status during the upper years of high school while girls' intellectual achievements are increasingly devalued during this period. Karamessinis (1980) confirms several aspects of the Austin and Draper study by concluding that: (1) there is evidence that gifted children exhibit higher self-concepts than nongifted; and (2) while gifted students may be more popular with peers during elementary school, peer esteem often diminishes during the high school years, perhaps because certain behaviors and peer conformity become highly valued in adolescence. Thus, it becomes even more apparent that the gifted youngster does not fit well.

Program Designs

School programs can enhance gifted students' social and emotional development. They achieve their best development when programs contain elements carefully devised to address social and emotional needs.

Modeling is a powerful strategy for influencing behavior. Experiences that pair gifted students with enthusiastic, energetic individuals in areas of expertise (one-to-one relationships between a student and an adult in a mentorship role) have proven quite successful.

Mentors act as adult models for students to emulate. The term *mentorship* comes from Greek mythology—Mentor was the faithful friend to whom Odysseus entrusted his son Telemachus. The unique relationship between student and mentor is a key to the success of this model. Boston (1976) identifies the goal of mentoring as transformation: "the learner realizes his potential in a situation in which there is motivation to learn, to seek the truth, and to develop a unique relationship."

There is a particular need for positive models. "The only adults most kids know are parents, relatives and teachers," says Nat Hentoff. "That's a narrow selection of the kinds of people they might grow up to be, so kids need other models" (Jackson, 1980, p. 1075).

Modeling

Some years ago, a third grade teacher complained that her students were unkind to one another. "They are so mean, so impatient," she said. Observation in that classroom revealed that the teacher, extremely creative and energetic, had little patience for the child who learned slowly. Her impatience was communicated to the students. Verbally, she encouraged the students to be kind to each other, but she demonstrated behavior that contradicted her words. Her students modeled her behavior and she shaped their attitudes not by what she *said*, but by what she *did*.

Because of their sensitivity and heightened awareness, many gifted children are vulnerable to hurt by others. Those who are highly verbal can easily articulate their feelings and assume that others can do the same. They sometimes come across as abrasive and insensitive. They may need direct instruction in listening skills so they will learn to hear and deal with others' feelings. Modeling listening skills would be important for such children. Other gifted children, though they also have a heightened awareness, have difficulty expressing their feelings in acceptable ways. They may withdraw or they may disrupt. Modeling can be useful in helping them express feelings. Gifted students may benefit from modeling to help them deal with individual differences so they can learn to moderate their intolerance or impatience with others who are less capable.

Benefits of mentorship include opportunities to provide models for students, to explore subjects more deeply than is possible in most classroom situations, to reveal previously unidentified talents, and to provide an alternative to conventional instructional methods. Mentor experiences also provide excellent career exploration opportunities. Mentorships can be organized in different ways, depending on needs and available resources. One focus of mentorship may be enhancement of academic learning through pursuit of a subject in depth.

Another important component of successful mentorships involves the affective dimension. Developing social skills, meeting responsibilities, communicating effectively, and decision making are all valuable aspects of these experiences. Mentorships give the gifted student an opportunity to work with stimulating experts who often have knowledge that surpasses that of teachers and allow him to practice self-directed learning.

Subject Exploration and Mentorships

Through mentorships, students can explore specific subjects of interest in greater depth than is possible in the classroom. Increasing demands on teachers make it more necessary than ever to identify outside resource persons to work with gifted students in specialized areas. Pairing a student with a mentor who respects and appreciates the student's talents can provide exciting experiences for both parties. Firsthand experiences and the opportunity to delve deeply into a specific area with the assistance and advice of an expert are valuable to the gifted student with a particular talent or ability. When asked how their creative abilities were developed, the recurring theme among a group of eminent scientists was that of a master-apprentice relationship (Maugh, 1974). Other successful people have identified a mentor experience as significant in their relationship (Stephens & Wolf, in preparation).

Many mentorship programs are presently operating around the country. While the academic gains are important, the benefits to these students' affective development may be even more significant. The students' special abilities are recognized and appreciated, and the opportunities to interact with experts and to work in real-life situations are invaluable. Exposure to different career options is also important. Mentor experiences are appropriate not only in professional fields but in the trades as well. Studs Terkel (1980) describes individuals across America, from all walks of life, who impart a sense of excitement and commitment to their chosen work—mechanics as well as dancers. People like these would be excellent mentors for gifted students.

Counseling the Gifted

By virtue of their special abilities, gifted students have some unique counseling needs. Typically, gifted students receive little attention from school counselors, who must spend their time with other school populations, usually those who are not achieving or who are behavior problems. Demands on counselors to handle class scheduling and other administrative duties also detract from time spent with the gifted. In addition, many school people believe the gifted will make it on their own and fail to understand their need for a support system. Gowan (1979) points out special guidance problems of gifted students:

1 They may face an embarrassment of riches, which make educational and occupational decisions difficult.
2 They may have problems related to upward social mobility.
3 They may become aware of developmental tasks before they have the physical resources to solve them.
4 They may have a greater need to develop the specialized interests that go with certain professional occupations.
5 They may have problems resulting from lack of adult models (p. 218).

Because gifted students often demonstrate high ability in many areas, they may have difficulty focusing on a career field. Since many choose careers that require long periods of special training, the need for an early focus may be crucial. Another problem area relates to expectations, which may work in several ways. Parents and teachers may press gifted students to choose prestigious or high status careers that do not coincide with their interests. Adults who recognize gifted students' high abilities may push them to commit themselves early to training in a specific area without allowing valuable exploration in other areas. Some parents whose educational experience has been limited or negative may limit their gifted children by insisting that they follow in their footsteps and pursue specific careers that do not match the students' abilities or interests.

Unique counseling needs arise for gifted females, minority gifted students, and gifted handicapped. Gifted females often suffer conflicts between career vs. traditional family roles. There has also been a lack of role models for bright women in professional roles. Barriers still exist in some fields for gifted women. These problems underscore the need for an organized counseling program for gifted females to help them deal with attitudes and emotions. Counseling can include a support group in which gifted females feel free to show their abilities and express their concerns.

Culturally different gifted students face potential conflict between values of their cultures and opportunities that may arise because of their ability and achievement.

Birch (1979) suggests making opportunities accessible to gifted handicapped students. Ramps for the physically handicapped, braille programs for the visually handicapped, and interpreters for those who would benefit can broaden the horizons of the gifted.

Ideally, schools should develop preventive programs to help gifted students deal with situational problems before they become issues requiring in-depth treatment. Such a program should deal with the affective needs of the gifted, to help them understand themselves, their differences, and develop skills for functioning better with others. Bringing together youngsters who express feelings of isolation and loneliness and helping them develop strategies for improving their interpersonal relationships can help prevent later crisis situations. DeLisle (1980) identifies several problems gifted students share: feeling different, alienation, dissatisfaction with interpersonal relationships, frustration over inadequate school curriculum, and occupational and career decisions. Preventive counseling is particularly effective in small groups, which can serve as support systems for gifted students.

Instructional Strategies

Counseling methods range from psychotherapy to behavior management, techniques that are appropriate for professional counselors. Teachers are not expected to be counselors; they are not trained to provide in-depth counseling for serious problems. In advising, guiding, leading, and teaching, however, it is obvious that a teacher can fill the counselor's role.

Much of the counseling with gifted students deals with problems of getting along with others and understanding themselves, for which we can use established strategies based on teachers' and counselors' knowledge of the characteristics and needs of the gifted. Bibliotherapy, humor, peer counseling/tutoring, and self-directed learning are possible strategies.

Bibliotherapy

Bibliotherapy focuses reading materials to help solve emotional problems and promote mental health. It is an effective technique for helping all children deal with problems of everyday living. Bibliotherapy is particularly valuable with those for whom books are so important. Through well-chosen books, gifted readers can increase self-knowledge and self-esteem and find relief from personal conflicts.

No single book can satisfy the literary talents and needs of the average child, let alone those of the gifted. Diverse materials are necessary. Shepard (1976) indicates that bibliotherapy can help children to think constructively and positively; talk freely about their feelings; analyze their attitudes and modes of behavior; realize that there is more than one way to solve a problem; find solutions or accommodations to problems that will lessen conflict with self and society; and to compare their problems with those of others. Wolf and Penrod (1981) point out that because of their aptitudes and interests, gifted children's unique needs and problems can be addressed effectively through bibliotherapy.

One category of books, biographies, have particular application for the gifted. Gifted children choose biographies as reading material earlier than their nongifted peers. Gallagher (1975) indicates that subjects of biographies can serve as important role models for the gifted, both for personal qualities and for career information and exploration. Gifted children identify with the accomplishments of those they read about and derive direction and comfort in reading about their experiences.

One resource for dealing with problems experienced by gifted students is S. S. Dreyer's *The Bookfinder: A Guide to Children's Literature about the Needs and Problems of Youth Aged 2–15* (Circle Pines, Minn.: American Guidance Service, 1977, 1981).

Bibliotherapy involves more than presenting books to students. The literature must be selected carefully according to students' needs, interests, and ability levels. A major key to this technique's success is the students' voluntary participation.

After a student reads a book, it is wise to provide opportunities for follow-up. The teacher or counselor can conduct individual discussions or create a small group to include the target students. The teacher must use a careful and thoughtful approach

Bibliotherapy is particularly valuable for the gifted, for whom books are so important, and biographies are often especially appealing.

when guiding a discussion in a sensitive area. Sometimes, being a good listener is far better than trying to probe for answers or feelings.

There are several ways teachers can identify problems children are having. Possible sources of information include parent/teacher conferences; the school counselor's awareness of specific problems; group discussions dealing with various elements of affective development; teachers' general knowledge of their students; students' diaries; and a sharing circle, in which students and teacher discuss common experiences. Bibliotherapy, if used wisely, with care and proper preparation, can address many problems and help improve students' personal and social adjustment. Bibliotherapy requires an awareness of the potential power of the written word and a practical knowledge of children's literature. It also requires sensitivity on the part of teachers and a willingness to deal with their students' affective development.

Humor As a Counseling Strategy

One approach to helping gifted students develop socially and emotionally in healthy ways is to relate instructional strategies to their characteristics. Many descriptions of the gifted refer to their well-developed sense of humor and their sharp wit. Rogers (1961) and Maslow (1954) both include a sense of humor as an important characteristic of self-actualized people. Thus, the use of humor in counseling the gifted may be particularly effective.

Berg and DeMartini (1979) describe the use of humor in counseling the gifted. They indicate that humor has been found useful in the counseling process with other populations as well. Humor has been used to increase spontaneity of expression; enhance self-esteem; expand flexibility and repertoire of responses; facilitate the development of creative thinking and problem-solving abilities; and increase self-directed behavior. They propose specific activities for using humor in counseling settings, including telling favorite jokes; drawing group cartoons; acting out fairy tales; writing satirical social essays; sharing humorous records, films, cartoons, and pictures; writing humorous cartoons; using humorous caricatures, overstatements, and understatements; and creating comic strips. Certain comic strips can be used to identify feelings; for example, when dealing with peer relations, selected Peanuts strips can stimulate directive questions:

When Lucy is mean to Charlie Brown, how do you think he feels? What can he do to change things? Have you been in a similar situation?

Exercise care when using humor. Trust between students and counselor should be firmly established. Always avoid sarcasm and ridicule. Humor can only be effectively used when the relationship between counselor and students is highly positive.

Peer Counseling and Tutoring

Gifted students can serve as counselors and/or tutors to other students. Allowing secondary students to serve as peer counselors gives them a chance to provide a service and enhance their self-perception. They can help with course selections, guide younger students, and provide academic help. Both students benefit from peer tutoring. Tutors feel their knowledge and expertise are useful and appreciated, and students being tutored receive necessary help. Teachers also have some relief from demands on their time.

Peer tutoring programs show that gifted students benefit through practicing and clarifying their own learning while at the same time gaining personal satisfaction and enhancing their self-images (Haun, 1975). Peer tutors can organize materials, keep records of completed skills, direct reading games, tell or read stories, and help with writing activities. They can also help younger children learn math facts or new words.

Peer counselors and tutors should not be assigned busywork. Use these strategies only when there are benefits for both students. In such activities, gifted students have opportunities for decision making, learning communication skills, enhancing and evaluating their schools, and appreciating individual differences.

Self-Directed Learning

Self-directed learning is a high priority for the gifted because they often become strongly independent at an early age. Torrance (1965) describes the gifted as independent, self-starting, and persevering.

Treffinger (1975) characterizes sound self-direction as organized, planned, and structured. In self-directed learning, the rate of instruction is changed and the nature of activities differentiated for gifted students. It does not imply that each student must work alone; there are opportunities to acquire social skills. Higher-level thinking skills, both cognitive and affective, should be built into the learning experience. Self-directed learning experiences should include an evaluation so that students can be involved in determining outcomes and measuring progress.

One type of self-directed learning, independent study, contributes to the development of positive affective characteristics. Students can develop self-discipline, be creative, satisfy personal interests, and practice decision making. Contracts can be developed for defining goals and methods and for pursuing an area of interest. Students learn to set goals, plan their time, and follow through to completion. They can then be given opportunities to share information with other students, assuming a teaching role and thus building important social interaction skills and creating positive feelings.

Treffinger (1978) proposes self-directed learning for solving practical problems. For example, students involved in decision making can help determine classroom rules, set reasonable schedules, and solve interpersonal problems.

Positive experiences with self-directed learning affect both the content and the process of learning. As gifted students become more skilled at self-management, that skill will carry over into experiences outside school. Gifted students need to learn to manage their time, not only for optimum learning to take place, but also so they can learn to enjoy leisure. Gifted adults sometimes become so involved in work and related activities that they do not know how to incorporate leisure time and recreation. Some gifted people exhibit such a high level of intensity and are so serious that they feel uneasy about spending time in leisure activities. By helping students become independent learners, giving them opportunities to manage their time and be involved in decision making, we help them learn the proper balance between work and play.

Administrative Arrangements

Since some teachers are also responsible for administering gifted programs, their awareness of alternative arrangements can be valuable for developing such programs. Some grouping arrangements allow more social and emotional development than do others. Grouping patterns that allow gifted students to interact with other gifted students, to learn from gifted people, and to mix with others who have common interests are likely to address their social and emotional needs. These grouping arrangements include alternative education, grade acceleration, advanced

Gifted students should not always work individually; they need opportunities to exchange ideas.

placement, and concurrent college enrollment. Regardless of the type of administrative arrangement used for serving gifted children, a systematic approach to developing social/emotional growth is necessary.

Structuring the Classroom Environment

Various methods of structuring the classroom environment can be beneficial to both cognitive and affective growth. At the elementary level, gifted children may benefit from opportunities to make decisions about their learning; for example, in learning centers they can work independently or in small groups, or choose from a plentiful supply of materials.

Individual research is best conducted in an area of the classroom that is quiet and free from distraction. (Research may also require easy access to library facilities.) Other sections of the room may have tables for interaction among students, teachers, or other adults.

Gifted students need many opportunities to interact with gifted peers, to exchange ideas, to share information, and to learn from one another. There should be a good balance between opportunities for individual and group work. Teachers should guard against allowing gifted students to work only individually; encouraging an excessive amount of individual work, such as book reports and workbook assignments, will make some gifted students feel isolated or even punished, and they will tend to avoid those activities.

To make both individual and small group activities effective, students should be responsible for their behavior. They also need to learn to track their progress and check their own work, to maximize individualized learning and free the teacher from many routine duties.

At both elementary and secondary levels, the key to serving the gifted is flexibility. Junior high and high school students need opportunities to make decisions about their own learning, to participate in groups with other gifted students, and to select advanced programs. If these provisions are made, it is possible to avoid the discipline problems that may arise as the student's way of communicating to teachers that things are not going well. Scheduling groups for counseling can also help prevent problems before they occur.

In arranging the classroom environment, consider also the match between gifted students and their teachers. All teachers are not suited to teaching the gifted, just as all are not equally skilled in teaching the handicapped.

Alternative Education

All students do not benefit from similar educational placements. Students with special talents, unusual aptitudes, and special needs often profit more from alternative education programs, such as community-based learning, where students have educational experiences outside school. Other learning opportunities include special interest clubs and apprenticeships.

Students, particularly at the upper grade levels, sometimes find community learning more beneficial than full-time school attendance. Emotionally, some gifted students profit from the wider options available in the community. School personnel can use community resources to meet the needs of the gifted by arranging for students to work and learn in community settings with adults who are interested or who specialize in a specific area. During released time from the school day, students pursue their special talents and interests.

Many community-based programs can help meet the needs of the gifted, as in libraries, museums, theaters, hospitals, radio and television stations, and in the workplace. Agencies and institutions can often provide specialized equipment or resources that are not available in most school systems; for example, resources for high-level creative and performing arts may be available through a local theater group and scientific equipment may be available at a local university. When developing community liaison programs, school personnel must address the problem of barriers to successful operation of the programs, such as scheduling, transportation, funding, supervision, and insurance coverage. They should also plan for ongoing evaluation.

By exposing gifted students to learning opportunities available in the community, we may interest them in activities that will carry over into leisure time. Many gifted children need extra stimulation and enrichment, but some have difficulty unwinding and enjoying leisure in informal settings with others. Community-based programs can be a vehicle for introducing gifted students to options for their free time, such as the symphony, drama groups, and science museums.

Other Alternatives for the Gifted

Alternative educational experiences can also occur inside the school. Open classrooms, experimental programs, and other nontraditional methods can be offered to selected students. But as in all special programs, it is important to make sure these alternative programs and the students match appropriately.

Grade Acceleration Grade skipping and early school admission can be responsive to gifted students' emotional needs. These are traditional but proven methods for giving students instruction suitable to their achievement levels. Placing students in settings with children and activities closer to their performance levels gives them better opportunities for healthy emotional development.

Early admissions, usually involving psychological testing and trial placement, permit students to enter school at earlier than usual ages (Braga, 1971). Students may skip kindergarten, entering directly into first grade, or may begin kindergarten one or more years early.

Grade skipping during the school years should be permitted only after careful individual evaluation. Certain transition points lend themselves more readily to skipping a grade, such as skipping the last year of elementary school to move into junior high, or compressing the junior high or middle school experience into two years and moving on to high school. Students may need supplemental instruction and personal assistance to smooth the transition to an accelerated grade.

Advanced Placement and Concurrent Enrollment Advanced placement (Gerritz and Haywood, 1965) courses at the high school level can also be responsive to gifted students' social and emotional needs. AP classes tend to be more homogeneous, with many bright students capable of handling college-level academic work.

In some schools with nearby colleges, selected high school students may take courses on college campuses in combination with their high school work. In other schools, students are permitted to skip one or more years of high school entirely and enter college early. The concurrent enrollment program is an example of a community-based program designed especially for the gifted.

Concurrent high school/college enrollment, or advanced standing programs for the gifted, is defined by the College Entrance Examination Board (CEEB) as "the pattern which enables superior students to receive appropriate placement, credit or both on the basis of the college level courses they have taken in high school" (Lynch, 1980). The courses may be taken on a college campus or as part of the Advanced Placement Program. College credit or advanced placement is granted on the basis of passing college level courses or by passing parts of the college entrance examination.

Concurrent high school/college enrollment has been used in various programs across the United States during the last three decades. As mentioned by Lynch (1980), these programs may include the following arrangements:

- High school students taking classes on a college or university campus;
- Students taking AP classes in high school and college on one campus;
- High school teachers teaching college-level classes in high school under college supervision; and
- The University Without Walls concept of instruction.

Throughout the 1960s and 1970s, various universities and colleges operated concurrent enrollment programs. Based on grade point averages of the concurrent enrollment students, many programs reported a high rate of success (Runquist, 1962; Wilbur and Chapman, 1977). Results of these programs indicated that a select group of high school students could successfully complete college-level classes taught on college campuses by regular teachers. These classes contained regular college students and expected college-level achievement. Some colleges and universities that have reported on their concurrent enrollment programs are Brooklyn College, The Ohio State University, UCLA, University of Illinois, University of Minnesota, University of Pennsylvania, Johns Hopkins University, Hamline University, the State University of New York system and 28 junior colleges in California.

The Study of Mathematically Precocious Youth (SMPY) at the Johns Hopkins University is a good example of a successful concurrent enrollment program (Stanley, George and Solano, 1977). On the basis of high SAT scores in math and expressed interest in the program, students from junior high age and above have opportunities to enroll in advanced math courses at the university. Data collected on this population over a period of several years indicate success in terms of both educational achievement and social adjustment. These students become better trained at a high level earlier in their school careers and have the potential to develop into prominent researchers earlier in their careers.

Concurrent enrollment populations contain many students who, by a variety of criteria, would qualify as gifted students. They are highly motivated, intellectually capable, and high achieving. This population is an excellent source of research data concerning the characteristics of bright students, their educational needs, their career goals, and their perceptions and attitudes about their school experiences. Information about this group of students would be useful to colleges and universities in recruiting gifted students and to public school decision makers in examining efficient ways to provide sound education to the gifted. Parents and school counselors can also learn from these data.

Challenging educational experiences such as concurrent enrollment give gifted students the chance to pursue appropriate academic interests. They also give them contact with others of like interests and talents. Although some gifted students may encounter social problems because of their youth and lack of experience, many young gifted students function well in the university environment.

Use of Affective Curriculum Materials

Sound social and emotional development must accompany cognitive development. While these are important goals for all children, they are particularly important for the gifted. Lacy (1979) believes that gifted students are more likely to achieve positions of power and influence as adults; thus, they should have worthy values and morality, emotional health, and good interpersonal and communication skills. The importance of these skills for the gifted lies in the assumption that the gifted have the potential to make significant contributions to society and to their own personal development.

Sound social/emotional development for the gifted can be promoted through strategies and materials that capitalize on their increased ability and special characteristics. Materials should stress feelings, interpersonal relationships, values, and personal growth. A sound affective curriculum may use a child-centered approach to address the following goals:

- To help students understand emotions, attitudes and values;
- To help students understand the effect of their environment on them;
- To help students understand the consequences of various emotions;
- To help students apply their knowledge of emotions, attitudes, and values toward positive real-life experiences.[1]

Academic achievement and classroom behavior are influenced by interpersonal relationships. A supportive environment enhances learning and promotes positive feelings. The concept that a classroom has a social climate is central to developing curricula that will enhance students' self-concepts and good interpersonal skills. Schmuck and Schmuck (1971) define classroom social climate as:

> One in which the students share high amounts of potential influence, both with one another and with the teacher; where high levels of attraction exist for the group as a whole and between classmates; where norms are supportive for getting academic work done, as well as for maximizing individual differences; where communication is open and featured by dialogue, and where the processes of working and developing together as a group are considered relevant in themselves for study. In such a classroom, we would expect to find student and teacher goal-directed activity and curiosity, feelings of self-esteem, feelings of security, rather than threat, high involvement in subject-matter learning, feelings of power arising from the ability to influence the teacher and other students, and a sense of belonging rather than of alienation from the school. (p. 18)

A systematic approach to affective instruction is vital. There is, of course, a close relationship between cognition and affect. Traditionally, it has been easier to develop

---

[1]Adapted from B. Eberle and R. Hall, *Affective direction: Planning and teaching for thinking and feeling* (Buffalo, N.Y.: D.O.K. Publishers 1979), p. X.

objectives for cognitive behaviors. Bloom et al. (1971) believe we have been hesitant to attend to the affective curriculum and discuss the problems associated with developing objectives for affective behavior. Recognizing these problems, Krathwohl et al. (1964) developed a taxonomy that allows the teacher to classify educational objectives that emphasize feelings and emotions. The objectives are arranged in a hierarchy from receiving, (attending), through responding, valuing, organization, and characterization. It is far easier to evaluate outcomes for cognitive objectives than for affective ones, although one can use observation, interviews and open-ended questionnaires. Students should feel that the affective curriculum allows free and open expression of feelings and attitudes.

Weinstein and Fantini (1970) suggest some sample activities to use in the classroom for dealing with feelings along with a list of resource materials for developing skills in interpersonal relationships.[2]

Sample Activities—Dealing with Feelings
Elementary Level: One Way Glasses

Purpose: To show that there are different ways of seeing the same situation and that one's state of mind influences perceptions. Each person creates his own world from his perceptions.

The teacher explains that different pairs of glasses (suspicious glasses, rose-colored glasses) will color the wearer's view of the world. The characteristics of each are explained and children volunteer to role play and tell others what they see. Other kinds of glasses can be used; gloomy, scared, boasting, hateful, stubborn, helpful.

Follow-up: Identify book or TV personalities and ascribe characteristics to them; for example, Batman.

Discussion and Evaluation: How did each type person make me feel? What happens when we always "wear the same type of glasses?"

Secondary Level: Making Positive Statements About Qualities and Accomplishments of Others[3]

1 Meet with the class and discuss the behavior of making positive statements about the qualities and accomplishments of others. Bring out in the discussion how everyone has both good and bad qualities, and that everyone has something he can do well. Talk about why it is better to be aware of a person's good qualities. When available, use stories, films, filmstrips, and other aids to stimulate discussion.
2 Identify specific behaviors to be modeled.
3 Model the behavior.
4 Provide opportunities for practice and discussion.

---

[2]Adapted from G. Weinstein and M. D. Fantini, *Toward Humanistic Education* (New York: Praeger, 1970), pp. 79–82.
[3]From Thomas M. Stephens, *Social Skills in the Classroom* (Columbus, Ohio: Cedars Press, 1978), pp. 270–71.

Resource Materials

There is a wide range of sources for resource materials for instruction in social and emotional development. Some materials are specifically designed for teaching social and emotional behaviors, and others can be adapted for such purposes. In the first group, materials are available that focus on the applied aspects of teaching as well as some that provide learning principles, theories, and philosophy. There are materials for teaching social skills and for encouraging social development at all grade levels, including educational sources such as reading texts, supplementary books, stories, and poems. Media and materials from the popular culture, such as cartoons, films, and news items, can also stimulate ideas and activities. Activities for teaching fall into two major categories:

- Models for Imitation—stories, poems, skits
- Problem Solving—cartoons, news items

Teachers can use stories from children's literature and basal readers for modeling experiences, selecting stories that provide examples of appropriate behavior models, or they can tell stories to students to serve the same purpose.

Cartoons provide a sequence of events for students to rearrange or complete. Students or teachers choose cartoon strips that provide examples of social behavior problems. Editorial cartoons are a rich source of material dealing with social issues. Newspaper articles are useful for encouraging students to suggest options for solving social behavior problems.

Working with groups is important to gifted students because much work requires cooperative behavior. Teachers can help students acquire cooperative behaviors by assigning group tasks, discussing the necessary cooperative behaviors, and demonstrating the behaviors. An excellent reference is B. Eberle and R. E. Hall's *Affective Education Guidebook: Classroom Activities in the Realm of Feelings* (Buffalo, N.Y.: D.O.K. Publishers). It contains an instructional model, learning activities, and community building activities for elementary and junior high students.

Values Clarification

Values clarification is an area of affective education that provides students with a process for examining their own lives, taking responsibility for their behavior, and articulating beliefs and ideas congruent with their own value system (Curwin & Curwin, 1974). Through value clarification activities, students have opportunities to deal with their feelings and concerns in order to explore their own values. Rath, Harmin, and Simon (1966) developed a model of valuing that forms the basis of teaching and curriculum development. The process they describe includes three elements:

- Choosing—A value is freely chosen from alternatives after careful thought of the consequences of each alternative
- Prizing—A value is cherished and prized enough to be affirmed publicly
- Acting—A value is acted upon, not only talked about, and becomes a pattern of life. (p. 30)

Sample Activities: Values Clarification[4]

Elementary Level: Values Box

Focus: The "Values Box" can help students discover and clarify values related to their feelings about themselves. They gather symbols of their values and present them to the class.

Materials: Two small boxes for each student, crayons, and paints. Use boxes about the size of a shoe box or hatbox.

Procedure: The students will use the two boxes to gather different objects that symbolize their values. They will then show the contents of their boxes to the class, explaining the meaning of different objects.

Directions: Give students these instructions:
1   Label one of your boxes "Me" and one box "Not Me."
2   Design or color your boxes any way you choose.
3   In the next week or two, collect some objects that show what you strongly believe in and put them in the "Me" box. If you believe in:
    a   luck or superstition, you might include a rabbit's foot or four leaf clover.
    b   being rich someday, you might include a coin.
    c   religion, you might include a religious object.
    d   creativity, you might include an original poem or drawing.
4   In the "Not Me" box, collect items that represent what you do not believe in, using the same procedure as for the "Me" box.
5   There are no limits to the items you may include in your boxes.
6   After the boxes are filled, you will each have a chance to show the class what you have collected and tell what each item means.

Questions for Discussion:
1   How difficult is it to determine what you believe in?
2   Do you think what you put in your boxes might change in the next year? How?
3   During the collection period, have you acted in any way that reflects the values in your "Me" box?
4   Have you done anything that reflects a value in your "Not Me" box?
5   Which box was more difficult to fill? Which had more items?
    You may wish to repeat this activity from time to time after intervals of at least a month, and then compare the results. With younger children, you may wish to provide more examples as a guide. Older children like to be creative and usually don't need many examples. If your classroom is designed for it, you may wish to have a "Values Box" center where each student can keep his boxes semipermanently, adding things or removing them throughout the year. In this way the "Values Box" records changes over time for students and teacher to observe.

---

[4]R. L. Curwin and G. Curwin, *Developing Individual Values in the Classroom* (Palo Alto, Calif.: Learning Handbooks, 1974), pp. 32, 33.

The teacher helps students use value clarification to explore goals, feelings, and concerns by providing a structure for clarification activities, including use of material and time built into the class schedule. The teacher's behavior and verbal messages must also be congruent. Rather than teaching his own set of values, the teacher must be willing to share values with the students while allowing for differences. Since teachers have their own sets of values, they need not try to maintain a neutral position, but should participate actively with students as members of the group.

Value clarification activities must take place in an atmosphere of trust and acceptance. Self-disclosure is not forced, but takes place as students feel comfortable. There is no evaluation of responses and confidentiality is honored. All students are treated with care and respect. Self-evaluation is a valuable tool for students to assess their interest, their level of participation in the discussion, what they learned, and how they feel about the activities.

Kohlberg's stages of moral development range from Stage 1, in which the individual does what is right to avoid punishment, and progress to Stage 6, in which the individual's idea of morality is defined by universal principles of equality and justice (Kohlberg, 1978). There is some evidence that high intelligence and a well-developed sense of moral judgment are related (Hoffman, 1977). Clark (1979) asserts that a sense of justice appears at an earlier age in gifted children and that they are often concerned with serious issues such as death, divorce, and world hunger in advance of their nongifted peers. Thus the need for exposing the gifted to values clarification exercises that promote self-understanding is particularly important.

Some values clarification activities can be geared to specific curriculum areas, as in the following examples.

Elementary Level: Words for Me[5]

Focus: If we approach the study of words as a value-rich area, we can develop numerous ways to help students examine their values as their vocabulary grows. This activity helps students personally relate to new vocabulary words and thus have a better chance to retain their meaning and spelling.

Materials: Paper, pencils, list of new vocabulary words.

Procedure: If you make the vocabulary circle part of your weekly lesson plan, you will find that the sensitivity and honesty of your students' responses will increase as time goes on.

Directions:
1 Have the students seated in a circle and provide them with paper and list of new words to be learned.
2 Using the new words, have them complete in writing a sentence such as the following:

---

[5]R. L. Curwin and G. Curwin, *Developing Individual Values in the Classroom* (Palo Alto, Calif.: Learning Handbooks, 1974), pp. 59–60.

a (For adjectives) The last time I felt _____ was when _____.

b (For nouns) A _____ is important to me because _____.

c (For nouns) At my house we use a _____ for _____.

d (For nouns). If I had a _____, I would _____.

e (For verbs) When I _____, I feel _____.

f (For verbs) If I could _____ as fast (well, quietly, etc.) as an _____, I would _____.

g (For adverbs) A time to move (talk, sit, etc.) _____ is when _____.

3 Go around the circle asking students to share their sentences. Ask each student his feelings about each word before moving on to the next word.

Note: As in all value clarification activities, you must respect the students' privacy. We find, however, that most students are eager to share a part of themselves in relation to new words. Occasionally you might want to have the students base a composition on one or more of their sentences.

Secondary Level: Illegal Behavior

Directions: Write out answers to the questions below. Later, you will have a chance to discuss your answers with a small group of students. You need not reveal your answers to anyone if you choose not to do so.

New Rochelle, N.Y., Oct. 27--When the red light turns to green and reads "Thank you" at any one of the automatic toll booths of the New England Thruway here, it does not always mean what it says. At least not if the motorist has short-changed the machine or dropped lead washers or foreign coins into it.

The state police reported today after a two-week campaign against toll cheaters that they had arrested 151 persons. They have been fined in City Court from $25 each for first offenders to $250 for multiple offenders.

Lieut. Thomas F. Darby reported that the offenders included a clergyman, a doctor, a dentist, an atomic scientist, lawyers and quite a number of engineers, advertising men and salesmen.

What the offenders did not know, the lieutenant said, was that the new toll-booth glass with one-way vision prevented them from seeing watchful troopers inside.

Neither did they know, the lieutenant continued, that the license plate of each offender was recorded, along with the objects he dropped into the machine.

1 Under what circumstances would you try to pass a toll machine without properly paying the fee? Check the most applicable reply below.

_____Only if I was certain that I would not be caught.

_____If I felt I had a good chance of not getting caught.

_____Never, under any circumstances.

_____Only if I needed the money desperately, like for family food supplies.

_____(Write any other choice that better suits you:)

> 2 Among the 151 persons arrested, there was only one clergyman, doctor, dentist, and atomic scientist. On the other hand, there were several lawyers, engineers, advertising men, and salesmen. Do you think this means that persons in the first group of occupations are more honest than those in the second group? Discuss.
>
> 3 Do you think that this behavior is serious? Do you think these persons are likely to be dishonest in other ways that would be more serious? Discuss.
>
> 4 Return to Question 1 and put an X by the reply that you would make to this: Under what circumstances would you keep a dime that was returned in error in a phone booth?
>
> 5 How do you account for any differences in your answers to Questions 1 and 4, if any?
>
> 6 Are you clear about how you feel about illegal behavior? Discuss.

This activity about illegal behavior, appropriate for young and old students, shows how a brief news item can be tied into a general theme. Note how the sequence of questions leads the student into the theme gently but interestingly.

Question 1 gets the student to take a position, often a useful clarifying tactic. Question 2 calls for some critical thinking and takes the heat off the student for a moment. Question 3 is similarly impersonal and calls for thinking about some of the consequences and correlates of slug passing. Questions 4 and 5 bring the issue back home, often dramatically, and point up possible inconsistencies in a person's stance. Noting inconsistencies is another important clarifying tactic and is especially useful before posing the jackpot question, number 6.

The Role of Parents

Parents of gifted children are eager to help them fulfill their potential. They need to be aware of the unique characteristics of the gifted, especially their variability across different areas of development. Some parents seek help with behavior management not because the nature of the problems differs from those of most children, but because the problems are often exacerbated when dealing with the gifted.

Because the gifted develop at a different rate than nongifted, parents may be baffled by the child who doesn't fit typical patterns of behavior and interests. The nine-year-old boy who questions everything, expresses himself like an adult, and pushes for privileges that seem inappropriate to his age may be a source of great worry to his parents. This is especially true if the same child exhibits an uneven growth pattern and is not advanced physically. Parents need help in understanding that decisions based on chronological age may not be appropriate for the gifted child.

Parents are often concerned with their gifted children's emotional development. These concerns often center around a child's making friends, pursuing extra-curricular activities, and using leisure time. Parents need help determining how much activity is enough, yet not too much, because of the common concerns about placing too much pressure on gifted children. They also need help in finding community resources to meet special interests.

Parents need to address the issue of expectations for their gifted children. Family priorities and role expectations will influence decisions about extracurricular or enrichment activities. Parents who value proficiency in the arts may tend to push an able youngster in that direction, while the child may be more interested in other pursuits. Career decisions may not be consonant with parental hopes and aspirations. School personnel are becoming more involved in helping parents become better equipped to deal with the problems of their gifted children both at home and at school.

Summary

Evidence concerning gifted children's social and emotional adjustment is not definitive. As is often the case in the social sciences, different studies produce different results. It is important for teachers to remember that there are wide variations among gifted children. Specific studies may show certain results for groups of gifted children concerning self-concept and social adjustment, but each student will need individual consideration. Program designs should include systematic instruction for enhancing social growth and emotional well-being, focusing on the development of healthy interpersonal relationships and good personal adjustment.

Resources

Bibliotherapy

Dreyer, S. S. *The Bookfinder: A Guide to Children's Literature about the Needs and Problems of Youth Aged 2–15.* Circle Pines, Minn.: American Guidance Service, 1977, 1981.
Annotates more than 1000 children's books, listed by subject and approximate grade level.

Teaching Feelings and Interpersonal Relationship Skills

Eberle, B., and R. E. Hall. *Affective Direction: Planning and Teaching for Thinking and Feeling.* Buffalo, N.Y.: D.O.K. Publishers, 1979.

Eberle, B., and R. E. Hall. *Affective Education Guidebook: Classroom Activities in the Realm of Feeling.* Buffalo, N.Y.: D.O.K. Publishers,
Contains an instructional model, learning activities and community building activities for junior and senior high students.

Fishter, C. *Dimensions of Personality.* Dayton, Ohio: Pflaum/Standard, 1972.
Graded activities for personal and social development. Workbooks, activity sheets for grades 4-6.

Stephens, Thomas M. *Social Skills in the Classroom.* Columbus, Ohio: Cedars Press, 1978.
Teaching strategies for 136 behaviors.

Weinstein, G., and Mario P. Santini, eds. *Affective-Humanistic Education: Toward Humanistic Education. A Curriculum of Affect.* New York: Praeger, 1970.

Wiggins, James D., and Dori English. *Affective Education: A Methods and Techniques Manual for Growth.* Washington, D.C.: University Press of America, 1977.
Compilation of strategies, activities, and procedures for an affective education program.

Teaching Social Behaviors

Cartledge, G., and J. Milburn. *Teaching Social Skills to Children.* New York: Pergammon Press, 1980. *Duso Kit.* St. Paul, Minn.: American Guidance Service, 1980.

Eisler, R. M., and L. W. Frederiksen. *Perfecting Social Skills: A Guide to Interpersonal Behavior Development.* New York: Plenum Press, 1980.

Goldstein, A. P., R. P. Sprafkin, N. J. Gershaw, and P. Klein. *Skill Streaming the Adolescent: A Structured Learning Approach to Teaching Presocial Skills.* Champaign, Ill.: Research Press, 1980.

Phillips, E. L. *The Social Basis of Psychopathology: Alternatives to Abnormal Psychology and Psychiatry.* New York: Grune and Stratton, 1978.

Shaftel, F., and G. Shaftel. *Role-Playing for Social Values: Decision-Making in the Social Studies.* Englewood Cliffs, N. J.: Prentice-Hall, 1967.

Staub, E. *Positive Social Behavior and Morality: Volume I, Social and Personal Influences.* New York: Academic Press, 1978.

Staub, E. *Positive Social Behavior and Morality: Volume 2, Socialization and Development.* New York: Academic Press, 1979.

Stephens, T. M. *Social Skills in the Classroom.* Columbus, Ohio: Cedars Press, 1978.

Stephens, T. M. *Social Behavior Assessment.* Columbus, Ohio: Cedars Press, 1980.

Wilkinson, J., and S. Canter. *Social Skills Training Manual.* New York: John Wiley, 1982.

Whitmore, J. R. *Giftedness, Conflict and Underachievement.* New York: Allyn and Bacon, 1980.

Values Clarification

Abramowitz, M., and C. Macari. "Values Clarification in Junior High School." *Educational Leadership* 29 (April 1972).

Curwin, G. et al. *Search for Values.* Dayton, Ohio: Pflaum/Standard, 1972.
A total curriculum for high school values clarification, also adaptable to students of other ages. Includes units in authority, competition, personal space, relationships, and time.

Curwin, R., and L. Fuhrmann. *Discovering Your Teaching Self: Humanistic Approaches to Effective Teaching.* Englewood Cliffs, N.J.: Prentice-Hall, 1975.
Geared to preservice teachers. Gives a model and many activities to help teachers become aware of their own values, goals, and self-perceptions. Activities have use with students.

Fraenkel, J. R. *Helping Students to Think and Value: Strategies for Teaching the Social Studies.* Englewood Cliffs, N.J.: Prentice-Hall, 1973.
Model for teaching social studies with a focus on thinking and valuing. Contains both theoretical framework and curriculum suggestions.

Harmin, M., H. Kirschenbaum, and S. Simon. *Clarifying Values Through Subject Matter.* Minneapolis, Minn.: Winston Press, 1973.
Examples of value clarification activities in many subject areas.

Harmin, M., H. Kirschenbaum, and S. Simon. "Teaching Science with a Focus on Values." *The Science Teacher* 37 (Jan. 1979).

Hawley, R., and I. Hawley. *A Handbook of Personal Growth Activities for Classroom Use.* Amherst, Mass.: ERA, 1972.
Many value clarification and personal growth activities.

Hawley, R., S. Simon, and D. Britton. *Composition for Personal Growth.* New York: Hart, 1973.
   English and language arts activities to help build awareness and personal growth.

Klein, R., et al. *Search for Meaning.* Dayton, Ohio: Pflaum/Standard, 1974.
   Activities for use with students of all ages; teachers' handbook, spirit masters, and activities ready for use.

Simon, S. "The Teacher Educator in Value Development." *Phi Delta Kappa* 52 (June 1972): 649-51.
   Makes a case for using value clarification in teacher education; includes examples of activities.

Simon, S., L. Howe, and K. Howard. *Values Clarifications: A Handbook of Practical Strategies for Teachers and Students.* New York: Hart, 1972.
   Compilation of values activities from articles and books, along with new activities.

References

Austin, A. B., and D. C. Draper. "Peer relationships of the academically gifted: A review." *Gifted Child Quarterly* 25 (1981): 129-33.

Bandura, A. *Principles of behavior modification.* New York: Holt, Rinehart and Winston, 1969.

Bandura, A. "Vicarious process: A case of no-trial learning." In *Advances in experimental social psychology.* Edited by L. Berkowitz.

Berg, D. H., and W. D. DeMartini. "Uses of humor in counseling the gifted." In *New voices in counseling the gifted.* Edited by N. Calangelo and R. T. Zoffman. Dubuque, Iowa: Kendall/Hunt, 1979.

Bernal, E. M. "The Education of the culturally different gifted." In *The gifted and the talented: their education and development.* Edited by A. H. Passow. Chicago: University of Chicago Press, 1979.

Birch, J. W. "An interview with Jack W. Birth." *The Directive Teacher (1979): 1-26.*

Bloom, B. S., J. T. Hastings, and G. F. Madaus. *Handbook on formative and summative evaluation of student learning.* New York: McGraw-Hill, 1971.

Boston, B. *The sorcerer's apprentice—A case study in the role of the mentor.* EMC Clearing House on Handicapped and Gifted Children. Reston, Va.: The Council for Exceptional Children, 1976.

Braga, J. "Early admission: Opinion vs. evidence." *The Elementary School Journal* (1971): 35-46.

Broverman, I. K., D. M. Broverman, M. M. Clarkson, P. S. Rosenkrantz, and S. R. Bogel. "Sex role stereotypes and clinical judgments of mental health." *Journal of Consulting & Clinical Psychology* 34 (1970): 1-7.

Browne, E. F. *Bibliotherapy and its widening applications.* Methuchen, N. J.: Scarecrow Press, 1975.

Clark, B. *Growing up gifted.* Columbus, Ohio: Charles E. Merrill, 1979.

Curwin, R. L., and G. Curwin. *Developing individual values in the classroom.* Palo Alto, Calif.: Learning Handbooks, 1974.

Delisle, J. "Preventative counseling for the gifted adolescent: From words to action." *Roeper Review* 3 (Nov/Dec 1980): 21-25.

Dreyer, S. S. *The bookfinder.* Circle Pines, Minn.: American Guidance Service, 1977.

Eberle, B., and R. Hall. *Affective direction: Planning and teaching for thinking and feeling.* Buffalo, N. Y.: D.O.K. Publishers, 1979.

Erikson, E. H. *Childhood and society.* 2nd ed. New York: W. W. Norton Company, 1963.

Gallagher, J. J. "Peer acceptance of highly gifted children in elementary school." *The Elementary School Journal* 58 (1958): 465–70.

Gallagher, J. *Teaching the gifted child.* New York: Allyn and Bacon, 1975.

Gallagher, J. *The gifted child in the elementary school.* Washington, D. C.: National Educational Association, 1959.

Gerritz, E., and E. Haywood. "Advanced placement: Opinions differ." *NEA Journal* 54 (1965): 22–24.

Gowan, J. C. "Guiding the creative development of the gifted and talented." In *New Voices in Counseling the Gifted.* Edited by N. Colangelo and T. D. Zaffran. Dubuque, Iowa: Kendall/Hunt, 1979.

Haun, D. "Where kids teach kids." *Teacher* 92 (1975).

Hoffman, S. "Intelligence and the development of moral judgment in children." *Journal of Genetic Psychology* 130 (1977).

Hollingsworth, L. *Children above 180 IQ.* Yonkers-on-Hudson, N. Y.: World, 1942.

Jackson, D. M. "Mentorships: What are they? Who needs them?" In *Readings in curriculum development for the gifted.* Guilford, Conn.: Special Learning Corporation, 1980.

Karamessinis, N. P. "Personality and perceptions of the gifted." *G/C/T* (May/June, 1980): 11–13.

Kircher, C. *Behavior patterns in children's books.* Washington, D. C.: Catholic University of America Press, 1966.

Kohlberg, L. "The cognitive-developmental approach to moral education." In *Readings in moral education.* Edited by P. Scharf. Minneapolis, Minn.: Winston Press, 1978.

Krathwohl, D. R., B. S. Bloom, and B. B. Masia. *Taxonomy of educational objectives: The classification of educational goals: Handbook 2, affective domain.* New York: David McKay, 1964.

Lacy, G. *The social and emotional development of the gifted/talented.* Albany, N. Y.: University of the State of New York, The State Education Department, 1979.

Lehman, E. B., and C. J. Erdwins. "The social and emotional adjustment of young intellectually gifted children." *Gifted Child Quarterly* 25 (1981): 134–37.

Maker, D. J. *Providing programs for the gifted handicapped.* Reston, Va.: The Council for Exceptional Children, 1977.

Maslow, A. *Toward a psychology of being.* Princeton, N. J.: Van Nostrand, 1961.

Maslow, A. H. *Motivation and personality.* 2nd ed. New York: Harper and Row, 1954.

Maugh, T. H. "Creativity: Can it be dissected? Can it be taught?" *Science* (June 21, 1974): 1273.

McConnell, J. V. *Understanding human behavior.* 2nd ed. New York: Holt, Rinehart and Winston, 1977.

Milgram, R. M., and N. A. Milgram. "Personality characteristics of gifted Israeli children." *The Journal of Genetic Psychology* 129 (1976): 185–94.

Raths, L. E., M. Harmin, and S. B. Simon. *Values and teaching: Working with values in the classroom.* Columbus, Ohio: Charles E. Merrill, 1966.

Reid, V. M., ed. *Reading ladders for human relations.* 5th ed. Washington, D. C.: American Council of Education, 1972.

Rogers, C. R. *On becoming a person.* Boston: Houghton Mifflin, 1961.

Runquist, O. The Hamline University Class Plan for St. Paul Developmental Program Students. A

Report of a Three-year Experiment of College Classes for Talented High School Students in Mathematics & Sciences. St. Paul, Minn.: Hamline University, 1962.

Stanley, J. C., W. C. George, and C. H. Solano, eds. *The Gifted and the creative: A fifty year perspective*. Baltimore, Md.: The Johns Hopkins University Press, 1977.

Stephens, T. M. *Social skills in the classroom*. Columbus, Ohio: Cedars Press, 1978.

Stephens, T. M., and J. Wolf. *Personal equations*, 1983 (in preparation).

Sweet, H. D. "A mentor program—possibilities unlimited." G/C/T (Nov./Dec. 1980): 40–43.

Terman, L. *Genetic studies of genius*. Stanford, Calif.: Stanford University Press, 1925, 1959.

Terkel, S. *American dreams: Lost and found*. New York: Pantheon Books, 1980.

Torrance, E. P. *Gifted children in the classroom*. New York: MacMillan, 1965.

Treffinger, D. J. "Teaching for self-directed learning: A priority for the gifted and talented." *Gifted Child Quarterly* 19 (1975): 46–59.

Treffinger, D. J. "Guidelines for encouraging independence and self-direction among gifted students." *Journal of Creative Behavior* 12 (1978): 14–20.

Weinstein, G., and M. D. Fantini, eds. *Toward humanistic education*. New York: Praeger, 1970.

Whitmore, J. *Giftedness, conflict and underachievement*. Boston: Allyn and Bacon, 1980.

Wilbur, F. P., and D. W. Chapman. "The Transferability of college credit earned during high school." *College & University* 52 (Spring, 1977): 280–87.

Wolf, J. S., and J. Gygi. "Learning disabled and gifted: Success and failure." *Journal for the Education of the Gifted* (Spring, 1981): 199–206.

Wolf, J. S., and D. Penrod. "Bibliotherapy: A classroom approach to sensitive problems." *G/C/T* (Nov./Dec. 1980): 52–54.

4

Meeting the Needs of Preschool Gifted Children

Nancy T. Goldman
Sylvia Rosenfield

More than sixty years ago, Walter Lippman stated that our real environment is "altogether too big, too complex, and too fleeting for direct acquaintance. And although we have to act in that environment, we have to reconstruct it on a simpler model before we can manage with it" (Lippman, 1922, p. 30; Erikson, 1977, p. 27).

Gaining control over the environment in all its complexity, and playing a self-satisfying role on one's own "stage" is, in fact, what all of human development is about. The "reconstructing" of our world begins at birth: on a small stage, to be sure, but nevertheless the beginning of each individual's adaptation to the world. As they develop, young children initially use fairly simple reconstructions of their world, much as the toddler builds simple models with wooden blocks. As development proceeds, reconstructions of the world become more complex until, in adulthood, they parallel an architect's highly sophisticated structures.

In this chapter, we will discuss how this development compares with development among gifted children and which programs are appropriate for this group.

A survey of the literature on child development reveals a certain consensus among theoreticians and practitioners on the relative importance of Piaget's and Erikson's theories in explaining the highly complex process of development. Jean Piaget, in the cognitive domain, and Erik Erikson, in the affective domain, have contributed greatly to our understanding of this journey to adulthood (Maier, 1978; Flavell, 1977; White, 1975; Bruner, 1966). As Maier states, these contributions are "yet to be utilized by many generations to come" (p. 88).

While other scientists and theoreticians may take issue with the concepts set forth in the two theories and with the basic assumptions on which they are based (Hunt, 1983), these two child developmentalists have provided a conceptual framework for others' work in the field. Their model includes two crucial aspects:

1 Each postulates a sequential pattern of development, a series of stages through which the child passes on the way to maturity.

2 Each focuses, at least in part, on the importance of the interaction between the developing structures of the child and the environment.

Although Piaget and Erikson studied different aspects of development, their conceptual frameworks and the stages they identify are strikingly similar. A synthesis of the two theories provides a fairly complete picture of the development of a total human being. Do their theories apply to gifted children as well? How do gifted children proceed through the complex process of development? In what ways, if any, does their development proceed differently?

Giftedness in Young Children

Since 1971, most programs in the United States have used the definition created by the United States Office of Education and put into law in the Elementary and Secondary Education Act of 1971, modified by the revisions of that law in 1978. This definition identifies gifted and talented children as those "who are identified at the preschool, elementary, or secondary level as possessing demonstrated or potential abilities that give evidence of high performance in such areas as intellectual, creative, specific academic, or leadership ability, or in the performing and visual arts, and who by reason thereof, require services or activities not ordinarily provided by the school." We repeat this definition here to focus on two factors: first, the definition specifically includes preschool children; second, the difficulty of identifying those abilities in preschool children must be highlighted.

Quite often, with the preschool child, we are examining potential rather than demonstrated abilities, since it is not usually possible to provide evidence of high performance in very young children. Thus, we think in terms of *potential* giftedness. This term, "potentially gifted," has often been applied to the underachieving gifted child; that is, the child who scores well on intelligence tests but does not demonstrate outstanding performance in any area. The term has also been used among those who work with students from culturally or economically different backgrounds to differentiate children who will show rapid development when provided with appropriate stimulation. In one sense, we talk about the preschool child as potentially gifted in the same way we discuss both the underachiever and the culturally different child: the outstanding ability, because of age, lack of motivation, stimulation, exposure, or some other factor, has not yet been demonstrated (it is latent). In another sense, however, we could say that applying "potentially gifted" to the preschooler should be extended to all gifted children, since it is not school performance we seek at all but the quality of the contribution the child will make as an adult. Each time we identify a child as gifted, we are making a probability statement about that child's future.

We have tended to identify as a gifted preschooler the highly verbal child who walks and talks early and is a self-taught reader. Recent research on young gifted children reveals quite a different picture. Although some gifted children may walk and talk earlier than their age peers and may be early readers, such developmental milestones as early walking and talking do not always correlate with advanced cognitive ability (Roedell, Jackson, & Robinson, 1980).

We increasingly recognize the individuality of the gifted child. The literature is replete with lists of characteristics to check off and add to to determine whether a particular child belongs in the gifted category. Only lately have Terman's early warnings about the wide variability among the gifted population (Terman & Oden, 1947) received serious attention from those seeking to characterize this population.

Evidence gathered from studying gifted preschoolers in two projects, in Washington State (Krinsky, Jackson, & Robinson, 1977) and in Boston (Willerman & Fiedler, 1977), shows there is no single portrait of a gifted child. There is greater variety among the gifted as a group than between the gifted and their nongifted peers (Roedell, Jackson, & Robinson, 1980). We can no longer talk about *the* gifted child, but about gifted children.

Research on older gifted children confirms that gifted children differ from each other in many ways. Whereas some researchers, most notably Lewis Terman (1925), found gifted children to be physcially superior to other children (Barbe, 1955), others have not found differences in physical stature between gifted and nongifted children from the same region (Frierson, 1965) or from the same family (Laycock and Caylor, 1964). Some researchers suggest that the physical superiority found in Terman's and others' studies may result from the fact that most of the gifted children in these studies came from higher socioeconomic backgrounds where nutrition and health care practices tend to be superior to those of the general population (Hildreth, 1954).

Likewise, gifted children have been described as more socially mature, happier, better adjusted, and more popular than their peers. In examining data from a broad range of studies, Gallagher (1975) found profound individual differences in personal and social characteristics among gifted children. Social maturity seems to develop at different rates among gifted children in the same way that other development occurs. Some gifted children seem to mature socially earlier than their peers; others do not. Recent research on very young gifted children indicates there is often a discrepancy between these children's understanding of social settings and their actual behavior in the settings (Roedell, Jackson, & Robinson, 1980). Some gifted children, for example, may have advanced understanding of how other people think and feel, called *social cognition* (Rubin, 1973; Shantz, 1975). They may also be able to see alternative solutions to conflicts in social situations, called *social problem solving* (Spivack & Shure, 1974). But this understanding is not always relfected in their behavior, or *social interaction* (Roedell, Jackson, & Robinson, 1980).

In terms of overall adjustment, studies seem to agree that children with moderately advanced intellectual skills do tend to be well-adjusted (Gallagher, 1975; Hollingworth, 1942; Terman, 1925). Some children with extremly advanced intellectual skills, however, seem to have more difficulty, perhaps because of the wide discrepancy between their chronological and mental ages (Hollingworth, 1942; Newland, 1976; Terman & Oden, 1947). In terms of popularity, some studies show gifted children to be isolated from their peers (O'Shea, 1960); others show them to be well-liked (Gallagher, 1958). The popularity of young gifted children seems to relate to individual differences in their social interaction skills, the type and degree of their ability, and availability of similarly able children (Roedell, Jackson, & Robinson, 1980).

Besides their variety, what else is true about young gifted children? In the Seattle Preschool Project, young gifted children were found to be *precocious* in one or more ways, and although the area of precocity varied greatly among the children, the fact that the children performed at the level of chronologically older children (children almost twice their age, in some cases) was uniform (Roedell, Jackson, & Robinson, 1980). Young gifted children, then, seem to perform at least in some ways as older children. Precocity is easier to recognize when one can use the developmental norms for the age group as a reference point.

Piaget's and Erikson's Theories of Child Development

The most salient features of the theories of Jean Piaget and Erik Erikson are these:
- Development seems to occur sequentially in an orderly process
- The stages of development are universal to all cultures, and the process unfolds in an increasingly complex way with each phase building upon the acquisitions of the previous one
- Development is essentially an interactive process with the environment.

In terms of the first point, development as an orderly process, the sequential phases of the two theories are almost parallel. Erickson's first five stages correspond with Piaget's five developmental phases. (The last three stages in Eriksons's conceptualization address adult development, an area that Piaget did not investigate.) The congruence of the two theories extends even to the approximate ages at which each phase occurs.[1]

Table 4-1 presents the first five phases of Erickson and the five phases of Piaget to illustrate the sequential nature of development according to the two theories.

The second salient aspect of the two theories is the increasingly complex way in which the process of development unfolds, with each phase building upon the acquisitions of the previous one. The beginning of the development of the notion of causality illustrates this point. In the sensorimotor phase, the concept of causality of the infant involves only a rudimentary understanding that some kind of connection exists between action and result. By the next phase, preconceptual thought, the young child now understands that she may be the potential cause of an action. In the next phase, where judgment is based on a single clue, the child reasons that an event *had* to happen. By the next phase, concrete operations, the child can begin to understand scientific explanations of the relationship between cause and effect. In the final stage, the individual can think about causality in a formal way, forming hypotheses and performing other logical operations internally.

---

[1]One criticism of Piaget's work has involved the failure in other studies to obtain his same data in regard to developmental ages. Piaget suggested that the findings of different average ages could be traced to environmental variations; it is more important that the sequence of developmental phases is the same (1951).

Table 4-1 THE PARALLEL DEVELOPMENTAL STAGES OF ERIKSON AND PIAGET

Erikson's Theory (Affect)	Piaget's Theory (Cognition)
Phase I: Acquiring a Sense of Basic Trust While Overcoming a Sense of Basic Mistrust, birth–18 months	Sensorimotor phase, birth–24 months
The infant develops a sense of expectancy toward his environment through a mixture of trust and mistrust. Through interaction with the primary caretaker (the first environment), the infant learns whether the universe is predictable and dependable and, thus, able to be trusted. The overall regularity and continuity in the child-parent relationship is of utmost importance if the child is to develop a sense of basic trust.	The infant's world is linked to desires of physical satisfaction within immediate sensory experience (autism). Actions or motor activities must be coordinated with the perception of the senses as the world is created into a whole. Within this phase are six stages, beginning with the use of the reflexes. The nature of reflexes provides spontaneous repetition for the child, who then repeats in increasingly complex ways, providing the first knowledge of patterns, sequentiality, causal relationships, and permanency. Active experimentation with these themes leads to the beginning of simple reasoning (*not* logic).

Table 4-1   Continued

Erikson's Theory (Affect)	Piaget's Theory (Cognition)
Phase II: Acquiring a Sense of Autonomy While Combating a Sense of Doubt and Shame, 18 months–3 years	Preconceptual Phase, 2–4 years
The young child is pulled between the dependency established in Phase I on his parents and the assertion of his or her own will. As the child tries to operate independently, he or she struggles to maintain a sense of power. Overstepping boundaries causes feelings of guilt and shame. Establishing wise limits to minimize these feelings is the most important parental function in this phase, if the child is to develop into an independent being.	Through continuous investigation, the child seeks to learn how and why things work as they do (primarily through play). Imitation of others and symbolic imitation become extremely important, as does language, another important vehicle of development. Thought and reason are egocentric, with the self as the reference point. Concepts are related to the child's subjective experience and involve the use of the senses. Judgments are made by outward appearance (perception). Identification with a model, usually a parent, occurs and the model is invested with tremendous power and held in awe. Anything that moves is assumed to be alive and may be feared.
Phase III: Acquiring a Sense of Initiative and Overcoming a Sense of Guilt, 3–7 years	Phase of Intuitive Thought, 4–7 years
The child is challenged to be active and purposeful, to master specific tasks, and to assume responsibility for himself or herself. The child begins to exercise a sense of initiative by responding to inner strivings, struggling at the same time with passivity (not going far enough) and guilt (going too far). A sense of self-identify, including the awareness of being a boy or girl, replaces the sense of egocentricity of the previous phase as the child gets involved in wider social spheres and tests new behaviors and roles.	This phase is an extension of the previous one, the two together covering the period of preoperational thought and forming a bridge between the child's passive acceptance of the world and the child's ability to act in it and react to it realistically. Whereas the child previously acted out thinking and reasoning with manipulation and playing, words now serve that role. Thinking is still egocentric, although intuition introduces a greater awareness of relationships among things. Attributes or properties are seen as absolutes.

Table 4-1 Continued

Erikson's Theory (Affect)	Piaget's Theory (Cognition)
Phase IV: Acquiring a Sense of Industry and Fending Off a Sense of Inferiority, 7–11 years	The Phase of Concrete Operations, 7–11 years
The child invests tremendous energy into producing, into mastering tasks, and into succeeding. The world of peers assumes a great importance, since peers are needed for self-esteem. They are also the criteria for measurement of success or failure. An opposing pull toward a previous level of lesser production plus the awareness of being a child, an incomplete person, brings feelings of inferiority. Later attitudes toward work and work habits are traceable to successful development in this phase.	The child acquires the concept of reversibility, now understanding that it is possible to return to the starting point of an operation and, therefore, to reverse it. Conservation occurs. Operations are concrete rather than formal, mental experimentation still dependent on perception. The relationship between a whole and its parts is understood, and systems of classification are established. Thinking shifts from induction to deduction, and time is now seen on a continuum rather than as "before" and "after".
Phase V: Acquiring a Sense of Identity While Overcoming a Sense of Identity Diffusion, Adolescence	The Phase of Formal Operations, 11–15 years
The individual struggles to make the choice of who he or she is to become while finding a place for keeps. Directions from within (self) and directions from without (the broader society) must be integrated in order to face as an equal the challenges of the adult world. The essential supports and value givers are the peer group as the individual struggles slowly to integrate himself or herself, leaving childhood behind.	The individual acquires the capacity to think and reason beyond his or her own world and beliefs and enters into a world of ideas and essences apart from the real world. Symbolism and the use of propositions are relied on in cognition, and a systematic approach to problems replaces random behavior. A concept of relativity emerges, and the ability to reason with hypotheses replaces reasoning with symbols.
Phase VI: Acquiring a Sense of Intimacy and Solidarity and Avoiding a Sense of Isolation	
Phase VII: Acquiring a Sense of Generativity and Avoiding a Sense of Self-Absorption	
Phase VIII: Acquiring a Sense of Integrity and Avoiding a Sense of Despair	

The two theorists explain the third aspect, the interactiveness of this dynamic process, differently. For Piaget, growth occurs as a result of disequilibrium between knowledge already mastered and the reality of the external world. The individual must adapt to this discrepancy through the interaction of assimilation (the individual's adaptation of the environment through integration) and accommodation (the impact of the actual environment on the individual, requiring him to change). For Erikson, each phase is characterized by internal conflict, a crisis of opposing forces that must be resolved as the individual interacts with the external world.

What is developmentally characteristic of the preschool child? If we accept these two theorists' phases and ages, preschoolers are struggling to acquire a sense of initiative while being pulled toward passivity (not going far enough) or guilt (going too far). A sense of identity is developing, as is the awareness of being either a boy or a girl. The child's social sphere has widened, perhaps to include a preschool experience or a play group situation with peers. In this wider sphere, the child tests new behaviors and roles and is exposed to a wider variety of people and experiences.

Cognitively, preschoolers are characterized by preconceptual or intuitive thought; they rely on what they perceive through the senses.

Recent Research on Child Development

Recent research using more sophisticated methodology has created a more impressive picture of the preschool child's thinking abilities. For example, while Piaget indicates that children are unable to conserve numbers until age six or seven, Gelman (1979) demonstrates that even three- and four-year-olds were able to do so when the experimental task was appropriately constructed. Her task utilized small sets of toy mice, two or three on a plate, and children were asked to identify "the winner." The younger children were able to conceptualize the winner and loser rows utilizing number concepts without being distracted by length or density, which in the usual Piagetian task lead to failure to obtain the correct solution. According to Gelman, the classical conservation task developed by Piaget is actually a more complex task and requires more in the way of cognitive processes and skills than the number knowledge it was designed to measure.

Bullock's work at the University of Pennsylvania with three-year-olds indicates that children this age understand the relationship between cause and effect, even though they can not articulate it (Hunt, 1982). Bullock arrived at these results by examining the children's nonverbal responses and reactions.

It appears that a child's level of performance may be affected by the language used in the task as well as by the way the task is structured. In assessing young children, Blank and her colleagues found that young children are more cognitively able than previously thought *if* we ask the right questions, since the level of complexity of the language used in the task correlated with the child's level of cognitive performance (Blank, 1979).

Flavell (1977) refers to this phase in the young child's life as characterized by an extraordinary amount of language development. He refers to the close association between this communicative development and the child's intellectual growth. Two types of communication develop during this period. The first type is informative in intent and has as its content facts and ideas. With this type of communication, the young child is able to receive, transmit, and manipulate information about the world. The ability to communicate to oneself as well as to others allows the child to symbolize, store, retain, and think about the products of daily experience. The second type of communication has a controlling intent and allows the young child to influence others' behavior. Through the use of these two types of communication, the child becomes, for the first time, an active trader in both information and interpersonal control.

Another Look at Preschool Gifted Children   There are two ways of viewing the unique developmental aspects of preschool gifted children. One view holds that gifted young children are simply more advanced than their age mates, and it is this precocity that sets them apart from their peers (Robinson, Roedell, & Jackson, 1979). Evidence for this view is based on observing young children's performance. Based on the observers' perceptions, these children do not appear to differ qualitatively in their thinking, but rather to demonstrate differences in rate of development.

Another view relates to their unique behavior and learning style, the possession and combinations of which results, in time, in qualitative differences in performance. While it is true that a child of three with the mathematical concepts of a seven-year-old appears *only* to be more advanced than peers in this area, that same child at the age of 12 or 13 may be functioning on a level that some adults could never master. That child is qualitatively different.

While gifted children appear at an early age only to be more advanced, this early advancement suggests the potential also for a qualitative difference in performance at a later stage of development. Very young children who learn quickly and easily *and* possess unusual memories *and* who are also able to develop highly systematic ways of relating, storing, and retrieving data may simply have more time to learn, remember, store, and manipulate both additional and more advanced information and processes. The result seems to be an effect of geometric progression on ability, performance, and competence.

Although there is no list of traits that every gifted child possesses, and although research illustrates the great variability within the gifted group (Roedell, Jackson, & Robinson, 1980), certain characteristics have come to be associated with gifted children. These characteristics are often found on checklists for identifying gifted children. Perhaps this phenomenon can be explained by the fact that developmental precocity (doing things earlier than one's same-age peers) is recognized behaviorally. Certain behaviors have been grouped into categories and associated with the gifted.

Unusual or Intense Curiosity   Some gifted children ask questions repeatedly, the answer to one question leading to another question. Other gifted children take objects apart to discover how they work, and often the objects are not what you would expect for their age (one 15-month-old was discovered dismantling a radio). Still other gifted children take apart ideas to discover their significance. The need for this behavior seems to come from inside them; they seem to want to know more than appears appropriate for their age. For example, M., at 3, became an expert on dinosaurs after looking through all the available books on the subject in the children's section of the public library. He went to the children's librarian to ask for more books. She let him look through books in the adult section and helped him find the information he wanted.

Unusual Sensitivity and Heightened Perceptual Skills Some gifted children seem to use their senses more actuely. They often notice or perceive things that other children do not: physical objects, details, nuances, changes in people's moods, smells, hues, resemblances to other objects or people. For example, L., at 20 months, recognized a stop sign from the back by its octagonal shape. H., at 2 or 3, noticed if the smallest item in a room had been moved (Hall & Skinner, 1980).

Advanced Conceptualization Some gifted children seem able to think abstractly far in advance of their chronological age, in making associations, systematizing, problem solving, and problem finding. This ability may display itself in the way they connect things or make associations and in the way they develop systems, organize objects or evaluate. For example, L., at 18 months, recognized a car of the same type as her mother's but of a different color ("That's Mommy's car, only it's red"). M., at 19 months, insisted the kitchen cabinet doors be closed when she saw them ajar because they were not "right." She became irate when a glass was replaced on the incorrect shelf.

Unusual Ability to Comprehend and Utilize Various Symbol Systems Some gifted children are able to understand and use with great ease different types of symbols (words in language, notes and phrases in music, numbers in mathematics). They often have early facility with the symbol (words, numbers, notes) and advanced understanding of the medium (language, math, music) as a system. For example, M., at 3½, showed her understanding of language in general and of bilingualism in particular by devising the strategy of speaking English in the living room and Spanish in the bedrooms and kitchen and then informing her mother of the strategy. A., at 3, was able to do complicated math problems in his head. By fourth grade, he had designed a new number system which he presented to his teacher for use in class. As an infant, N. was unusually sensitive to sound. Her mother reported that she cried when funeral music came on the radio and stopped when her mother shut it off. As a preschooler, she corrected her mother's singing when it was off-key or incorrect, and in elementary school she was able to repeat perfectly complicated musical phrases and patterns after hearing them once.

Unusual Memory and Avid Interest in A Variety of Topics Some gifted children surprise you by what they remember and for how long. They seem to have a highly developed filing system in their heads and place all types of information in it in "mental trays" for quick retrieval. They easily become experts on topics; after they exhaust a topic to their satisfaction, they move on to a new topic and explore it in depth. They often seem to know a lot about a wide range of topics that interest them. For example, at 3½, S. had an avid interest in airplanes. Although he was unable to read, he looked through any book he could find with information on the topic. This interest lasted about a month; then he moved on to shells.

Unusual Degree of Independence in Thought and Action   Some gifted children are described as "marching to the beat of a different drummer." These children often have difficulty accepting help, even when they need it, because they are so insistent on doing things for themselves. Completing tasks on their own gives them needed satisfaction. They sometimes take positions or stances that do not conform to others' standards, because they set their own. For example, L., at 20 months, insisted on going down the slide into the pool at the camp where her father worked for the summer. Since the water was over her head, her mother prepared to go down the slide with her. Unwilling to be thwarted in her attempt to accomplish the task on her own, L. tried to bite her mother's hand in order to loosen her mother's grip on her. M., at 3, insisted on trying to print his name himself, even though his fine motor coordination was not sufficiently developed to allow him to succeed at this task. S., as an adult, recounted his frustration over the fact that he could not get out of his crib as a toddler. He remembers feeling "locked up in his body," a prisoner of his own limited coordination. S. was 13 or 14 months old at the time.

Unusual Task Commitment or Motivational Perseverance: Drive to Perfect   Some gifted children seem to be able to concentrate for a longer period of time than their peers. They will stay with an activity for as long as it interests them, often spending hours on one topic or activity. They usually stay with the task until the job they do satisfies them. They are often not satisfied with the standards others set for tasks or jobs, and instead set impossibly high standards for themselves. The job they do must be perfect. They become devastated by their failure to be perfect. This drive, although it takes a great emotional toll, is one of the factors that contributes to their creating exceptional products. For example, even at 2, N. had to do a perfect job on everything she attempted. When a stuffed toy she played with refused to sit up alone on her tricycle in her parade, she flung it across the floor and told her mother she was angry at it. L., at 20 months, sometimes hit herself on the head when she was unable to do something she wanted to do: riding a two-wheeler or tying her own shoes, for example.

Unusual Leadership Ability   Gifted children sometimes appear to be natural leaders; they seem to command followers without trying and are often puzzled by their ability in this area. Since they often play with children older than themselves (with similar abilities) or prefer the company of adults, they learn interpersonal skills that put them in a leadership position with their age-mates, whom they often find "too babyish." They often organize and lead the activities in a group even when the group is composed of older children or adults. Often they are able to exert their will over others. For example, B., the youngest child in her preschool class, tells many of the other preschoolers where to sit and what to play with. According to her teacher, she organizes activities and fantasy play with one particular group of children, and the group misses her when she is absent. Some of the children seem almost lost without her.

Unusually Developed or Sophisticated Sense of Humor   Some gifted children see humor in situations where others do not and are able to use sophisticated forms of humor in communications with others. They like puns and riddles and enjoy playing with words. They are not easily fooled (if warned) and can turn situations around in humorous ways to their own benefit. Even before they understand the "joke," they are able to use funny phrases and punch lines correctly in their speech. For example, L.'s mother relates the story of her daughter's reply, at 22 months, to a question a neighbor asked her with the negative response, "No way, José."

In exhibiting some of these behaviors, gifted children seem to develop in ways that are both similar to and different from the development norms for their age group. As we have said, there is no single profile of a gifted child. Young gifted children are characterized by wide variations in characteristics and abilities and in the areas of precocity. A young gifted child might function as a seven-year-old in reading, math, or music, but act very much a three-year-old in every other way. Second, development among children tends to be very uneven, so that much of a gifted child's development may correspond to the developmental norms for the age.

Developmental norms are helpful for two reasons. First, they help us to see where a young child's development might be precocious. Second, they remind us that young gifted children are *children* first and *gifted* second and, therefore, have the same needs and growth patterns as their age-mates. Expectations for their behavior must always be viewed in these terms.

Preschool Programming

An impressive amount of literature documents the importance of the preschool years in a child's later development. It is during the early years that a child develops the attitudes and habits that significantly affect not only current functioning, but later functioning as well (Karnes, 1980). Burton White (1979) states that a child's informal education from infancy to age three has a tremendous impact on later intellectual development. Newland (1976) refers to underachievement as a habit that can begin early. Bloom (1964) concludes that early environment is critical to development for three reasons: the rapid growth of selected characteristics in the early years; the sequential nature of human development (what happens early affects what happens later); and the nature of learning itself (learning well initially is easier than stamping out later what is learned poorly).

The importance of the early years is attested to by the massive effort, initially undertaken by the federal government in 1965, to provide educational intervention for one subgroup of this population at special risk, economically disadvantaged preschoolers, through Operation Head Start. While the need for preventive intervention for this particular group was readily acknowledged, the notion that all preschoolers might be developmentally at risk was not. White (1975) estimates, however, that no more than 10 percent of preschoolers are "as well educated and developed as they can and should be" (p. 103).

Although recent literature on early intervention and the critical effect of an early positive environment clearly suggests the importance of the preschool years, there has been little research on gifted three-, four-, and five-year-olds or on the critical period of intervention for them (Karnes, 1980). The assumption of the indestructibility of children's talents and gifts has, however, been seriously questioned (Karnes, 1980; Gallagher, 1975). Havighurst (1962) indicates that children become superior through the combination of being born with superior potential and being raised in a superior environment. If learning is too simple and too familiar, the child will fail to develop and withdraw in boredom (Hunt, 1969). Reason tells us what research has not yet documented: young gifted children need a positive early environment.

Programs for Gifted Preschoolers

As of 1980, literature showed that 17 programs for preschool gifted existed nationally (Jenkins, 1979; Kaplan, 1980; Roedell, Jackson & Robinson, 1980); however, the type and level of services varied greatly. In one instance, the program constituted providing educational planning information directly to parents of gifted preschoolers. In another, the needs of gifted preschoolers were met in regular classrooms, serving much the same function as a nursery or day care center.

Given the wide variability in structure among the programs cited in the literature, one might have considerable difficulty distinguishing between programs appropriate for gifted preschoolers and those appropriate for preschoolers generally. Kaplan (1980) urges taking into account two concepts when establishing programs for gifted preschoolers:

1 Because gifted and talented preschoolers are like their same-age peers in many ways, all theories regarding young children are applicable to these children as well; and

2 Because gifted and talented preschoolers differ from their same-age peers in significant ways (rate of learning, level of commitment to task, exceptional ability in an area), regular programming which is appropriate for preschoolers generally must be altered or modified in order to take into account the specific differences

Thus, programs for gifted preschoolers must first address the needs of this *age group*, such as mastery of specific tasks, experimentation with new behaviors and roles, manipulation of concrete objects, and development of expressive language. (You may want to refer to the theories of Erikson and Piaget in Table 4-1.)

Programs for gifted preschoolers must also address the *special needs* of this group by modifying instruction to account for each child's individual learning style and pace and unique traits, interests, and areas of precocity. Such modifications might include teaching reading to one gifted three-year-old, exposure to science lab equipment and training to another, and training analytical and evaluative skills. It might also include special attention to a handicapping condition.

Of the several program models developed for this group of children, Schaffer (1980) suggests a developmental-interaction approach, in which children actively participate in their own development through direct interaction with, and exploration of, their environment. This model assumes that children expand and develop in the presence of appropriate opportunities and experiences. Another model is a combination of the Structure of Intellect model and the open classroom (Karnes, 1980). Kaplan (1980) further cites Taba's teaching strategies, Gagné's hierarchical types of learning, and Ennis's aspects of critical thinking. Herbert Thelen's Group Investigation Model and J. R. Suchman's Inquiry Approach have also been used successfully with young gifted children (Ellenhorn, 1983).

Despite the number of models available, there is no evidence to indicate which program model is most effective (Roedell, Jackson, & Robinson, 1980). No one model has been demonstrated to be superior to the others (Karnes, 1980). Follow-up studies of the various Head Start program models, undertaken by David Weikart (1977), showed that all models were effective when teachers were committed to the model and dedicated to the children (Roedell, Jackson, & Robinson, 1980). This principle may or may not hold true for programs designed to serve gifted preschool children, although the use of a conceptual model does seem to be an important element (Karnes, 1980). Programs that adopt a conceptual model are likely to be more consistent and organized than programs that work without one (p. 111). We will discuss several programs, each of which was designed for a different population of gifted preschoolers: a general population, a culturally-different population, and a handicapped population.

Three Model Programs

The Seattle Preschool Project (WASHINGTON) The Seattle Preschool Project, also known as the Child Development Preschool, at the University of Washington in Seattle is a university-affiliated and research-oriented program for a general population of gifted preschoolers. It has been cited as a model program with funding from the Office of the Gifted and Talented and the Spencer Foundation. The program is the first step in a sequence of services available for intellectually and academically advanced children in Seattle.

Focus was on the development of children with different types of advanced intellectual and academic skills using learning experiences that encourage thinking skills, intellectual curiosity and persistence, creative expression, academic and social skills, and large and small muscle coordination and dexterity. Activities and goals in the curriculum are based on Piaget's theory of logical thinking.

The Pippi Program (NEW YORK) The Pippi Program, located in East Harlem in New York City, is an urban program for gifted culturally different and bilingual preschoolers, funded by the Office of the Gifted and Talented and the Philippson and Lipper Foundations. Fordham University was a consultant for the program.

The focus in this program was to develop critical, creative, and logical thinking, and problem solving skills (including social problem solving) through process-training activities and units or topics appropriate for advanced three- and four-year-olds. The program simultaneously trained parents. The curriculum was based on a Bloom's Taxonomy model with an understanding of cognitive and affective development as described by Piaget and Erikson.

The Chapel Hill Gifted-Handicapped Project (NORTH CAROLINA) The Chapel Hill Gifted-Handicapped Project in Chapel Hill, North Carolina is affiliated with the University of North Carolina. The project was designed to meet the needs of a gifted-handicapped population by providing a combination of small-group activities, individual activities, and therapy. It was funded by the Bureau for the Handicapped as a demonstration (model) project.

The focus was to provide a balance between enrichment programming and remedial programming to enhance special abilities or strengths and develop areas of weakness. The program used a unit-topic approach with curriculum based on a Bloom's Taxonomy model. Activities for each child were based on his or her disability and developmental age. The family component was an integral part of the program, including training parents and parent participation in the classroom and in assessment, program design, and evaluation.

Common Factors   These three programs have several common factors. All were cited as model projects and received funding from outside sources. All had some type of affiliation with, or services provided by, a university. All based curriculum and activities on the developmental literature and had a strong conceptual base. All addressed the needs of the individual children by tailoring activities and skills training to individual needs, developmental levels, and abilities. All relied on parent involvement, either encouraging active parental participation in the classroom or at home or utilizing parental information and input. Finally, all focused on developing cognitive skills such as observing, predicting, classifying, analyzing, synthesizing, evaluating, and social problem solving. Although each program was designed for a different group of gifted preschoolers, their similarities are striking.

Principles of Programming for Gifted Preschoolers

Certain principles relating to the programmatic needs of gifted preschoolers have become apparent:

- The program should be holistic, addressing both cognitive and affective aspects of development.
- The approach should be individualized to provide an optimal match between the learning environment and the children's unique characteristics and abilities, previous learning and experiences, and needs as preschoolers and gifted children (and, in some cases, their handicapping condition).
- Academic skills should be integrated into the program, but only to provide children with necessary tools.
- A parental component is necessary for both parental support and parental education or training, to help parents facilitate their child's development.
- The identification model must relate to the type of differentiated program provided.
- The teacher should have certain characteristics and skills and should model the behavior that is the goal for the children.

Table 4-2 compares the way a gifted program addresses the characteristics of gifted children to the special requirements of a gifted preschool program.

Holistic Programs

Since uneven development is often characteristic of young gifted children (Roedell, Jackson, & Robinson, 1980), discrepancies between cognitive competence and social and emotional maturity often occur. These discrepancies can place children in situa-

Table 4–2   GIFTED AND GIFTED PRESCHOOL PROGRAMS

Children's Characteristics	Gifted Program	Preschool Program
An unusual amount of curiosity	Wide exposure to a variety of topics	Topics not usually done at this age
A great deal of independence in thought and action	Provision for working alone; allowance for differing ideas and opinions; provision for exploring self-selected topics	Independent study; training activities in creative thinking and creative problem solving; allowance for own time frame
Task commitment; ability to work until self-satisfied	More flexible time arrangements; allowance for task completion	Provision in day for longer work periods
Ability to see concepts more easily	Inclusion in curriculum for higher level thinking (analysis, synthesis, evaluation)	Appropriate activities for developing thinking
Ability to learn more quickly and easily	Less stress on basic skills	Reading and math skills development less important than concept development
A wide variety of interests	Exploration of many topics	Unit study; trips and materials on various topics
An unusual degree of sensitivity	Discussions on "values" topics; activities to help develop self-evaluation	A lot of understanding; discussions of many topics; help with seeing oneself honestly
A sense of humor	Appreciation of humor in situations	Appreciation of humor

tions where they are considered "different," in the negative sense. Children thus need special help in nurturing their advanced abilities while developing their average skills in other areas.

The program must address both the cognitive and affective aspects of development. The children need to develop such cognitive skills as classification or grouping, seriation or sequencing, patterning, and spatial and temporal relations. Thinking skills and strategies, including creative and critical thinking, should be included in the program in a sequential and systematic way. Although all good preschool programs give some attention to thinking skills (Roedell, Jackson, & Robinson, 1980), not all programs approach such training systematically. A systematic approach is especially important for cognitively advanced children, to provide immediate challenge and to develop effective tools for the future. All three model programs focused on systematic development of these skills.

Social skills training, an essential part of every good preschool program, was an important focus in the Seattle Preschool Project. This project found that intellectually advanced preschoolers with average social skills have difficulty making friends, communicating with same-age peers, or overcoming social differences between themselves and older children who are intellectual peers (Roedell, Jackson, and Robinson, 1980).

Young children who are noticably different have particular difficulty forming social relationships and often develop maladaptive behavior patterns. Social problem solving can be especially effective with these children (Shure & Spivack, 1974). In this approach, the children's cognitive abilities are used to solve social and interpersonal problems that occur both within and outside of the classroom. (This approach was particularly successful in the Pippi Program [Goldman & Rosenfield, 1979].)

Individualizing

Because of the wide variability among young gifted children and the unevenness of their development, the program must be individualized to meet their various needs. In effect, this means an individual program plan for each child. Several "matches" need to be taken into account in such planning.

First, one must remember that these children are preschoolers, and are therefore similar in many ways to their age peers. For example, most children at this age regard adult actions as fair. They perceive obedience to adults as synonymous with goodness, and disobedience with badness. Although they may reflect cooperation and respect in both their play and speech, neither is necessarily present in their thinking. Cognitive advancement does not preclude the need for structure and limits, praise and support, and constructive criticism and honest feedback. Nor does it preclude developmental immaturity in other areas. Any program approach or model should take into account such developmental aspects.

Second, remember that the children are gifted and may therefore differ from their age peers and from each other in many ways. Their faster rate of learning may require a more advanced, faster paced curriculum of greater depth, and taught differently than might be appropriate for their age mates (Fox, 1979). Also, their different areas of giftedness or precocity may require one type of treatment or program and their average areas another.

Third, since the children are gifted, they have some characteristics commonly associated with giftedness (for example, heightened perception or a drive for perfection). All the children do not possess the same characteristics in the same combinations, however. Curriculum and activities must be matched with individual characteristics as well.

Fourth, previous learning experiences and acquisitions must be considered and built upon for new learning to take place. Referring to this problem, Hunt (1969) states that "in order for a given experience to alter a child's level of understanding, that experience must have an appropriate relationship to information already learned from previous experience. If new learning is too simple and too familiar, the child will fail to develop and withdraw in boredom. If the new learning is too complex and too demanding, he will withdraw in fear or explode in anger" (p. 38). Hunt counsels that the best indicators of a good match are the child's emotional responses.

An optimal match requires individualized planning, according to Robinson, Roedell, and Jackson (1979), and ought to encourage development of strengths as well as help improve less advanced skill areas.

Academic Skills

Unfortunately, many programs for exceptionally able children focus on developing academic skills for the wrong reason: to "show off" their participants. The purpose of developing academic skills in preschoolers is not to use the children in an adult performance, but to provide them with tools to use in their investigations, studies, and explorations.

Most cognitively precocious children will learn to read, for example, given adequate instruction. Some will learn to read by themselves; others will have difficulty grasping such subjects as reading and math for a variety of reasons. Reading and other academic skills should be taught to young gifted children when they are ready for it and require it as an educational tool.

Teaching academic skills for the skills' sake alone is not appropriate in a good gifted preschool program, since time is better spent developing such cognitive and affective skills as problem solving, social problem solving, and social interaction.

The Parent Component

Although no research exists on the effect of parental involvement in preschool gifted programs, ample evidence in child development literature and in follow-up studies of Operation Head Start attest to the impact of parental involvement on a child's development.

The informal education that families provide for their children "makes more of an impact on a child's total educational development than the formal educational system" (White, 1975, p. 4). White further states that "if a family does its job, the professional can provide effective training. If not, there may be little the professional can do to save the child from mediocrity" (p. 4).

Milner (1951) cited two factors in the parent-child interaction that affect reading readiness upon entrance to school: (1) a warm, positive family atmosphere where the adult is seen as positively reinforcing; and (2) extensive opportunity to interact verbally with adults in the family. When both of these conditions were met, children were ready to read, motivationally and cognitively.

The impact of parent involvement in various Head Start programs was presented by Hess (1976): (1) the more the program concentrated on parents, the greater the impact of the program on the child; (2) a one-to-one teacher/parent relationship produced greater gains than when parents were taught as a group; (3) home visits were particularly effective; and (4) the degree of structure in the activities parents used related positively to the program's impact on the child.

These results were considered in planning the parent component of the Pippi Program. Lack of professional and financial resources eliminated the possibility of frequent home visits and one-to-one teacher/parent relationships, at least in terms of training. The program did, however, concentrate on parents in the sense that they were expected to participate in structured training sessions once a month.

Each training session was devoted to a specific topic, such as the characteristics of the gifted, what constitutes a good gifted program, patterning as an analysis skill, evaluation activities to do at home with the child, and values clarification. These topics were developed sequentially, so that knowledge from previous sessions was built upon in succeeding sessions. Parent evaluations revealed the effectiveness of this model (Goldman & Rosenfield, 1979).

The impact of the family on a child's development is greater than that of the formal educational system.

Each session also devoted time to talking informally about the specific problems parents of young gifted children face. This time gave parents support for actions and practices they now used effectively with their children. (See the chapter Appendix for sample parent materials and evaluation forms.)

Parent participation was also an integral part of the Chapel Hill program. This program's family component included parent involvement in assessment, program planning, and evaluation; parent training; and parent participation in the classroom and on the advisory board.

Identification

One goal in planning a program is to match the children to the particular program. Identification plans are based on the assumption that the program addresses the needs and capabilities of only a certain group of preschoolers. If the program were equally applicable to all preschoolers, there would be no reason to go to the time and expense of carrying out an identification plan.

Identification of the gifted preschool child, as with identification of any other group, is essentially a measurement task. As such, it relies on a set of specific measurement variables. After making decisions about the definition of giftedness the program is willing to build its program around, the two key measurement concepts of reliability and validity must be addressed.

Operational Definition

We have discussed the variety of definitions of giftedness; however, there is a substantial difference between the conceptual definitions and an operational definition. To identify a human attribute accurately, one must have a precise operational definition. Unfortunately, there is no precise, universally accepted operational definition of giftedness (Hagen, 1980). Giftedness is not a unitary trait like tallness, where we can agree on what tallness means and on appropriate procedures for measuring it. Part of the difficulty in identifying gifted children is that giftedness cannot be observed directly, but must be inferred from observing the behavior of individuals either in naturally occurring situations or in situations constructed specifically to elicit the desired types of behavior (Hane, 1980).

The characteristics we look for as indications of giftedness in young children must be carefully selected. Among the many characteristics that young children exhibit, only some are related to the potential for high level achievement. Further, those characteristics related to achievement in one area may or may not relate to achievement in other areas. Finally, it is not just the presence or absence of a characteristic in a given child, but the relationship among the characteristics that determines the child's capacity for high level achievement.

To reach an operational definition, it is first necessary to pinpoint the areas in which one is going to search for potential giftedness. Hagen (1980) suggests that at the preschool level, we designate general rather than specific areas for selection of gifted characteristics. At this stage of development, one could identify children with above average academic achievement, but we are less able to recognize children with a specific area of academic potential, such as scientific aptitude.

A second decision relates to the degree of exceptionality. How high a score must a child have to be considered precocious? Must the child be exceptional in one area or in more than one area? Since there is no typical gifted child, there is considerable variability among the characteristics that any given child might exhibit. Children do not do all things equally well: children who seem to be exceptionally advanced in one area of functioning may not be so in all areas. Thus, the system one uses to make decisions must take this developmental unevenness into account.

Reliability   Several sources of error may interfere with the reliability of a child's scores. The preschool child is notorious for unreliable performance—for behavior that may vary considerably from hour to hour, place to place, and person to person. For examiners who try to test a preschool child who resolutely remains mute while the baffled parent explains that the child never stops talking at home, the situation can be frustrating. Therefore, assessment should not be confined "to single observations, either of time or measure" (Lidz, 1977, p. 133). Consider Lidz's experience over a two-week period: "There were many instances when children showed a great deal of stress and inhibition or acting up during the early sessions and would have been declared untestable if limited to those times; but, during the second week, many showed a dramatic change and became quite accessible" (p. 133). In testing preschool youngsters for gifted programs, one must give special attention to the conditions of testing, to the need to test over a period of time, and give each child the time to adapt to the testing situation. Even then, with the difficulties inherent in testing young children, one must take great caution in assuming that one has obtained the child's true score. Always consider the following two principles when testing young children (Anderson, 1967):

- The earlier in development measurements are made, the less reliance should be placed on single measures or observations to predict later development.
- The earlier in development assessment is conducted, the more one should consider the possibility of such factors as negativism and refusal as contributing to error in measurement.

Validity   The ability to measure intellectual capacity with any degree of long-term consistency based on preschool assessment is also an issue. According to Bayley (1967), intelligence is "a dynamic succession of developing functions, with the more advanced and complex functions in the hierarchy depending on the prior maturing of earlier simpler ones" (p. 403). While individual intelligence tests are reliable (that is, relatively consistent in an individual's scores over a period of years), validity is particularly questionable if the first test is administered during the preschool period. The relationship of one intelligence test score to that of later scores becomes stronger as the child becomes older, but the scores of three- to five-year-olds are not good predictors of scores at age eight or twelve. While measurement is possible with this age group, it requires a certain reservation about the validity of the outcome.

Usability   A third criterion, along with reliability and validity, is often applied to assessment techniques (Goodwin & Driscoll, 1980). Usability—an efficient, inexpensive, and acceptable system for identification—is a serious problem. For example, group tests cannot be used with this age group. It is often difficult to be efficient, as children may be more or less willing and able to accommodate quickly to the demands of the testing situation. A certain playfulness and unwillingness to conform to the demands of the examiner in a standardized test situation is a common occurrence.

Roedell, Jackson & Robinson (1980) encourage having each applicant participate in all stages of the selection process, rather than using a screening system in which some nominees are systematically excluded along the way. Since individual test sessions are necessary for measurement of advanced cognitive skills, lack of a screening method adds considerable expense to the system.

Although no identification system will be perfect, Roedell, Jackson & Robinson (1980) suggest that in designing a system, the following questions be asked:

1 Does the standard test component of the identification system include measures of a child's abilities in each area relevant to the content and goals of the program?
2 Are all the measures included in the identification relevant to the program?
3 Are the standard tests known to yield reliable and valid estimates of abilities for children who are likely to perform at levels far beyond those expected for their age group?
4 Does the system include consideration of information about a child's everyday behavior collected from parents or others who know the child well?
5 Are those who are a part of the identification process trained to consider all aspects of the available information, such as the adequacy of the test session or special features of the child's background?
6 Are all components of the identification system appropriate for use with children from the cultural groups represented among the applicants?
7 Can a child qualify for the program despite a low score on an individual component of the identification battery if performance is very strong on other components?
8 Can the identification process be accomplished with the time, staff, and funds available? (p. 64)

Attempting to obtain the most satisfactory answers to each question will insure the most accurate results possible, given the imperfect state of the art.

Developing a Model Identification Plan

Each identification plan should include a basic concept of the type of giftedness the program will be designed to accommodate. For example, many preschool programs for the gifted are built on a definition of intellectual precocity. After defining the area, the staff must determine what characteristics will be examined as indications of giftedness. If the program is based on a definition of academic excellence, for example, what criteria will the staff define as indications of academic excellence? One indication might be mathematical reasoning ability. The next stage is to identify the sources from which to gather that information. A variety of sources is available, but the sources are more limited for preschoolers than for school-age children. Obviously, young children have had less experience and fewer opportunities to develop and demonstrate a potential for giftedness. The more information available, the more accurate the identification is likely to be. Helpful sources of information in the identification of preschool gifted children include the child, the child's caretakers, and teachers (if the child is in a preschool program).

Next, decisions must be made regarding the specific methods or instruments; for example, which intelligence test best meets the program's specifications. Data can be collected through tests, observations of the child, ratings or questionnaires given to those who know the child, and the child's products, such as artwork. Robinson et al. (1979) suggest three considerations when collecting data on preschool gifted children. First, there must be an opportunity for children to display extremely advanced skills: "Thus, many of the 'readiness' tests used to identify children who are not adequately prepared for the typical kindergarten or first grade program are wholly inadequate for identifying preschool children with advanced abilities" (Robinson et al., 1979, p. 145). Second, given the difficulty in obtaining reliable performances from children of this age, they suggest presenting the child with a broad range of tasks, to encourage the possibility that the child's strongest performance will be captured. Related to this, the examiner should collect evidence as to "what the child can do, and not be discouraged by what the child cannot, or will not do" (p. 146). Finally, they urge that identification include a detailed parent report in addition to an evaluation of the child, since "even the most comprehensive battery of tests, administered by the most skillful of testers, may not provide a good estimate of a young child's capabilities" (p. 146).

Finally, another crucial decision concerns how the various information and scores will be combined and evaluated. The use of matrices, for example, may result in the inclusion of less able individuals into programs, and the exclusion of the extremely able whose ability lies in only one area. Will each measurement in the battery receive the same weight? The purpose of identification is to determine which children will do best in a special preschool program, and the answer needs to be defined empirically for each community and each special program (Shwedel, 1980).

Selection of Instruments   Tests are most often used to identify children according to the criteria of intelligence, academic aptitude, and creativity.

Simply stated, intellectual giftedness can be defined within the cognitive domain as an exceptional potential for learning, along with outstanding ability to "assimilate, manipulate and utilize abstract concepts and factual information in problem solving" (Whitmore, 1980, p. 61). According to Whitmore (1980), the intellectually gifted child is defined by the possession of superior ability in the area of cognitive processing. The preschool child begins to become recognized as a thinker towards the end of the second year (White, 1975). The underlying processes that may be the hallmark of the gifted preschool child have gained increasing respect in the past several years with the recognition that these cognitive processes are more complex than previously thought (Gelman, 1979). These skills are usually measured by a standardized general intelligence scale, such as the Stanford-Binet or the Wechsler Preschool and Primary Scale of Intelligence (WPPSI). There is general consensus that if a single measure is to be relied upon for identifying intellectually gifted children of preschool age, the best single measure would be a test of general intelligence (Roedell et al., 1980).

The Stanford-Binet Intelligence Scale, revised in 1960 (Terman & Merrill, 1960) and renormed in 1972, is the test usually selected for testing a young child's intellectual competence (Hagen, 1980; Roedell et al., 1980; Martinson, 1981). While the WPPSI (Weschsler, 1967) has been used as well, it does not appear to differentiate the top two or three percent as well as does the Binet (Hagen, 1980; Rellas, 1969; Sattler, 1982), because of its limited ceiling. On some of the WPPSI subtests, gifted preschoolers obtain the maximum possible scores (Rellas, 1969).

While individual intelligence tests are noted for their psychometric properties, there is often a tendency to attribute too much to the score the child receives. In the Seattle Preschool Project, follow-up studies demonstrated that individual Stanford-Binet IQs of children tested at the age of two or three did not show much stability at age four or five, although the group as a whole tended to demonstrate increases in performance level (Roedell et al., 1980). The differences went in both directions: children who scored well on the first test decreased in performance and children who scored less well increased in performance. (This finding is consistent with the earlier literature cited in the discussion of validity.)

The question remains as to whether differentiation of young children's cognitive abilities into specific abilities is appropriate (Hagen, 1980). The major intelligence tests differ as to their reliance on a single score or a score differentiated into specific abilities. While the Stanford-Binet taps different kinds of abilities in its various test items, it yields only a single score, called an IQ. On the other hand, the WPPSI provides two scales, a verbal and performance scale, as well as specific subtests within each.

A second area in which giftedness may be demonstrated via test performance is academic aptitude. Generally, the best predictor of outstanding academic achievement is the current level of achievement, but this indicator cannot be easily applied to the preschool child. Some children of preschool age develop advanced skills in the tool subjects of reading and arithmetic, but it is unclear whether these early advanced academic skills indicate giftedness, as the long-term predictiveness of early reading and math skills has not been validated (Roedell et al., 1980). The data suggest that children who read early are likely to be good students later (Durkin, 1966) and that good readers are well represented among the intellectually precocious children of preschool age (Terman & Oden, 1947). Many very bright children do not demonstrate early academic precocity, however, and the lack of these skills in a preschool child should not be considered a negative indicator.

Measurement of reading skills can be informal or formal. While reading tests are not standardized for preschool children, it is not difficult to evaluate a child's reading skill with individual tests of reading such as the Peabody Individual Achievement Test (PIAT) (Dunn & Markwardt, 1970). Reading readiness tests should not be used for this purpose, however, because of their inability to discriminate among children with average and above average skills. Experience with such instruments in the PIPPI Program clearly illustrated the failure of this type of evaluation instrument to provide differentiated information about gifted young children.

Arithmetic questions are generally included on intelligence tests for young children, and some indication of mathematical precocity can be gleaned from these subtests or items. Roedell et al. (1980) suggest that a combination of items from the Stanford-Binet and the WPPSI Arithmetic Subtest provides an estimate of the preschool child's mathematical ability. When more extensive data are needed, they suggest the mathematical section of the PIAT or the Keymath Diagnostic Arithmetic Test (Connolly, Nachtman, & Pritchett, 1971).

Another approach to identifying mathematically precocious preschoolers involves a Piagetian base, through which the child's understanding of the logical principles underlying the number system and computation techniques are assessed: "Children's comprehension of the principles of seriation, class inclusion, and invariance of quantity (conservation) is related to their readiness to master mathematical skills" (Roedell et al., 1980, p. 45). Tests available to tap young children's conservation abilities include the Concept Assessment Kit (Goldschmidt & Bentler, 1968) and the Cartoon Conservation Test (DeAvila, 1979).

A child may also demonstrate advanced abilities in creative or divergent thinking. Measuring creativity through the use of tests is complicated by the difficulties in defining the construct and in finding indications of its presence in the child. This problem is particularly acute in the preschool period, since it is hard to evaluate the production of very young children in terms of creativity. The levels of skill and development often preclude the child's ability to demonstrate creative production in any meaningful way. As for the validity and reliability of tests of creative thinking, Gallagher, Aschner, and Jenne (1967) comment: "one of the best but least likely things that could happen would be for investigators to avoid assiduously the term creativity in referring to these embryonic measures" (p. 93).

Weaknesses in the reliability and validity of most creative thinking measures at any age suggest caution in their use with the preschool child for identification purposes. Results of instruments such as the Torrence Test of Creativity (1966), Make a Tree (Circus, 1974–75), and Starkweather's (1971) research battery should be considered cautiously when used for selection purposes. While one may be impressed by the "cleverness and unusualness of the test tasks . . . validity information remains meager" (Goodwin & Driscoll, 1980, p. 241). It is useful to keep track of the results of these tests and to develop a procedure to determine what, if anything, these measures add to the success of identification methods used with preschool children.

It has been suggested that the performance of preschool children on creative thinking measures be scored qualitatively as well as quantified:

> By employing productive thinking tasks as stimuli to engage a child's interest and inspire verbal or pictorial responses that need not be limited to a predefined "correct answer," the sensitive examiner may gain meaningful insights into a child's capabilities that are, indeed, quite different from those revealed by intelligence tests (Roedell et al., 1980, p. 51).

We have found this to be true with two items from the Torrence Tests of Creative Thinking (1966), Clouds and Alternate Uses, which were modified for use with preschool children. A wide range of scores in fluency, flexibility, and originality suggests that preschool children respond differentially to these tasks along a number of dimensions; however, the reliability and predictive validity of such an approach needs further investigation.

With the limitations of the tests currently used, parent questionnaires and rating scales probably provide the most objective sources of information for identifying gifted children. There is ample evidence that parent ratings are useful for identifying young gifted children (Jacobs, 1971; Martinson, 1981; Robinson et al., 1979; Roedell et al., 1980). In fact, the preliminary findings of Robinson and his colleagues (1979) suggest that parent information may be a better estimate of later intellectual functioning than early test scores. Some children who exhibited average ability on test scores at age two, but for whom parent reports indicated extraordinary ability, were functioning at higher levels by age four. These results deserve serious consideration.

In the Seattle Preschool Project, Robinson et al. (1979) examined a variety of ways in which parents can provide information about their children. The first is parent referral of the child to the program. The findings confirm that parents exercise considerable self-selection in nominating their children as gifted, a finding consistent with other studies involving parent nomination (Jacobs, 1971; Goldman & Rosenfield, 1979). Some differences have been found among socioeconomic groups (Cheyney, 1962; Ciha et al., 1974; Roedell et al., 1980), with parents of lower socioeconomic levels more apt to nominate their children as gifted than parents of upper socioeconomic levels. It has been suggested that well-educated parents from homogeneous, affluent communities tend to be unrealistically stringent in their standards for giftedness (Roedell et al., 1980).

A second way to tap parent information is by means of a checklist of characteristics thought to be typical of gifted children. This approach presents problems, especially regarding the difficulty for parents of making clear decisions on such items as "quick mastery" of information (Roedell et al., 1980). The checklist format may not provide specific enough information for parents to use accurately.

A third approach is the use of a questionnaire to focus on the intellectual and academic abilities children display. The gifted child may be more remarkable for *how* she does things rather than *what* she does, and the need to ask a manageable number of questions may exclude some of the ways a child displays exceptional talent. For this information, an open-ended or structured interview format is often useful (Goldman & Rosenfield, 1979; Roedell et al., 1980).

Parents have been used as informants in all the areas in which testing has been used, and are also useful for describing the child's affective characteristics that are considered important for maximizing the child's advanced capabilities. Factors such as task commitment and motivation can be assessed by asking parents to complete questionnaires. The Thomas and Chess (1977) temperament questionnaire has been used for this purpose (Goldman & Rosenfield, 1979). One of the temperament characteristics measured—persistence—has been found to relate to success in a gifted program (Burk, 1980).

Models for Identification

Most professionals agree that multiple criteria should be used for identification. Models have been developed for three different populations: general; minority/culturally different; and handicapped.

The first approach was developed by the Seattle Preschool Project (Robinson et al., 1979; Roedell et al., 1980), a longitudinal study of children with advanced intellectual abilities who are identified at preschool age. More than 300 children, originally nominated by their parents on the basis of some demonstrated intellectual ability prior to age five, have been evaluated. Besides a variety of revised parent questionnaires to improve the nominating process, the project developed a battery of tests to evaluate the children's functioning. The battery includes measurements across a wide variety of areas:

- A measure of general intellectual ability, measured by a short form (the starred items) of the Stanford-Binet Intelligence Scale
- Measures of spatial-perceptual reasoning skill involving the Block Design and Mazes Subtests of the WPPSI and, to provide a higher ceiling for children who do exceptionally well on these two subtests, the Wechsler Intelligence Scale for Children–Revised (WISC–R), developed for older children; for two- and three-year-olds, the Sequin Form Board to estimate spatial reasoning ability
- Reading and mathematical achievement, using a brief informal reading inventory and the Arithmetic Subtest of the WPPSI
- Short-term memory as measured by the numerical memory subtest from the McCarthy Scales of Children's Abilities

The domain of intellectual ability has been translated into a set of behaviors a child might perform, and these behaviors form the basis for the parent questionnaire and interviews to give a picture of the child's functioning.

An outstanding contribution of the Seattle project was the development of a "best performance" philosophy for handling the information accumulated through the battery of measuring instruments: "the most meaningful aspect of a young child's test performance is not the child's average level of performance across a wide range of tasks, but the most advanced performance demonstrated" (Roedell et al., 1980, p. 129). The long-term usefulness of the various measurements used in Seattle and the best performance philosophy require continued evaluation.

The PIPPI Program, a preschool program for culturally different preschool children, also developed an identification plan based on a composite battery and a best performance philosophy (Goldman & Rosenfield, 1979). Assessment is embedded in a total process of evaluation that involves the individual child as well as the child in relationship to other children, a preschool teacher, and a school psychologist. Parent nomination is the program's primary referral source, although Head Start and day care teachers were also invited to nominate children. Parents provided a valuable source of referrals; 75 percent of the children referred by parents scored one standard deviation or better above the mean on the Stanford-Binet Intelligence Scale.

Once nominated, each child is scheduled for a group classroom interview. In small groups of six to eight, the PIPPI teacher conducts two activities: an art activity and a story telling session. Free play is allowed briefly before the structured activity, until all the children arrive, and for a brief period after the activities. The staff observes both free play sessions.

The children are invited to return individually with a parent. At the second session, the child is given an individual psychological examination by the school's psychologist. Parents are interviewed by either the director or the program's psychological consultant, using a structured format, but allowing the parent to describe the child's play and social behavior in some detail. The parent also fills out the Temperament Questionnaire (Thomas & Chess, 1977), which is scored to determine the child's persistence level.

After the data are collected and scored, each child is evaluated for entrance into the program based on readiness for a structured preschool program and capacity to benefit from a program that focuses on higher level thinking skills. The Stanford-Binet has proven to be a valuable predictor of performance for these lower socioeconomic children. A cut-off point of 120 has been established. Scores on the Binet have predicted not only which children the teachers would evaluate for the program, but also seem to relate to the child's subjective feelings of comfort and satisfaction in the program, as reported by parents on their program evaluations.

In the third year of the PIPPI program, it was extended to a bilingual school, which required a revision of assessment procedures. Staff members were also interested in developing additional measures of cognitive ability because of a continuing concern that the community's lower socioeconomic level could limit some children's ability to obtain high scores on the Stanford-Binet. They selected the Raven Coloured Progressive Matrices as a potentially useful measure. The manual suggests that it be used with a language measure when it is being administered as an intelligence test, so the Boehm Test of Basic Concepts (Boehm, 1971), with both an English and Spanish version, is also included. Despite an extensive history of use of the Ravens, relatively little work had been done with the measure at the preschool level. One of the issues of concern with the use of the Ravens with very young children is its reliability, so it was also considered necessary to develop reliability data, for which two groups of children participated in a study (Roper, 1980). A gifted monolingual English-speaking PIPPI group of 22 children, aged 4 to 5½, were administered the Ravens, Boehm (in English), and the Stanford-Binet. A group of 12 children, aged 4½ to 6½, received the Ravens and the Boehm (in English or Spanish, depending upon their dominant language). Both groups were retested with the Ravens after one month. The test-retest correlation for the monolingual groups was .70, and for the bilingual group, .60; these moderate correlations were not high enough to suggest using the test without considerable concern as to whether a child's score on a second administration would be similar to that on the first. The slight difference in reliability between the two groups, in favor of the monolingual children, was in line with the subjective perception of the school psychologist who tested all the children. She found the bilingual children more difficult to test, more playful, and less willing to conform to the demands of the test situation. Results of the analysis for the monolingual children yielded correlations of .37 between the Binet and the Ravens, and .31 between the Binet and the Boehm, indicating that the Binet is indeed measuring something different from either the Raven or the Boehm.

After exploring a number of other strategies, a best score philosophy was established for the PIPPI Program. When a child is sufficiently English-dominant to take the Stanford-Binet, the cut-off score of 120 became increasingly valuable as indicating the necessary cognitive level to benefit from the curriculum. One bilingual child who was not testable on the Binet because of his limited English, scored in the 75th percentile on the Ravens, and was accepted into the program. This score was particularly remarkable because of his impoverished infancy. Several children whose scores and behavior were outstanding in some respects were not accepted into the program because they were not ready to be in school, or because their parents were not ready to have them leave home. Preschool programs are not in the best interest of every child, including some gifted, at age three or four; for such children, it may be better to develop parent training programs. The PIPPI program asked these questions to evaluate its parent training program:

1 What specific skills did you learn in the PIPPI parent meetings this year? Please describe.
2 What things do you handle differently with your child as a result of our meetings? Please describe.
3 How has the way you look at your child changed as a result of our parent meetings? Please describe.
4 Do you handle your other children or your own life differently in any way as a result of our meetings? Please describe.
5 Do you handle such issues as death, religion, sex differently with your child/children as a result of our meetings? Please describe.
6 How have our meetings been helpful to you personally? Please describe.
7 For next year, what skills would you like to learn?
8 What topics would you like to see covered?
9 What specialists or speakers would you like to hear?
10 What other suggestions would you make to help us design a parent program next year which will meet your needs?

The qualitative analysis of the parent interviews related to the child's performance on the intelligence test. Children who scored well on the test had usually displayed behavior the parent could describe, when asked to talk about the child's play behavior or social interaction, which marked the child as unusually precocious. Parents described bright children, for example, as "adult-like" in conversational abilities from an early age. This is consistent with White's (1975) finding that "one of the characteristics of the well-developed three-year-old is a tendency to hold conversations with adults as if they were peers" (p. 173). These parents reported this pattern at an even earlier age. Although developmental milestones such as age of walking or talking did *not* relate highly to other indications of intellectual ability, the parents did consistently note that they could treat the child as much older.

The Chapel Hill Gifted-Handicapped Program (Leonard, 1978) uses a four-step process of identification of program participants. In the first stage, potential candidates are referred for further study by means of a checklist of characteristics that provides space for a brief description of how these traits are manifested. Next, further evaluation is conducted to document *above average* performance or potential for such on one or more standard instruments. Test selection is individualizedd for each child depending on the handicapping condition. Table 4–3 lists some of the tests used. If information is limited or the use of a standardized test is inappropriate at this second stage, the child is evaluated by an interdisciplinary team at the Division for Disorders of Development and Learning at the University of North Carolina.

Additional information is gathered in the third stage by observing the child's play or by interviewing parents or teachers regarding skills and play preferences. No criteria are applied to these techniques, although this step of the process provides helpful information about each child.

Finally, acceptance into the program is determined by a consensus of Gifted-Handicapped Staff, based on all available information. Most of the children demonstrated abilities at least one year above their chronological age in some developmental area.

Table 4-3 STANDARDIZED TESTING FROM THE CHAPEL HILL GIFTED-HANDICAPPED PROJECT

Environmental Handicap	Physical Handicap	Hearing Impairment/ Language Impairment	Visual Impairment
Wechsler Preschool & Primary Scale of Intelligence Leiter International Performance Scale	Peabody Picture Vocabulary Test Columbia Mental Maturity Scale French Pictorial Test of Intelligence	Leiter International Performance Scale Performance section of the Wechsler Preschool & Primary Scale of Intelligence	Interim Hayes Binet Intelligence Scale Verbal section of the Wechsler Preschool & Primary Scale of Intelligence Maxfield-Buchholz A Social Maturity Scale for Blind Preschool Children Merrill Palmer Scale of Mental Tests

The staff has developed certain guidelines, including the need to train teachers who will be referring children to the program. These guidelines may help in identifying other gifted-handicapped children for a program:

- Each test item presented to a child is one in which the child has the sensory ability to comprehend the task; the physical ability to make the required response; and the experience necessary to perform the task.
- Performance of handicapped children on standardized tests should be compared with the performance of other children with similar handicapping conditions, in addition to comparisons with normal children.
- Because of the nature of the population, the problems inherent in testing handicapped children, and the developing concept of gifted-handicapped, no specific criteria or scores should be established for determining giftedness other than the general criterion that the child should exhibit unusual abilities despite the handicapping condition.

Identification: State of the Art

The programs we have described have several common factors. All use multiple sources of information about each child, as is the case with most identification programs for gifted children. Each relies on individual testing conducted by a trained staff member or psychologist. All the programs value parent information. On the negative side, the programs rely on instruments that do not have strong measurement characteristics for either the age group or type of population (the handicapped group) to obtain information about desired abilities. The need for additional study of these techniques is an ongoing concern of all the programs.

Given the limited state of the art for assessing preschool gifted children, any identification program's adequacy should be continually reassessed. Follow-up studies should involve those who have been identified as gifted as well as those who have not. The identification plan should be modified by refining, adding, and eliminating methods procedures on the basis of the evaluation data. Continual re-examination of children both in and out of the programs should allow for opportunities to reclassify them in either direction. Some children who demonstrate early promise do not seem to develop, even under optimal circumstances, in that direction; others, whom we might classify as late bloomers, come into their own at a later age. We have relatively little understanding of how this process occurs; the identification process only measures the child within a limited time span. Classification may also change depending upon the type of program offered, which can result in a different definition of giftedness.

Although we have highlighted some of the difficulties in identifying preschool gifted children, the importance of developing efficient and accurate procedures should not be underestimated. The use of multiple criteria and continual re-evaluation of the process and of the children will contribute to better identification procedures. In many respects, the problems discussed here reflect those in any identification procedure for identifying gifted children and/or preschool children; it is the combination of preschool and gifted (and, in some cases, handicapped) that requires caution.

Major Elements of the Program

The Teacher

In attempting to assess the importance of the teacher in the education of gifted children, Renzulli (1968) canvased twenty experts in the field and found that the teacher, the curriculum, and the student selection procedures were rank-ordered 1, 2, and 3, respectively, as important elements of the program. Gallagher (1975) referred to the general consensus among the experts that the teacher and the curriculum need "special attention" (p. 72).

What skills and traits should a teacher of young gifted children have? Newland (1976) states, "The teacher of the gifted must possess in abundance those characteristics which can be particularly contributive to the learning to be done by the gifted" (p. 147). Kaplan (1980) lists several characteristics needed by the teachers of the gifted: "a given teacher should possess a significant number of them, though not necessarily all to the same degree" (p. 120), among which she includes:

- Good health and high energy level
- Desire to work with young gifted children
- High level of intelligence

- Good mental health and interpersonal skills
- Knowledge of child development and experience with young children
- Keen sense of humor
- Sensitivity to individual differences
- Enthusiasm
- Maturity
- Wide interests and at least one demonstrated area of talent
- Commitment to family involvement
- Participation in the community
- Creativity
- Eagerness to learn
- Good self-concept
- Training (p. 121)

Examination of these traits reveals that the teacher's characteristics relate to both the characteristics and the behavior of young gifted children. They also refer to the teacher's need to be a model for these children, both in the sense of possessing similar characteristics and in the sense of behaving in ways that are similar to the children's ideal performance.

The concept of the teacher as a model is important to all programs for gifted children. If the teacher differs qualitatively from the students, they find it hard to relate to him and to give credence to his methods of operation. But a teacher they view as "one of them" is better able to teach in the Socratic notion of the term.

We often find in programs for gifted children that the teacher is highly organized, with well-developed analytical skills, and is able to model the strategy known as critical thinking in both his behavior and in classroom activities. With this strategy, he does a highly effective job of teaching the children how to operate. Or, the teacher may be highly creative, supporting the development of fluency and originality, and providing the kind of environment in which the children's creative thinking abilities flourish. Rarely, however, does the teacher possess and utilize both these modes of behavior in the classroom, with the result that the children learn well how to use only one type of thinking behavior when they need to comprehend, use, and develop both types. Good preschool programs for gifted children include experiences with both critical and creative thinking, to match the children's cognitive needs and abilities.

The Curriculum

A theoretical base developed from the knowledge we have about thinking is essential in planning a preschool curriculum for gifted children. One such conceptualization for teaching young intellectually gifted children is that of teaching the thinking skills. As Sigel (1977) documents, "the class of social experiences most significant are those which serve to demand participation, planning, reconstruction of previous experiences, and in essence, separate the individual from the immediate and concrete present. These behaviors are and will be referred to as *distancing behaviors*" (p. 2).

Sigel's model of training arises from a Piagetian-based understanding of the preschool child. He recommends distancing strategies in the form of inquiry techniques, including:

- Asking good questions
- Posing alternatives
- Pacing
- Responding to children's questions
- Arrangement of the classroom
- Using a variety of contexts

To ask good questions means to minimize those that require little mental activity (What color is this block? What is the first, second, or third thing that will happen?) in favor of questions that require greater mental activity on the part of the respondent, and that are likely to be followed by genuine exchanges of information and opinion (Tell me about that; Why do you think that?). Sigel suggests that questions that activate thinking help the child focus her mental energies on the issue at hand and thus construct the relevant concept for herself.

A second distancing strategy is to pose conflicting issues or alternatives (Would you rather build a house with blocks or with wood scraps?). In choosing among two or more alternatives, the child must carefully examine each possibility, if the choices are mutually exclusive, and if there is some consequence in having made the choice. When these two conditions are met, the child is likely to be motivated to be thorough. Sigel adds, however, that questions here help the child to consider pertinent details, make inferences, and relate pieces of information. Questions thus become a strategy for helping the child learn how to weigh options.

A third aspect of the use of distancing strategies involves pacing. A good initial question can be lost by "not waiting long enough between question and answer, by showing approval only for correct answers, or by accepting answers without posing alternatives" (p. 27). Again, questioning can help determine how strongly the child holds the response and establish a basis for the child's developing point of view. Sigel believes that when a child is given the opportunity to test knowledge for himself, he may change beliefs on the basis of the results. His guiding principle is to, whenever feasible, "let the child discover the consequences of the action himself." The teacher's role is to help maintain safe conditions for testing consequences and to help children notice and analyze consequences.

A fourth aspect of distancing strategies is to respond to child-initiated questions. How the teacher responds serves as a model to the child for developing a genuine dialogue. One technique is to avoid answering a child's question with a factual response, but to instead help the child figure out the answer. Replies such as "that's a good question; let's figure it out" help free the child from dependence on the teacher.

A fifth strategy involves the physical arrangement of the preschool classroom. Activities should be arranged so that possibilities for integration are obvious to the child, for example, placing blocks near the dramatic play area. When materials are within the children's reach and storage areas are labeled with pictures so the children know where things are kept, they have more control over their environment and can more easily use classroom resources for solving problems. Sigel suggests materials that lend themselves to a variety of purposes, such as blocks and construction materials. He also advocates introducing novel materials to stimulate discussion and exploration and using stories that will elicit ideas from the children.

Finally, Sigel urges using distancing behaviors in a variety of contexts, since children must be able to use their cognitive abilities in understanding "why rules have been set in resolving disputes with other children, in estimating physical prowess, and in evaluating one's own preferences as well as in learning about school-related topics" (p. 27).

Sigel sees sound reasons for using these strategies with preschool children to develop cognitive thinking skills: "inquiry, by its very nature, has demand characteristics which help the respondent activate, orient, and organize his or her thinking (p. 16)." He notes that it is difficult for most teachers and parents to ask open-ended questions, maintain a waiting attitude, and then, when the answer comes, ask another question without killing the conversation. Our point is that learning to engage a child in distancing behaviors requires training for the teacher. But it is precisely this element, the *approach* used with the children, rather than classroom content or activities, that differentiates a gifted program. The way in which a lesson or activity is carried out is of paramount importance.

One sequence in the PIPPI Program illustrates this approach. In this case, the thinking skill is patterning. Cognitive scientists are beginning to recognize the importance of this skill as "another way in which our minds are predisposed to organize the welter of incoming experience" (Hunt, 1982). Here is an excerpt from this sequence:

- Step 1   At the front of the room, line up the children who are wearing clothing with patterns. Ask "Tell me why I have these children in a line." Ask additional questions to elicit as many responses as possible.
- Step 2   Hold up a simple pattern in two colors (made on large chart). Ask "Can you think of any ways in which this design is like the children's row/clothing?" Elicit as many responses as possible.
- Step 3   Using colored cubes, make a simple three-color pattern. Ask "Is there another way I can do this? Are there any other patterns we could make?"
- Step 4   Using clapping rhythms, ask "How many different patterns can we make? How are these patterns alike/different? Tell me about this pattern."
- Step 5   Ask "Can you find any patterns in our day (the week, the month, the year, the seasons)?" Present similar patterns and ask "What can you tell me about this?"
- Step 6   Ask "Can you design a pattern for someone else to complete?"
- Step 7   Ask "Can you make patterns with rubber stamps, parquetry blocks, unifix cubes? What other objects in the room could you use?"
- Step 8   In the block and play areas, ask the children to notice any patterns that occur.
- Step 9   Design a pattern museum in the classroom. Ask the children to design the museum itself and to include patterns of their choice.
- Step 10   Ask "What can you tell me about patterns?"

Similar sequences have been developed for grouping, associating, and sequencing. A unit on evaluation has been designed along similar lines.

Evaluation

Evaluation is the act of making judgments. It occurs, according to Norris Sanders in *Classroom Questions: What Kinds?*, in two steps. The first is to set up appropriate standards or values and the second is to judge how closely an object or item meets these standards.

We agree with his description but call these two steps *setting up criteria* and *meeting the criteria*. We teach very young children to follow these steps by giving them lots of practice with meeting criteria we set up, by helping them set up criteria and allowing them to meet the criteria, and by asking them to set up their own criteria and then meet them. Thus, the two steps are broken down into three additional and sequential steps.

Because many of the children at this age don't read, we use a symbol system and a questioning pattern that is appropriate for their skills level. That is, the children ask:

Does this picture have _____?
Does this picture have _____?
Does this picture have _____?

The answer should be YES when they see a large green circle above the symbols and NO when they see a large red circle with an X inside above the symbols. Thus, a task is shown symbolically in the following way on the board:

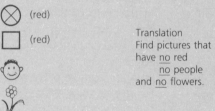

Translation
Find pictures that
have <u>no</u> red
       <u>no</u> people
and <u>no</u> flowers.

Having Children Meet Criteria You Set Up for Them

Activity 1

Say, "Today we are going to be looking for certain pictures in magazines. You know we have done this many times. We have cut out our pictures, pasted them on paper, and put them up around the room. We have made pictures of *groups* and of *patterns*. [Reinforce previous skills in *analysis*.] Can anyone think of any other types of pictures we have cut out?

"Today we are going to cut out pictures that *do not* have certain things in them. [Pictures without certain criteria are easier than pictures that contain three criteria for very young children.] We want to find pictures that have no red, no people and no trees." This task is written on the board symbolically in the following way:

"I'm going to pass out magazines to everyone. You look through your magazine and when you find a picture that has no red, no people, and no trees in it, please bring it to me."

Have children look through magazines to find pictures. Children bring up their magazines one at a time. You ask each child to look at his/her picture again and question, "Does it have no red? Does it have no people? Does it have no trees?" Then ask, "Does it meet our criteria?" If it does, give child scissors or help child cut out picture. Let each child paste his/her picture on a large piece of display paper (use PRIT or other glue stick; it's easier for children of this age to manipulate) and label each picture.

Display the children's work and allow any child who wishes to do so to describe his/her picture and explain how it meets the criteria.

Activity 2

Remind children of previous activity. Point out picture on the wall. Describe criteria in that picture. Then say, "Today we are going to meet our criteria in a different way. This time we are looking for pictures that have red, a person, and a tree." The task is shown on the board symbolically as follows:

(green)

(red)

Ask the children if that means their pictures can't have blue or another color in it beside red, or if their pictures may contain more than one person or tree.

Pass out magazines and use the same procedure you used in Activity 1. Label each child's picture and display the work in the room or in the hallway. Tell the children that they can add to this display if they find other pictures in magazines at school or at home. Note: Use your own judgment as a teacher (evaluate, in other words) how much experience and practice with these two types of activities your group of children need before you proceed to the next level. Alter or modify the activities as needed.

Helping Children Set Up Criteria to be Met

Activity 1   Setting up criteria (attributes) for members of a group or set (reinforcement of previous skills training in grouping)

Begin by reviewing what a group is (a set or collection of items that have certain attributes in common). Recall with them work they have already done in forming food groups: meats, dairy, grains, fruits, and vegetables. Tell them that you are going to use the vegetable group today to set up three criteria. Say, "Let's use green vegetables. That means we already have two criteria: (1) vegetables (2) that are green [place on board]. Ask them what your third criterion could be. It might be green vegetables (Criteria 1 and 2) that (3) can be eaten raw or are used in salad or are eaten in summertime. List the criterion they choose as a group.

Have them find pictures that meet these three criteria in books and magazines. Let them cut out the pictures from magazines and draw or copy the pictures from books. Display work with each child's contribution labelled.

Activity 2

Have the children pick the group (Fruits, Toys, Vehicles, Animals, etc.). List the attribute of membership as Criterion 1. Have the children decide Criteria 2 and 3. Find pictures and display work as outlined above.

Activity 3   Setting up criteria to evaluate a specific thing (e.g., a good paper or a good report)

Explain that you and they have been evaluating their work since the beginning of the year. [Obviously, you can't say this unless it's true, so make sure you do it. This can be done simply by having them tell you their judgment for each piece of work they do, by writing their judgment of their own work on it, and by adding your evaluation underneath. Don't *ever* underestimate their ability in this area. They are painfully aware of the quality of the job they do and resent it when you tell them everything is "wonderful" when they know it isn't. So be honest and they will be also. As Michael, one of our first PIPPI youngsters, said when asked to evaluate his work, "Put GOOD TRY and give me some paper to take home for practice."]

Explain, further, that you and they will continue to do so, but that you are going to concentrate now on evaluating a specific piece of work. Choose a piece of work they will do that day. Ask them to describe the things they will have to do to do a good job. List the standards on the board:

Criteria	Evaluation			
	by child		by teacher	
1. Is my work neat?	YES	NO	YES	NO
2. Is my work complete?	YES	NO	YES	NO
3. Is my work correct?	YES	NO	YES	NO
Evaluation: Did I do a good job?	YES		NO	

Activity 4

Do Activity 3, but assign specific point values to the criteria and to each correct answer. Use a graph or number line to show the evaluation of each child's work. Keep a graph for a week of one sample per day of each child's work. Ask each one to describe the *pattern* of work the graph shows. (This is an excellent way to reinforce the work you have done with the *analysis* skill of *pattern*.

Activity 5   Classify according to criteria

Using the empty product boxes, cans, and containers that the children have brought in for use in the housekeeping corner, play the game "What's My Criteria?" This game can be set up simply by clearing one shelf or tabletop in the room and by arranging a small number of items together because they meet the same criteria. For example, an empty orange juice container, an empty milk container, and an empty grapefruit juice container would meet the following criteria: (1) liquids (2) that we drink (3) cold. Remove the milk container and substitute it with an empty pineapple juice container and you have: (1) citrus fruit (2) drinks (3) in cardboard containers (4) that we drink cold.

Play the game by setting up criteria in advance and then placing items that meet the criteria on the shelf and play the game by placing items on the shelf and having the children guess the criteria. Be sure to let the children place the items and let you and the other children find the criteria.

Activity 6   Classify animals according to criteria

Order a set of wildlife cards from Weekly Reader Books (1250 Fairwood Avenue, P.O. Box 16615, Columbus, Ohio 43216). This set contains 900 cards classified alphabetically, zoologically, geographically, and ecologically. Use them with the children to classify animals. Set up simple categories for them initially: mammals, fish, birds, reptiles and amphibians, and insects. Then set up criteria for these categories: For example:

Mammals

Criteria

1. Nurse young
2. Are warm-blooded
3. Born in actual form (rather than egg form)

As an independent activity, children evaluate a small number of cards according to whether they meet the criteria of the category.

Activity 7   Conducting simple science experiments according to criteria (example: boiling water)

Boil water with the children. Ask them what they notice. They will probably say they see bubbles and they see steam. Use a thermometer to measure water temperature. Show them the temperature. List the criteria you have discovered:

Criteria for boiling water

1. Has rolling bubbles
2. Makes steam
3. Has a temperature of 212° F or 100° Centigrade

Boil water every day with the children for one week. Compare what they see each day with the criteria listed the first day. Ask if the criteria were met. At the end of the week, ask them if they notice a pattern. Explain that scientists look for patterns when they develop theories and establish scientific laws. Discuss the pattern with them. Ask if they could describe the law for boiling water.

Do other science experiments in the same way (the Law of Gravity, for example). Ask them if anyone has a theory they would like to test. If so, test it with the class or have the child test it as an independent study with your help as a facilitator.

Having Children Set Up Their Own Criteria and Meet Them

Work individually with the children, having them set up criteria, evaluating these criteria, resetting them up, if necessary, and then meeting them. *You* function as a facilitator. This process can be reinforced when they do independent studies.

The importance of this kind of approach cannot be overstated. The child becomes aware of herself as a thinking being and is in control of the task. For intellectually gifted children, that is a substantial goal for the preschool program to move towards.

Summary

The needs of preschool gifted children reflect in large measure the needs of other gifted children of different ages. Developmental issues, difficulties in reliably measuring performance, and the problem of finding measures with long-term predictive validity are unique to this period. Programming for very young children also has its unique aspects. Working with parents takes on special importance with the preschooler. Not all preschool children are in school, or even ready for a group setting, and it is difficult to convince communities that these children need special assistance. One must keep in mind that it is not a long-range economy to stint on providing resources to the most potentially productive members of our society, as the results of Head Start have so clearly shown. As we gain increasing respect for the young child's thinking capacity and the interaction of cognitive with environmental factors in the development of high levels of achievement, we may be more willing to acknowledge the need to nurture the gifted preschool child.

References

Anderson, J. "The limitations of infant and preschool intelligence tests." In *Behavior in infancy and early childhood.* Edited by Y. Brackbill and G. Thompson. New York: Free Press, 1967.

Barbe, W. B. "Characteristics of gifted children." *Educational Administration and Supervision* 41 (1955): 207–17.

Bayley, N. "The growth of intelligence." In *Behavior in infancy and early childhood.* Edited by Y. Brackbill and G. Thompson. New York: Free Press, 1967.

Blank, M., S. A. Rose and L. J. Berlin. *The language of learning: The preschool years.* New York: Grune & Stratton, 1978.

Bloom, B. S. *Stability and change in human characteristics.* New York: John Wiley, 1964.

Boehm, A. *Boehm test of basic concepts.* New York: Psychological Corporation, 1971.

Bruner, J. S., R. R. Oliver, P. M. Greenfield et al. *Studies in cognitive growth.* New York: John Wiley, 1966.

Burk, E. *Relationship of temperamental traits to achievement and adjustment in gifted children.* Unpublished doctoral dissertation, Fordham University, 1980.

Cheyney, A. B. "Parents view their intellectually gifted children." *Peabody Journal of Education* 40 (1962): 98–101.

Ciha, R. E., T. E. Harris, C. Hoffman, and M. W. Potter. "Parents as identifiers of giftedness, ignored but accurate." *The Gifted Child Quarterly* 18 (1974): 191–95.

Connolly, A. J., W. Nachtman and E. M. Pritchett. *The key math diagnostic arithmetic test.* Circle Pines, Minn.: American Guidance Service, 1971.

DeAvila, E. *Cartoon conservation scales.* Corte Madera, Calif.: Linguametrics Group, 1979.

Dunn, L. M., and F. C. Markwardt, Jr. *Peabody individual achievement test.* Circle Pines, Minn.: American Guidance Service, 1970.

Durkin, D. *Children who read early.* New York: Teachers College Press, 1966.

Ellenhorn, J. *A staff development plan for the design of learning environments.* Doctoral dissertation, Teachers College, Columbia University, 1983.

Erikson, E. *Toys and reasons: States in the ritualization of experience*. New York: W. W. Norton, 1977.

Flavell, J. H. *Cognitive development*. Englewood Cliffs, N. J.: Prentice-Hall, 1977.

Fox, L. "On Torrance's 2004 Utopia." *G/T/C* (Jan./Feb., 1979): 3.

Frierson, E. C. "Upper and lower status gifted children: A study of differences." *Exceptional Children* 32 (1965): 83–90.

Gallagher, J. J. "Peer acceptance of highly gifted children in elementary school." *Elementary School Journal* 58 (1958): 465–70.

Gallagher, J. J. *Teaching the gifted child*. Boston: Allyn and Bacon, 1975.

Gallagher, J. J., M. J. Aschner, and W. Jenne. *Productive thinking of gifted children in classroom interaction*. Reston, Va.: Council for Exceptional Children, 1967.

Gelman, R. "Preschool thought." *American Psychologist* 34 (1979): 900–5.

Gelman, R. "The nature and development of early number concepts." In *Advances in child development and behavior*. Vol. 17. Edited by H. W. Reese. New York: Academic Press, 1972.

Goldman, N., and S. Rosenfield. *Identification procedures for the bilingual preschool gifted child: A model*. Paper presented at Council for Exceptional Children, Dallas, April 1979.

Goldschmid, M. L., and P. M. Bentler. *Manual: Concept assessment kit–Conservation*. San Diego, Calif.: Educational and Industrial Testing Service, 1968.

Goodwin, W., and L. Driscoll. *Handbook for measurement and evaluation in early childhood education*. San Francisco: Jossey-Bass, 1980.

Guilford, J. P. *The nature of human intelligence*. New York: McGraw-Hill, 1967.

Hagen, E. *Identification of the gifted*. New York: Teachers College Press, 1980.

Havighurst, R. J. "Increasing the pool of talent." In *The gifted child: The yearbook of education*. Edited by G. G. Bareday and J. Lawverys. New York: Harcourt, 1962.

Hess, R. *Effectiveness of home-based early education programs*. Paper presented at American Psychological Association, Washington, D.C., September, 1976.

Hildreth, G. "Three gifted children: A developmental study." *The Journal of Genetic Psychology* 85 (1964): 239–62.

Hollingworth, L. S. *Children above 180 IQ*. New York: World, 1942.

Hunt, M. "How the mind works." *New York Times Magazine* (Jan. 24, 1982): 30.

Hunt, J. McV. *The challenge of incompetence and poverty: Papers on the role of early education*. Chicago: University of Illinois Press, 1969.

Jacobs, J. C. "Effectiveness of teacher and parent identification of gifted children as a function of school level." *Psychology in the Schools* 8 (1971): 140–42.

Kaplan, S. *Educating the preschool/primary gifted and talented*. Ventura, Calif.: Ventura County Superintendent of Schools, 1980.

Karnes, M. B. "Elements of an exemplary preschool/primary program for gifted and talented." In *Educating the preschool/primary gifted and talented*. Edited by S. Kaplan. Ventura, Calif.: Ventura County Superintendent of Schools, 1980.

Krinsky, R., N. E. Jackson and H. B. Robinson. "Analysis of parent information in the identification of precocious intellectual development in young children." In *Identification and nurturance of extraordinarily precocious young children*. Edited by H. B. Robinson et al. Seattle: University of Washington, Children Development Research Group, 1977 (ERIC ED 151 095).

Laycock, F., and J. S. Laylor. "Physiques of gifted children and their less gifted siblings." *Child Development* 35 (1964): 63–74.

Leonard, J. *Chapel Hill services to the gifted/handicapped.* Chapel Hill, N.C.: Chapel Hill Training-Outreach Project, 1978.

Lidz, C. "Issues in the psychological assessment of preschool children." *Journal of School Psychology* 15 (1977): 129–35.

Lippman, W. *Public Opinion.* New York: Macmillan, 1922.

Maier, H. W. *Three theories of child development.* New York: Harper and Row, 1965.

Martinson, R. *The identification of the gifted and talented.* Reston, Va.: Council for Exceptional Children, 1975, 1981.

Meeker, M. *The structure of intellect.* Columbus, Ohio: Charles E. Merrill, 1969.

Milner, E. A. "A study of the relationship between reading readiness in grade 1 school children and patterns of parent-child interaction." *Child Development* 22 (1951): 95–112.

Morgan, H. J., C. G. Tennant, and M. J. Gold. *Elementary and secondary level programs for the gifted and talented.* New York: Teachers College Press, 1980.

Newland, T. E. *The gifted in socio-educational perspective.* Englewood Cliffs, N. J.: Prentice-Hall, 1976

O'Shea, H. "Friendship and the intellectually gifted child." *Exceptional Children* 26 (1960): 327–35.

Piaget, J. *Play, dreams and imitation in childhood.* London: Heinemann, 1951.

Raven, J. C. *Colored progressive matrices.* New York: Psychological Corporation, 1947.

Rellas, A. "The use of the Wechsler preschool and primary scale (WPPSI) in the early identification of gifted students." *California Journal of Educational Research* 20 (1969): 117–19.

Renzulli, J. "What makes giftedness? Reexamining a definition." *Phi Delta Kappa* (1978) 180–84, 261.

Robinson, H. B., W. C. Roedell, and N. E. Jackson. "Early identification and intervention." In *The gifted and talented: Their education and development.* NSSE Yearbook. Edited by A. H. Passow. Chicago: University of Chicago Press, 1979.

Roedell, W. C., N. E. Jackson, and H. B. Robinson. *Gifted young children.* New York: Teachers College Press, 1980.

Roper, R. *Assessment of preschool bilingual gifted children.* Paper presented at the American Psychological Association, Montreal, September 1980.

Rubin, K. H. "Egocentrism in childhood: A unitary construct?" *Child Development* 44 (1973):102–10.

Sattler, J. *Assessment of children's intelligence and special abilities.* 2nd ed. Boston: Allyn and Bacon, 1982.

Schaffer, M. C. "Child development principles and the gifted preschooler." *Roeper Review* 3 (1980): 7–9.

Shantz, C. U. "The development of social cognition." In *Review of Child Development Research.* Vol. 15. Edited by E. M. Hetherington. Chicago: University of Chicago Press, 1975.

Sigel, I. *Consciousness raising of individual competence in problem solving.* Paper presented at the Third Vermont Conference on the Primary Prevention of Psychopathology, Burlington, Vt., June 1977.

Shure, M. B., and G. Spivack. *Social adjustment of young children.* San Francisco: Jossey-Bass, 1974.

Shwedel, A. *A new direction in the identification of children for a preschool gifted program.* Paper presented at the American Educational Research Association, Boston, 1980.

Stackweather, E. K. "Creativity research instruments designed for use with preschool children." *Journal of Creative Behavior* 5 (1971): 245–55.

Tannenbaum, A. J. *Gifted children: Psychological and educational perspectives.* New York: Macmillan, 1983.

Terman, L. M. *Genetic studies of genious: Mental and physical traits of a thousand gifted children.* Vol. 1. Stanford, Calif.: Stanford University Press, 1925.

Terman, L. M., and M. Merrill. *Stanford-Binet intelligence scale.* Boston: Houghton Mifflin, 1960.

Terman, L. M., and M. H. Oden. *Genetic studies of genious: The gifted child grows up: Twenty-five years' follow-up of a superior group.* Vol. 4. Stanford, Calif.: Stanford University Press, 1947.

Thomas, A., and S. Chess. *Temperament and development.* New York: Brunner/Mazel, 1977.

Torrance, E. P. *Torrance tests of creative thinking.* Lexington, Mass.: Personnel Press, 1966.

Wechsler, D. *Manual: Wechsler preschool and primary scale of intelligence.* New York: Psychological Corporation, 1967.

White, B. *The first three years of life.* Englewood Cliffs, N.J.: Prentice-Hall, 1975.

Willerman, L., and M. F. Fiedler. "Intellectually precocious preschool children: Early development and later intellectual accomplishment." *Journal of Genetic Psychology* 131 (1977): 13–20.

Part Two

Four Essential Content Areas

The four chapters of Part Two address major subject areas: reading, writing, arithmetic, and social studies. Each chapter presents concepts essential to the study of the field and discusses approaches for elementary and secondary level students.

Central themes of Part Two relate directly to curricular goals: what, when, and how to teach the material. Each chapter emphasizes the basic skills as prerequisite tools for later performance. Highlighting performance at mental rather than chronological age levels and focusing on higher level thinking directs the content toward the gifted and talented. The need for preliminary assessment is coordinated with the goals of the curriculum. The overlap of skills and abilities are related to both content and student performance in each area.

A major theme running through this section is the similarity of approaches among the four content areas. Inquiry, inductive and deductive reasoning, problem solving, and the research method are emphasized throughout. The section pinpoints the so called "Fourth R" for the gifted.

While the content varies, the processes are similar. The content changes, calling for strategy shifts, but the underlying current is that of research and scientific method.

One aspect of instructional strategy and curricular differentiation is the altered environment in which learning is facilitated. Math and science encourage similar environments. They are more structured, and the learning processes are best facilitated in settings that encourage acquisition of the structures. Social studies and language arts, on the other hand, encourage easy and rapid exchange of ideas. The classroom and the teacher capitalize on such interchanges.

Both the process and the content come together with the environment in a three-way locus of impact. Each tempers the other in a "give and take" fashion, and the learner becomes the fourth participant in the exchange. In this way, differentiation based on learner, content, and process emphasize both particular differences and generic similarities.

5

Mathematics for Gifted Students

M. E. Kersh
F. K. Reisman

Mathematics instruction for gifted students sometimes occurs in the mainstream, sometimes in special classes for the gifted. Whatever the setting, instruction has often been limiting in terms of viewing mathematics as creative and reflexive experiences. In this chapter, we will review the current status of mathematics as it applies to the gifted in elementary and secondary schools, and examine those factors that inhibit creativity in mathematics. We will also describe a generic approach to mathematics for gifted learners and present a profile of a gifted student with learning problems in mathematics. We will discuss four diverse views of mathematics needed by gifted learners, as well as strategies appropriate for teaching the gifted and activities that have been successful with gifted learners. There is an annotated resource list for future mathematics material development at the end of the chapter.

Essential Concepts for Mathematics Programs for Gifted Learners

Factors Limiting Mathematical Development of Gifted Learners

Circumstances have often limited the opportunities of the gifted to experience mathematics as a creative, divergent discipline. Administrative policies that encompass the pressure of standardized tests and adherence to selected textbooks, along with minimal teacher knowledge of mathematics and lack of mathematics text series for the gifted are factors that inhibit mathematical creativity. Another limiting circumstance is student dislike of mathematics, which results in mathematics avoidance and learning problems, even among those who show evidence of high intellectual ability.

Administrative Policy   The mathematics curriculum, for the most part, is remarkably standard in content and sequence throughout American schools. In general, school districts' administrative policies require adoption of a limited set of mathematics text series, and teachers tend to use these in a page-by-page sequence. There is probably greater consensus on grade placement of topic and sequence of topics within grades in mathematics than in any other subject area. Some of the pressure for adherence to a standard mathematics curriculum doubtlessly arises from district use of standardized mathematics achievement tests. Accountability for pupil performance on such tests influences teachers' decisions on what to emphasize in the mathematics curriculum, as well as when to teach a topic. Knowing, for example, that many fifth graders perform poorly in addition of fractions, a teacher would provide drill on these problems immediately before administration of a standardized mathematics achievement test. Although it is true that mathematics achievement tests are constructed to reflect content taught at grade level, it is equally true today that they exert subtle pressures that tend to hinder curricular changes in topic and sequence of presentation through the grade levels as well as within a grade. These restraints severely limit teachers when they attempt to differentiate mathematics for the gifted.

Within the confines of a set mathematics curriculum, some teachers do attempt to differentiate mathematics for able students. Offering the gifted more mathematics practice is one common, if ineffective, mode of differentiation. A bright youngster who completes one page of multiplication problems is given another of the same to complete. The child soon learns to pace her work completion to coincide with her peers, once more successfully masking her giftedness.

Another common procedure for coping with gifted students in mathematics is to move them through the regular curriculum at a faster pace. Advocates of a fast-paced curriculum usually view mathematics as a body of knowledge to be covered, and in their opinion, differentiation for the gifted means progressing through the body of mathematics as quickly as possible. While this eliminates much of the waiting time for others to catch up, it also means that the gifted student merely goes faster through an inappropriate curriculum. Why inappropriate? In most texts, the yearly overlap in topics and review chapters provides unneeded repetition, while the quantity of drill and practice is excessive for most gifted learners. Gifted learners often find the directed instruction that entails incremental learning steps tedious and unnecessary. Furthermore, most of the sequence rationale is based on expert opinion of a logical analysis of how concepts must be sequenced, rather than on research into how students learn.

Reisman offers an example of traditional sequencing versus that based on research.

> Let us consider teaching the skill of telling time to the precision of a minute. The traditional approach is to teach time on the hour first, then to the half-hour, and next to five minutes after the hour. The child is not guided to tell time to the minute until the last step in the sequence. In fact, many elementary school mathematics texts introduce the fractional idea of "half after" and "a quarter after" the hour prior to the concept of "so many minutes after." However, when looking at how children learn to count, we see that a child learns to count by ones first. Yet, he does not learn to tell time to the minute, which is based on counting by ones, until the latter part of the time-telling sequence, a point which usually is reached during second or third grade. This seems in opposition to the natural mathematical development of counting. Also, it is possible that children become fixated on the positions of time to the hour and to the half hour, thus making it more difficult for them to learn to tell time to the minute. When we analyze the task from a mathematical view and mesh our findings with our knowledge of how a child first learns to count, we discover that our sequence of instruction has been backwards.
>
> Further investigation, making use of Bruner's enactive level of learning, has indicated that children can reproduce time on a clockface before they can identify it. Thus, setting time on a clockface should precede reading time on a clockface. This sequence usually is ignored and, in fact, time-telling instruction often starts at Bruner's iconic or picture level which is exemplified by pictures of clockfaces in arithmetic texts or workbooks. (1978, p. 4)

Reisman's research (1978) shows that the more effective sequence for telling time to the nearest minute is to match minutes to a number line 1–60, match number line minutes to hours on a clock face, analyze a clockface and describe the function of each part, use of the minute hand, then use of the hour hand.

In another effort to differentiate the mathematics curriculum, teachers often assign more challenging problems for the gifted. With the advent of mainstreaming, some textbooks have come to include challenge sections for brighter students. While these are interesting and sometimes do challenge the gifted, they are usually only momentary diversions in otherwise dull material.

Teacher Knowledge of Mathematics   A principal reason for the rather slavish adherence to an established mathematics curriculum is that most teachers do not feel competent in the subject. Most elementary teachers have less than three years of high school mathematics and usually one year of college mathematics, which includes some methods in teaching mathematics (Overview, NACOME Report, 1975). Contrast this preparation with that of preparation in the language arts. Generally, all teachers have taken four years of high school language arts (English, speech, etc.), two years of college courses, and reading and language arts methods classes.

Furthermore, the courses teachers take in mathematics tend to reinforce their views of mathematics as a deductive system of rules, the purpose of which is to produce one correct answer. Their convergent experiences, combined with a lack of depth in mathematics, constrain most teachers from attempting creative, divergent learning activities in their mathematics teaching. Thus, in full-time classes for the gifted, teachers are often content to use a standard basic mathematics curriculum, reserving creative lessons for other subject areas.

In resource or pull-out programs, mathematics is often omitted or restricted to a few miscellaneous pages from one of the numerous commercial booklets dealing with enrichment mathematics. This mathematics curriculum thus becomes a discontinuous set of activities, diverting, yet unrelated to the main body of the curriculum in any meaningful way. Again, the teacher's lack of background in mathematics is a major factor for neglecting mathematics in a pull-out program. Teachers for such programs are usually chosen to teach the gifted on the basis of creative and unusual teaching abilities in subjects other than mathematics for the reasons we mentioned.

Resource teachers are also admonished to use curriculum beyond that regularly taught. Thus they develop materials that build on their own strengths and that capture the interest of gifted learners, resulting too often in the neglect of mathematics.

Student Attitudes Toward Mathematics   Many gifted students, not unlike their regular peers, initially like mathematics in the primary grades, but acquire more negative feelings as they progress through school. This often results in mathematics avoidance by the very learners who can most benefit from further mathematical experiences. The deleterious effects of negative attitudes toward mathematics and subsequent mathematics avoidance are especially evident with gifted women and most minorities.

The Study of Mathematically Precocious Youth (SMPY) project at Johns Hopkins (Fox, 1975) found far more males than females who are exceptionally gifted in mathematics. After reviewing research on sex differences in mathematics, Fox ascribes three factors that may contribute to this difference in numbers: (1) differential career interests and expectations; (2) encouragement from significant others; and (3) early identification and educational opportunities for the gifted female. Bright girls tend to self-select themselves out of advanced high school mathematics courses (Haven, 1971). Yet Fennema and Sherman (1977, 1978) found that when females choose to take mathematics courses, they do as well as males. In relation to attitudes, the perception of the usefulness of mathematics seems to relate to the participation of gifted females in mathematics classes. If gifted females see math as useful in their career choice, the more likely they are to continue its study (Haven, 1971). Programs that have attempted to provide special math classes for gifted females have focused on one or more of these factors: awareness of the usefulness of mathematics, cooperative rather than competitive learning, increased confidence in doing mathematics, female role models, and spatial ability (Cook & Kersh, 1980; Fox, 1975).

Casserly (1980) studied 20 public schools where males and females consistently scored equally well in mathematics assessments. Though the schools are diverse, they share common features:

1   Teachers have a strong science and mathematics background.
2   Teachers openly express love and appreciation of mathematics.
3   Bright students are grouped together in mathematics classes.
4   Teachers emphasize reasoning and counsel students.

The overview of mathematics achievement and attitudes of minorities (excepting Oriental males) is much the same as that for females. A low mathematics achievement profile, negative mathematics attitudes, and subsequent mathematics avoidance after mathematics participation becomes optional is the pattern, with even more dramatic score differences from white males than is the case for females. Research on gifted minorities in relation to mathematics is uncommon. A recent review (Olstad, et al., 1981) of research findings related to factors that inhibit achievement by ethnic minorities in science and mathematics makes the following recommendations:

- Early exposure to experiential science and mathematics
- Use of instructional strategies that accommodate the variety of cognitive styles seemingly associated with minority groups
- Inclusion of minorities in quality high school math and science courses
- Career awareness courses to expand professional aspirations among minorities
- Provision of academic role models in math and science

Clearly, further efforts are needed to identify gifted women and minorities early enough to influence their attitudes, aspirations, and expectations, and to develop appropriate curricula to accommodate various learning modes.

Restructuring the Mathematics Program to Accommodate Gifted Learners

There are two approaches to mathematics curriculum to overcome the factors that tend to limit it for gifted learners. The first approach employs generic or core factors that influence learning to establish a profile of the gifted learner and to select content and develop instructional strategies.

The second approach to restructuring the mathematics curriculum views the field from four aspects: as topics (arithmetic, algebra, geometry, etc.), as language, as logical structure, and as processes mathematicians employ. Inherent in each of these facets of mathematics are elements for organizing a curriculum.

Generic Factors Influencing Mathematics Learning

Awareness of generic influences helps teachers understand why some gifted young-sters learn mathematics easily and why others perform well below their expected achievement level. These influences on learning can aid in content selection and in decisions about instructional strategies. Reisman and Kauffman (1980) introduced generic factors to teaching mathematics to children with special needs, including the gifted, with the following explanation:

> For a teacher, it does not necessarily help to know if a child is profoundly, severely, or moderately retarded, or "gifted." These labels do not tell what mathematics the child could learn, and they do not tell how to teach. Instead, it is helpful to know that one of the core influences on learning is the rate at which one acquires knowledge. Knowing the scope of mathematics that a child may be expected to learn in a given span of time provides guidance for selecting those topics that are most relevant for a particular child. Each of the generic or core factors . . . may be applied to intellectually handicapped as well as talented learners. These generic factors in their extreme have a profound impact on a child's learning mathematics. The child's ability to see relationships, to engage in abstract thinking, to use symbol systems and to problem-solve will affect his or her acquisition of mathematics ideas. (p. 3)

Others allude to generic factors that influence mathematics learning by describ-ing gifted students. For example, Menchinskaya and Moro (1975, pp. 161–69) described Russian students with high aptitude for arithmetic as motivated to accom-plish school tasks, able to learn school material at quick tempo, having a higher level of mental activity characterized by "more highly developed analysis and synthesis, generalization, abstraction, and concretization" (p. 162), able to discern essential features of problems, and make use of rules and principles. The Russian pupils were also described as "displaying organization and concentration in their studies . . . they begin by preparing the work space . . . Some . . . whisper or reason out loud in order to facilitate their own understanding" (p. 168). In describing gifted Russian students, the authors pointed out that those capable of high intellectual activity may at the same time be hindered by an "insufficiently responsible attitude toward study" or display a "slowness in switching from one method of operation to another" or "be guided by inessential, external criteria" (p. 169).

Sattler (1982) described a nine-year-old gifted child as using "extensive vocabu-lary . . . Expressing himself clearly in a very adult fashion . . . showed unusual sophis-tication in his use of humor . . . greatest strength lies in conceptual thinking" (p. 438).

Blake (1981) listed these intellectual characteristics of gifted students: "Gifted and talented pupils acquire complex discriminations, memorize, and form concepts faster and to a higher level than normal pupils do. They also solve problems better" (p. 326).

Reisman (1981) proposed generic factors as an alternative assessment pro-cedure to cognitive stages, pointing out that "implications for applying Piagetian theory to teaching have been strongly supported by Furth and Wachs (1974), ques-tioned by Smedslund (1977), and vigorously opposed by Engelman (1971)" (p. 5). Reisman proposes these generic factors to describe gifted students:

- Learning at rapid rates
- Attending to salient aspects of situations
- Conserving (e.g., relates transformation and accompanying invariant)
- Retaining information with minimal repetition
- Understanding complex materials
- Constructing relationships, concepts and generalizations (p. 5)

One may develop profiles to portray students' strengths and weaknesses, including those of gifted children who have difficulty in mathematics. Figure 5-1 shows Reisman's profile of a learning disabled gifted student. This student is in really good shape. His major need is for ample practice. Another gifted student might have difficulty attending to salient aspects of situations. Such a student would need cues to help direct attention. It is important for teachers to be aware that gifted students may be gifted in many areas, but not in mathematics. Or, students may have an aptitude for mathematics, but because of anxiety, lack of exposure to mathematics, or gaps in

Figure 5-1 PROFILE OF A GIFTED CHILD WITH A LEARNING DISABILITY—RAPID RATE OF COGNITIVE DEVELOPMENT.

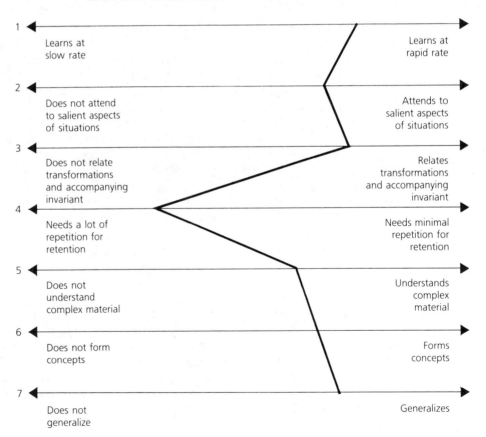

mathematics foundation, they may perform below their expected level of achievement.[1]

Diverse Views of Mathematics. Mathematics may be approached as a body of knowledge organized into nominative categories of study: as a language complete with symbol systems, syntax and grammar; as a logical structure of relationships between figures and forms; or as a set of processes engaged in by one who thinks mathematically.

Most students, particularly in the United States, experience the topical or nominative view of mathematics. The path of mathematical learning commonly begins with arithmetic, with a brief introduction to geometry, proceeding to algebra, formal geometry, calculus, analysis and so on. Each subdivision of mathematics is a course of study in itself and over the K–12 school experience, learners have the opportunity to sample the broad field of mathematics. There are positive aspects to this topical organization. A tightly sequenced course on one topic permits learners to focus on the salient features of that mathematical branch. A restricted course focus usually yields consensus by experts on course topics and topic sequence, which results in uniformity of textbook coverage. In our mobile population, consensus on course content and placement is an advantage for the student who must transfer schools.

While many topics are "covered," in the topical or nominative view, the interrelationships between mathematical subjects are omitted or mentioned only incidentally. This can be a disadvantage to gifted children who seek to bridge topics. As a generic skill, they construct relationships, concepts, and generalizations. In effect, they are able to synthesize the unrelated. Unless the relationships among mathematical topics are explicit, the bridges the gifted student constructs may not be valid. The gifted, then, need to go beyond sampling a broad range of mathematical topics to see other views of mathematics not commonly emphasized.

Another view of mathematics is as a language. Mathematics uses a special language, or uses language in a special way, and learning mathematics involves learning new linguistic patterns.

Little research has been done on the linguistic aspects of mathematics. Henkin (1972) has cited several linguistic problems that mathematics presents to learners. One difficulty arises from the subtle requirements and sophisticated terminology required to distinguish between use and mention of given symbols within the same context. For example, in the equation $2x + 3 = 0$, the student is taught that x is the unknown and 2 is the coefficient. In $ax + b = 0$, a becomes the coefficient, with x again the unknown. But what happens to the student's formative concept of an unknown and a coefficient in the equation $2a + 3 = 0$? Linguistically, the student must understand that the unknowns are not determined by the equation, but are "givens." Initially, instead of telling the student to solve the equation, the instructor should tell him to find a number x such that $2x + 3 = 0$.

Order of operation and punctuation is as essential in understanding mathematics as in understanding verbal communications. For example, the sentence, "Shall I

---

[1]From F. K. Reisman, *Teaching Mathematics: Methods and Content,* 2nd ed., Copyright © 1981, Houghton Mifflin Company. Used by permission.

put the stamp on myself?'' or ''Shall I put the stamp on, myself?'' is certainly ambiguous in terms of how much postage might be required. In the same way, the mathematical expression $3 \times 5 - 2 + 4 \div 2$ requires punctuation to determine whether the expected response is 3, 6, 11, or some other number.

A review of studies on mathematics and language (Earp and Tanner, 1980) indicates that mathematics should be part of children's oral communication. Children should discuss mathematics, rather than work on it only individually. Time should be devoted to building a mathematical vocabulary in context, and techniques from reading and language arts should be applied to mathematical vocabulary building. Earp and Tanner also believe that mathematical statements in textbooks are beyond children's reading levels and should be rewritten in a more meaningful context. Current theorists conjecture that metalinguistics, the ability to think about language, is a prerequisite for learning to read (Mattingly, 1972; Elkonin, 1971; Pfrimmer, 1980). Research on metalinguistics in relation to mathematical language is thus indicated.

We know that young children learn linguistic patterns in the first years of life. There is thus an obvious need to experiment with mathematics as a language with young children, particularly young gifted learners who are capable of more complex linguistic patterns at a younger age.

In its broadest view, mathematics can also be seen as a science of significant form, a science of pattern and structure. Felix Browder (1975) describes this view of mathematics as one of a world as governed by objective laws of form, which can be discovered only by the interaction between an individual's creative insight on the one hand, and objective testing of the consequences of the intuitive insight or fantasy on the other. Browder offers as an illustration the development and application of the theory of groups.

A group is a collection of elements—numbers, figures, objects—and an operation for combining them such that the system observes the rules of closure, identity, associativity, and inverse. Work with groups originated in the study of the roots of algebraic equations by Lagrange and Galois in the late 18th and early 19th centuries. Group theory is now used to express the physical event of elementary particle collision. Indeed, the theory provides a structural link between arithmetic, algebra, geometry, coding theory, crystallography, quantum mechanics, and elementary particle physics. Thus, mathematical ability in this global sense is the ability to analyze significant form in one domain of experience and apply it to illuminate apparently unrelated contents.

This view of mathematics far exceeds technical utility. It requires the learner to detect patterns in natural occurrences, and to investigate the stability of such patterns as well as their modifications. Whitehead maintains that mathematics is the most powerful technique for understanding and analyzing patterns (Whitehead, 1929).

Gifted learners need to construct, analyze, and evaluate systems and their transformations. They are capable of looking at reality to discover systems and then to use the systems to interpret reality. This equivalent relationship is a union of order with spontaneity and creativity that is so necessary for gifted learners.

The approach in the fourth view of mathematics is from the perspective of process, in which the question becomes, ''What does one do in thinking mathematically?'' Scandura (1971) details six processes that describe mathematical thinking.

- Ability to Detect Regularities
  To detect regularities involves perceiving a pattern and abstracting the common elements among the components. This skill is essential in inductive reasoning. Examples in number series alone would provide gifted learners ample practice in this skill.
- Ability to Construct Examples
  This skill is the inverse of discovery. It requires the student, given the rule of generalization, to construct new examples. Implicit in this skill is the idea of verifying conjectures. Often, with gifted learners, teachers acknowledge the generalization they develop, but do not have them verify their own educated guesses, to see whether the idea will actually work. Constructing a magic square or developing story problems that illustrate the expression $3 (5 + 7) = ?$ involves students in divergent production, which is rare in elementary mathematics classes, where the focus is on the convergent production of one right answer.
- Ability to Interpret Mathematical Descriptions
  Reading the precise and efficient technical language of mathematics often presents students with seemingly insurmountable difficulties. Indeed, not all symbol systems are universal in mathematics. Thus, the writer must precisely define each symbol, and the reader must comprehend the vocabulary of symbols before reading the mathematics. Both reading and comprehending in context are involved in interpretation. Gifted learners should know the conventions in mathematical terminology and the arbitrary assignment of meaning to symbols. In addition, they could develop new systems to convey mathematical descriptions.
- Ability to Describe Mathematical Ideas
  This skill requires the student to read mathematics in its symbol form and translate the symbols in one or more ways into meaningful descriptions. Descriptions may be verbal, symbolic, or figurative. They are usually less precise than the mathematical statement and require the students not only to know *what* to do, but to describe how they did it. The ability to describe mathematical ideas is important in problem solving, in fixing an idea for retention, and in general communication.
- Ability to Make Logical Inferences
  This skill is essential in deductive reasoning. Most students can study and memorize published proofs, but gifted students, even those with only passing interest in mathematics, should be able to develop simple proofs in geometry, algebra, or number theory. Fourth and fifth grade gifted learners have also been successful in learning formal logic (Suppes, 1969). Most gifted learners, however, require explicit instruction in logical inference.
- Ability to Construct Axiomatic Systems
  Recognition of key or basic ideas or assumptions is essential to this process— those that are logically independent, that is, not derived from other ideas. Informally, learners construct axioms when they distinguish data that are

essential for problem solution from data that are superfluous. Identifying first principles in debate, revealing inconsistencies in arguments, and re-organizing knowledge to retain maximum facts with minimum memorization are activities in which it is helpful to construct axioms.

The ability to detect regularities, construct examples, interpret mathematical descriptions, describe mathematical ideas, make logical inferences, and construct axioms are a mathematician's process skills.

The major benefit to gifted learners in approaching mathematics as a set of process abilities is that they can behave or act as a mathematician, using content appropriate to their own level of development. They can assume the role of scholar, a role often considered appropriate for the gifted in other subject areas, but seldom offered to them in mathematics.

The four approaches—the topical, the linguistic view, mathematics as form and structure, and mathematics as process—together offer a multidimensional aspect to mathematics that gifted learners should experience.

Presently, we do not have curriculum materials to promote a multidimensional perspective. Hence, teachers, as the orchestrators of mathematics curricula, must select materials and activities that will allow students at least to glimpse these various mathematical aspects. Teachers must analyze mathematical activities that have been successful with the gifted to identify the mathematics aspects involved in the activity. Such analyses will reveal not only the aspects of math that are emphasized, but will also indicate which aspects are receiving insufficient coverage. Continued analyses of successful mathematical activities may show that some content promotes a specific aspect. As mentioned, the study of groups promotes mathematics as form and structure. Certain instructional strategies may promote other aspects—integrative strategies could promote linguistic aspects, for example.

Mathematics for the Elementary School

As a result of limited mathematical experiences at the elementary level, gifted learners commonly view mathematics as a set of rule-based algorithms one applies to converge on the one correct solution. Indeed, to most gifted, mathematics and arithmetic are synonymous (with minor deference to geometry, as regards shape recognition and measurement). Because there are many views of mathematics, however, gifted learners deserve to experience it as more than a unidimensional discipline.

During the primary and middle grades, gifted learners should become proficient in rational number calculations as well as in basic mathematical concepts. Numeration, classification, seriation, customary and metric measurement, shape recognition, area and volume, ratio and proportion, and understanding of rational number operations are the standard topics in both gifted and average classes. Additional topics for enriching the mathematical curriculum for the gifted might include base systems other than ten, exponents and roots, scientific notation, logic, mental arithmetic shortcuts, flow charts, samplings, statistics, probability, and cryptoanalysis (codes). In addition, many topics of elementary number theory, such as finite dif-

Gifted elementary students should be able to proceed through the standard mathematics curriculum at an accelerated pace.

ference techniques, number sequences, Pascal triangle patterns, modulo arithmetic, divisibility rules, primes and composites, continued fractions, and introduction to irrational and complex numbers are all appropriate topics of inquiry for gifted learners. Algebraic notation can be introduced as an extension of arithmetic computation; for example, finding a missing addend is written as $8 + N = 17$, and the number sequence 1, 4, 9, . . . can be understood as N^2. Students can also work with transformations such as slides, rotations, and flips in geometry. Coordinate geometry, symmetry, tesselations, and projections are all within the understanding of gifted elementary students.

Calculators and computers open additional mathematical opportunities for gifted learners. Computer software presently concentrates primarily on developing lower level skills; however, these programs could be used in computer assisted instruction (CAI) to accelerate an individual learner through simple mathematics. (This usage assumes that further enrichment acivities would be available to the CAI user.) Calculators and computers allow gifted learners to attempt to solve problems that require difficult or intricate computation, or mathematical knowledge beyond the learner's range—knowledge of trigonometric functions, for example. The learner can use these computer operations without a complete understanding of the functions themselves. The learner is the problem solver and the computing device is a tool to facilitate calculations. Using computers this way may require some knowledge of programming, a skill well within the range of attainment for gifted learners. While computers have mathematical uses, they should not be viewed solely as mathematical aids. Software is also available for language arts, social studies, and science.

The proposed mathematical topics for gifted elementary students include acceleration through a standard mathematical curriculum and enrichment of the standard fare. Gifted learners assimilate facts quickly; this talent should be tapped in moving learners through fundamental mathematics skills. The gifted would be given less time to become proficient in basic computation and the fundamental mathematical concepts required for all elementary students. Additional time would thus be available to enrich the learners' understanding of the complex field of mathematics, and enrichment topics would capitalize on talents other than rapid fact assimilation. A talent for building relations among diverse facts is necessary to pattern-finding. Intense interest, long attention span, and desire for elaboration contribute to independent investigations of complex mathematical concepts. The problem in developing appropriate mathematical curricula for the gifted is not a choice between acceleration or enrichment, but blending and accommodating both acceleration and enrichment of mathematical ideas.

Secondary Concepts

At the secondary level, there are more available textbooks, articulated programs, and program options for the gifted.

The Comprehensive School Mathematics Program, *Elements of Mathematics*, is a six-year mathematics program for gifted secondary students. The series consists of fifteen books (0–12, A, B) that deal with operations of rational numbers, probability, number theory, algebra, geometry, logic, topics in analysis, computer programming, and measure theory. The series was developed through CEMREL, a regional educational laboratory, and has been used with gifted secondary school students throughout the country by specially prepared teachers.

Another secondary mathematics program also successful with the gifted is the Unified Mathematics Course developed by the Secondary School Mathematics Curriculum group. This six-year program for grade 7–12 was designed for college preparatory students and uses common concepts fundamental to the branches of mathematics to unify its study. Students experiment with and investigate mathematical situations, then generalize and defend their conclusions.

The scope of mathematics for the SSMCIS are described by Howard Fehr (1968), the program director:

> The number system of the cardinals, the integers, the rationals, the reals, and the complex; the structure of the group, the ring, the field, the ordered field, and the algebraic-geometric (or geometric-algebraic) structure of vector spaces and their linear algebra. In each of these structures one investigates the properties of the operations, the expressions and functions on the set of elements, the solution of sentences (equations, inequations, with absolute values, etc.), gradually developing these notions in a formal algebra of functions and formal solutions of sentences, once the real-number field has been obtained. Probability with statistical inference, the calculus, and elementary numerical analysis, provide a fitting and satisfying climax for the last years of secondary-school study.[2]

Proposed mathematics content for gifted secondary students is accelerated in terms of content and pace. Able students generally begin formal study of algebra in grades seven or eight. In the SMPY (1975) program, precocious students can master more than a year's algebra in six weeks. This pace allows students to study mathematical topics that are usually introduced at the college level, often at an advanced or graduate level.

Computer use with gifted secondary students is already widespread. Software now coordinates with secondary mathematics textbooks, presenting text problems for solution on the computer. Computer use will undoubtedly alter some of the ways teachers present mathematical material. In calculus, for example, the computer algorithm for solving certain integrals differs from the algorithm that is efficient for paper-pencil integral solution. Should both algorithms be taught, or only one?

The Advanced Placement Program, administered by College Board Publications, offers secondary students an opportunity for either advanced standing or college credit with advanced standing in a variety of subject areas, including sciences, mathematics, English language, foreign languages, and art. The Advanced Placement Program offers teachers' guides, sample courses, suggested textbooks, and teacher workshops. Course instructors are expected to have sufficient background prepara-

---

[2]H. F. Fehr, "Mathematical Education for a Scientific, Technological, and Industrial Society," *The Mathematics Teacher* 61 (1968): 665–71.

tion in their discipline. To qualify for advanced standing, students must earn a score of 3 or better (from a range of 1 to 5) in the Advanced Placement examination.

Honors programs at the local level have long been available in larger secondary schools. Participation is usually based on school achievement as assessed by grade point averages or high mathematics course grades. Honors classes in mathematics may even begin in junior high school, allowing honors course participants to take five or six years of college preparatory mathematics.

Honors courses are usually rigorous treatments of mathematical topics. The course content is telescoped to allow students classes in analysis, precalculus, computers, or other advanced topics as part of their secondary school program. An incentive for enrollment in these intensive courses is the likelihood that students will achieve advanced status in college mathematics courses, and earn exemption from first-year courses or perhaps even the first college calculus series.

Under the auspices of Johns Hopkins University, the Study of Mathematically Precocious Youth, a group headed by Julian Stanley, (Keating, 1972, 1976) has identified exceptionally talented students ages 12 to 14, and provided mathematics programs for them. In general, the study has shown the value of standardized tests for discovering mathematically brilliant youth. The students are then placed in fast-paced mathematics classes, which include grade-skipping, part-time enrollment in college courses, Saturday classes, and early entrance to college. The SMPY model is now used in several school districts and cooperating universities across the country.

Throughout elementary and secondary school, gifted learners should be encouraged to perceive the divergent creative aspects of mathematics. To encourage divergence, teachers should include several instructional strategies in their repertoire.

Strategies of Teaching Mathematics to Gifted

An instructional strategy is a plan of action for presenting curriculum. The purpose of an instructional strategy is to maneuver students into the most advantageous position for acquiring skills or concepts.

No single instructional strategy is most effective in teaching mathematics to the gifted, nor is there a strategy effective *only* with the gifted. The following strategies, however, should receive greater emphasis in a gifted program to promote problem solving, critical thinking, creativity, synthesis, and other behaviors associated with higher levels of thinking.

Problem-Solving Strategy

Problem solving extends beyond routine application of a rule or algorithm to solve verbal or word problems. Problem solving encompasses nonroutine problems as well as applications of mathematical principles to real problems, and constitutes the heart of mathematics.

In general, a mathematical problem poses a question based on given information or conditions. The problem solver does not perceive an immediate solution to the problem and actively engages in a search, using trial and error or some organized search process. The National Council of Teachers of Mathematics says "Problem solving must be the focus of school mathematics for the 1980s."

Polya (1958) describes the four phases of problem solving as (1) understanding the problem; (2) devising a plan; (3) carrying out the plan; and (4) looking back. Variations on these four phases constitute much of the research on problem-solving behavior.

The general recommendations that promote problem solving suggest framing the problem in such as way as to excite curiosity, so that problems become the learners' problems and are not imposed. To provide young children with initial practice in problem solving, Dienes (1963) recommends inventing stories that have mathematical structures and taking advantage of hidden mathematical qualities of children's own games and conversations. For older learners, practice in problem solving that focuses on process as well as solution is appropriate. Again, situational, nonroutine problems are more accepted than standard word problems, which merely provide drill on previously learned algorithms. (The National Council of Teachers of Mathematics' *Sourcebook of Applications of School Mathematics* offers background information for constructing situational problems.)

Questioning Strategy

With Bloom's cognitive taxonomy, questions, like behaviors, can be classified into hierarchical categories of thinking. Asking higher level questions requires students to use higher level thinking skills. A teacher who is adept at asking questions over the full range of the taxonomy of questions can improve the intellectual climate of the classroom by directing questions to the higher, more challenging categories. In mathematics, teachers often ask questions in the form of "what" or "how much." Rephrasing the question to ask "how" or "how many different ways" allows divergent answers and emphasizes process.

Getzels (1979) urges that we begin to teach questioning or problem finding in schools. Schools emphasize problem solving, in which the problem, process, and solution are already known by the teacher; it is usually not until graduate study, however, that the student is responsible for defining a new problem or attempting new solutions.

Getzels offers the following example to illustrate the differences among directed teaching, guided discovery, and problem finding.

In a directed teaching situation the instructor teaches that the area of a rectangle is the product of its length and width, $A = l \times w$. Students are shown an example and then asked to complete a worksheet to find the area of rectangles, given length and width.

In a guided discovery lesson, students might be shown various rectangles with numbers on a grid and questioned to assure that each finds the generalization $A = l \times w$.

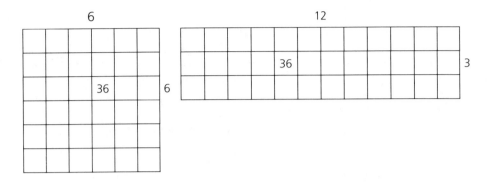

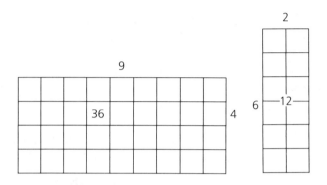

The teacher can ask:
- What might we call these figures?
- How are the figures shown alike? different?
- What might the numbers on the outsides of the figures represent?
- How are the numbers on the inside found?
- How are the numbers on the outside and those on the inside related?
- How could we express that relationship mathematically?

In a problem-finding activity, the teacher should show students the grids and ask, "What might we ask about these shapes?" All possible questions would be recorded, then labeled into overlapping categories, such as: questions for which we perceive immediate answers; questions we can't answer, but know an answer source; questions with open-ended answers; questions we would like to answer, and so on. Through such practice, students learn to ask questions, and to seek the pattern and the anomaly or inconsistency.

The development of questioning strategies in children seems to be age-related (Mosher and Hornsby, 1966). Six-year-olds ask questions that are really specific answers (Is it five?), while eleven-year-olds ask constraint questions (Is it less than ten?). Eleven-year-olds can use negative responses more effectively.

Gifted learners are questioners. Often, however, their questions are parried, ignored, or punished; as a result, many gifted students give up inquiring in school. Instruction in the art of questioning would enhance their natural assets. Reason can answer questions, but imagination asks them. (Teachers who wish to build their own skills in questioning techniques should consult sources such as Hunkins [1972] or Carin [1971].)

Induction Strategy

Inductive learning requires the student to work through specific problems to determine generalizations or principles. Polya (1957) states that mathematics in the making is an inductive science. Inquiry strategies include discovery learning, in which students not only make new (to the learner) generalizations, but also learn about learning, or the art of discovery.

The teacher's role in inductive learning is to place the students in the problem situation, ask key questions, and act as a resource. Induction emphasizes discovery; it is the opposite of didactic or direct teaching. Students are actively involved in inductive learning, in which they learn by doing.

Inductive learning is appropriate for gifted learners because it requires them to bring order to an ambiguous problem situation, seek patterns among complex data, abstract patterned regularities, and describe them. The Fraction Pattern Activity (p. 171) is one example of a discovery strategy appropriate for gifted learners in the intermediate grades. Much of the material from the Madison Project (Davis, 1964) and the mathematical material of Zolton Dienes (1963) focus on activities for mathematical discovery and inquiry.

Mastery Learning Strategy

Mastery learning refers to a genre of learning strategies based on the belief that a student can *master* certain objectives if she spends the necessary amount of time. Time is a factor in any mastery learning strategy: time needed to learn, time spent in learning, and time available for learning. Basic to the strategy is the attempt to maximize the variables that influence learning—opportunity to learn, aptitude for a task, perseverance, quality of instruction, and ability to understand instruction.

Individualized instruction programs are often designed around a mastery learning model, although mastery learning has also been successfully used in group or class learning situations. Generally, the sequential steps in the strategy are:

1 Specification of objectives
2 Designation of mastery score for summative evaluation
3 Unit teaching
4 Formative tests
5 Immediate feedback
6 Diagnosis of errors
7 Alternative procedures

8 Retest

9 Summative evaluation

To the extent that mastery learning strategies allow gifted students to study only that which they have not yet mastered and at a pace adjusted to them, mastery learning can be beneficial. No mastery learning units specifically designed for the gifted have been published, but there is an audience for them. Most mastery learning units concentrate on lower level cognitive objectives; for the gifted, however, mathematics objectives might focus around the categories of application, analysis, synthesis, and evaluation.

Games Strategy

Games that illustrate mathematical principles and enhance skill practice have long been a part of school instruction. Games appeal to students' interests, require active involvement, promote social interaction, and offer an opportunity to integrate mathematics with other subjects. As either a total class, small group, or individual activity, games fit well in classrooms. Learners can often use the games independently in learning centers or laboratory settings. When selecting mathematical games, teachers should identify their educational purpose and be able to demonstrate the game's educational significance. (See the annotated reference list at the end of this chapter.)

Games have additional educational potential for gifted learners, who can focus on analysis of successful game strategies. For example, in one version of the game NIM, two players begin with a number N, and the rule that a player can subtract up to a certain number S from N. The player forced to subtract the last number loses. The major mathematical benefits for gifted learners, after they learn the game, lie in determining which numbers insure that a player will win. Students analyze the game rules and seek rules about the rules. The games, then, become a starting point for activities involving a higher level of thinking.

Gifted learners are often quite creative in designing games to fit educational needs. A pair of fourth-grade gifted students developed a Facts card game for primary children who were having trouble with sums. They then modified the game for third graders who had difficulty remembering the sevens and nines multiplication tables.

Many gifted students are presently involved in learning with microcomputers. Instead of using commercially available software games and activities, most gifted children prefer to program their own activities. Since storage of extensive commercial programs is unnecessary, it is possible to purchase cheaper microunits with less memory capacity for gifted learner use.

The work of Papert (1980), which enables children to program the computer, is based on computational geometry. The approach of this LOGO group at MIT is: "In order to learn something, first make sense of it." Children teach the microcomputer to draw, and while teaching it to draw a circle, the child sees that the commands result in "forward a little and turn a little," a cluster of ideas at the heart of calculus.

(Programming books appropriate for teachers and students are now available, several of which are described in the resource list at the end of the chapter.)

Integrative/Interdisciplinary Strategy

The goal of integrative/interdisciplinary education is to pull together the hetero-geneous principles, theories, and concepts of the various disciplines into a meaningful whole. Integration involves more than merely putting subjects together or using one subject area as the tool of another. One hopes to provide a unified and related pattern of experience for each student.

Developing an integrative curriculum is not easy, but neither is it impossible. One begins with the discipline one knows well, and moves from related fields of study to more remote disciplines. The developer should first describe the major ideas and structure of the discipline he knows best, then talk to experts in other disciplines. One should begin to note those processes, terms, and concepts that extend across disciplines. For example, each major field of study is concerned with change and unity, with some ordering principle, and with the coexistence of complexity with simplicity. Many disciplines even use the same vocabulary to describe similar con-cepts. These similarities can become themes for integrative curriculum.

An integrative approach increases the opportunities to explore interrelation-ships of realities and abstractions. Whatever the field of study, it should be recognized that the most abstract systems (symbolic systems) are human-made, arbitrary, and subject to change. This view enhances the dynamic quality of growth in knowledge, whether in artistic endeavors, spatial relationships, language, or social institutions.

When you have an idea for an integrative theme, focus first on the field you know best, to trace the development of the concept in familiar territory, and begin to note possible learning activities for later exploration and elaboration.

Then, explore a discipline closely related to yours, so you can develop the selected theme in a closely allied field. For example, from biology, move to biochemis-try; from art, to architecture or design; from history, to anthropology or sociology.

As your knowledge of the theme increases, begin to examine fields that are less familiar. With this step, your conception of the theme will become more generalized. There are several practical ways to become more knowledgeable in an unfamiliar discipline:

1 Collect definitions of the field.
2 Find out how the field is organized by consulting several introductory textbooks and looking at the chapter headings. Consult a colleague in that field to learn its major theories.
3 Attempt to relate your own field to the one you are investigating. Describe those elements, forms, or situations that relate to your field, and compare the forms and structures of each.

Now you will be ready to work on the gifted curriculum unit. For a project as extensive as an integrative curriculum, plan to ask for help from many specialists. Specialists from diverse disciplines, teachers of various grade levels, and evaluation experts are all necessary to the development of a successful integrative curriculum unit.

Themes for integrative units are symmetry, patterns, constraints and variations, and transformations. Each of these themes occurs in humanities, arts, sciences, and social sciences. For example, consider the concept of transformation.

The verb "to transform" comes from the Latin *transformare*, meaning to change in shape. The current definition extends beyond a mere change in shape to include change in form, character, condition, function, or nature. Most major fields of study include this concept, and the term appears in various disciplines as: bacterial transformation; genetic transformation; mathematical transformations; transformation of various countries, cities, continents, and governments; transformational drama; transformations in folk literature; and transformations in humans (a psychoanalytic perspective). Each discipline or major field of study modifies the definition for its specific use. For example, in linguistics:

> The process of converting a syntactic construction into a semantically equivalent construction according to the rules shown to generate the syntax of the language.

In mathematics:

> To alter a figure or expression to another differing in form, but equal in quantity or value. [In mathematics there are some 19 separate definitions of transformation in calculus, geometry, group theory, and statistics.]

In physics:

> To change one form of energy into another.

And, regarding electricity:

> To change a current in potential.[3]

Some fields describe transformation by different names. Musical transformations involve theme and variations; historical and economic transformations are cycles or trends; physical sciences often refer to transformations as principles of constraints and variables. All disciplines say, however, that to study transformations is to study change, the goal of which is to determine which qualities change and which remain the same. Since transformation occurs in most disciplines, it is considered a universal concept suitable as an organizing topic for an integrative curriculum.

The student alone, of course, must do the integrating. Only the student can organize his own experience into some way of dealing with the diverse stimuli and problems that confront him; however, an integrative curriculum makes it possible, or easier, for him to integrate his experience.

If the teacher or curriculum developer provides the integration theme, what is the probability that this specific integration will be the same for the student? Although an external scheme of integration cannot be imposed, it can motivate an individual to develop one's own unique integrative structure. The structure can be encouraged by focusing attention on the integrative scheme in all phases and in all stages of the educational process. As teacher and curriculum strive to unify experiences, the probability increases that the student will attempt to model the teacher in integrating experiences.

---

[3]Definitions are from *The Oxford English Dictionary*.

Environment to Promote Mathematical Learning

Classroom Atmosphere

Just as a repertoire of teaching strategies is necessary to promote maximum development for gifted learners, so is the proper selection of learning environments. Environmental conditions that are particularly important to mathematical learning are those that encourage tolerance for ambiguity, promote risk-taking, reward multiple solutions to problems, encourage reflection and verification, and probe error responses for new conceptualizations. The setting should promote discovery, construction of clear examples, and projection of logical inferences. To promote such an

Most elementary mathematics textbooks require the teacher to supplement with enrichment activities for the gifted.

atmosphere for mathematical thinking, teachers must ensure a safe environment where no one ridicules ideas, where risk taking is encouraged, and where the class becomes a community of scholars sharing the excitement of learning. Teachers should encourage expression of feelings about mathematics, ranging from frustration and anxiety over blocked progress, to confidence and pride in new learning. This way, mathematics, often considered a purely cognitive endeavor, is united with its affective components.

In this milieu, the teacher assumes in turn the roles of expert, guide, and learner. The role of expert appears when the teacher structures the learning situation, organizes the learning activities, and establishes criteria for evaluating student work. As the unit continues and as students initiate individual investigations, the teacher assumes the role of guide to references and resources. Teacher and students then learn from the discoveries of other students. Through this mutual sharing of student learning, students and teachers remain alert to knowledge while engaged in the process of mathematics.

The physical setting should be flexible enough to allow privacy for individual and small group work as well as open space for larger group activities, with instructional materials and resources readily available. Human resources should not be overlooked; it can be helpful to have a mathematics expert talk with a gifted learner and follow her work. The consultant can identify lines of inquiry within the main body of mathematics and suggest steps for investigation. University mathematics and mathematics education professors, high school mathematics teachers, or mathematicians in industry are usually willing to devote time to young learners and inquiring teachers in their mutual search for mathematical knowledge.

Classroom Activities

Elementary mathematics textbooks do not illustrate the innovative content and instructional strategies discussed in this chapter, so the following activities are offered as examples. Each activity is labeled as appropriate for primary or intermediate grade students and includes objectives for learners, special materials needed, instructions for the teacher, and tangents or follow-up activities. Each activity provides a starting point of inquiry into mathematics.

Classifying the Class (Primary)

Objectives:
    Students will use a matrix to collect and analyze data.
    Students will quantify categories to determine class preferences.

Procedure:
  1 Record on a class matrix (see Figure 5–2) on the board, the order of each child's preferences in five subject areas from most favorite to least favorite, using these symbols:
               A—Art
               L—Language Arts

M—Mathematics
C—Science
O—Social Studies

2   Decode individual student's order of preference. OMCLA would mean that child's preference order is (1) Social Studies, (2) Mathematics, (3) Science, (4) Language Arts, (5) Art.

3   Assign points to each preference.

1st position—5 pts.
2nd position—4 pts.
3rd position—3 pts.
4th position—2 pts.
5th position—1 pt.

4   Total the values of the whole class for each subject area. (See Figure 5–3.)

5   Rank order the class's preferences to form a class consensus.

6   Discuss how individual preferences might be accommodated in the class; why people might think differently; and how the matrix could be used for collecting other data.

7   Some other preference categories could be: poems, artwork, periods of the day.

LAOMC	ACOLM			LMAOC
LACMO		CMLOA	COLMA	ALMOC
MCAOL	ACLMO	MCLOA	LOCAM	CMOLA
CMLAO	q	ACOLM	ACLMO	AMCOL
ACMOL	CMLAO	AMCOL	MACLO	MLACO
MCALO	MACOL	MCALO	MCOLA	LOCMA

Figure 5–2   A CLASS MATRIX

ART (A)
4 + 5 + 0 + 0 + 3 = 12
4 + 0 + 1 + 1 + 5 = 11
3 + 5 + 1 + 2 + 1 = 12
2 + 2 + 5 + 5 + 5 = 19
5 + 2 + 5 + 4 + 3 = 19
3 + 4 + 3 + 1 + 1 = 12
                  ‾‾‾‾
                  85 pts.

LANGUAGE ARTS (L)
5 + 5 + 0 + 0 + 3 = 13
5 + 0 + 3 + 3 + 4 = 15
1 + 3 + 3 + 5 + 2 = 14
3 + 5 + 2 + 3 + 1 = 14
1 + 3 + 1 + 2 + 4 = 11
2 + 1 + 2 + 2 + 5 = 12
                  ‾‾‾‾
                  79 pts.

MATHEMATICS (M)
2 + 1 + 0 + 0 + 4 = 7
2 + 0 + 4 + 2 + 3 = 11
5 + 2 + 5 + 1 + 4 = 17
4 + 3 + 1 + 2 + 4 = 14
3 + 4 + 4 + 5 + 5 = 21
5 + 5 + 5 + 5 + 2 = 22
                  ‾‾‾‾
                  92 pts.

SCIENCE (C)
1 + 4 + 0 + 0 + 1 = 6
3 + 0 + 5 + 5 + 1 = 14
4 + 4 + 4 + 3 + 5 = 20
5 + 4 + 4 + 4 + 3 = 20
4 + 5 + 3 + 3 + 2 = 17
4 + 3 + 4 + 4 + 3 = 18
                  ‾‾‾‾
                  95 pts.

SOCIAL STUDIES (0)
3 + 3 + 0 + 0 + 1 = 7
1 + 0 + 2 + 4 + 2 = 9
2 + 1 + 2 + 4 + 3 = 12
1 + 1 + 3 + 1 + 2 = 8
2 + 1 + 2 + 1 + 1 = 7
1 + 2 + 1 + 3 + 4 = 11
                  ‾‾‾‾
                  54 pts.

FIGURE 5–3   PREFERENCE FOR SUBJECTS—CMALO

Streets and Intersections (Primary)

Objectives:
Students will interpret graphic displays as numerical relationships, collect data on different graphic displays, and generalize beyond the data.

Procedure:
Draw seven parallel line segments on the board and one line segment that intersects the other seven. All line segments are streets, and each intersection has four corners.

In the 7–1 arrangement, how many corners are there?	(Answer: 28)
In a 6–2 arrangement, how many corners are there?	(Answer: 48)
What arrangement will make the most corners?	(Answer: 4–4)
What arrangement will make the least number of corners?	(Answer: 8–0 or 0–8)

If we use 9, 10, 11 . . . line segments, how can we decide on the arrangement that will give us the most or the fewest corners?

One Chip, Two Chip, Three Chip, Four (Primary)

Objectives:
The students will find several procedures for exchanging chips at specified rates and will determine the fastest rate of exchange to acquire a yellow chip.

Materials Needed:
Counters or chips of four colors
1 die per team

Procedures:
Form teams with two or three members on each team. Two teams compete to get a yellow chip. Two green chips can be exchanged for one red chip; two reds for one white chip; two whites for one yellow chip. A member of a team rolls the die and the team receives the same number of green chips as there are spots on the die. As a team accumulates chips, they may be exchanged at the rate specified above. When the game has been learned, rates of exchange are raised to 3 for 1, 4 for 1, etc. Students share strategies for chip exchange, seeking shortcuts. For example, in a 3 for 1 game, if a team has two greens and rolls a five, the team might

1 count out 5 green; put 5 with 2 already in hand and fair exchange
2 count 5 dots and say 5 green equals 1 red and 2 green; 2 green plus 2 green equals 1 red plus 1 green
3 count dots and say 5 dots plus 2 green is 7 green; 7 green equals 2 red plus 1 green

The play may be reversed such that each team has one or two yellow chips. They roll the die to determine how many green to take away. The team that gives away all its chips first wins.

After teams have played with various chip exchange rates, students should be able to determine which game plays fastest—the two, three, or four exchange game.

Running the Hundred (Primary)

Objectives:

Students practice single-digit addition.

Students will devise a way to record successive addition problems and work as a coordinated team to achieve a goal.

Procedure:

Teams of four students roll one die successively, keeping a running total until the team accumulates 100 points. The team devises a way to record the successive moves to check their work, and each team member must individually make a record of the play. Teams race to reach a total of exactly 100.

After the teams have devised recording systems and played several rounds, winning teams will share their systems and techniques with the class.

Making Six a Hundred (Primary)

Objectives:

Students practice addition and discover more than one combination of digits to achieve a total of one hundred.

Materials:

Deck of playing cards with the tens and face cards removed.

Procedures:

Two, three, or four players may play. Each player receives six cards from the deck and attempts to combine them through addition to get as close to 100 as possible. All six cards must be used.

Example: Player is dealt 1 - 1 - 2 - 4 - 5 - 6 and combines them as

$$\begin{array}{r} 64 \\ 25 \\ +\ 11 \\ \hline 100 \end{array}$$

Players will discover that various combinations of these six cards will yield 100. They could attempt to discover all possible ways to get 100 for any six cards.

Copycat (Primary)

Objective:
Students will increase visual imagery skills and evaluate factors that make the task more difficult.

Materials:
Geometric pieces—at least two pieces of several shapes and several colors with sides of equal length

Procedure:
1 Set up a barrier between you and your partner.
2 Create a pattern using no more than six pieces. (When you become an expert at this game, you can increase the number of pieces you use.)
3 Make sure the necessary duplicate pieces for copying this pattern are available for your partner to use.
4 Take the barrier down for ten seconds and let your partner study your pattern.
5 Put the barrier back up and let your partner try to make the pattern from memory. (Peeks are allowed only if both partners agree to it!)
6 Try to discover why some patterns are easier to remember than others.

Rotations of Shapes (Intermediate)

Objectives:
Students will be able to plot points on a graph by their x and y coordinates and connect these points with line segments.
Students will be able to determine where corresponding points will fall when the original shape is rotated 180°, 90°, 270°, around the centerpoint (5, 5).
Students will complete at least three rotational designs.

Materials:
8½" × 11" half-inch graph paper
Graph paper transparencies

Procedure:
1 Students select a category under which they collect related words.
2 They collect three-letter, four-letter, five-letter, etc., through ten-letter words that fit that category. For example, under astronomy: sun (3), star (4), Pluto (5), Saturn (6), Jupiter (7), Universe (8), asteroids (9), Copernicus (10).
3 Then, using the chart below, the letters in each word are changed to numerals in a modulo ten system.

```
1 2 3 4 5 6 7 8 9 10
A B C D E F G H I J
K L M N O P Q R S T
U V W X Y Z
```

sun → 9–1–4; star → 9–10–1–8; Pluto → 6-2-1-10-5; Saturn → 9–1–10–1–8–4; Jupiter → 10–1–6–9–10–5–8; Universe → 1–4–9–2–5–8–9–5; asteroids → 1–9–10–5–8–5–9–4–9; Copernicus → 3–5–6–5–8–4–9–3–1–9

4 For each word translated into numerals, a shape can be made by pairing adjacent numerals as x and y coordinates, plotting points on a graph, and connecting these points to those preceding and following. To do this, write down the numerals corresponding to the word. Repeat the first two numerals that start the sequence so the line segment path will close and return to the starting point. Thus, for the word "sun," the corresponding numerals 9 1 4 will extend to 9 1 4 9 1. You are now ready to pair adjacent numerals: 9 pairs with 1 to become (9, 1), 1 pairs with 4 to become (1, 4), 4 pairs with 9 to become (4, 9), and 9 pairs again with 1 to become (9, 1), thus returning to the original two numerals. These x and y coordinates are then listed vertically in the first of four columns:

$$(9,1)$$
$$(1,4)$$
$$(4,9)$$
$$(9,1)$$

(Note: When working with longer numerical chains derived from longer words, there will be one more set of coordinate points than there are in the sequence.)

5 The coordinate pairs are then plotted. The first, or x, coordinate directs the number of spaces you go right and the second, or y, coordinate directs the number of spaces you go up before placing the point.

6 At this point, students are asked to construct the same figure rotated 180°. After plotting several coordinates rotated 180°, students are asked to develop a process for rotating 180°, 90°, and 270°. Several processes are possible, such as rotating a transparency of the figure.

7 This step was developed by fifth-grade gifted learners. Each point is then connected to the previous point by a line segment. Completing steps 1–5 results in beginning a shape that will be rotated 180°, 90°, and 270°.

    a To rotate the original shape 180°, the coordinate pairs for plotting this rotation are derived from the coordinate pairs in the first column, those that were used to form the original shape. From all the first-column numbers in the x position, we will compute what number is needed to make each number 10. The number to add becomes the x coordinate recorded in the third column. (At this time, the second column remains blank.) It is a similar operation for the y position numbers; that is, determine what number is needed to make the y position number in the first column 10 and record that number in the y position in the third column. Here is what the first and third column would look like for the word *sun*:

$$(9, 1) \quad (1, 9)$$
$$(1, 4) \quad (9, 6)$$
$$(4, 9) \quad (6, 1)$$
$$(9, 1) \quad (1, 9)$$

These coordinate pairs are plotted and line segments connected to previous and following points, thus completing the 180° rotation of the original shape.

    b The coordinates for rotating the original shape 90° are found in the first and third columns and recorded in the second column. The y coordinates from the first column become the x coordinates for the second column and the *x* coordinates from the third column become the second column's *y* coordinates. For *sun*:

(9, 1)	(1, 1)	(1, 9)
(1, 4)	(4, 9)	(9, 6)
(4, 9)	(9, 6)	(6, 1)
(9, 1)	(1, 1)	(1, 9)

The same drawing procedure used with the original and the 180° rotation are now used to draw the 90° rotation.

c The coordinates for rotating the original shape 270° are found by taking the *x* coordinates and *y* coordinates in the second column, finding those addends that give the sum of 10, and recording those numbers in their respective places in the fourth column. This is the same procedure used to find the third column coordinates from the first. Here are the coordinates for the 270° rotation of the word "sun" and those in the second column from which they came:

(	)	(1, 1)	(	)	(9, 9)
(	)	(4, 9)	(	)	(6, 1)
(	)	(9, 6)	(	)	(1, 4)
(	)	(1, 1)	(	)	(9, 9)

The 270° rotation is drawn as before, finishing all four of the rotations. Figures 5–4, 5–5, and 5–6 illustrate these rotations.

Figure 5–4

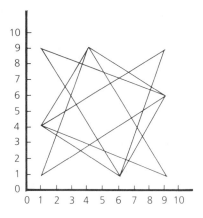

1. SUN   (9,1)(1,1)(1,9)(9,9)
   9 1 4 9 1   (1,4)(4,9)(9,6)(6,1)
                (4,9)(9,6)(6,1)(1,4)
                (9,1)(1,1)(1,9)(9,9)

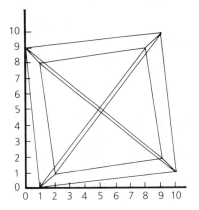

2. STAR   (9,10)(10,1)(1,0)(0,9)
   9 10 1 8 9 10   (10,1)(1,0)(0,9)(9,10)
                        (1,8)(8,9)(9,2)(2,1)
                        (8,9)(9,2)(2,1)(1,8)
                        (9,10)(10,1)(1,0)(0,9)

Figure 5-5

Figure 5-6

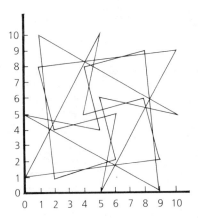

3. PLUTO   (6,2)(2,4)(4,8)(8,6)
   6 2 1 10 5 6 2   (2,1)(1,8)(8,9)(9,2)
                       (1,10)(10,9)(9,0)(0,1)
                       (10,5)(5,0)(0,5)(5,10)
                       (5,6)(6,5)(5,4)(4,5)
                       (6,2)(2,4)(4,8)(8,6)

Base Number Systems (Intermediate)

Objectives:
  Students convert the same sequence of numerals in different bases to base ten numerals.
  Students generalize on the base ten equivalent of successive bases.
  Students develop strategies to determine an unknown base.

Procedures:
  Have students complete the following sequence:

$$11201_{nine} = \underline{\hspace{1cm}} \text{ ten}$$
$$11201_{eight} = \underline{\hspace{1cm}} \text{ ten}$$
$$11201_{seven} = \underline{\hspace{1cm}} \text{ ten}$$
$$11201_{six} = \underline{\hspace{1cm}} \text{ ten}$$
$$11201_{five} = \underline{\hspace{1cm}} \text{ ten}$$

  Students then develop a generalization from this work.
  Students should determine whether their generalization is true for negative bases; for fractional bases.
  When the students understand bases and numeration systems, they can request any base ten equivalent in an unknown base system, then determine the unknown base. Strategies for determining the base should be developed. For example, if the unknown equivalent for 25_{ten} is 100, the unknown base is either $\pm$ five.

PEX: Plus Equals Times (Intermediate)

Objectives:
  Students can determine a pattern from specific examples, construct examples to illustrate the pattern, and describe the mathematical pattern.

Procedure:
  Students are given the following examples:

$$0 + 0 = 0 \times 0$$
$$2 + 2 = 2 \times 2$$
$$4 + 1\tfrac{1}{3} = 4 \times 1\tfrac{1}{3}$$
$$2\tfrac{1}{3} + 1\tfrac{3}{4} = 2\tfrac{1}{3} \times 1\tfrac{3}{4}$$

The student must find two more such examples and develop a rule for finding all such examples.

Solution:

$$\text{If } \frac{a}{b} + \frac{c}{d} = \frac{a}{b} \times \frac{c}{d}$$
$$\frac{ad + cb}{bd} = \frac{ac}{bd}$$
$$ad + cb = ac$$

$$\frac{ad}{ac} + \frac{cb}{ac} = 1$$

$$\frac{d}{c} + \frac{b}{a} = 1$$

Therefore, to find a match for $1\frac{1}{5}$ ($\frac{6}{5}$), ask:

$$\frac{5}{6} + ? = 1 \qquad \text{(Answer: } \frac{1}{6}\text{)}$$

Check:

$$1\frac{1}{5} + 6 = 1\frac{1}{5} \times 6$$

$$\frac{6}{5} + \frac{30}{5} = \frac{6}{5} \times 6$$

$$\frac{36}{5} = \frac{36}{5}$$

Problem Solving on a Grid That Uses Powers of Two Primes as the Basis of its Construction (Intermediate)

Audience:
Fourth or fifth grade gifted class.

Objectives:
Students will:

1   Construct a grid using the powers of 2 and 3.
2   Listen to the directions given by the teacher about finding the starting point, transferring the stated operations to directions, and following correspondingly on their grid, recording the ending part by its number.
3   Solve the following problems by using the chart:
  a   multiplication of whole numbers
  b   division of whole numbers
  c   factoring a number
  d   reducing fractions
  e   finding greatest common factor
4   Expand the chart to include fractions.
5   Solve these kinds of problems with the use of an expanded chart:
  a   multiplication, using fractions and mixed numbers as terms
  b   division, using fractions and mixed numbers as terms
6   Construct other charts using the powers of other one-digit primes.
7   Solve similar problems to B, C, D, and E above using the newly constructed charts.

Materials:
8½″ × 11″ sheets of one-inch graph paper
Pencils
Transparencies of completed grids

Procedure:
    1   In the middle of an 8½″ x 11″ sheet of one-inch graph paper, have students make an array of 5 x 5 (25) dots, one inch apart. Use the intersections of graph lines for this purpose. Connect all dots orthogonally by line segments (see Figure 5–7).

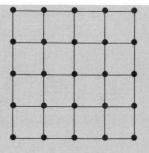

FIGURE 5-7

2 To the right and slightly above the upper left dot, place a 1, representing 2 to the zero (2^0) power. Have students label horizontally the four other dots in that top row by the other powers of 2: 2, 4, 8, 16 (see Figure 5–8).

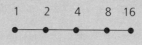

FIGURE 5-8

3 Return to the 1; tell students that 1 is also 3 to the zero power. Have them label vertically the four other dots in that first column by the powers of 3: 3, 9, 27, 81.

4 Complete the numbering of the graph. If a dot is horizontally to the right of another dot, multiply the number above the first dot by 2. If a dot is vertically below another dot, multiply the number above the first dot by 3 (see Figure 5–9).

1	2	4	8	16
3	6	12	24	48
9	18	36	72	144
27	54	108	216	432
81	162	324	648	1296

FIGURE 5-9

5 After a beginning point has been designated, follow a multiplication path on the chart traveling right one line segment between dots if multiplying by 2, traveling vertically one line segment between dots if multiplying by 3. For example: $4 \times 2 \times 2 \times 3 \times 3 \times 3 =$ _____, start at 4, travel 2 spaces right, 3 spaces down, ending at 432.

   6   Follow a division path on the chart. Designate a beginning point; travel left when dividing by 2, travel up when dividing by 3.

   7   Multiply two numbers on the chart by using the configuration of a number as the multiplier.

   a   Choose a number for a multiplier.

   b   Draw a path from 7 to that number. The possible directional elements are down and right.

   c   Choose a number for a multiplicand.

   d   Draw the same configuration from the multiplicand that was drawn from 1.

   e   The ending dot with its designated number gives the students the product.

   8   Divide a larger number by a smaller one, using only numbers on the chart.

   a   Choose a number for a divisor.

   b   Draw a path from that number to 1. (The possible directions are up and left.)

   c   Choose a larger number for a dividend.

   d   Draw the same configuration from the dividend that was drawn from the divisor. The ending dot gives students the quotient.

   9   To factor a number, students draw a configuration (a point, line, rectangle, or square) this way:

   a   Choose a number on the dittoed chart. Place a pencil point on the dot that signifies that number.

   b   If there are dots above, draw a line segment to the furthest dot. If there are not, remain where you are.

   c   From that position, if there are dots to the left, draw a line segment to the furthest dot left. If not, remain where you are.

   d   From that position, if there are dots below, draw a line segment down, the same length drawn in step **b**. If not, remain where you are.

   e   From that position, if there are dots to the right, draw a line segment to the dot where you started. If not, remain where you are.

   f   If the resulting configuration drawn is a dot, the only factor is 1.

   g   If the configuration drawn is a line segment, the numerically designated dots on that line are the factors of that number.

   h   If the configuration drawn is a rectangle or square, the numerically designated dots on the perimeter and those in the interior are the factors of that number.

   10   Reduce fractions using this procedure. Record the fraction not in its simplest terms. Put your right index finger on the numerator, your left index finger on the denominator, and travel left one line segment simultaneously with both fingers until you cannot travel any further left. Then, travel up with your right finger until you cannot travel up any further. Your right index finger will then give you the reduced term of the numerator, your left index finger the reduced term of the denominator.

   11   The greatest common factor of two numbers on the chart can be found by drawing the configuration for both numbers and examining each to see the greatest number occurring as a factor in *both* configurations.

   12   The chart used previously is expanded so that it has four quadrants. Before, if you traveled horizontally right, each number would be multiplied by 2, and if you traveled vertically down, each number would be multiplied by 3. With the new chart, the inverse is also used. If you travel horizontally left, each number is divided by 2. If you travel vertically up, each number is divided by 3. (Figure 5–10 shows the resulting chart.)

$\frac{1}{1296}$	$\frac{1}{648}$	$\frac{1}{324}$	$\frac{1}{162}$	$\frac{1}{81}$	$\frac{2}{81}$	$\frac{4}{81}$	$\frac{8}{81}$	$\frac{16}{81}$
$\frac{1}{432}$	$\frac{1}{216}$	$\frac{1}{108}$	$\frac{1}{54}$	$\frac{1}{27}$	$\frac{2}{27}$	$\frac{4}{27}$	$\frac{8}{27}$	$\frac{16}{27}$
$\frac{1}{144}$	$\frac{1}{72}$	$\frac{1}{36}$	$\frac{1}{18}$	$\frac{1}{9}$	$\frac{2}{9}$	$\frac{4}{9}$	$\frac{8}{9}$	$1\frac{7}{9}$
$\frac{1}{48}$	$\frac{1}{24}$	$\frac{1}{12}$	$\frac{1}{6}$	$\frac{1}{3}$	$\frac{2}{3}$	$1\frac{1}{3}$	$2\frac{2}{3}$	$5\frac{1}{3}$
$\frac{1}{16}$	$\frac{1}{8}$	$\frac{1}{4}$	$\frac{1}{2}$	1	2	4	8	16
$\frac{3}{16}$	$\frac{3}{8}$	$\frac{3}{4}$	$1\frac{1}{2}$	3	6	12	24	48
$\frac{9}{16}$	$1\frac{1}{8}$	$2\frac{1}{4}$	$4\frac{1}{2}$	9	18	36	72	144
$1\frac{11}{16}$	$3\frac{3}{8}$	$6\frac{3}{4}$	$13\frac{1}{2}$	27	54	108	216	432
$5\frac{1}{16}$	$10\frac{1}{8}$	$20\frac{1}{4}$	$40\frac{1}{2}$	81	162	324	648	1296

FIGURE 5–10

Try to discover how you could use the new chart to multiply and divide when one or two of the terms are fractions or mixed numbers.

Using powers of 2 horizontally and of 5 vertically, complete the chart in Figure 5–11.

	1	2	4	8	16
5					
25					
125					
625					

FIGURE 5–11

Make a list of other one-digit prime pairs you could use. If time permits, make these charts and work these kinds of problems:

a   Multiplication of whole numbers
b   Division of whole numbers
c   Factoring
d   Reducing fraction
e   Finding GCF

Fraction Patterns (Intermediate)

Objectives:
   Students will seek patterns or rules for finding the sum of two fractions, describe the rule, and generalize the rule for any fraction.

Procedure:
   The instructor places addition of two fractions on the board with the correct sum.

Example 1: $\dfrac{1}{4} + \dfrac{1}{5} = \dfrac{9}{20}$

   Then another.

Example 2: $\dfrac{1}{2} + \dfrac{1}{3} = ?$

   Most students will immediately respond "⅚." Now switch the examples to the addition of a unit fraction and another common fraction that is *not* a unit fraction

Example 3: $\dfrac{1}{2} + \dfrac{2}{5} = ?$

   Usually, everyone will see the pattern for the denominator (2 x 5), but responses for the numerator will differ. ⁷⁄₁₀, ¹²⁄₁₀, ¹³⁄₁₀ are often mentioned, along with the correct response, ⁹⁄₁₀. Have a student explain several of the incorrect responses. Do not allow explanation of the correct response. Indicate the correct response for Example 3 is ⁹⁄₁₀, stating that the rule for finding ⁹⁄₁₀ will not be verbalized. Each student must continue to search for the rule. Give another example.

Example 4: $\dfrac{2}{3} + \dfrac{2}{5} = ?$

   Again accept responses. Emphasize that *all* the examples, 1–4, use the *same* rule, even Examples 1 and 2, the two unit fraction examples. Suggest that the students re-examine all the examples for a common pattern.
   Ask: How can 1, 4, 1, 5 be combined to get 9?
            How can 1, 2, 1, 3 be combined to get 5?
            How can 1, 2, 2, 5 be combined to get 9?
   Indicate the correct solution of Example 4 as ¹⁶⁄₁₅.
   Do *not* allow the students who find the rule to verbalize it for others. Involve those who know the rule by allowing them to suggest good examples.

When most students can solve the examples with numbers, give for solution the example

$$\frac{a}{b} + \frac{c}{d} = ?$$

Note that some examples are not reduced to simplest terms. As an extension of this activity, ask students to modify the general solution to insure a solution in simplest terms. Another extension of this lesson is to introduce complex fractions.

This activity should precede any instruction in adding fractions, even fractions with like denominators. If some work on fractions addition has already taken place, change the form of this activity from

$$\frac{1}{2} + \frac{1}{3} = \frac{5}{6}$$

to

$$(1,2)\ (1,3) \rightarrow (5,6)$$

When the lesson has been completed, translate the examples to fractions.

Summary

At the elementary grade levels, a number of critical deficiencies must be alleviated to offer gifted learners a rich divergent program of mathematics. Gifted elementary learners need mathematics textbook materials that have continuity and in a sequence based on curriculum research. Teachers at these levels need to improve their general mathematics background and become proficient in several skills areas. Increasing technological demands require teachers of the gifted to learn about and use computers and to teach simple programming commands. Teachers must also develop skills in assessing generic factors that influence mathematics, along with a repertoire of teaching strategies and a classroom environment that promotes optimum mathematical learning. Learning activities should integrate affective as well as cognitive expectations.

Mathematical concerns for the gifted at the secondary level revolve around teachers, content, and learners, but with dimensions that vary from elementary grade-level concerns. Textbooks and programs for the mathematically able are available, but offer a topical view rather than a process, language approach, or structural view of mathematics. Additional hardware and software to promote computer proficiency are also necessary at the secondary level.

Studies on identification of mathematical talent as well as characteristics of those gifted in mathematics have been informative for program development. There are, however, important curricular questions yet to be answered in relation to mathematics curriculum for the gifted; for example:
- Which instructional strategies produce specified mathematical outcomes for groups of gifted students with similar generic profiles?
- What is an efficient distribution of time spent on selected strategies to produce specified mathematical outcomes?

- What kinds of mathematics curriculum topics are most amenable to selected strategies?
- Can mathematics curricula be developed to enable the gifted to view mathematics in its diverse facets?

Resources

The following materials have proven useful as resources for mathematics programs for gifted learners. None of the materials would, by themselves, constitute an adequate mathematics program for the gifted, but all offer enrichment experiences. Materials appropriate for primary, intermediate, or secondary gifted learners are labeled. No label indicates the materials can be of some value at any level.

Ahl, D. H., ed. *BASIC Computer Games (Microcomputer Edition)*. Morristown, N.J.: Creative Computing Press, 1981.
  101 games for the microcomputer, most written in Microsoft 8080 BASIC. Each game is briefly described and microcomputer programs listed.

Ahl, D. H. *More BASIC Computer Games*. Morristown, N.J.: Creative Computing Press, 1979.
  84 games for the microcomputer in Microsoft BASIC.

Baker, M.O. *Syllogisms*. Pacific Grove, Calif.: Midwest Publications, 1981.
  Series of three booklets (A = easy, B = medium, C = difficult) for analyzing syllogisms. Problems designed to be solved through class discussion. (Intermediate, Secondary)

Banwell, C.S., K.D. Saunders, and D.G. Tahta. *Starting Points*. London: Oxford University Press, 1972.
  Collection of activities for mathematics to use as beginning points for investigations by children. (Primary, Intermediate)

Barr, S. *Experiments in Topology*. New York: Thomas Y. Crowell, 1964.
  Interesting topological problems posed, discussed, and explained. (Intermediate, Secondary)

Beard, R.S. *Patterns in Space*. Palo Alto, Calif.: Creative Publications, 1973.
  Unique geometric designs with directions for construction.

Bezuszka, S. et al. *Applications of Finite Differences*. Chestnut Hill, Mass.: Boston College Press, 1976.
  One of a series of booklets from the Boston College Mathematics Institute Motivated Math Project Activity. Problems are of interest to students in grade 4 and above and involve finite differences as a solution technique. (Intermediate)

Bezuszka, S., M. Kenney, and L. Silvey. *Designs from Mathematical Patterns*. Palo Alto,Calif.: Creative Publications, 1978.
  Mathematics of symmetrics, designs, and patterns explored through activities. (Primary, Intermediate)

Bezuszka, S., M. Kenney, and L. Silvey. *Tessalations: The Geometry of Patterns*. Palo Alto, Calif.: Creative Publications, 1977.
  Exercises review informal geometry and extend it to investigations of tiling patterns. (Intermediate)

Black, Howard, and Sandra Black. *Figural Analogies*. Pacific Grove, Calif.: Midwest Publications, 1981.
  Series of three booklets to improve visual discrimination and figural reasoning skills. (Intermediate)

Bond, J.M. *Let's Try: First Year Papers in Reasoning*. London: Thomas Nelson and Sons, 1973.
  Booklet of 22 activities, each with 30 questions. Object of activities is to enable the teacher to assess, at regular intervals, a child's reasoning ability. (Primary)

Bourgoin, J. *Arabic Geometrical Pattern and Design*. New York: Dover, 1973.
  Set of 190 linear plates of basic patterns underlying Arabic designs to use for symmetry study as well as relating math, art, and culture.

Brownlee, J. *Tangram Geometry in Metric*. Hayward, Calif.: Activity Resources, 1975.
  Series of activities involving tangrams that are more advanced than the various shapes to be made from the seven tangram pieces. (Primary, Intermediate)

Buchanan, S. *Poetry and Mathematics*. Chicago: The University of Chicago Press, 1962.
  By treating poetry mathematically and mathematics poetically, the author shows the mutual reflections of each. Figures, numbers, proportions, equations, functions, and symbols are examined for their poetic and mathematical content. (Secondary)

Cohors-Fresenborg, E., D. Finke, and S. Schütte. *Dynamical Mazes*. Osnabruck, Germany: Universitat Osnabrück, 1979.
  Exciting new kit to teach sorting and networks. Consists of a pegboard surface, building "bricks" (or roadway connections), and programmed texts to teach construction. Children learn to build networks to sort various collections, including numbers. (Primary, Intermediate)

Dantzig, T. *Number. The Language of Science*. New York: Macmillan, 1930.
  Requires mathematics only through the high school level for understanding. Deals with symbol and form; presents evaluation of number as a human story, but is not a history of number. (Intermediate, Secondary)

Davis, R.B. *Discovery in Mathematics*. Reading, Mass.: Addison-Wesley, 1964.
  Exercises for children to practice axiomatizing as well as logical deduction. (Primary, Intermediate)

Dienes, Z.P., and E.W. Golding. *Geometry Through Transformations*. New York: Heider and Heider, 1967.
  Series of three booklets (I, Geometry of Distortion; II, Geometry of Congruence; III, Groups and Coordinates). Each begins with background information for the teacher, then presents learning activities for students. (Intermediate)

Dienes, Z.P., and E.W. Golding. *Exploration of Space and Practical Measurement*. New York: Heider and Heider, 1966.
  Conceptual material for teachers' understanding comprises first third of book. Approaches measurement in terms of comparisons; explores geometry topologically and then through geometric transformations. Over 60 games for learning measurement and geometry. (Primary, Intermediate)

Dienes, Z.P., and E.W. Golding. *Sets, Numbers and Powers*. New York: Heider and Heider, 1966.
  Explanation of sets, numbers, and powers for the teacher, with thirty games leading to an understanding of sets and numbers. (Primary, Intermediate)

Droze, D. *Asking Questions; Finding Answers*. San Luis Obispo, Calif.: Dandy Lion, 1979.
  Activities that allow children to use their own questions as starters for investigations. (Intermediate)

Genise, L.R., ed. *Games and Enrichment Activities. A Look at Mathematics Through Models*. New Rochelle, N.Y.: Cuisenaire Company of America.
  Classroom activities involving nonverbal mathematics, spatial relations, patterns, and matching. Some activities require Cuisenaire rods and geoboards. (Primary, Intermediate)

Gidley, R., and D.G. Seymour. *Eureka-Math Enrichment*. Palo Alto, Calif.: Creative Publications, 1968.
  Math activities covering wide range of topics and levels of difficulty. Teacher's Guide with solutions is available. (Intermediate)

Ginther, J. *Math Experiments with Pentominoes*. Pacific Grove, Calif.: Midwest Publications, 1976.
  Activities using pentominoes (five squares joined) to form specified shapes. (Primary, Intermediate)

Graham, L.A. *The Surprise Attack in Mathematical Problems*. New York: Dover, 1968.
  Examination of the unexpected approaches to problem solving in mathematics that are simple, yet elegant. (Secondary)

Greens, C., J. Gregory, and D. Seymour. *Successful Problem-Solving Techniques*. Palo Alto, Calif.: Creative Publications, 1977.
  Expands Polya's four phases of problem solving to 9 steps. Provides specific problem-solving techniques and sample problems for each technique. Only general mathematics skills are necessary for problems. (Intermediate)

Greens, C. et al. *Techniques of Problem Solving: Gifted Decks*. Palo Alto, Calif.: Dale Seymour, 1980.
> Problem cards comprised of the most difficult problems from the total TOPS cards. Problems appropriate for gifted learners, grades 3 through 6. (Intermediate)

Greenwood, D. *Mapping*. Chicago: The University of Chicago Press, 1941.
> Reading, interpreting, and making your own maps. (Intermediate)

Hadamard, J. *The Psychology of Invention in the Mathematical Field*. New York: Dover, 1945.
> Essays on the interaction of conscious and unconscious in the preparation, incubation, and illumination processes in problem solving. (Secondary)

Harnadek, A. *Basic Thinking Skills*. Pacific Grove, Calif.: Midwest Publications, 1977.
> Series of 13 booklets covering analogies, antonyms, synonyms, conservation paths, following directions, transitivity, and patterns. (Intermediate)

Harnadek, A. *Critical Thinking*. Pacific Grove, Calif.: Midwest Publications, 1976 (Book 1); 1980 (Book 2).
> Critical thinking refers to a broad range of problem-solving procedures and is not limited to mathematics. Addresses logic, errors in reasoning, propaganda, and probability of truth and falsity; includes activities and practice exercises. (Intermediate)

Harnadek, A. *Inductive Thinking Skills*. Pacific Grove, Calif.: Midwest Publications, 1979.
> Eleven booklets covering cause and effect, figure relations, inferences, reasoning by analogy, and spatial perception. (Intermediate)

Harnadek, A. *Mind Benders (Deductive Thinking Skills)*. Pacific Grove, Calif.: Midwest Publications, 1978.
> Thirteen booklets for promoting deductive thinking in reading and mathematics. A-level booklets are easy; B-level medium difficult; C-level very difficult. Students should work through A and B levels before attempting C. (Intermediate)

Harnadek, A. *Word Problems*. Pacific Grove, Calif.: Midwest Publications, 1979.
> Three booklets of general mathematics word problems. Problems are clearly stated and arithmetically mixed so that students do not automatically know the required operation for solution. (Intermediate)

Hofstadter, D.R. *Godel, Escher, Bach: An Eternal Golden Braid*. New York: Basic Books, 1979.
> Connects a number of disjointed disciplines (logic, biology, psychology, linguistics) into a meaningful whole to investigate the nature of thought processes. Contributes to the view of mathematics as a language. (Secondary)

Holmberg, V.L., M. Laycock, and Dale Seymour. *Aftermath I, II, III, IV*. Palo Alto, Calif.: Creative Publications, 1975.
> Four booklets offering miscellaneous exploratory activities in mathematics. (Primary, Intermediate)

Hughes, B. *Thinking Through Problems. A Manual of Mathematical Heuristic*. Palo Alto, Calif.: Creative Publications, 1976.
> Present problems from number sequences, algebra, and analytic algebra, and techniques for solving them. Most problems could be presented to intermediate grade gifted learners. (Intermediate)

Jacobs, H. *Mathematics. A Human Endeavor*. San Francisco: W. H. Freeman, 1970.
> Author attempts to present what mathematics is really like. Originally intended for able but unmotivated secondary students, the text has been used successfully with gifted intermediate learners in the intermediate grades. (Intermediate)

Jenkins, L., and P. McLean. *It's a Tangram World*. Hayward, Calif.: Activity Resources, 1980.
> Uses tangram shapes to teach fractions. (Primary)

Johnson, D.S., V.P. Hansen, W.H. Peterson, J.A. Rudnick, R. Cleveland, and L.C. Bolster, *Applications in Mathematics, Course A*. Glenview, Ill.: Scott, Foresman, 1972.
> Intended for a pre-algebra course. Offers six units, each designed for about 6 weeks of instruction. Includes Functions & Graphs, Relations & Geometry, Sampling & Statistics, Estimation & Measurement, Prediction & Probability, Algebra. (Intermediate)

Judd, W. *Patterns to Play on a Hundreds Chart*. Palo Alto, Calif.: Creative Publications, 1975.
> Demonstrates concepts such as place value, operations on whole numbers, and fractions, using a standard hundred chart. (Primary)

Kadesch, R.R. *Math Menagerie*. New York: Harper and Row, 1942.
Twenty-five experiments in mathematics using only inexpensive materials such as rulers and graph paper. (Intermediate)

Kennedy, J., and D. Thomas. *Kaleidoscope Math*. Palo Alto, Calif.: Creative Publications, Inc., 1978.
Activities with hinged mirrors; most activities are exploratory and appropriate for intermediate grade students. (Intermediate)

Kenney, M.J. *The Incredible Pascal Triangle*. Boston: Boston College Press, 1976.
One of the series of the Motivated Math Project Activity Booklets (see Bezuszka). Presents various sequences and patterns based on the Pascal Triangle—combinatorials, summations, binomial expansions, Fibonacci numbers are some of the topics. (Intermediate)

Krulik, S., and J.A. Rudnick. *Problem Solving: A Handbook for Teachers*. Boston: Allyn and Bacon, 1980.
Activities, problems, and games for teaching skills and subskills for successful problem solving.

Laycock, M., and R.A. Schadler. *Algebra in the Concrete*. Hayward, Calif.: Activities Resources, 1973.
Uses concrete manipulative materials to demonstrate sequences, algebraic expressions, and linear equations. (Intermediate)

Laycock, M., and G. Watson. *The Fabric of Mathematics: A Resource Book for Teachers*. Hayward, Calif.: Activity Resources, 1975.
Supplemental material pertinent to learning (1) number, (2) numeration, (3) measurement, (4) geometry, and (5) sets and logic. Under each topic (or thread), lists behavioral objectives, published (and thus readily available) manipulatives, games, activities, A-V materials, children's references, Teacher's references, and assessment questions with publishers' addresses for each material.

Laycock, M., and M.A. Smart. *Solid Sense in Mathematics: Problem Solving*. Hayward, Calif.: Activity Resources, 1981.
Three booklets offering problems in elementary mathematics appropriate for grades 4–9. Uses Cuisenaire rods. (Intermediate)

Laycock, M., and C. Johnson. *The Tapestry of Mathematics*. Hayward, Calif.: Activity Resources, 1978.
Provides secondary teachers with the same resource service as *The Fabric of Mathematics* provides for elementary teachers. Activities and materials are organized around operations, functions, model making, measurement, and logic. Covers algebra, geometry, trigonometry, and elementary calculus topics.

Lund, C., and M.A. Smart. *Focus on Calculator Math*. Hayward, Calif.: Activity Resources, 1979.
Calculators are used for more than checking drill problems; students explore patterns and clarify rules of arithmetic. Includes estimation activities. (Primary, Intermediate)

Malone, L., and J. Johnson. *BASIC Discoveries. A Problem-Solving Approach to Beginning Programming*. Palo Alto, Calif.: Creative Publications, 1981.
Presents computer programming in BASIC for grades four and above through an exploratory and problem-solving approach. Activities follow a five-step cycle of explore, solve, predict, investigate, and review. (Intermediate, Secondary)

McCutcheon, G.B. *The McCutcheon Math Series*. Skokie, Ill.: National Textbook, 1975.
Ten booklets, each dealing with a different mathematical topic. Student books and teacher guides are available. Topics covered: equations, number bases, residues, logarithms, functions, determinants and probability. (Intermediate)

Page, D.A. *Maneuvers on Lattices*. Watertown, Mass.: Educational Services, 1965.
Using various arrangements of number lattices of whole numbers and fractions and a code of arrow operations, students discover number relations. (Primary, Intermediate)

Perl, T. *Math Equals. Biographies of Women Mathematicians Plus Related Activities*. Menlo Park, Calif.: Addison-Wesley, 1978.
Examines the lives of women who have made significant contributions to mathematics. Provides activities relating to the areas of mathematics in which the women worked. Not sequential in concept or level of difficulty.

Rozsa, P. *Playing with Infinity: Mathematical Explorations and Excursions*. New York: Dover, 1957, 1976.
> Written for nonmathematicians. Presents concepts of differentiation, infinite series, and the creative role of form. No formulae; all concepts are built-up. Chapters are sequential and must be read in order. Gifted elementary grade students contributed to the book. (Intermediate, Secondary)

Ranucci, E.R. *Seeing Shapes*. Palo Alto, Calif.: Creative Publications, 1973.
> Discovery exercises in spatial abilities. (Primary, Intermediate)

Ranucci, E.R., and J.L. Teeters. *Creating Escher-Type Drawings*. Palo Alto, Calif.: Creative Publications, 1977.
> Step-by-step explanation of the basic geometric ideas underlying Escher drawings. Worksheets. (Intermediate)

Raths, L., J. Wassermann, and S. Wasserman. *Thinking Skills Development Program*. Westchester, Ill.: Benefic Press.
> Identifies 12 kinds of thinking activites and provides practice in the form of job cards for each kind of activity. (Intermediate)

Row, T. S. *Geometric Exercises in Paper Folding*. New York: Dover, 1966.
> Exciting exercise book for high school and college geometry classes. Demonstrates theorems for the square, equilateral triangle, and other regular polygons. (Secondary)

Saaty, T.L., and F.J. Weyl, eds. *The Spirit and the Uses of the Mathematical Sciences*. New York: McGraw-Hill, 1969.
> Essays dealing with mathematics both as creative thought and as a tool in science and technology.

A Sourcebook of Applications of School Mathematics. Prepared by a Joint Committee of the Mathematical Association of America and the National Council of Teachers of Mathematics. Reston, Va.: NCTM, 1980.
> Three types of problems: (1) short, (2) medium length, (3) time-consuming. Data are realistic, computations feasible, and problems cover the topics of advanced arithmetic, algebra, geometry, trigonometry, logarithms, combinatorics, and probability.

Scholastic Dynamath. Englewood Cliffs, N.J.: Scholastic.
> Mathematics magazine of puzzles and problems published nine times during the school year. (Primary, Intermediate)

Seymour, D., and M. Shedd. *Finite Differences. A Problem-Solving Technique*. Palo Alto, Calif.: Creative Publications, 1973.
> Problems that can be solved using the finite difference technique. Explains the technique simply enough for gifted elementary students.

Steinhaus, H. *Mathematical Snapshots*. New York: Oxford University Press, 1969.
> Demonstrates mathematical phenomena through diagram and photograph. Activities could be used when teaching the necessity of visualizing mathematics.

Stein, S. K. *Mathematics. The Man-Made Universe. An Introduction to the Spirit of Mathematics*. San Francisco: W.H. Freeman, 1975.
> Exploits concreteness of mathematics to introduce the general reader to mathematics. Designed to give students an appreciation of the beauty, extent, and vitality of mathematics. Offers exercises to promote mathematics as form and structure. Exercises for routine application and challenge problems.

Taylor, A. *Math in Art*. Hayward, Calif.: Activities Resources, 1974.
> Activities to promote discovery of concepts in mathematics and art. Topics appropriate for intermediate grades.

Zaslovsky, C. *Africa Counts*. Boston: Prindle, Weber and Schmidt, 1973.
> Examines mathematical contributions of the African peoples using number and pattern as an organizing principle.

Zullie, M. E. *Fractions with Pattern Blocks*. Palo Alto, Calif.: Creative Publications.
> Activities for use with Pattern Blocks to promote fraction concept development. Materials have been used with primary and intermediate grade students. (Primary, Intermediate)

References

An Agenda for Action. Recommendations for School Mathematics of the 1980s. Reston, Va.: National Council of Teachers of Mathematics, 1980.

Blake, K. A. *Educating Exceptional Pupils*. Reading, Mass.: Addison-Wesley, 1981.

Block, J. H., ed. *Mastery Learning Theory and Practice*. New York: Holt, Rinehart and Winston, 1971.

Bloom, B. S. "Learning for Mastery." *Evaluation Comment* 1 (1968): 7–12.

Browder, F. E. "Is Mathematics Relevant? And, if so, to what?" *The University of Chicago Magazine* 67 (1975).

Callahan, C. M. "The Gifted and Talented Woman." In *The Gifted and the Talented*. The 78th Yearbook of the National Society for the Study of Education. Chicago: The University of Chicago Press, 1979.

Carin, A. A., and R. B. Sund. *Developing Questioning Techniques*. Columbus, Ohio: Charles E. Merrill, 1971.

Casserly, P. L. "Factors Affecting Female Participation in Advanced Placement Programs in Mathematics, Chemistry, and Physics." In *Women and the Mathematical Mystique*. Edited by L. H. Fox, L. Brody, and D. Tobin. Baltimore, Md.: The Johns Hopkins University Press, 1980.

Cook, N., and Kersh, M. E. "Improving Teachers' Ability to Visualize Mathematics." In *The Proceedings of the Fourth International Conference for the Psychology of Mathematics Education*, 1980.

Daniel, E. D., and R. B. Guay. *Spatial Abilities, Mathematics, Achievement, and the Sexes*. Paper presented at the annual meeting of the American Educational Research Association, San Francisco, 1976.

Dienes, Z. *An Experimental Study of Mathematical Learning*. London: Hutchinson, 1963.

Earp, N. W., and F. W. Tanner. "Mathematics and Language." *Arithmetic Teacher* 28 (1980).

Elements of Mathematics. St. Louis, Mo.: CEMREL, 1973.

Elkonin, D. B. "Development of Speech." In *The Psychology of Preschool Children*. Edited by A. V. Azporozhets and D. B. Elkonin. Cambridge, Mass.: MIT Press, 1971.

Engelman, S. "Does the Piagetian Approach Imply Instruction?" In *Measurement and Piaget*. Edited by D. R. Green, M. P. Ford, and G. B. Flamer. New York: McGraw-Hill, 1971.

Eysenck, H. J. *Know Your Own I.Q.* New York: Bell, 1962.

Fehr, H. F. "Mathematical Education for a Scientific, Technological, and Industrial Society," *The Mathematics Teacher* 61 (1968): 665–71.

Fehr, H. F., J. T. Fey, and T. J. Hill. *Unified Mathematics Course I-IV*. Menlo Park, Calif.: 1972.

Fennema, E., and J. Sherman. "Sex-related Differences in Mathematics Achievement, Spatial Visualization, and Sociocultural Factors." *Journal of Educational Research* 14: 51–71.

Fennema, E., and J. Sherman. "Sex-related Differences in Mathematics Achievement and Related Factors: A Further Study." *Journal for Research in Mathematics Education* 9 (1978): 189–203.

Fox, L. H. *Sex Differences: Implications for Program Planning for the Academically Gifted*. Paper presented at the Lewis M. Terman Memorial Symposium on Intellectual Talent, Baltimore, Md., November 1975.

Furth, H. G., and H. Wachs. *Thinking Goes to School*. New York: Oxford University Press, 1974.

Getzels, J. W. *Problem-Finding and the Nature and Nurture of Giftedness*. Paper presented to the Third World Conference on Gifted, Jerusalem, Israel, 1979.

Glennon, V. J., ed. *The Mathematical Education of Exceptional Children and Youth*. Reston, Va.: The National Council of Teachers of Mathematics, 1981.

Haven, E. W. *Factors Associated with the Selection of Advanced· Academic Mathematics Courses by Girls in High School*. Unpublished doctoral dissertation, University of Pennsylvania, 1971.

Harvey, J. G. "Problem Solving in Mathematics: 1969–1978." In *Problem-Solving Studies in Mathematics*. Edited by G. Harvey and T. A. Romberg. Madison, Wisc.: Wisconsin Research and Development Center for Individualized Schooling, 1980.

Henkin, L. "Linguistic Aspects of Mathematical Education." In *Learning and the Nature of Mathematics*. Edited by William E. Lamon. Chicago: Science Research Associates, 1972.

Hunkins, F. P. *Questioning Strategies and Techniques*. Boston: Allyn and Bacon, 1972.

Jensen, J. *Bias in Mental Testing*. New York: The Free Press, 1980.

Keating, D. P., and J. C. Stanley. "Extreme Measures for the Exceptionally Gifted in Mathematics and Science." *Educational Researcher* 1 (1972).

Keating, D. P., ed. *Intellectual Talent: Research and Development*. Baltimore, Md.: The Johns Hopkins University Press, 1976.

Kersh, M. E. *Mastery Learning in Fifth Grade Mathematics*. Unpublished Ph.D. dissertation, University of Chicago, 1971.

Kempe, A. B. *How to Draw a Straight Line*. Reston, Va.: The National Council of Teachers of Mathematics, 1977.

Kilpatrick, J. Problem Solving and Creative Behavior in Mathematics. In *Studies in Mathematics* Vol. XIX. Edited by J. W. Wilson and L. R. Carry. Stanford, Calif.: School Mathematics Study Group, Stanford University, 1969.

Kilpatrick, J. "Problem Solving in Mathematics." *Review of Educational Research* 39 (1970): 523–34.

Kim, H. *Learning Rates, Aptitudes, and Achievements*. Unpublished Ph.D. dissertation, University of Chicago, 1968.

Mattingly, I. G. "Reading, Linguistic Process and Linguistic Awareness." In *Language by Ear and Eye*. Edited by J. K. Kavanagh and I. G. Mattingly. Cambridge, Mass.: MIT Press, 1972.

Menchinskaya, N. A., and M. I. Moro. "Questions in the Methods and Psychology of Teaching Arithmetic in the Elementary Grades." In *Soviet Studies in the Psychology of Learning and Teaching Mathematics*. Vol. XIV. Edited by J. R. Hooten. Chicago: University of Chicago, 1975.

Meyers, P. J., II, G. Vredeveld, J. Lewis, and P. Harrington. *Choice: Suggested Activities to Motivate the Teaching of Elementary Economics*. Stevensville, Mich.: Educational Service, 1975.

Mosher, F., and J. R. Hornsby. "On Asking Questions." In *Studies in Cognitive Growth*. New York: John Wiley, 1966.

Olstad, R. G., J. R. Juarez, L. J. Davenport, and D. L. Haury. *Inhibitors to Achievement in Science and Mathematics by Ethnic Minorities*. Unpublished paper, College of Education, University of Washington, 1981.

Osborn, R., M. V. DeVault, C. C. Boyd, and W. R. Houston. *Extending Understandings of Mathematics*. Columbus, Ohio: Charles E. Merrill, 1969.

Overview and Analysis of School Mathematics K–12. Conference Board of the Mathematical Sciences. National Advisory Committee on Mathematical Education, 1975.

Papert, S. *Mindstorms: Children, Computers, and Powerful Ideas*. New York: Basic Books, 1980.

Pfrimmer, M. E. *The Relationship of Metalinguistic Awareness to Reading Achievement.* Unpublished Ph.D. dissertation, University of Washington, 1980.

Platts, M. E. *Challenge: Suggested Activities to Motivate the Teaching of Mathematics in the Intermediate Grades.* Stevensville, Mich.: Educational Service, 1975.

Platts, M. E. *Plus: Suggested Activities to Motivate the Teaching of Mathematics in the Primary Grades.* Stevensville, Mich.: Educational Service, 1975.

Polya, A. *How To Solve It. A New Aspect of Mathematical Method.* Garden City, N.Y.: Doubleday, 1957.

Polya, G. *Mathematical Discovery.* New York: John Wiley, 1962.

Rasmussen, P. *Mathtiles: Manual. A Concrete Approach to Arithmetic and Algebra.* Berkeley, Calif.: Key Curriculum Project, 1977.

Reisman, F. K. *A Guide to Diagnostic Teaching of Arithmetic.* 3rd ed. Columbus, Ohio: Charles E. Merrill, 1982.

Reisman, F. K. *Teaching Mathematics: Methods and Content.* 2nd. ed. Boston: Houghton Mifflin, 1981.

Reisman, F. K., and S. H. Kauffman. *Teaching Mathematics to Children with Special Needs.* Columbus, Ohio: Charles E. Merrill, 1980.

Sattler, J. M. *Assessment of Children's Intelligence and Special Abilities.* 2nd ed. Boston: Allyn and Bacon, 1982.

Scandura, J. M. *Mathematics. Concrete Behavioral Foundations.* New York: Harper and Row, 1971.

Smedslund, J. "Symposium: Practical and Theoretical Issues in Piagetian Psychology III— Piaget's Psychology in Practice." *British Journal of Educational Psychology* 42 (1977): 1–6.

Suppes, P., and C. Ihrke. *Accelerated Learning in Elementary School Mathematics—The Fourth Year.* Technical Report #148. Stanford, Calif.: Stanford University, Institute for Mathematical Studies in the Social Sciences, 1969.

Terman, L. M. *Mental and Physical Traits of a Thousand Gifted Children, Genetic Study of Genius.* Vol. 1. Stanford, Calif.: Stanford University Press, 1925.

Ward, J. et al. *The Curriculum Integration Concept Applied in the Elementary School.* Austin, Texas: University of Texas Press, 1960.

Webster's New World Dictionary. New York: World, 1958.

Wescott, A. M., and J. A. A. Smith. *Creative Teaching of Mathematics in the Elementary School.* Boston: Allyn and Bacon, 1967.

Whitehead, A. N. *The Aims of Education.* New York: Mentor Books, 1929.

Youngpeter, J. M., and D. P. Davan. *Meter.* Stevensville, Mich.: Educational Service, 1975.

6

Science

Carolyn M. Callahan

In a society increasingly characterized by dependence on science and technology, educators of gifted children face the challenges that plague science educators in general, but which become magnified in light of the roles the gifted are expected to assume in the advancement, understanding, management, and utilization of scientific knowledge. Educators have tried to meet these challenges by focusing on how best to develop and implement curricula that will maximize understanding of scientific knowledge, give students an appreciation of the scientific process, and actively engage students in the search for further knowledge. Heavily funded research and development efforts during the 1960s resulted in many curricular models, materials, and training packages for use in elementary and secondary science programs, and in modification of many science textbooks. Further, teacher education programs and methods textbooks have adopted a process orientation to science instruction (Harbeck and Marcuccio, 1978). Yet, a recent study by the National Science Foundation (1980) described a disappointing impact of these efforts on actual science instruction. Much of science teaching still relied heavily on didactic approaches to instruction and failed to incorporate the strategies and concepts of the curriculum development efforts into classroom practice. The current back-to-basics movement, which tends to focus on reading, writing, and arithmetic, and which directs funds to curriculum in those areas, is detrimental to other areas, especially those that require specialized materials, equipment, and inservice training (Harbeck & Marcuccio, 1978). Unfortunately, science falls into this category.

All children stand to lose from the lack of opportunity to develop an understanding and appreciation of the process of science, but gifted children will exhibit a wider gap between potential and actual achievement unless steps are taken to adopt process approaches to curriculum and modify the curriculum according to the specialized needs of this exceptional population.

Science for the Gifted

To discuss the need for modifying science programs to meet the needs of the gifted, one must first consider the population to be served. As in any other subject area, it is important in science to consider both those of higher general intellectual ability and those who have specific academic abilities. Selecting the appropriate educational program depends upon the type of giftedness to be served.

Students of High Intellectual Ability

The primary approach to defining and identifying the gifted has focused on the search for children of high general intellectual ability: those who score high on an intelligence test (Gallagher, 1975; Renzulli, 1979). This definition and identification process led to the identification of children who had characteristics such as a large vocabulary, an exceptional memory, a large store of information, a good sense of humor, good verbal facility, and rational problem-solving ability (Gallagher, 1975). Even though this narrow definition of giftedness, based solely on general intellectual ability, has given way to more expanded definitions, such as that incorporated in P.L.

183

95–561 (Section 902),[1] many school districts still identify and place children according to the one criterion, and expect a differential curriculum across subject matter will be sufficient for these children.

Students With Specific Academic Ability

More expanded definitions of giftedness often include reference to a population of children with specific academic aptitudes, that is, special achievement and/or special abilities in only one or two specific discipline areas. Identification of children with specific aptitudes has received impetus from two divergent approaches to gifted education. The first movement that drew attention to the need to identify the gifted child with a specific academic ability was the Johns Hopkins Study of Mathematically Precocious Youth (1974). This program showed the need to identify children with outstanding potential in mathematics and to provide them with rapid acceleration. The parallel movement in science would be to identify children with outstanding potential in science and provide a rapidly accelerated science program. This approach to the definition of specific aptitude in science would seek to identify children who can absorb scientific information and grasp complex concepts usually taught to older children.

Students with specific ability in science may or may not also have high general intellectual ability. The relationship between these two groups is best considered intersecting sets.

Renzulli (1979) provides an alternative approach to identifying students with specific academic abilities. He abstracted the characteristics of gifted adults to construct a definition based on the identified clusters of traits. This definition has been labeled the "three-ring" definition of giftedness.

The literature describing gifted adults (for example, Terman and Oden, 1947; Terman, 1954; Roe, 1952) strongly suggests that the achievement of giftedness in adults is a function of a combination of factors rather than simply a function of a high IQ. Brandwein (1958) suggested that besides genetic factors, at least two other factors are necessary for developing high ability in science: *activating* and *predisposing* factors. Activating factors are those associated with an inspirational teacher (which we will consider later); predisposing factors are divided into two clusters of traits labeled *persistence* and *questing*. Persistence is characterized by "a marked willingness to spend time, beyond the ordinary schedule on a given task. A willingness to withstand discomfort. A willingness to face failure."[2] Questing is that trait which causes an individual to seek more precise and accurate explanations of phenomena; it is a discontent with current explanations (or lack of explanations) for the way the world works. According to Brandwein, all these factors are necessary for

---

[1] For the purposes of this part, the term 'gifted and talented children' means children and, whenever applicable, youth, who are identified at the preschool, elementary, or secondary level as possessing demonstrated or potential abilities that give evidence of high performance capability in areas such as intellectual, creative, specific academic, or leadership ability, or in the performing and visual arts, and who by reason thereof, require services or activities not ordinarily provided by the school. (Sec. 902)

[2] P. F. Brandwein, *The Gifted as Future Scientist* (Ventura, Calif.: Ventura County Superintendent of Schools, 1981), p. 10.

developing high ability in science; no one factor is sufficient in itself. LaSalle (1977) would argue that the persistence factor should weigh most heavily in the combination.

In the most exhaustive study of the personality and intellect of successful scientists, Roe (1952) found the most striking characteristic to be a high IQ, but she also identified personality characteristics that coincided with those discussed by Brandwein and reported by the National Science Foundation (LaSalle, 1977). Among these are:

- A general need for independence, autonomy, and personal mastery of the environment
- Attraction to facts such as might appear mutually contradictory and delight in finding a way to reconcile them
- A precocious self-confidence about solving intellectual problems

Renzulli (1979) examined this literature along with extensive studies of giftedness across many disciplines, and concluded that giftedness is characterized by interaction among three traits: above average ability, creativity, and task commitment.

In using the term "above average ability" to describe the first component of his definition, Renzulli notes that ineffectiveness of intelligence test scores (above intermediate score levels) in predicting individual success in creative/productive endeavors. He calls for a definition that recognizes that individuals who score slightly lower on standardized tests of general mathematical ability, specific aptitude, or achievement, may well be the more likely to be recognized as gifted adults. In identifying the gifted, therefore, we should look at students who have above average, but not necessarily the highest scores, on tests of general intellectual ability, specific aptitude, or achievement. Success in any field of endeavor, however, depends on the presence of the other two factors.

The second factor, creativity, is difficult to define (Renzulli, 1979). By creativity, Renzulli does *not* mean earning high scores on tests of divergent productive or ideational fluency, but rather the ability to meet the criteria for creative performance within specific performance areas as established by the persons accomplished in that area. Further judgments of creativity should be made by persons qualified to judge those areas on the basis of performance or products. A prototype would be scientists' judging science fair projects on the basis of their originality of thought and freshness of approach.

Finally, an individual must also exhibit task commitment, "a refined or focused form of motivation . . . energy brought to bear on a particular problem (task) or specific performance area. One might metaphorically define the role played by this cluster of traits as the psychological 'yeast' that activates the manifestation of creative productivity" (Renzulli, 1979, p. 17).

The interaction of these three clusters of traits is crucial to the final definition. First, each cluster is equally important in the constitution of the "gifted" person; that is, a person with high aptitude in math but little creativity or task commitment in that area is unlikely to develop into a "gifted mathematician." Similarly, a child with great task commitment and interest in science but with little aptitude or creativity is unlikely to be a "gifted scientist." Second, the three traits must be brought to bear on some

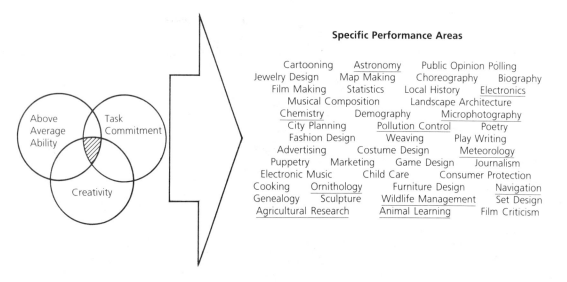

General Performance Areas

Mathematics   Visual Arts   Physical Sciences
Philosophy   Social Sciences   Law   Religion
Language Arts   Music   Life Sciences   Movement Arts

Specific Performance Areas

Cartooning   Astronomy   Public Opinion Polling
Jewelry Design   Map Making   Choreography   Biography
Film Making   Statistics   Local History   Electronics
Musical Composition   Landscape Architecture
Chemistry   Demography   Microphotography
City Planning   Pollution Control   Poetry
Fashion Design   Weaving   Play Writing
Advertising   Costume Design   Meteorology
Puppetry   Marketing   Game Design   Journalism
Electronic Music   Child Care   Consumer Protection
Cooking   Ornithology   Furniture Design   Navigation
Genealogy   Sculpture   Wildlife Management   Set Design
Agricultural Research   Animal Learning   Film Criticism

Above Average Ability   Task Commitment   Creativity

Figure 6–1 GRAPHIC REPRESENTATION OF THE DEFINITION OF GIFTEDNESS

potentially valuable area of human performance—that is, for giftedness to manifest itself and be recognized, the individual must bring the traits to bear in specific performance areas. Figure 6-1 is a schematic representation of the definition, with examples from the area of science underlined for emphasis.

Implications For Curriculum Development

Referring to the literature's figural representations of the definitions of giftedness, we see in Figure 6–2 that we need to serve three groups through differentiated science programs. Despite long-standing debates over who is "truly gifted," there remains the fact that the needs of all three of these groups are sadly neglected in most science programs, particularly at the elementary and middle school levels.

Characteristically, students who fall into the category of exceptional general intellectual ability will learn the concepts of the science curriculum more rapidly than the average child; the same is true of the child with exceptional specific aptitude in

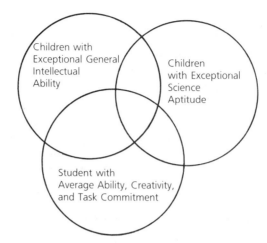

Figure 6-2   THE "THREE-RING" DEFINITION OF GIFTEDNESS

science or unusually high achievement areas in science. These children tend to be bored by instruction geared to teach already familiar concepts or to reinforce concepts for slower students. Thus, the science teacher must look for alternative enrichment activities or acceleration to meet these children's needs. (It cannot be assumed that they will be interested in or motivated to pursue additional work in these areas.)

Children with exceptional general intellectual ability should have opportunities for enrichment or acceleration activities in science.

Enrichment or acceleration activities can take the form of presentation of new areas for exploration at the same difficulty level (enrichment), presentation of more in-depth study of the same topical area (enrichment), or movement to more advanced units that would normally be taught later in the year or at another grade level. On the other hand, Renzulli (1977) presents a problem-oriented curriculum for the child who meets his criteria for giftedness.

Essential Concepts

The primary concern in planning instruction for the gifted revolves around setting objectives that will address their needs and choosing activities that will help the children achieve those objectives. Setting appropriate objectives depends on a number of variables: (1) what is in the regular science curriculum; (2) the children's intellectual and developmental levels; (3) what programming and curricular options are available and acceptable to the school community; and (4) the children's levels of interest and motivation.

Developmental Considerations

A common error about the gifted child is the assumption that because she has an extraordinary IQ and/or achievement score in science, she is also at a higher cognitive level, as described by Piaget. The literature does not support this assumption, and therefore, it is inappropriate to plan science lessons that presume a young gifted child has achieved the formal operational stage of reasoning ability. We are often misled into making these assumptions about gifted children by their ability to recall complex relationships and information about science phenomena. For example, gifted children often recite complicated explanations of weather phenomena that they have heard on television or read in the newspaper. It is natural for the listener to be impressed by the vocabulary, sentence structure, and sophistication of ideas, but probing the actual understanding of the phenomena may or may not yield a solid base of comprehension.

The implications of these developmental concerns are fourfold.

1 The teacher must assess the developmental level of the gifted children in the class. Children who have not yet mastered formal logical reasoning will need concrete examples and manipulatives to reach full understanding of the concepts.

2 Do not forget the possibility of horizontal and vertical décollage which result in differential achievements of cognitive levels, as described by Piaget, depending on the area considered.

3 Even though gifted children may not be at a more advanced stage developmentally, their ability to process larger amounts of information and rapidly manipulate symbols suggest that they will use their inquiry and discovery approaches quickly and efficiently, and less structure will be necessary, since the gifted create their own efficient structures for information processing (Koran & Lehman, 1981). They will also not need as many examples before they make generalizations; they will not need many repetitions to reinforce concepts; and they will be capable of attaining more complex concepts and understanding more complex relationships.

4   Simple acceleration or grade skipping will cause difficulty if the instructional techniques and materials do not take into account these developmental concerns. Gifted students may be astute at learning to state principles and concepts at a knowledge level (because of their extraordinary memory ability), but may not gain a real understanding of the discipline.

Principles of a Differentiated Curriculum for the Gifted

To help teachers develop curricula for the gifted, the National/State Leadership Training Institute on the Gifted and Talented brought together leaders in the field of education of the gifted to establish principles of curriculum development (Kaplan, 1979). They drew up thirteen rules for selecting content and activities:

- Present content that is related to broad-based issues, themes, or problems
- Integrate multiple disciplines into the area of study
- Present comprehensive, related, and mutually reinforcing experiences within an area of study
- Allow for the in-depth learning of a self-selected topic within the area of study
- Develop independent or self-directed study skills
- Develop productive, complex, abstract, and/or higher level thinking skills
- Focus on open-ended tasks
- Develop research skills and methods
- Integrate basic skills and higher level thinking skills into the curriculum
- Encourage the development of products that challenge existing ideas and produce "new" ideas
- Encourage the development of products that use new techniques, materials, and forms
- Encourage the development of self-understanding, i.e., recognizing and using one's abilities, becoming self-directed, appreciating likenesses and differences between oneself and others
- Evaluate student outcomes by using appropriate and specific criteria through self-appraisal, criterion referenced and/or standardized instruments[3]

Broad-Based Themes

Science activities for the gifted should pertain to generic or comprehensive topics. Rather than focusing on the specific examples of a food chain, for example, emphasis should be on ecological systems, then on the general concept of systems and the impact on a system of altering or removing one of its components. Or, instead of simply introducing insects and their characteristics, the teacher might consider introducing the question of the impact on the environment of new components, the removal of existing components, or the alteration of components. For example, the impact of the appearance of the Mediterranean fruit fly in California might be used to begin the discussion.

---

[3]S. N. Kaplan, *Inservice Training Manual: Activities for Developing Curriculum for the Gifted and Talented* (Ventura, Calif.: Ventura County Superintendent of Schools).

Multidisciplinary Approach

Introducing broad-based issues, themes, or problems allows for integration of other disciplines into the study of science. Science educators, and educators in general, have called for interdisciplinary study for many years, but the prevailing approach has been to teach science as distinct and separate from other disciplines. For the gifted child who can easily recognize the relationships among disciplines and the problems of those relationships, it is extremely important for the teacher to seek ways of tying science to all disciplines: math, social studies, art, music, physical education. Science study provides an excellent takeoff point for a multidisciplinary approach to curriculum study. Consider that advances in scientific knowledge and technology have implications for all disciplines. As with the example of the Mediterranean fruit fly, the teacher can easily expand a discussion of the insect to include ecological systems and systems in general; the implications of decisions by political leaders to spray or not to spray, to lead to a discussion of political systems; the economic impact, to lead to discussions of economic systems; and mathematics discussions of the notion of the geometrical increase in the fruit fly population. According to the children's level, you can introduce notions of estimating the number of fruit flies in a whole area by sampling only a limited area. Of course, the "biological science" discussion can be expanded to the physical sciences at the high school level by introducing the chemistry of insecticides, or possibly into meteorology by discussing the ideal conditions for spraying and how to predict when those conditions will exist.

Mutually Reinforcing Experiences

As with all curricula, a curriculum for the gifted should be more than a series of unrelated experiences dependent on chance occurrences, random availability of films, or unrelated "interesting" or "fun" activities demonstrated at conferences or included in packages of instructional materials. Rather, it should reflect comprehensive

Figure 6–3 TWO TEACHERS' LESSON PLAN BOOKS

planning of related activities that build on and reinforce previous learnings. Consider the contrast between the lesson descriptions in the two teacher's planning books in Figure 6–3.

In-depth Learning Within A Self-Selected Topic

A crucial aspect of a well-developed program for gifted students—especially those who have specific aptitudes in science or who meet Renzulli's three-ring criteria—is the opportunity for a student to pursue a topic of his choice in depth. Often this principle translates into "Go to the library, read about _____, and write a report." This unfocused and unmotivating assignment is unlikely to inspire gifted children. Instead, the teacher should help the child explore areas that interest him, and help him focus on a topic in which he can make discoveries. So, instead of assigning "Insects" as a study topic and having one child study wasps, another, ants, and a third, mosquitoes, the teacher might suggest broad topics such as "Genetic Engineering" or "Voyager II and the Rings of Saturn."

Developing Independent or Self-Study Skills

Allowing in-depth study of a self-selected topic requires the students' ability to pursue knowledge independently and to use self-study skills. Not all gifted children will necessarily have these skills, especially in light of the highly structured nature of science instruction which depends on textbook information and/or highly directive laboratory exercises. It will thus be necessary in many cases to help students develop these skills through highly structured contract systems and initially close monitoring. To help students structure their independent study, one might use a contract such as that in Figure 6–4.

Figure 6–4   AN INDEPENDENT STUDY CONTRACT

Name: _____

General Area of Study: _____

Specific Question(s) to be Answered or Hypothesis to be Tested: _____
_____

First Steps or Initial Research Strategies to be Tried: _____
_____

Resources/Materials Needed: _____
_____

Anticipated Product: _____
_____

How This Product Should be Evaluated: _____
_____

Anticipated Date of Completion: _____

Open-ended Tasks

One characteristic of gifted children is their ability to go beyond the assigned task, to see new questions and new relationships, and to seek more sophisticated information. Activities should allow each student to maximize her potential by taking a concept or idea as far as possible. The following example illustrates the introduction of an open-ended unit of study.

> In London, Ontario, Mr. Hendricks's fourth-grade students enter their classroom after lunch to find an array of glasses, bottles, bells, wooden boxes of different sizes (with holes in them), tuning forks, xylophones, and small wooden flutes. These objects are spread about the room, and the students spend a few minutes playing with them, creating a most horrendous sound, while Mr. Hendricks watches.
>
> After a few minutes they begin to settle down and one of them asks, "What's going on here, Mr. Hendricks? It looks like you've turned the place into an orchestra."
>
> "Well, in a way," he smiles. "Actually, for the next few weeks this is going to be our sound laboratory." He moves across the room and picks up an instrument made of wood and wires and plucks one of the wires. At the same time he uses a spoon to strike a soft drink bottle on the desk next to him. "Do you notice anything about these sounds?" he asks, and repeats his plucking and striking.
>
> "Hey," says one of the girls, "they sound the same, but different."
>
> "Do it again," suggests one of the students, and Mr. Hendricks obliges. Soon all of the students have noticed that the sound is at the same pitch or level.
>
> "Your problem," explains Mr. Hendricks, "is to find out what makes sound vary and to describe that variation. Given the limitations of the devices we have in this room, I want you to organize yourself to conduct some experiments and present me with sets of principles that you think describe the variations. When you're finished, I want you to be able to describe to me how you would design an instrument with certain capabilities. I'll tell you what I want the instrument to be able to do and you can tell me how to make it. Then we'll begin to test your ideas. Now, I think we ought to organize ourselves into groups and decide how we're going to go about this. Does anybody have any ideas?"
>
> "Well," Sally ventures, "I've noticed that the things are made out of five different kinds of materials. Maybe we could get into five groups, and each group would experiment with those for awhile. Then we could share what we've learned and trade sound and check out the thinking of the other groups. After that we could decide what to do next."
>
> Someone joins in with another suggestion, and the class spends the next half hour planning how the study will begin.[4]

A student in this classroom will obviously be trying to deduce some fundamental principles of sound. At the same time, opportunities for students to accumulate deeper information, to construct original experiments, and to explore related areas in the physical sciences are also clearly available at the students' discretion.

Developing Complex or Higher Level Thinking Skills and Research Skills and Methods

Science programs for the gifted have adopted many of the curriculum materials developed for regular classroom use during the 1960s. These programs had been abandoned or ignored or judged "too difficult" for the regular classroom, but turned

---

[4]From B. Joyce and M. Weil, *Models of Teaching*, 2nd ed. (Englewood Cliffs, N.J.: Prentice-Hall, 1980), pp. 130–31. This scenario is based on the Biological Science Inquiry Model.

out to be highly appropriate for gifted children. For example, Hammill (1979) reports on use of the *Elementary Science Study* materials in the elementary science program in Prince George's County, Maryland; Woolever (1979) notes the usefulness of *Science—A Process Approach* in planning elementary curricula for the gifted; and Kearney (1979) discusses the value of *Science Curriculum Improvement Study* materials. The goals of these programs closely parallel the principles of gifted education: development of higher level thinking and research skills and familiarity with scientific methodologies. With regard to high school curricula, Karplus notes:

> As might be expected, the gifted, scientifically oriented, high school student has derived the greatest benefit from the courses, because they provide a much more appropriate challenge for him than did traditional courses. (1969, p. 37)

The science programs and methods textbooks that advocate a process approach identify concepts and skill objectives almost identical to those in curriculum guides for gifted students. Cain and Evans (1979), for example, consider this list of skills the core of "sciencing" for the elementary student:

1 Observing
2 Classifying
3 Measuring
4 Using spatial relations
5 Communicating
6 Predicting
7 Inferring
8 Integrated processes (defining operationally, formulating hypotheses, interpreting data, controlling variables, and experimenting) (Cain and Evans, 1979, p. 7)

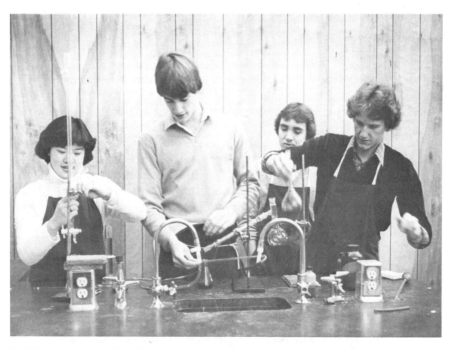

It is important to allow gifted students to work as "practicing scientists."

By now you should recognize the importance of allowing gifted students to become "practicing scientists." Their experiences should lead them to a point at which they can question the "factual statements" of their science texts, pose new questions, and construct experiments to test their ideas.

The teacher should introduce gifted students to alternative ways of communicating their learnings, discoveries, and accomplishments. Students might produce reports in the format the scientist uses to communicate research findings, such as the format of the leading professional journals, or produce demonstrations, create and construct audiovisual presentations, participate in debates on controversial scientific issues, or give oral presentations such as those one might see at a professional meeting. Teachers should not require written reports based on encyclopedia articles or "All About . . . " books that will be both boring to write and boring to read.

Self-Understanding   A gifted child often has difficulty understanding the degrees of likeness and difference between herself and other children. Through the study of growth and individual differences in biology, the teacher has the ideal opportunity to generate discussions that will help the gifted child understand these likenesses and differences.

Appreciation of differences is often particularly difficult for the gifted child at the middle school level, when students face considerable peer pressure to conform. The wish to conform and the desire for acceptance may cause them to hide their abilities and refuse to be identified as exceptional, and recognition may embarrass them. These factors have particularly negative implications for females in science and math (Callahan, 1980). Many gifted females accept cultural stereotypes and abandon their interest in science (Fox, 1975). Instead, they need exposure to appropriate female role models from the science fields.

Evaluation

Evaluation plays an important role in curriculum planning, and the ways we evaluate reflect our *true* values and goals for gifted students. To encourage independent, self-directed study and then grade according to scores on multiple-choice exams is contradictory; it tells students that we really value the ability to learn a common core of knowledge rather than the degree to which they challenge ideas, produce new products, or use new techniques. Further, it is not only the teacher who should evaluate a student's work; the student should participate as well. Self-evaluation skills are crucial to the creative scientist. Evaluation of student outcomes should: (1) be based on appropriate and specific criteria, jointly established by teacher and student; (2) emphasize student self-appraisal; (3) use criterion-referenced and/or standardized test instruments only when appropriate; and (4) use alternative assessment strategies, such as checklists, rating scales, and contracts, whenever they are more appropriate.

Basic Concepts and Objectives for the Gifted

The *basic* organizing concepts for science for the gifted are:
- The process of formulating scientific questions
- Methods of scientific inquiry

- The structures of the disciplines of science
- The interrelationships between the sciences and other disciplines
- The history of science
- The use of intuition in science
- The use of inductive and deductive reasoning in scientific problem solving
- The language of science
- Patterns in science

These principles suggest implicit goals. If we translate the principles into objective terms and apply them specifically to the sciences, we might come up with a list like this:

1   The student will be able to select a topic for independent study and focus that topic into a manageable study.
2   The student will use self-directed study skills in independent study and/or experimental research.
3   The student will develop productive (creative), complex, abstract, and/or higher level thinking skills and apply them to science problems.
4   The student will develop the research skills and methods of the sciences.
5   The student will be able to apply both basic skills and knowledge and the higher level thinking skills to problem solving.
6   The students will challenge existing ideas in science.
7   The students will produce "new" knowledge and ideas in science.
8   The students will create products that reflect the use of new techniques, materials, and forms.
9   The students will develop self-understanding.

These general statements reflect primarily cognitive goals, although goals for the gifted must extend to affective and psychomotor skills. Affective goals are necessary if we expect these individuals to become intelligent citizens in a technological world or creative producers in the sciences. Affective goals include a respect for scientific processes, an appreciation of the scientific literature, and questioning of scientific "fact." Psychomotor goals should be based on developing skills for using the equipment necessary for scientific investigations.

Many of these goals may appear to be those of the regular science curriculum; however, although these goals often appear in the science literature, the teacher often does not translate them into instructional plans. Also, although the regular curriculum seeks to have students understand the scientific process by leading them through the scientific process in laboratory demonstrations, there are subtle but important differences in the kinds of classroom activities developed for the gifted. The first difference has to do with area of experimentation. Process approaches for the regular classroom emphasize discovery, with materials and kits for guiding teacher and child through a set of activities and questions leading to a predetermined conclusion that illustrates a fundamental concept. The skills taught through this process are valuable to all children and are likely to result in a more thorough understanding of the concepts and techniques of scientific inquiry. But the procedures fail to allow for the development of two other, more fundamental skills and fail to round out the development of the gifted/creative scientist. The first of these is the skill of "question asking" or "problem focusing" (Gallagher, 1975; Goetzels, 1980). The predetermined structure of the activities fails to give the student practice in identifying scientific questions of merit; predetermined laboratory exercises or discussion patterns often deteriorate into a game of twenty questions, and gifted students quickly learn that they can find the "right" answers by reading a few pages ahead in the textbook or checking in another text.

The second skill the traditional approach overlooks is that of creating and implementing scientific experiments. The student who is led through only predetermined laboratory experiences will not have practice in the creative problem solving skills necessary to solve science problems.[5] Thus, objectives that differentiate a science program for the gifted are those that help the student reach the point of becoming an investigator of new scientific questions.

Unfortunately, the predetermined activities do not fall into either of the categories of curriculum differentiation models recommended for the gifted: acceleration and enrichment. Within each category, a number of models have received considerable attention and application.

Acceleration and/or Enrichment

Shall we provide enrichment activities for gifted children or shall we develop an acceleration program to meet their needs? This frequently asked question oversimplifies the issues involved. First, the question of acceleration vs. enrichment suggests a simple matter of administrative arrangements. That is, do children stay at the same grade level or do they skip grades? This conception represents only the narrowest application of acceleration. Second, the dichotomy between acceleration and enrichment is in many ways artificial. In science, it is nearly impossible to provide meaningful enrichment and involve students in in-depth study of new areas without at some point offering concepts and skills normally taught in later years. On the other hand, it is nearly impossible to provide a purely accelerated program, until students have reached the stage of formal operations, because of developmental issues. The formal, abstract thinking required in upper-level science programs may be beyond the reach of many gifted children. Besides the concern with intellectual development, there is considerable debate over the social implications of acceleration programs that place children with groups of older students.

Acceleration:

Although acceleration has been regarded as an administrative arrangement, it is really an important *curricular* option for the gifted. Briefly, acceleration is any option that provides for delivery of more advanced content to younger students. The most frequent acceleration alternatives are early admission to school, grade-skipping, telescoping, and early admission to college.

One way to differentiate curriculum is to group students for more rapid progression through the science curriculum. Abeles (1977) suggests the arrangement

---

[5]This is not to imply that students do not need instruction in basic laboratory skills and techniques, but rather that these skills can be learned through a variety of approaches—teacher-structured and student-structured.

Table 6-1 AVERAGE AND ACCELERATED SCIENCE PROGRAMS

Grade Level	Average Program	Accelerated Program
7	Life Science	Life and Physical Science
8	Physical Science	Earth Science
9	Earth Science	Biology
10	Biology	Chemistry
11	Chemistry	Physics
12	Physics	Advanced Course (e.g. Astronomy, Geology, Human Physiology, or Advanced Placement in Physics, Chemistry or Biology)

shown in Table 6–1 as one possible way of telescoping through the junior/senior high school years. It would be possible to further accelerate the curriculum to include advanced placement courses earlier, or instead of the regular courses for some students.

Issues and Problems of Acceleration in the Sciences

There are many advantages to acceleration techniques, but some problems with implementation in the sciences. The first drawback lies in many elementary and middle school teachers' lack of training in the sciences, particularly the physical sciences. If telescoping is to be handled within the regular classroom, the teacher must become familiar with science concepts taught at several succeeding levels of the school program. Second, acceleration depends on a strong commitment to provide this option from kindergarten through twelfth grade. As Morgan et al. (1980) note, many students who have been accelerated in elementary and/or middle school go on to a very traditional high school program where they are presented with the same concepts and skills they have already mastered at lower levels.

From our discussion of the principles of a differentiated curriculum, it is apparent that simple acceleration in science as it is currently taught (NSF, 1980) fails to incorporate activities that meet these standards. Science tends to remain compartmentalized at the elementary school level and departmentalized at the secondary school level, thus inhibiting the likelihood that a pure acceleration approach will address broad-based issues, themes, and problems, or integrate other disciplines with science. Rapid progression through a structured curriculum also tends to inhibit the opportunity for in-depth study of a self-selected science topic as well as the development of independent and self-directed study skills. Topics and activities tend to be teacher-selected and directed. Because much of science instruction remains textbook- and knowledge/content-oriented (NSF, 1980), there will also be little opportunity to develop complex, abstract, and/or higher-level thinking skills or to encounter open-ended tasks where the student can use creativity. Logically, if higher-level thinking skills are not introduced, it is not feasible to integrate them with basic skills. Finally, acceleration does not automatically lead to development of products that challenge existing ideas and produce "new" ideas. Acceleration usually focuses on attaining current knowledge of content and process.

Enrichment

Enrichment programs for the gifted are more common than acceleration programs. These programs attempt to provide activities that introduce concepts and skills not ordinarily encountered in the regular curriculum. Several models of enrichment curricula have been used for planning activities for the gifted, among which are Bloom's *Taxonomy of Educational Objectives: Cognitive Domain* (Bloom et al., 1956); Guilford's Structure of the Intellect Model (Guilford, 1968); Williams's Model (1969); and the Enrichment Triad Model (Renzulli, 1977).[6]

Essentially, Bloom's Taxonomy was developed as a means of classifying test questions. It was then translated into a guide to teachers for formulating objectives and questions for classroom discussions and tests that would draw on many thinking skills, rather than simply memory or knowledge.[7] While fundamental knowledge of the discipline and its structure is important, the abilities to understand the information, apply the knowledge and skills, analyze scientific concepts and ideas and see relationships among them, combine ideas in new ways, create new approaches to scientific study, and make judgments about the value of scientific methods, scientific studies, and theory are also crucial to the scientist's development.

Unfortunately, the Taxonomy falls short as a curriculum model (as it has been popularly applied) because (1) it does not give guidance in selecting appropriate content for study; (2) it does not suggest a plan for sequencing content; and (3) it does not represent discrete thinking processes that can be taught one at a time. Few professionals in science would suggest that they can separate each of these levels in their actual thinking processes. The tendency has been to compartmentalize thinking skills much as we compartmentalize the disciplines, creating artificial or trite questions and activities.

Higher level thinking skills form the objectives of the new science programs, such as ESS and SAPA, and many materials for teaching these thinking skills in science are already available to the elementary and secondary school teacher. In an enrichment program, however, the teacher should seek to identify areas of study outside the regular curriculum to which these skills can be applied. It is impossible to state exactly which activities might constitute "enrichment" for any grade level, because "enrichment" depends upon what is "regular."

The following sample science unit represents an attempt to introduce a new area of study and apply the higher level thinking skills, without presenting unrelated activities. Most of the activities require the student to use more than simple memory skills while acquiring a broader background of scientific information. The activities also introduce multidisciplinary concepts.

---

[6]The term *curriculum* is used here as it is in the literature in education of the gifted, rather than in the stricter sense in which it might be used in the curriculum field; curriculum model refers here to any guide for establishing goals for the gifted and/or to plan activities.

[7]For further reading on developing this skill, see *Classroom Questions* by Norris M. Sanders (New York: Harper & Row, 1966).

The Pros and Cons of Space Colonization

Subject: Honors Science

Grade: 9

Goal: To provide an in-depth study of space colonization—its physical properties, its technological advancements, and its human and social implications.

Teaching Objectives:
    To provide learning experiences that will enable the students to:
- Use science concepts, process skills, and values in making everyday decisions.
- Distinguish between scientific evidence and personal opinion.
- Identify the relationship between fact and theory.
- Understand the interrelationships among science, technology, and other facets of society, including social and economic development.
- Recognize the limitations as well as the usefulness of science and technology in advancing human welfare.
- Recognize that science cannot be divorced from the critical realities of contemporary life and society.
- Equate the cost of scientific and technological advancement within the context of the future benefits to society.

Teaching Strategies:
    This is an eight-week unit designed to provide an opportunity for students to assess the human and economic implications as well as the technical feasibility of space settlements.
    The basic reference tool for building background information is the 185-page National Aeronautics and Space Administration (NASA) report *Space Settlements: A Design Study* (Washington, D.C.: 1977). This report grew out of a ten-week program in engineering systems design held at Stanford University and the Ames Research Center of NASA. The purpose of this program was to construct a picture of how people might permanently sustain life in space on a large scale, and then to answer the question "Is it feasible to do so?"
    Students will study the report and then make a value judgment as to the social and scientific-technological feasibility of space colonization.

Teaching Procedure
    I. Student orientation to and overview of the unit.
        The class is introduced to the NASA report *Space Settlements: A Design Study*
        The foreword by James C. Fletcher (Oct. 1, 1976), NASA administrator, is read and discussed.[8]
        The class will function as a group of scientists and engineers reviewing and evaluating the report of the Stanford-Ames Research Center symposium.
        After intensive study of the evidence, the class will then debate the pros and cons of space colonization.

---

[8]National Aeronautics and Space Administration, *Space Settlements: A Design Study* (Washington, D.C.: NASA, 1977), p. v.

II. Topics to explore in class and pursue as independent research include:
Colonization of space
    The overall system
    Design goals
    The history of an idea
Physical properties of space
    The topography of space
    Solar radiation
    Matter in space
    Meteoroids and space habitats
    Ionizing radiation in space
Human needs in space
    Weightlessness
    Atmosphere
    Food and water
    Combined environmental stress
    Environmental design to reduce stress
    Small size and isolation
    Design criteria
    Psychological and cultural considerations
    Space requirements of various community activities
Choosing among alternatives
    The shape of the habitat
    Shielding
    What if criteria change?
    Fabrication techniques
    The people in the colony
    Life support
    Satellite solar power stations
    Where the colony should be located
    Mining, transport, and processing in space
    The transport system
    Material properties for design
    Parameters of habitability
    Mass as a measure of structural cost
View of the future
    Benefits not related to energy
    Research in deep space
    Rocket engines for deep space
    Transport
    Asteroidal resources
    New methods of construction
    Habitat design
    Automation and productivity
    Limits to growth
    Some economic considerations
Recommendations and conclusions
    Recommendations for research and development in critical subsystems
    Recommendations for space ventures
    Conclusions

III. The students prepare to debate the pros and cons of space colonization in the immediate future by considering the following:

Isaac Asimov, writing in *National Geographic* (July 1976) stated that "We can build space colonies . . . in the near future (which) would fulfill functions that are now fulfilled by cities on the surface of the earth."

T. A. Heppenheimer, in his book *Colonies in Space* (Stackpole), states:
Colonies in space is the next giant step for mankind, evolutionary in its impact—thousands of people living and working in attractive, earthlike space communities and eventually solving the world's energy problems. This is not fantasy, not just a vague outline of future possibilities.

Thousands of prominent individuals—scientists, industrialists, writers and editors, members of Congress—are now aware of this all-but-inevitable exciting human reality that can start becoming fact before the end of the twentieth century.

Space is mankind's new frontier. Serious and careful studies have shown that large space colonies can be built soon.

Ray Bradbury, in the introduction to *Colonies in Space*, attempts to discredit the short-sightedness of those who question spending billions on space colonization so long as poverty and want torture and enslave millions here on earth.

The U.S. Congress is vested by the U.S. Constitution with the power "to lay and collect taxes, duties, imposts and excises, to pay the debts and provide for the common defense and general welfare." In establishing the hierarchy of need, Congress must make value judgments. The question must be asked, in the light of the Constitution, which needs (defense, social, economic, etc.) are of the greatest import. On what bases should value judgments be made? The complexity of today's society precludes simplistic answers.

An informed citizen who is functionally literate must be competent to relate the lessons of history to the human quest for understanding and for solving contemporary problems. For example:
Excessive taxation was a contributing factor to the decline and eventual fall of the Roman Empire.
Excessive taxation was a contributing factor in precipitating the American Revolution.
Excessive taxation—property tax collection per person increased 111 percent in the ten-year period 1966-1976—has led to a nationwide taxpayers' revolt with the first shot being fired in California on June 6, 1978, when the California voters, by a two-to-one margin, amended the state constitution to slash property taxes by 57 percent and to erect high barriers against major increases in state and local levies for years to come.

Following the revolt of the California voters on June 6, 1978, President Carter (*U.S. News & World Report*, June 19, 1978) stated: "The people of California have reflected a strong national dissatisfaction with taxes that unfairly burden middle-income taxpayers and demonstrate their impatience with the steadily increasing cost of government."

In the light of the evidence from the past, namely, that governments topple when taxes become oppressive, and in the light of contemporary evidence of taxpayer revolt, is it logical to "buy" Heppenheimer's prediction that space colonization will be subsidized by tax dollars before the end of the twentieth century? (Clendening & Davies, 1980, pp. 281, 283–285).

Guilford's Structure-of-the-Intellect

Perhaps the most important contribution of the Structure of the Intellect model is its emphasis on developing the young scientist's creativity. Developing creativity is a goal for all children, but it is an integral component of scientific inquiry. The following activities for primary age students are based on the Structure of Intellect model.

Unit Plan: Rocks and Minerals

Purpose: To develop a knowledge of and an understanding of one of classificatory systems in science, develop creative thinking skills, and develop observation skills

Rationale: Many children naturally begin their own "rock collections" when they pick up "pretty" rocks from their yards, the beach, other vacations, etc. They will thus be likely to have something of their own to contribute to the study or can easily find specimens to contribute.

Vocabulary

rock
mineral
hardness
sedimentary
igneous

Activities

Day One: Take the children on a walking tour looking for

1 Different kinds of rocks (cognition). (Have the children collect specimens as they walk.)
2 Different uses of rocks and minerals (cognition). Have children bring rock collections.

Day Two: Display the children's rocks on a table in front of the room. In small groups ask the children to come up with as many different ways as they can to group the rocks. Give color as an example. (divergent production)

Introduce the concept of hardness by showing the children that one rock will scratch a second rock but not vice versa.

Explain to the children that scientists use this technique to classify rocks. Ask them if they can guess the name of the hardest rock. Ask children to brainstorm all the ways that they can think of to use a rock. (divergent production)

Day Three: Review the concept of hardness (memory). Ask the children to develop a plan for arranging their rock collection from softest to hardest (convergent production and evaluation). This task will give practice in hypothesizing, observing, collecting data, and drawing conclusions.

Day Four: One of the categories which probably emerged in the classification activity was classification by feel or shiny vs. dull. Use this as an introduction to observing type of rock as categorized by origin (sedimentary vs. igneous). All children to discuss possible ways that rocks might be formed. There are many good books with illustrations of this process and pictures which show how different rocks were formed. Ask the children to categorize the rocks according to origin (evaluation).

Day Five: have the children pick up their favorite rocks and sit quietly in a circle with one of these rocks in their hands with their eyes closed. Begin by asking the child to remember where they found the rock.
"Make a picture in your mind of the place where you found the rock." (Ask each child to describe that place to you.)

"Now imagine you are that rock. What does it feel like to be a rock in this place? Is it hot? Is it cool? Are you being stepped on?" (Ask each child what he/she feels like. Urge the child to elaborate on his/her description.)

"Now imagine what it was like to be picked up and moved to the classroom. How did you feel about being taken from your home? Do you want to go back or do you want to stay? Why?"

"Now imagine you are a huge piece of stone which is going to be a part of a building project. What kind of building would you like to be? (Give each child a chance to respond.) Why?"

"Now imagine you are a precious rock like a ruby or a diamond. How does that feel? What would you like to do with your life?"

Expand this exercise with *your* imagination. (divergent production)
At the conclusion of this series of activities, explore with children their individual interests in continuing to study rocks and minerals as a lead to individual study and projects.

Williams Model

Frank Williams has developed curricular materials that focus directly on the development of creativity (1969). In addition to the cognitive behaviors of fluency, flexibility, originality, and elaboration derived from the SOI model, Williams adds the affective behaviors to his set of desirable outcomes. He devised a set of teaching strategies for application across math, social studies, science, language arts, music, art, and other subjects for developing these behaviors. This model was designed for use in the regular classroom for all students, but has been adopted by many teachers of the gifted for use with this special population. The following example is one of the science activities.

To Encourage: Original Thinking

Through: Science

Using: Strategies No. 8—Organized random search
No. 10—Tolerance for ambiguity
No. 14—Evaluate situations
No. 18—Visualization skills
 The group will be asked to design a package that will protect an egg from breaking when dropped from the roof of the school.
 To carry this further, encourage students to build their designs and hold a contest to determine successful designs.

Other Enrichment Materials

There are many other ready-materials which can be used to develop the process skills discussed in Bloom's Taxonomy, the SOI model, and Williams's model. *The Almost Whole Earth Catalog of Process Oriented Enrichment Materials* (Stewart & Dean, 1980) is a compendium of these materials categorized by process skill and subject matter area.

The Enrichment Triad Model

The models described thus far have been criticized for a number of reasons. First, they are not truly curricular models, but rather learning models or models of intelligence. Second, there is no reason to believe the skills taught by means of these models are not appropriate for all children—in fact, they were generally intended for that purpose. Finally, there is some question as to how the models have been applied. Do we tend to behave as if thinking occurs in a vacuum, separate from content? Can divergent production occur without memory and cognition? One critic of these models points out that the result of their misapplication has been the creation of many disconnected activities that children consider "fun" but which do not really promote any new knowledge, thinking skills, or attitudes (Renzulli, 1977). As an alternative, Renzulli proposes a model for differentiating curriculum that he calls "The Enrichment Triad Model" (1977).

Assumptions and Goals

The type of gifted student to be served by the Enrichment Triad model is the child described by Renzulli's three-ring definition of giftedness. Thus, in science, we would serve children who exhibit the combined traits of above-average ability, creativity, and high task commitment to a scientific investigation. The child who simply learns facts and information well in science would *not* be successful in a program that uses this model, and alternative programming should be considered. Activities in this curriculum are based on student interest and learning style, rather than teacher interest or teaching style. This approach will require considerable behavioral change in many teachers. Finally, the model is product-oriented; while it considers the development of necessary knowledges and skills, its ultimate goal is to have children engage in activities that resemble as closely as possible those of professionals in the discipline—the student actually assumes the role of "producer" of knowledge rather than "consumer" of knowledge. For example, rather than simply learn what chemists have learned in their labs, students will engage in investigation that either extends the body of knowledge in chemistry to some new area of application, or in presenting that knowledge in some new way to a new audience.

Renzulli's major goal for the gifted is to help the child become an actual investigator of a real problem or topic using appropriate methods of inquiry. He incorporates that goal and his assumptions into two program objectives:

1 For the majority of time spent in the gifted programs, students will have an opportunity to pursue their own interests to whatever depth and extent they do desire; and they will be allowed to pursue these learnings in a manner that is consistent with their own preferred styles of learning. (Renzulli, 1977, p. 5)

2 The primary role of each teacher in the program for gifted and talented students will be to provide each student with assistance in (a) identifying and structuring realistic solvable problems that are consistent with the student's interests, (b) acquiring the necessary methodological resources and investigative skills that are necessary for solving these particular problems, and (c) finding appropriate outlets for student products. (Renzulli, 1977, p. 10)

Description of the Model: Preparation As we see in Figure 6–5, there is no inherent sequence to the order in which the different activities are introduced. As with all other aspects of the model, the point at which we begin depends on children's needs and interests. Further elaboration on the model as it relates to individualizing programs for the gifted (Renzulli & Smith, 1979) suggests that some preliminary assessment is important for planning subsequent activities.

In assessing a child for program planning, Renzulli and Smith suggest that one first assess the child's intellectual and achievement level to determine the areas of strength. For example, assuming that children are demonstrating above-average science achievement as shown in standardized achievement tests, grades, and/or teacher ratings, we should plan to do either formal or informal diagnosis relative to upcoming science units. The teacher may use either the diagnostic tests available in science textbook series or an informal interview to determine the degree to which students have knowledge and understanding of the concepts and skills to be introduced. The teacher can then determine which concepts or skills need to be taught and which can be assumed, and therefore, not retaught.

We thus relieve the gifted child of the boring task of relearning already mastered concepts. For example, assume that you are about to introduce an activity, Electric and Magnetic Interactions from the SCIC materials, in which students are to invent electrical models using dry cell batteries, wire, and a light bulb (SCIS, 1970).

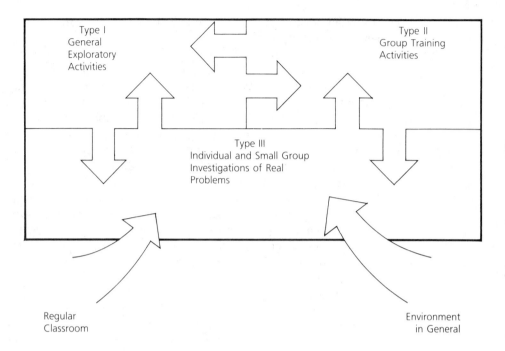

Figure 6-5 RENZULLI'S ENRICHMENT TRIAD MODEL

Many gifted children with an interest in science will have already experimented at home with these materials and will have a good understanding of the concepts. You can easily assess the child's mastery by having him complete a worksheet such as that in Figure 6-6. Students who demonstrate ability to predict outcomes should not have to complete the activities, and should be given enrichment activities instead. The time that is freed from activities that teach what the child already knows (in science or other areas) can be used for enrichment activities.

In the Enrichment Triad Model, the type of enrichment activities depends on further assessment of the child's interests and learning style. A child who has achieved in science is likely to have an interest in science phenomena; an interest inventory will help you identify specific interests. Renzulli (1977) has constructed an "Interest-A-Lyzer" to help the teacher narrow the child's interests. These are several items from the scale:

2. Pretend that someday you will be the famous author of a well-known book. What type of book will it be (History, Science, Poetry, Fiction, Fashion, etc.) and what will the book be about?
   Type of Book _____
   The book will be about _____
   _____
   Can you think of a good title for your book?
   _____

Bulb and Batteries

Look at the diagrams below. Under each diagram, indicate whether the electrical arrangement illustrated will result in a completed circuit with the light bulb lit up. Write yes or no to indicate your prediction.

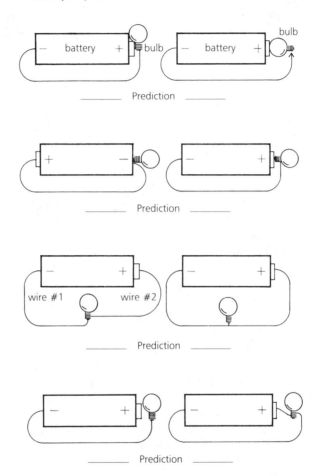

Figure 6–6 AN SCIC TYPE I ACTIVITY

3. Pretend that you can invite any person in the world to be a teacher in the special program for two weeks. Who would you invite?
First Choice _____
Second Choice _____
Third Choice _____

4. Pretend that a new time machine has been invented that will allow famous persons from the past to come back to life for a short period of time. If you

could invite some of these persons to give a talk to your class, who would you invite?

First Choice _____

Second Choice _____

Third Choice _____

5. Are you a collector? Do you collect stamps, seashells, baseball cards, or other things? List the things that you collect and the number of years you have been collecting.

Things I Collect	Number of Years I have been Collecting
_____	_____
_____	_____
_____	_____

6. What are some of the things you would like to collect if you had the time and money?

_____

_____

There is also a scale to help teachers identify the children's learning styles (Renzulli and Smith, 1979).

After the teacher has accurately assessed the child, planning can begin for enrichment activities, identified as Type I, Type II and Type III activities.

Type I Activities: General Exploratory Activities   The general exploratory activity is designed to introduce students to a new or extended area of study. Topics for exploratory activities should derive from the students' interests, the potential for suggesting projects for Type III activities, and the potential for introducing children to the discipline's structure and methodology. To generate enrichment activities, one must be familiar with the regular curriculum. Renzulli has suggested that the faculty who know the discipline best should brainstorm a list of enrichment topics that might be associated with regular curricular activities, and the list may be added to the other disciplines; for example:

- To coordinate with the study of heat, consider the study of *cryogenics* (the study of the effects on matter of extremely low temperatures)
- To extend a study of traditional energy forms, consider a study of solar energy by looking at solar architecture
- To enrich a study of sound, consider introducing acoustics

Figure 6–6 is an example of a Type I activity. Other sources of exploratory topics are current science magazines and/or journals. New areas of study do not appear in textbooks and published educational materials for many years.

Public and commercial television are excellent sources for introducing new areas of science research, presenting information on the process of science, and developing a sense of the history of science (an excellent exploratory topic in itself). For example, the NOVA series is a continual source of ideas for enrichment topics not likely to be covered in current curricula. Other special series serve as sources of bibliographic material, show how scientists gather evidence, how they generalize from data, and how they face cultural resistance to new ideas. *Search for Solutions* examines scientific processes in detail and *Connections* explores the historical connections between scientific/technological events and sociological/cultural events. Many series are accompanied by teachers' guides or other printed materials. Newspapers and news magazines also offer new ideas as well. The general topic areas from these sources may need further refinement and narrowing according to the students' interests and availability of resources.

Of course, identifying a topic does not complete the process. The teacher must then construct activities to introduce students to the discipline, from among options such as learning centers, readings, films, field trips, speakers, slide tapes, laboratory problems, simulation games, and magazine articles. For example, if a child has expressed interest in electricity, the teacher might locate a biography of Thomas Edison, present a series of somewhat complex electrical problems in a learning center, and order a film about electrical particles. The focus of the exploratory activity should be on the "how" of the discipline rather than the "what".

At the end of an exploratory activity, the teacher should discuss possible investigations by asking if students have questions they might like to find answers to, ideas for new experiments they would like to try, or if there are products they might like to create. For one elementary school student, interest in electricity resulted in construction of an electrically powered robot.

Type II Activities: Group Training Activities   Process activities—cognitive, psychomotor and affective—fall in the category of Type II activities. Renzulli does not deny the importance of skills acquisition; however, he argues that these skills are best learned when applied to real-life problems, and are appropriate for all children. He therefore recommends that teachers nurture these skills as much as possible through regular classroom activities, and reinforce and expand them as the student begins to work on investigations and needs additional process skills not taught in the regular classroom. Materials developed as part of the recent science curriculum studies are excellent sources of process activities.

Process activities also help develop and reveal interests. Teachers should be alert for extraordinary student involvement and achievement in the process skills, perhaps by keeping a log of activities and names of students who do more than required by the assignment, who ask many questions, or who give creative answers and suggestions.

Type III Activities: Individual and Small Group Investigations of Real Problems   The Type III activity is actually this model's method of differentiation for gifted education. The goals of Type III activities are to:

- Assist youngsters in becoming actual investigators of *real* problems or topics by using appropriate methods of inquiry.
- Provide students with opportunities for taking an active part in formulating problems to be investigated and the methods by which the problem will be attacked.
- Allow students to use information as *raw data* rather than reporting about conclusions reached by other persons.
- Provide opportunities for students' inquiry activity to be directed toward some tangible product.

- Provide students with an opportunity to apply thinking and feeling processes to real situations rather than structured exercises.[9]

The best examples of this type of activity in science are the National Science Fair competitions. Although these students' projects are at the most sophisticated level, the principles are the same for all projects and investigations performed as Type III activities.

The first steps in planning Type III projects is to focus the problem into one that can be answered or investigated with the tools available. One way to help the student focus the problem is to lead her through the questioning process the professional scientist would use. With younger children, the products of investigation are likely to go in many directions other than strictly scientific, but creating them will still help them acquire knowledge and experiment with problem solving.

A second step is to identify appropriate methodology and data gathering techniques. Formulating real problems will rule out a traditional trip to the encyclopedia to write a paper. Students will probably use background information to help formulate their problems, but they should be creating new products.

The third step is to identify an appropriate audience for the products. In this model, the teacher is no longer the only audience. Students must share their products as would professionals, perhaps through:

- Presentations, learning centers, or science magazines for children
- Presentations to science clubs or scientific societies
- Publication in science journals
- Competition in science fairs
- Newspaper or magazine articles
- Presentations to industrial leaders

Perhaps the best way to understand the kinds of scientific inquiry that might result in Type III activities is to look at two examples of Enrichment Triad Model activities (one group and one individual). The first unit resulted in a Type III activity, after explanatory and group process training; the second Type III activity grew out of the regular curriculum.

The following science "unit" met most of the criteria of the Enrichment Triad Model and was used with elementary school students.[10]

Elementary Science Unit, Type III Activity

This unit can be used with groups of gifted children who have an interest in biological studies, as a way to introduce them to potential areas of study (marine biology, oceanography, ecology) as well as to the Enrichment Triad Model itself.

Exploratory Activities

It is common to find at least one life science unit in elementary school programs that addresses the characteristics of "aquatic plants and animals"; for example, the ESS (Elementary Science Study) units on pond water and crayfish and the SCIS (Science

---

[9]From D. M. Eberly.
[10]This unit is a modification of a unit described by Gary Awkerman and Paul Teller in "Mess Management for Gifted Students," *Science and Children* (March 1979): 10–11.

Curriculum and Improvement Study) units on life in an aquarium. Students who indicated an unusually strong interest in studying the characteristics and environments of aquatic animals but had already mastered the basic concepts and skills of the unit were given the opportunity to explore a more specific area of study. To go beyond the activities and topics of the regular classroom, the teacher looked for a related exploratory topic which allowed for (a) more in-depth study, (b) the introduction of topics not covered in the regular school curriculum at some other time, and (c) the potential generation of ideas for real-life problems for the children. The community was coastal, so a natural extension was to the ocean and its inhabitants. Recognizing children's interests in things with which they were somewhat familiar, the teacher began the unit by asking these students whether they had ever had a "seafood platter." After students listed the various seafoods on the platter, he asked what they knew about the characteristics and environments of these animals. As expected, their knowledge was limited. He asked if anyone knew who studied these animals and what they studied. To answer the questions, he invited a marine biologist to discuss how marine animals are studied and scheduled a trip to the aquarium to observe marine life in natural habitats.

Obviously, all schools are not geographically located to make a trip to the ocean convenient, so alternative exploratory activities will be necessary:

- A learning center where students are presented with (1) task cards containing descriptions of various marine life forms and pictures to match with the descriptions; (2) a creative writing task asking students to write a poem or a short story about or from the point of view of a crayfish, crab, or other marine form; (3) a set of shells from various crustaceans for identifying three similarities and three differences in the shells; and (4) books on marine biology and oceanography
- Films about the ocean and its animals, or, perhaps, a videotape of one of the Jacques Cousteau or Nova television specials about marine life
- A reading center displaying *National Geographic* or *Science* magazine articles about various fish or crustaceans, or about beach erosion, or about threats to marine life
- A slide-tape presentation of marine life
- A sea-life aquarium can be set up so students can make observations about the similarities and differences in environments, plants, animals, and the interactions of this aquarium compared to a fresh-water aquarium. An experiment altering a single variable (amount of available light, or water temperature) can be set up to illustrate the importance of the balance of environmental factors as well as an example of how a marine biologist might do an environmental impact study. (Materials for setting up aquariums are available from biological supply houses. An alternative, of course, is to focus on locally available food fish.)

The following considerations are important in choosing materials for the exploratory activities:

1 Activities should give children a sense of the *process* involved in the study of these animals. For example, *National Geographic* explains in detail how evidence is gathered and how information is classified and analyzed, and presents pictures and descriptions of various phenomena.

2 Exploratory activities should reflect children's learning styles. Field trips are usually motivating, but if there will be only classroom materials available, then high interest *options* should be available also.

3 Try to incorporate the use of the *process* or Type II activities into exploratory

activities whenever possible. For example, articles on beach erosion and threats to marine life can lead to discussions of values clarification issues relating to environment versus economic factors, or the learning center activity on poetry or short story writing can develop creative writing skills as well as affective objectives.

Science process skills of observation, description, measurement and categorization can be reinforced by matching descriptions to pictures or in the process of identifying similarities and differences.

4   They should reflect student interest, not teacher interest.
5   They should involve students in activities similar to those engaged in by professionals in the field. For example, a marine biologist would classify animals, observe the conditions affecting stability of an environment, etc.

Process-Oriented Activities

A number of process-oriented activities were discussed as part of the exploratory activities, but additional activities included:

- A library research activity where students are sent on a scavenger hunt to find the names of particular plants or animals meeting certain descriptions.
- A brain-storming activity where students are asked to list all the possible uses for clam shells, mussel shells, lobster shells, etc.
- Creation of decoupage with shells where pictures are formed using the shell shapes.

Real-Life Products

As a result of a brainstorming activity, the children were able to generate many ideas for the kind of real-life problems they might like to work on. Examples of ideas for real-life products that emerged from this unit included:

- Production of placemats that were printed and sold to local restaurants. The placemats had drawings of the fish and crustaceans served on a typical seafood platter and "facts" of interest. In an actual implementation of this project, students developed a questionnaire to find out what was common knowledge so they could provide new information. In the process of developing the questionnaire, they attained knowledge objectives (they had to learn about the animals themselves); process skills (construction of appropriate data-gathering instruments, sampling, data analysis); and writing skills (how to present their questions and answers in an interesting and accurate format).
- A newspaper article about the local seafood industry and the impact of a recent hurricane
- A study of the effects of various chemicals that were being dumped by the area's industries into the ocean
- A plan for cleaning up an inlet area that had become an unauthorized and illegal garbage dump
- A learning center for younger children or a library display
- A book of poems, short stories, and artwork about marine life
- A survey of the community (or people in a restaurant) as to which seafood they like best and how they like it cooked, for presentation to the local restaurant association

Note that students might integrate other of their talents or involve students gifted in art or writing in some of these projects.

These projects could represent either individual or group work, but each should have an appropriate audience identified by the children. The teacher can ask questions such as:

- Who would like the placemats?
- Who would like to know what we have learned about marine life? How can we best share our information?
- Where can we display our findings?
- Who would like to read our poems and short stories?

A middle school physical education teacher related an example of one way in which science can easily be integrated with other disciplines through applications of the Triad Model. One child had often expressed personal dislike for team sports, and rarely became involved in class activities with any degree of enthusiasm. In an attempt to motivate the child to take an active part in a unit on basketball, the teacher began his usual lecture on the importance of exercise to physical health and happiness. The child responded with the counternotion that the activities taught in physical education class are relatively useless to life-long physical health because they were all team sports, and after one leaves school, there is little occasion to play football, volleyball, or basketball except in a league. He also said he ''had read somewhere'' that these sports often did not provide good cardiovascular exercise and body conditioning, especially considering that the best athletes in the class got most of their exercise in team sports anyway. ''What about individual sports or a running program or a program of individual exercise?'' he asked. Fighting back the desire to argue for the sports' contribution to developing team spirit, the teacher asked the student, ''What do you propose we do about this problem?''

After considerable discussion, the student, the physical education teacher, and the science teacher agreed upon a management plan. The process of filling out the management plan up to this point and designing the experiment to verify assumptions required the student to use the skills of problem focusing, experimental design, generating testable hypotheses, perceiving possible solutions, and organization. Specific persons and titles of books and journals were to be filled in after further investigation by the teachers and the student. Filling in these specifics required the use of library search skills.

In implementing the project, the student applied these Type II skills:

- Use of existing knowledge (to generate an alternative plan)
- Creativity (in developing an exercise plan)
- Collection of raw data
   Observing
   Counting
   Charting
- Questionnaire Design
- Data analysis skills
- Planning and organizing

This project gave the student the opportunity to study the cardiovascular system, create a physical education program appropriate to his stated goals, and use a scientific process to test achievement of the program's goals.

This particular investigation did not require an exploratory activity, but is an example of an investigation arising directly from the regular curriculum.

Cautions

Enrichment, like acceleration, faces many obstacles to its proper implementation. As mentioned earlier, many elementary science teachers feel inadequate, in knowledge and preparation, to teach the regular science curriculum (National Science Foundation, 1980). Thus, developing activities that go beyond the scope of the regular curriculum is likely to cause a great deal of frustration. Grade-skipping at least offers the likelihood that students will be with individuals versed in more advanced science content and process skills.

For elementary teachers to successfully implement a differentiated science classroom using an enrichment model, they must accept the following premises:

1 Many students with specific ability and interest in science will know more about some (or many) topics than you do. Do not be threatened by their knowledge, but learn from them and with them.

2 Stay current with major scientific events and breakthroughs. Part of children's fascination with science arises from what they see on television, in newspapers, and in magazines, which are also excellent sources for ideas for enrichment topics.

3 Seek out others who are more knowledgeable in science than you are to help particularly advanced children. Establish a school resource file (other teachers, administrators, librarians, who are directly involved in science teaching or have science-based hobbies (such as gardening or building electronic equipment) and a community resource file.

At the middle school and secondary levels, enrichment techniques encounter a different challenge. At this point, science content often becomes the predominant theme, and emphasis is directed toward amassing great amounts of *information*. The science teacher at this level must step back and examine some values. What "knowledge" of science is most basic and most important for students to know? What is the purpose of the laboratory? The middle school and secondary teacher must also be concerned about the process of science and structuring activities for the gifted student that allow him to develop as a scientist rather than as an information sponge.

Modifications of Instructional Strategies

In modifying curriculum for the gifted, one must also consider the instructional strategy to be used. Referring to the importance of the method of content presentation, Gallagher (1975) notes that "the process of thinking or the style in which a youngster approaches difficult problems appears important" (1975, p. 74). He goes on to say that it is not only what the teacher presents, but how he presents it that is important in instructing gifted children. Joyce and Weil (1980) concur with Gallagher's judgment:

> There is a considerable array of *alternative* approaches to teaching. Many of these are practical and can be implemented in schools and classrooms where students and teachers have both skill and will. Further, these models of teaching are sufficiently different from one another that they change the probability that various kinds of

outcomes will result if they are used. Thus, . . . *methods make a difference in what is learned as well as how it is learned.* (p. 461)

Joyce and Weil also emphasize the importance of recognizing that the various approaches to instruction can be combined, and a variety and blending of instructional approaches is often necessary to achieve all our goals and prevent boredom. Usually, a balance of instructional models is required to achieve our goals. The models and objectives discussed thus far suggest a need to abandon exclusive use of traditional lecture or information-giving strategies and predetermined laboratory exercises in favor of strategies that allow for the use of thinking skills and encourage students to develop the attitudes, values, knowledges and investigative skills of the scientist. Of the models for instruction that Joyce and Weil present, those that seem appropriate to these ends include inquiry, concept attainment, inductive thinking, advance organizers, biological sciences inquiry model, and synectics. Table 6–2 lists the instructional and nurturant effects of these models.

Table 6–2 INSTRUCTIONAL AND NURTURANT EFFECTS OF TEACHING MODELS

	Instructional Effects	Nurturant Effects
Inquiry	Scientific process skills Strategies for creative inquiry	Spirit of creativity Independence or autonomy in learning Tolerance for ambiguity
Concept attain-ment	Nature of concepts Improved concept-building strategies Specific concepts Inductive reasoning	Awareness of Alternative perspectives Tolerance of ambiguity (but appreciation of logic) Sensitivity to logical reasoning in communication
Inductive thinking	Concept formation process Specific concepts	Attention to logic Sensitivity to language Awareness of the nature of knowledge
Advanced organizers	Conceptual structures Meaningful assimilation of information and ideas	Interest in inquiry Habits of precise thinking
Synectics	General creative capacity Creative capacity in subject domain	Achievement in subject domain Group cohesion and productivity
Biological science inquiry model	Process of research biology	Scientific knowledge Commitment to scientific inquiry Open-mindedness Cooperative spirit and skill

Adapted from *Models of Teaching* (Joyce and Weil, 1980).

The lesson ideas we have mentioned incorporate some of these strategies; the rock and mineral unit uses synectics in the imagination exercise and the activity using the biological science inquiry model on p. 202. Examples of the other approaches can be found in *Models of Teaching* (Joyce and Weil, 1980), *Sciencing* (Cain and Evans, 1980) and other methods textbooks in science education.

Preschool/Primary Programs

The literature on preschool and primary science programs for the gifted reflects both the smaller number of programs at this level and the lack of attention to science instruction at this level. The programs that do exist reflect attempts to broaden the students' exposure to science concepts in general and to develop thinking skills.

Generally, programs for the gifted at this level emphasize enrichment rather than acceleration. Descriptions of programs or curricula at these levels are very sparse. Two of the best documented programs are those of the preschool/handicapped project in Chapel Hill, North Carolina, and the Astor Program in New York City, discussed in chapter 4. The Astor Program's units in science are presented in Table 6-3. This is a full day program, and the units were used for both skills and enrichment

Table 6-3   SCIENCE CONCEPTS PRESENTED IN THE ASTOR PROGRAM

Level I	Level II	Level III
Magnetism	Natural Sciences in New York City	Methods of Scientific Investigation
Gravity	Wheels	Body Science
Earth in Space	Roots—Trees, Plants, Teeth, Vegetable	Basic Needs of Man
Environmental Health	Gravity/Balance	Origin of Man
Fossils	Endangered and Extinct Species	Inter-Dependence of Plant and Animal Life
Air	Amphibians and Reptiles	Classroom Gardening
Reproduction	Nutrition	Electricity
Animal Adaptations to Habitats	Sound	Senses
Plant Development	Structures—Architecture	
Change in Nature	Birds—From Dinosaurs to Birds	
Water—Water Cycle	Skeletons—Differences Between Man and Animal	
Sound		
The Solar System		
Reptiles		
Insects		
Colors		
Light—Shadows		
Birds' Nests		
Icthyology		
Microscope		
Evaporation and Condensation		

concepts. The Astor Program incorporated units from the M.A.P.S. Science Units of Study (Ehrlich, 1978); the units relating to science in the Chapel Hill program were medicine, diet, pets, birds, plants, insects, and the zoo (Malley-Crist, Hoyt & Leonard, 1977).

Secondary Programs

The two most available options in high school science programs for the gifted are honors courses and/or advanced placement courses. The difference between the two options lies in the specified purpose of advanced placement courses to provide preparation to take examinations to earn credit for courses at the college level in biology, chemistry, and physics (two courses) (CEEB, 1979). The College Entrance Examination Board provides outlines of topics and curriculum guides for teachers of advanced placement courses. The courses are not intended as substitutes for beginning courses, but rather are built on introductory courses. The advanced placement biology course is dependent on introductory chemistry courses, advanced placement chemistry is dependent on introductory level concepts in physics and mathematics, and the advanced placement physics courses are dependent on mathematics (physics requires calculus) (CEEB, 1979). The student who seeks advanced placement credit can study in designated advanced placement courses, an honors class, or can work independently. Standardized examinations in each course provide scores for college entrance and placement officials to consider in determining possible credit. Both honors courses and advanced placement courses seek to provide selected students with more advanced and complex information and laboratory skills. Honors courses are conducted at the discretion of the school and the teacher, so they may be similar to advanced placement courses as general biology, chemistry, or physics courses, or they may be specifically developed around a narrower area of science (for example, microbiology) or an enrichment area (for example, geology or history of science), or they may be multidisciplinary seminars with science as one component.

A teacher may also opt to provide enrichment activities within a regular biology class using any of the curricular models we have described. Table 6–4 shows how a biology course can be modified to provide enrichment activities. The left column shows units and topics to be covered in the regular sequence; the right column describes activities for use with gifted students to extend their knowledge, thinking skills, and investigative skills, which can lead to Type III activities.

Special Schools

Special schools are another option for gifted science students. Among the best known special schools are the Bronx High School of Science, the Brooklyn Technical High School, and the North Carolina residential school for students gifted in science and mathematics. A description of the program at the Bronx High School of Science shows an emphasis on microbiology, with an opportunity to speculate, hypothesize, and design experimentation in that area at the ninth-grade level. At the tenth-grade level, emphasis is on recognition and selection of scientific problems with individual study (such as one student's experiment with the effects of differing concentrations

Table 6–4 ENRICHMENT OF A BIOLOGY CURRICULUM[1]

OVERVIEW OF UNITS	ENRICHMENT ACTIVITIES

Unit I: The Nature of Life
  I. The Science of Life
    A. Describe significant biological advances in history
	1. Development of whole problem-solving sequence if given a problem

B. Identify and use scientific methods of research	2. If given proper data about present social and biological situations, students will identify areas needing scientific research
C. Demonstrate knowledge of the structure, function, care, and use of the compound microscope	3. Students will analyze research procedures (either their own or those recorded) and be able to identify variables, evaluate conclusions
II. The Living Condition A. Differentiate between living and nonliving things	1. Investigate the meaning of death in a biological organismal level and contrast that with a clinical or moral definition
B. Identify the parts of the cell and their relationship to the total organism	2. Express their own concept of death and its meaning with a view toward transplant technology and life support machinery
C. Contrast the processes of spontaneous generation and biogenesis	

III. The Chemical Basis of Life
    A. Describe matter and energy and their interrelationships
    B. Identify elements and their structures
    C. Name and describe chemical compounds
    D. Demonstrate understanding of chemical basis of life	

IV. The Structural Basis of Life
    A. Correlate cellular structure and function
    B. Compare and contrast the structures of plant and animal cells	

[1]From Halifax County Public Schools, Halifax, Va.

Table 6–4   *continued*

OVERVIEW OF UNITS	ENRICHMENT ACTIVITIES

V. The Cell and Its Environment
   A. Describe the mechanisms of homeostasis
   B. Compare and contrast osmosis and diffusion
   C. Describe the process of pinocytosis
VI. Photosynthesis, Respiration, and Cell Energy
   A. Identify and describe the steps of the process of photosynthesis
   B. Describe process of respiration
   C. Be able to state energy requirements of cellular respiration
VII. Nucleic Acids and Protein Synthesis
   A. Relate the historical significance of the discovery and structure of DNA	

	1. Students would evaluate the potentials of genetic engineering; research present techniques of genetic engineering; be able to discuss successful engineering work
B. Identify and describe the DNA molecule, the processes of transcription, and replication	2. Formulate as a class a set of guidelines under which genetic engineering research could continue but that would guarantee the safety of the general public*

C. Describe the mechanism of protein synthesis
   D. Define and describe the mechanisms of genetic engineering
VIII. Cell Growth and Reproduction
   A. Describe simple cell division—fission
   B. Process of mitosis—name five stages
   C. Compare and contrast asexual and sexual reproduction
   D. Be able to describe the importance of chromosome number
   E. Demonstrate understanding of process of meiosis	

*These ideas would be particularly appropriate for the development of Type III Activities: Individual or Small Group Investigations as described in the *Enrichment Triad Model* (Renzulli, 1977).

Table 6–4 continued

OVERVIEW OF UNITS	ENRICHMENT ACTIVITIES

Unit II: The Continuity of Life
  IX. Principles of Heredity
    A. Describe Gregor Mendel's work and his contributions to the study of heredity
    B. Use Mendel's hypothesis and applications
  X. The Genetic Material
    A. Identify the gene hypothesis
	1. Use population sampling techniques (of school population, community, or family) to determine occurrence of sex-linked or sex-determined traits such as colorblindness, baldness, etc. Be able to collaborate research data with genetic mapping.

B. Describe and identify sex determination and sex linkage in genes	2. Use pre-determined sex-linked trait carrying Drosophila and map transmission of trait through subsequent offspring
C. Describe and apply concepts of nondisjuntion, gene linkage, crossing over, and mutation theory	3. Formulate a legal guideline to be used in counsel for persons who have a sex-linked trait; how can continuous transmission of that trait be controlled (or indeed should it be controlled and by whom?)*
XI. Genes in Human Populations A. Determine population samples and gene pools	1. Correlate the facts of population samples and gene pools with the process of natural selection; use research to provide good examples and examples where the organism was at a disadvantage due to his gene pool
B. Compare and contrast fraternal and identical twins	2. Design family pedigree for a single trait and describe that trait transmission through three or more generations by information available from family; use genetic principles to explain that transmission pattern

Table 6–4   continued

OVERVIEW OF UNITS	ENRICHMENT ACTIVITIES
C. Determine the pattern of inheritance of blood types	
D. Describe cases of inherited diseases	3. Research ethnic groups to identify specific genetic diseases (i.e., Tay Sachs, etc.)
	4. Formulate a directive to a hypothetical family to counsel them on the advisability of future pregnancies; use genetic principles to explain to the parents the rate of incidence, the chances of occurrence in their case, considerations of the quality of life
XII. Applied Genetics	
A. Correlate application of genetic principles to the improvement of plants and animals	1. Identify genetic hybridization examples that have changed the nature of plants and animals
B. Describe the significance of Luther Burbank's contributions to plant breeding	2. Identify possible hybridization of organisms to solve problems of crop production and food manufacture to ease worldwide hunger
XIII. The Diversity of Life	
A. Identify significant contributions of Linnaeus to classification systems	
B. Use scientific names of plants and animals	
C. Determine classification of living things	
D. Determine problems in classification	
Unit III: Microbiology (Survey)	
XIV. The Viruses	
A. Contrast living and nonliving properties	
B. Describe disease-causing properties	
XV. Bacteria and Related Organisms	
A. Identify structure and correlate function of bacteria—common forms	1. Collect samples of common bacteria from surfaces, isolate bacterial colonies, and deter-

Table 6-4   *continued*

OVERVIEW OF UNITS	ENRICHMENT ACTIVITIES
	mine antibody that works best for combating a specific disease germ

B. Describe economic importance
XVI. Infectious Disease
    A. Describe how diseases are
       caused, spread
	1. Investigate the programs that are underway in this community to combat diseases; correlate amount of funding to the program efficiency; identify areas of where improvement is needed or programs overlap

B. Compare structural, cellular, antibody and chemical defenses against diseases
    C. Define immune therapy
    D. Define chemotherapy
XVII. The Protozoans
    A. Compare and contrast the structure and function of Amoeba, Paramecium, and Euglena
XVIII. The Fungi
    A. Identify characteristics of Fungi
XIX. The Algae
    A. Identify characteristics of Algae
Unit IV: Multicellular Plants
    XX. Mosses and Ferns
    A. Correlate structure and life cycle of mosses
    B. Correlate structure and life cycle of ferns
    C. Show relationship between mosses and ferns and higher plants
    XXI. The Seed Plants
    A. Summarize seed plants including species, structure, woody vs. herbaceous plants
    XXII. The Leaf and its Function
    A. Compare and contrast kinds of venation and blades
	1. Use paper chromatography to separate leaf pigments; use different leaf sources to compare and contrast the pigmentation and predict leaf color change in the fall

Table 6-4 continued

OVERVIEW OF UNITS	ENRICHMENT ACTIVITIES
B. Identify leaf structure C. Correlate leaf function and structure D. Describe leaf coloration and modifications XXIII. Roots and Stems A. Correlate structure, development, function of roots	1. Use woody winter twig key to identify unknown species of tree by structures

B. Correlate structure, development, function of stems
    C. Identify structure of woody winter twigs
XXIV. Plant Reproduction
    A. Describe methods of vegetable reproduction and propagation
	1. Propagate plants using techniques of layering, grafting, and root sprouting; be able to describe each step of the process from a plant organismal level and to determine variables in each method of propagation. Prepare a guide for others on best techniques

B. Identify flower structure
    C. Correlate flower function in sexual reproduction
    D. Describe development from fertilization to seed formation	

Unit V: Biology of the Invertebrates
XXV. Sponges and Coelenterates
    A. Identify characteristics of sponges and coelenterates
    B. Describe economic importance
XXVI. The Worms
    A. Correlate structure and life styles of platyhelminthes
    B. Correlate structure and life cycles of nemathelminthes
    C. Correlate structure and functions of Annelida
    D. Identify parasitic worms and describe their effect on man
XXVII. Mollusks and Echinoderms
    A. Correlate structure and functions of mollusks	

Table 6–4   *continued*

OVERVIEW OF UNITS	ENRICHMENT ACTIVITIES

B. Correlate structure and functions of echinoderms
C. Describe relationships between animals—evolutionary links
XXVIII. The Arthropods
    A. Correlate structure and basic functions of crustaceans
    B. Distinguish between Diplopoda and Chilopoda
    C. Identify characteristics of spiders
XXIX. Insects—Familiar Arthropods
    A. Describe general structure of insects
    B. Describe metamorphosis and life cycles
    C. Describe economic importance—beneficial and harmful
Unit VI: Biology of the Vertebrates
    XXX. Introduction to the Vertebrates
    A. Describe characteristics of vertebrates
    B. Identify vertebrate systems
    C. Describe complex vertebrate behavior
XXXI. The Fishes
    A. Correlate general structure and functions of fishes
XXXII. The Amphibians
    A. Describe characteristics of amphibians
    B. Identify different types of amphibians
    C. Correlate the structure and behavior of the frog
XXXIII. The Reptiles
    A. Identify reptile characteristics
    B. Name types of reptiles
    C. Describe the amniote egg
XXXIV. The Birds
    A. Identify characteristics of aves
    B. Correlate development and structure of egg
XXXV. The Mammals
    A. Survey of different types of mammals including mammalian characteristics	

Table 6–4 *continued*

OVERVIEW OF UNITS	ENRICHMENT ACTIVITIES

Unit VII: Human Biology
  XXXVI. Human History
    A. Brief survey of ancient man
  XXXVII. The Body Framework
    A. Identify types of body tissues
	1. Use techniques of compara-
	tive anatomy to compare and
	contrast skeletal structures of
	vertebrates

B. Correlate structure and function
      of skeletal system
    C. Correlate structure and function
      of muscular system
	2. Use cellular and organismal
	understanding to determine
	causes of cramping, fatigue,
	and tetany

XXXVIII. Nutrition
    A. Identify nutrients and describe
      their function in the body
	1. Conduct original research on
	eating habits of specific teen-
	agers for a month; determine
	if nutritional needs, calories,
	and vitamin intake are suffici-
	ent for individual activities;
	recommend changes and de-
	fend recommendations from
	physiological studies

B. Describe structure of man's
      digestive system
    C. Analyze the process of chemical
      digestion
    D. Describe absorption and utiliza-
      tion of digested food
  XXXIX. Transport and Excretion
    A. Correlate the structure and func-
      tion of blood
	1. Investigate the use of the di-
	alysis machine; describe
	mechanics of blood cleansing
	and determine frequency of
	visits required; identify haz-
	ards and benefits of dialysis.
	Prepare a "handbook" for
	doctors to give to dialysis pa-
	tients and their families

B. Correlate the structure and func-
      tion of the heart
    C. Identify blood types and describe
      transfusions
    D. Correlate man's circulatory sys-
      tem and his other systems	

Table 6–4 *continued*

OVERVIEW OF UNITS	ENRICHMENT ACTIVITIES

E. Correlate the structure and function of the kidneys
F. Correlate the structure and function of the skin
G. Describe interrelationships of skin, blood, kidneys, and heart and their role in homeostasis
XL. Respiration and Energy Exchange
    A. Identify structures of man's respiratory system
    B. Contrast breathing and cellular respiration
    C. Describe oxygen debt
XLI. Body Controls
    A. Describe the structure of nerves and the nervous system
    B. Correlate the structure and function of the brain
    C. Describe the function of the senses of touch and taste, and identify the structures of the eye and ear
    D. Describe interrelationships of the nervous system and other systems
XLII. Tobacco, Alcohol, and Drugs
    A. Brief survey including effects on human systems
XLIII. Body Regulators
    A. Identify the location of endocrine glands
    B. Correlate hormones and their control over certain body functions
    C. Describe results of over and under secretions
XLIV. Reproduction and Development
    A. Describe genetic significance of sexual reproduction
    B. Compare and contrast male and female anatomy
    C. Describe ovarian and uterine cycle
    D. Describe fertilization
    E. Describe development of human embryo	

Table 6–4   *continued*

OVERVIEW OF UNITS	ENRICHMENT ACTIVITIES
F. Describe birth process G. Identify venereal diseases and describe their symptoms, treatment, and results if untreated XLV. Ecology A. Compare and contrast five major biomes	1. Select a specific area (such as eroded, vacant lot) and recommend procedures to restore that area to ecological balance; research costs and procedures recommended and determine other factors that influence conservation practice*

B. Identify concepts of habitat and ecological niche
    C. Describe components of ecosystem
    D. Describe components in resource conservation
    E. Determine procedures for control of pollution; water, noise, and air
    F. Determine problems of solid waste disposal and radioactive waste containment
    G. Correlate concepts of competition, food chains, survival of fittest
	2. Investigate and document methods used in standard municipal water treatment
	
	3. Use random sampling of quadrants to determine percent cover of plant species and competition; record data and calculate percents

*Indicates individual or small group investigations.

of auxin on the growth rate of oats). At the eleventh-grade level, students focus on library research, learning how to read scientific papers and how to use *Biological Abstracts,* the *Index Medicis,* and other scholarly references. Each student works on an individual project throughout the year; the projects are then submitted to the school's Science Congress, to the New York Biology Teacher's Congress, the Science Fair, and the Westinghouse Science Talent Search. Selected papers are published in the department annually (Kopelman, Galasso, & Strom, 1977). (Note how this program parallels some of the basic tenets of the Enrichment Triad Model.)

Extra School Activities

The Talcott Mountain Science Center is an example of an extra school program (which, incidentally, also offers an elementary program). The Saturday program for gifted students (from about 25 Connecticut communities at any given time) focuses on individual or small group research projects on topics the students choose. Students work with the staff to select a research topic and a plan of attack, then conduct their research using the Center's equipment. Projects have included a study of granulation characteristics of a glacial deposit (published in *Geotimes*); a study of wind climatology, including a report to the State Department of Transportation on potential traffic exhaust pollution on a nearby reservoir, and design, construction, and operation of an unexplained weather satellite viewing station (Atamian and Danielson, 1977). The underlying philosophy of this program also resembles that of the Enrichment Triad Model.

Summary

We have seen throughout this chapter how programs such as SAPA, ESS, and science process materials have been adopted and adapted for programs for the gifted. Programs at the secondary level also make use of the process materials such as BSCS, PSSC, Project Physics, and Chem Study (Clendening and Davies, 1979). These materials provide a basis for instructing students in the process skills necessary for scientific investigation (Gallagher, 1975).

Science for the gifted can best be approached by generally upgrading science curricula to provide process skills to all children, then emphasize for gifted students further development of the skills of scientific investigation. Students must then have opportunities to apply these skills to more advanced content levels and to independent scientific investigations that will extend scientific knowledge.

References

Abeles, S. "Science education for the gifted and talented." *Gifted Child Quarterly* 21 (1977): 75–79.

Atamian, G., and E. Danielson. "Programs for the gifted at Talcott Mountain Science Center." *Gifted Child Quarterly* 21 (1977).

Bloom, B. S. et al. *Taxonomy of educational objectives, Handbook I: Cognitive domain.* New York: David McKay, 1956.

Brandwein, P. F. et al. *Teaching high school science: A book of methods.* New York: Harcourt, 1958.

Burke, J. *Connections.* Boston: Little, Brown, 1978.

Cain, S. E., and J. M. Evans. *Science: An involvement approach to elementary science methods.* Columbus: Charles E. Merrill, 1979.

Callahan, C. M. "The gifted girl: An anomaly?" *Roeper Review* 2 (1980): 16–20.

College Entrance Examination Boards. *Advanced placement course descriptions*. Princeton, N. J.: College Entrance Examination Board, 1979.

Clendening, C. P., and R. A. Davies. *Creating programs for the gifted: A guide for teachers, librarians, and students*. New York: R. R. Bowker, 1980.

Ehrlich, V. Z. *The Astor Program for gifted children*. New York: Teachers College and the Board of Education of New York City, 1978.

Fox, L. H. *Sex differences: Implications for program planning for the academically gifted*. Paper presented at the Lewis M. Terman Memorial Symposium on Intellectual Talent, Baltimore, Md., November, 1975.

Fox, L. H. "Programs for the gifted and talented: An overview." In *The gifted and talented: Their education and development*. Edited by A. H. Passow. Chicago: University of Chicago Press, 1979.

Gallagher, J. J. *Teaching the gifted child*. 2nd ed. Boston: Allyn and Bacon, 1975.

Gardner, M. "10 trends in science education." *The Science Teacher* 46 (January, 1979): 30–32.

Goetzels, J. *Problem finding and originality*. Presentation at the Fifth Annual Northern Virginia Conference on Gifted/Talented Education, Alexandria, Va., March 1980.

Guilford, J. P. *Intelligence, creativity and their educational implications*. San Diego, Calif.: Knapp, 1968.

Hammill, S. "Nothing is more unequal than the equal treatment of unequals." *Science and Children* (March 1979): 12–15.

Harbeck, M. B., and P. Marcuccio. "Science in the lives of children." *Childhood Education* (November/December 1978): 94–98.

Joyce, B., and M. Weil. *Models of teaching*. 2nd ed. Englewood Cliffs, N. J.: Prentice-Hall, 1980.

Kaplan, S. N. *Inservice training manual: Activities for developing curriculum for the gifted and talented*. Ventura, Calif.: Office of the Ventura County Superintendent of Schools, 1979.

Karplus, R. "What's new in curriculum—physical sciences." *Nations Schools* 84 (1969): 35–36.

Kearney, E. I. "Several routes to excellence." *Science and Children* (March 1979): 42–43.

Kopelman, M., V. Galasso, and P. Stron. "A model program in science." *Gifted Child Quarterly* 21 (1977): 80–83.

Koran, J. J,. and J. F. Lehman. "Teaching children science concepts: The role of attention." *Science and Children* (January 1981): 21–22.

LaSalle, D. "Guest editorial." *Gifted Child Quarterly* (1977): 1–4.

Malley-Crist, J., M. S. Hoyt and J. Leonard. *A planning guide for gifted preschoolers*. Chapel Hill, N. C.: Chapel Hill Training Outreach Project, 1977.

Morgan, H. J. et al. *Elementary and secondary level programs for the gifted and talented*. New York: Teachers College, 1980.

National Science Foundation. *What are the needs in precollege science, mathematics, and social science education? Views from the field*. (Report No. SE80-9) Washington, D. C.: National Science Foundation, Office of Program Integration Directorate for Science Education, 1980.

Renzulli, J. S. *The enrichment triad model*. Mansfield Center, Conn.: Creative Learning Press, 1977.

Renzulli, J. S. *What makes giftedness? A reexamination of the definition of the gifted and talented*. Ventura, Calif.: Ventura County Superintendent of Schools Office, 1979.

Renzulli, J. S. *Son of triad: Inservice training worksheets for the enrichment triad model.* Storrs, Conn.: University of Connecticut, undated. (mimeo)

Renzulli, J. S., and L. H. Smith. *A guidebook for developing individualized educational programs for gifted and talented students.* Mansfield Center, Conn.: Creative Learning Press, 1979.

Roe, A. *The making of a scientist.* New York: Dodd, Mead, 1952.

Schwab, J. J. *Biology teachers' handbook.* New York: John Wiley, 1965.

SCIS Teacher's Guides. Chicago: Rand McNally, 1970.

Stanley, J. C. et al. *Mathematical talent: Discovery, description, and development.* Baltimore, Md.: Johns Hopkins University, 1974.

Terman, L. M. "Scientists and nonscientists in a group of 800 gifted men." *Psychological Monographs* 68 (1954): 1–41.

Terman, L. M., and M. H. Oden. *The gifted child grows up: Twenty-five years' follow-up of a superior group. Genetic studies of genius.* Vol. 4. Stanford, Calif.: Stanford University Press, 1947.

Williams, F. E. *Classroom ideas for encouraging thinking and feeling.* Buffalo, N. Y.: D.O.K. Publishers, 1969.

Williams, F. E. "Assessing creativity across Williams 'cube' model." *Gifted Child Quarterly* 23 (1979): 748–56.

Woolever, J. D. "Pine View's departmentalized program." *Science and Children* (March 1979): 30–32.

7

Social Studies

Emily D. Stewart

Teaching social studies to gifted and talented students takes place in a broad and ever-shifting context. Our views of the world are changing, bringing an inevitable change in our views about relating to one another—person to person as well as nation to nation. We refer to today's era as the postindustrial age, the communication age, the information age, and the space age; metaphors for today's world include "global village" and "spaceship earth." Yet, we frequently see a return to provincial national views even as cultural diversity within nations increases. While shockingly rapid changes sometimes seem to take us close to the terrifying prospect of total self-destruction, rapid technological change has also given us new potential to decide how we will live and how we will change our lives. Such changes bring a new urgency to the role of social studies in developing responsible citizens and leaders capable of vision and sensitivity.

> The most important factor in the complex equation of the future is the way the human mind responds to crisis. In *A Study of History* Arnold Toynbee points out that the greatest historical forces are set in motion when people decide to pit themselves against serious challenge. Human experience is not a closed circle. It is full of magnificent defenses and sudden departure from predicted destinations. (Cousins, 1981, p. 51)

Agreement is widespread on the important role of social studies in preparing young people to respond to possible societal crises as well as to solve current problems. Similar agreement focuses on the need for developing the ethical sensitivity and leadership potential of students who show unusual promise in the area of social studies. Questions continue to arise, however, about the specific nature and goals of social studies in general education as well as in the education of gifted students, including concerns about content, teaching methods and strategies, and procedures for identifying students with unusual potential.

What Is Social Studies?

When a single goal is proposed for social studies, citizenship education is the most frequently mentioned (Morrissett & Haas, 1982; Fontana & Mehlinger, 1981; Barr, Barth & Shermis, 1977; Joyce, 1972). The argument over whether social studies is a unitary field or a federation of subjects has continued, however, since the early NEA report (1916). Those who support the view of social studies as a federation of subjects have proposed to continue the focus on basic citizenship education while maintaining the integrity of individual subjects. In practice, this has frequently meant primarily teaching history (Hertzberg, 1982; Popham, 1971). Proponents of a unitary approach have based curriculum on contemporary problems, issues and principles. There are few attempts, however, at a sophisticated integration of the social studies curriculum for either elementary or secondary classrooms (Ponder & Hirsh, 1981; Superha, Hawke & Morrissett, 1980).

Areas upon which social studies draws include history, geography, economics, anthropology, sociology, psychology and political science (Mitsakos, 1981; Smith, 1979). Besides these major areas, social studies may include law-related education, career education, and a number of other areas as well (Allen, 1981). Current

Table 7–1 THE THREE SOCIAL STUDIES TRADITIONS

	Social Studies as Citizenship Transmission	Social Studies as Social Science	Social Studies as Reflective Inquiry
Purpose	Citizenship is best promoted by inculcating right values as a framework for making decisions.	Citizenship is best promoted by decision making based on mastery of social science concepts, processes, and problems.	Citizenship is best promoted through a process of inquiry in which knowledge is derived from what citizens need to know to make decisions and solve problems.
Method	Transmission: Transmission of concepts and values by such techniques as textbook, recitation, lecture, question and answer sessions, and structured problem-solving exercises.	Discovery: Each of the social sciences has its own method of gathering and verifying knowledge. Students should discover and apply the method appropriate to each social science.	Reflective Inquiry: Decision making is structured and disciplined through a reflective inquiry process which aims at identifying problems and responding to conflicts by means of testing insights.
Content	Content is selected by an authority interpreted by the teacher and has the function of illustrating values, beliefs, and attitudes.	Proper content is the structure, concepts, problems, and processes of both the separate and the integrated social science disciplines.	Analysis of individual citizen's values yields needs and interests which, in turn, form the basis for student self-selection of problems. Problems, therefore, constitute the content for reflection.

From C. L. Mitsakos, The nature and purposes of social studies. In *Education in the 80s: Social Studies*, ed. J. Allen. Washington, D.C.: National Education Association, 1981. Used with permission.

approaches increasingly emphasize ingredients such as cultural pluralism and interdependence, societal changes brought about by urbanization, and the now compelling requirement of assuming a global perspective (Allen, 1981). Decision making and values clarification continue to be mentioned as essential components of social studies.

Despite the mention of citizenship education as the purpose of social studies, Mitsakos (1981) believes there are three equally distinctive views of social studies: (1) the social sciences simplified for pedagogical purposes; (2) citizenship transmission, and (3) training in critical thinking. Table 7–1 shows his characterization of the three viewpoints.

Aims of Social Studies

No aim is more clearly focused in the history of social studies reform than that of educating citizens for a democracy. Since the National Education Association's Committee of Ten report (1873), this has been the central role assigned to the social studies. In 1964, the National Council for the Social Studies issued this statement:

> The most inclusive aim of social studies as a part of general education in the United States is to help young people learn to carry on the free society they have inherited, to make whatever changes modern conditions demand or creative imagination suggests that are consistent with its basic principles and values, and to hand it on to their offspring better than they received it. (p. 20)

The central role of social studies is to educate citizens for a democracy.

Arthur Ellis (1977) outlines the overriding concerns of social studies educators in the Reflective Inquiry tradition:

1 Social studies should help learners to come to a greater awareness of themselves, to clarify and examine their views, and to establish a sense of self-identity.
2 Social studies should provide learners with an understanding of past events and persons and of their roles in shaping present-day lives.
3 Social studies should promote in learners a concern for the development of an understanding and acceptance of others with different values and life styles.
4 Social studies should provide learners with a knowledge of human systems in the areas of economics, government, and culture.
5 Social studies should provide learners with the skills necessary to carry out the independent investigation of problems and to react critically to the solutions posed by others.
6 Social studies should provide learners with an awareness of possible futures and the roles they might play in shaping those futures.
7 Social studies should provide learners with an appreciation of people's efforts to improve the human condition through creative expression and problem solving.
8 Social studies should provide learners with an understanding of the decision-making processes involved in human interaction and with the skills necessary to become effective decision makers.
9 Social studies should provide learners with the ability to utilize both cooperative and competitive circumstances for the achievement of goals.
10 Social studies should provide learners with a sensitivity toward their own potentials and toward the potentials of their fellow human beings. (p. 17)

Ellis also comments that the day-to-day enactment of these goals is the real measure of a social studies program's worth.

The National Council for the Social Studies (1979) suggests in its revised guidelines for the 1980s that social studies programs should

- Directly relate to the age, maturity, and concerns of students
- Deal with the real world
- Draw from currently valid knowledge about human experience, cultures, and beliefs
- Carefully select objectives and state them clearly in a form that will furnish direction to the programs
- Engage students directly and actively in the learning process
- Rely on a broad range of learning resources
- Facilitate the organization of experience
- Evaluate program objectives in a useful, systematic, comprehensive, and valid way
- Receive vigorous support as a vital and responsible part of the school program

Current Classroom Practice

Despite the best intentions of social studies educators, recent research on current classroom practice shows what John Goodlad (1983) calls "curricular sterility." His research indicates that while teachers list as intended learnings such skills as drawing conclusions from data, testing hypotheses, and deriving concepts from related events, few activities actually occur to develop these skills. In social studies classrooms, much like classes for other subjects, students listened, while teachers "out-talked" their classes by a ratio of about three to one. Students seldom plan or initiate anything. They read short sections of textbooks, but rarely anything of some length. They seldom create their own products, speculate on meanings, or talk about alternative interpretations. In direct contrast to the obvious goals of social studies, students work alone most of the time, seldom engaging in projects that require collaborative effort.

Social studies shares this lack of instructional variability with most other school subjects; however, students rate social studies to be of low interest relative to other subject fields (Ehman, Mehlinger & Patrick, 1974; Goodlad, 1983; Hertzberg, 1982; Mitsakos, 1981). Goodlad (1983) speculates on the reason for this rating:

> The topics that come to mind as representing the natural and social sciences appear to be of great human interest. But on the way to the classroom they are apparently transformed and homogenized into something of limited appeal. (Alfred North Whitehead's words on the uselessness of inert knowledge come to mind.) (p. 468)

Considerable evidence shows that despite the stated goals, in social studies instruction, as in most other school subjects, the typical mode of instruction is recitation (Hertzberg, 1982). Teaching continues not to be individualized, but aimed at the classroom group as if it were a uniform whole (Bloom, 1981; Fancett & Hawke, 1982; Goodlad, 1983: Weiss, 1978). There are, of course, adjustments of standards for some students and adjustments for different rates of progress, but for the most part, "each individual is instructed as a member of a group with some notion that all are to get as nearly equal treatment as the teacher and the instructional material can supply" (Bloom, 1981, p. 88).

The wide gap between stated goals and current classroom practice is not a new phenomenon; the discrepancy has persisted since the early efforts at social studies reform at the beginning of the century. Attempts to move social studies methods away from recitation and toward inquiry began with the first methods textbook in the 1880s.

The gap between goals and practice may be partly accounted for by the fact that most classroom time in social studies is spent with textbooks; there is very little use of other instructional materials or variety of approaches (Hertzberg, 1981). Although today's textbooks use slick graphics and eye-catching pictures, most of them are largely factual (Patrick & Hawke, 1982); very little of the material helps students think critically (Wiley, 1977). Furthermore, textbooks are generally organized around study topics that were established more than 60 years ago (Lengel & Superka, 1982). A recent review of social studies textbooks is sharply critical: "Our conclusion, that social studies texts are not now and have never been appropriate for the gifted, can be extended to suggest that they are also not appropriate for anyone else" (Shermis & Clinkenbeard, 1981, p. 21).

Current social studies education seems geared to only a narrow spectrum of its goals. This profile of the classroom setting is unfortunate for all students, but it imposes an extremely heavy penalty on the gifted. Bloom (1981) reports "very few instances in which talent development and schooling function to enhance each other'' (p. 94). Those few instances where school experiences served as a major source of support for developing talent involved teachers who actively and energetically pursued a new program or method of instruction, principals who recognized quality work and went out of their way to offer individual encouragement, support from peers in school, or public events in the schools that made the work real and gave a chance to demonstrate achievement. Special efforts to provide these dimensions in the school setting are essential to recognizing and developing the talents of students gifted in social studies.

Social Studies in Education for the Gifted

Social studies education has received much attention in the field of special education for gifted and talented students. The objectives of both fields frequently overlap— encouraging inquiry, critical thinking skills, creative thinking skills, decision-making skills, investigation of real problems, and leadership skills. Ponder and Hirsh (1981) go so far as to suggest a ''kid glove fit'' of the rationales of the new social studies and education for the gifted as delineated in Renzulli's Enrichment Triad, a model for developing programs for the gifted and talented.

Current practice in the education of gifted students, especially in ''pull-out'' programs, makes use of methods frequently advocated by social studies educators. Students often engage in small group projects, group exercises for training critical thinking skills, and creative problem-solving activities. Independent student investigations often focus on social problems or issues that are considered social studies content. Educators of gifted students have much to gain by recognizing the natural overlap of their goals and methods with the field of social studies.

Identifying Students Gifted in Social Studies

Identifying students with unusual talent in social studies is complicated by the scope of the field and the diverse skills necessary for the various social sciences that comprise the field of social studies. Many of the characteristics that lead to outstanding achievement in social studies can be developed, given the right setting, even though they might not be evident initially.

Plowman (1980) suggests that social studies teachers look for certain characteristics to identify the gifted and talented, students who:

- Are conceptually advanced for their age
- Are a storehouse of advanced, technical, or very specific knowledge
- Enjoy difficult or complex tasks
- Set high standards for independent projects
- Are recognized by classmates as a source of new ideas and knowledge and recognized as group strategists or organizers
- See humor in human relationships and are able to laugh at themselves
- Tell or write imaginative stories
- Have wide-ranging and/or highly focused interests

- See relationships that other people do not
- Absorb knowledge easily and in a minimum time
- Are advanced, intensive, and extensive readers—at least two grade levels above class placement
- Use self-survival mechanisms—e.g., fantasy when the pace of learning is too slow, the generalizations are too simple, the content is too mundane, or the instruction is geared at a depressingly low conceptual-comprehension level (p. 14)

The behavioral objectives suggested for focusing the social sciences curriculum to gifted children in California schools (California State Department of Education, 1977) sound remarkably similar to the characteristics in Plowman's identification checklist:

- Applies problem-solving procedures gained from the social sciences to every-day situations
- Shows unusual ability to organize complex tasks
- Demonstrates prolonged attention when working on independent investigations
- Displays evidence of curiosity and attempts experimentation
- Finds relationships between apparently unrelated concepts across several subject disciplines
- Displays intellectual honesty in an intense search for truth (pp. 2–3)

Since the talents for which we are looking and the skills we are trying to develop are so similar, any effort to identify students gifted in social studies should also help to develop those traits in a wider range of students. This interactive view of what it means to be gifted is consistent with the recent research supporting a broadened conception of giftedness (Getzels & Dillon, 1973; Guilford, 1977; MacKinnon, 1978; Renzulli, 1978; Wallach, 1976). Increasingly, researchers suggest that creative productivity may be more strongly influenced by nonintellectual factors (motivation, personality, participation in extracurricular activities) than by measures of school achievement or ability (Barron, 1963; Bloom, 1963; Munday & Davis, 1974; Wallach, 1976).

Renzulli's Revolving Door Identification Model (Renzulli, Reis & Smith, 1981) takes into account the interactive nature of giftedness. This model's flexibility makes it particularly helpful in identifying students gifted in social studies.

The Revolving Door Identification Model (RDIM) is based on Renzulli's definition of giftedness, focusing on the interaction of above-average ability, creativity, and task commitment the student brings to bear on a topic. It includes the premise that giftedness is not "an absolute concept—something that exists in and by itself, without relation to anything else" (p. ix), but that it can be a relative or situational concept. Students with above-average ability may be responsive to activities that develop interests or produce creativity, and consequently may begin to display the creative, productive behavior typical of the gifted. Renzulli et al. (1981) suggest

We can serve gifted students more effectively if we (1) expand the number and variety of opportunities, (2) make the opportunities available to more students, (3) do not require every child to follow through on every activity and (4) provide supplementary services at the time and in the areas where a child shows the eagerness to follow through. In other words, our identification procedures should place as much emphasis on the ways in which children interact with experiences (i.e., action or performance information) as they do on the ways in which children respond to structured questions or ratings (i.e., status or psychometric information). (p. x)

Use of RDIM begins with selecting a talent pool of approximately 20 percent of the school population. These students receive special services, including compacting and streamlining of regular classroom material, exposure to a wide range of learning activities not ordinarily included in the regular classroom, and training in creative and critical thinking skills. The activities frequently take place in the regular classroom, where all students have the opportunity to benefit from them. Students in the talent

Figure 7-1   ENTRY AND EXIT CRITERIA FOR THE REVOLVING DOOR MODEL

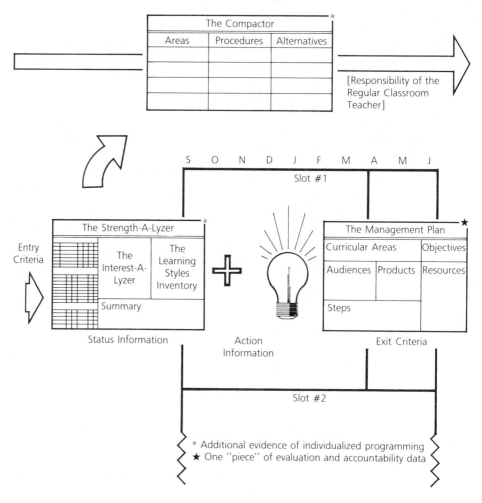

From J. S. Renzulli, S. M. Reis, and L. H. Smith, *The revolving door identification model* (Mansfield Center, Conn.: Creative Learning Press, 1981). Used by permission.

pool who respond to these activities or other classroom experiences with an interest in investigating a topic in some depth, "revolve" into a special resource setting where they receive intensive help. Approximately 5 percent of the school population takes part in this advanced level enrichment at any given time. As students complete their individual or small group investigations, they revolve back into the regular classroom.

Figure 7–1 illustrates Renzulli's identification model. Identification procedures use the usual "status information," including test scores and teacher ratings, but also rely heavily on current "action information," such as a student's expressed desire, enthusiasm, or interest in pursuing a topic further. Figure 7–2 shows how the regular classroom teacher plays a key role in spotting a high level of student interest and in communicating this to the specialist teacher in the resource setting.

Identifying students who are gifted in the area of social studies, then, becomes

Figure 7–2 TEACHER COMMUNICATION OF HIGH STUDENT INTEREST

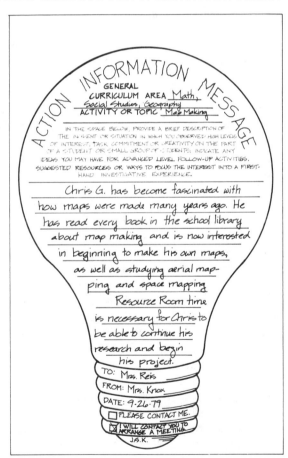

From J.S. Renzulli, S.M. Reis, and L.H. Smith, *The revolving door identification model* (Mansfield Center, Conn.: Creative Learning Press, 1981). Used by permission.

a process of looking for unusual potential from among a wide range of students who have ample opportunities to interact with materials and thus give hints of outstanding capability. It is a process of developing talent while we are attempting to recognize it, then following up with intensive help and encouragement as a student's gifts and talents become evident.

Essential Concepts

In designing social studies programs appropriate for gifted and talented students, educators must not only decide how such programs should differ from common classroom practice, but must answer a more difficult question as well: How should social studies programs for the gifted differ from the best social studies practices advocated for all students? The answers to both questions must be a natural out-growth of gifted students' characteristics. According to Kaplan (1979), this poses a twofold problem: "differentiating the curriculum for the general characteristics of the gifted and adapting the curriculum for individual manifestations of these characteristics" (p. 163).

Common classroom practice is insufficient to challenge gifted and talented students. Most teachers have not had the training that "would make them respond 'instinctively' to the fruitful observation or the penetrating question of a thoughtful student" (Stake & Easley, 1978, p. 16). Although each social studies teacher has a different set of purposes, the most common and vigorously defended purpose is that of socialization. Teachers see this purpose as "intimately related to observance of the mores of the community, submitting personal inclinations to the needs of the community, conforming to the role of the 'good student,' and getting ready for the next rung on the educational ladder" (Stake & Easley, 1978, p. 16). The highly talented and creative student clearly requires more latitude for questioning and exploring ideas, more emphasis on critical thinking skills, and more opportunities for creative problem solving. Many other students could benefit from these changes, as well.

How, then, should social studies for the gifted differ from good social studies education? The answer is tied to the learning-style characteristics of gifted students, but even more importantly to our goals in educating the gifted and talented. The primary goal in the education of gifted and talented students is to develop "creative producers" (Renzulli, 1977; Ward, 1961). Social studies for the gifted should focus on developing creative producers in the social sciences, persons who might add something new to a discipline or even change its direction. It should also encourage creative producers who can bridge social science disciplines, synthesize them, and give us visionary leadership.

Relevant learning, according to Jerome Bruner, is "what you know that permits you to move toward goals you care about" (1971, p. 114). Recent social studies critics (Johns, 1983; Shaver, 1977) suggest that goals of social studies reformers concerning learning the structure of the discipline (that is, learning the tools to be a historian rather than learning about history) may not be relevant or appropriate for all students. Shaver (1977) calls for a shift in emphasis from attention to social sciences data (note the Social Science tradition in Table 7–1), to a concern with values and political-ethical decision making (note the Reflective Inquiry tradition in Table 7–1). Such a need seems evident. Bruner (1966), as well, suggests that "structure must always be related to the status and gifts of the learner. Viewed in this way, the optimal structure of a body of knowledge is not absolute but relative" (p. 41).

Students derive a substantial amount of their knowledge about social issues from sources other than school (Wronski, 1981), and in one recent study, reported that on the social issue of energy use "they obtained little or nothing in the way of knowledge, attitudes or decision-making ability from their elementary and secondary school experiences" (p. 121). Johns (1983) points out the importance of beginning with students' interests and current levels of knowledge. He suggests that students will not integrate social studies content if it is too far removed from their level of self-understanding.

Many attempts at social studies reforms have been defeated by trying to get everyone involved to take one approach. The goal of teaching the structure of the discipline (social studies taught as social science) may be more appropriate for gifted and talented students than for students in general education. Research on learning styles of gifted and talented students indicates their preference for independent work (Stewart, 1977). This characteristic, coupled with the goal of becoming a creative producer, fits well with the process of learning the structure of the discipline—of becoming a young social scientist.

Reaching the Goals of Social Studies for the Gifted

The first step in providing for gifted students in social studies is to recognize and encourage those areas of general education that provide linkage, that are important initial steps in developing special talent in social studies. Whitehead's (1929) "romance stage" of learning is such a bridge. Paul Torrance (1981) refers to it as "encouraging children to 'fall in love' with something and develop bigger, richer, more accurate images of the future" (p. i). Other bridges to talent development are training critical thinking skills, creative thinking skills, and decision-making skills. Models developed by Ward (1982), Taba (1971), Williams (1970) and Taylor (1968) give specific help for developing these thinking skills.

The most significant bridge to talent development may be the organization and management of a school or classroom. Common sense, as well as recent research (Hamilton, 1983; Bronfenbrenner, 1979; Peshkin, 1978; Cusick, 1973; Deal & Kennedy, 1983; Brookover, Schweitzer, Beady, Flood & Wisenbaker, 1978; Goodlad, 1983b; Grabe, 1981), supports the view that the structure of the school environment does a great deal of "teaching" quite apart from the planned instruction that takes place. Research on school and classroom ecology focuses on the "hidden curriculum"—the implicitly taught values, behavior, and social systems. The hidden curriculum is perhaps a more powerful teaching tool for social studies than for any other school subject. The importance of opportunities for leadership and democratic participation in the school setting can hardly be overemphasized, especially for developing outstanding talent in the social sciences. Research from the American College Testing Service (1974) suggests that participation in extracurricular activities may predict success in adult life more accurately than either school grades or test scores.

Besides the usual activities such as student government and the school newspaper in secondary schools, students can also become more directly involved in solving school or classroom problems through creative problem-solving techniques.

The next step in social studies programming for the gifted is to provide the specialized and distinctive help necessary for a student who demonstrates outstanding ability or potential, the young person who is not only capable of learning and applying the tools of the social scientist creatively but who also is interested in doing so. Renzulli's Enrichment Triad Model (1977) is an excellent guide for this process.

Creativity is integral to the outstanding historian or any other social scientist. Compelling curiosity about a topic is the first step to creative thinking, the starting point to a thorough and thoughtful investigation. Willingness to wonder and imagine allows bright young historians to see afresh the images of the past. The inclination to question brings about new combinations of recorded material. The drive to investigate and to speculate may bring new and insightful interpretations of historical data. The creative process is more than a set of steps or exercises to make learning more enjoyable; it is the driving force of the productive social scientist. Gifted youth in the social sciences need to examine their own learning styles and creative powers at the same time they immerse themselves in content. Gifted and talented students can best profit from social studies when an understanding of creativity is interwoven with the study of content and the investigation of real problems. In this way, creativity becomes the most important tool of the young social scientist.

Models for Working with Gifted Students

Several educational models can be applied to social studies programming for gifted and talented students. Their primary value is to help educators organize their thinking about how to work with individual students as well as groups so they can move closer to the goal of recognizing and developing talent.

The Enrichment Triad Model

The Enrichment Triad Model (Renzulli, 1977) is a broad-based and comprehensive model for developing defensible programs for gifted and talented students. Its objective is to enable students to become true inquirers in their areas of interest. The primary focus of the students' time is on investigating real problems in a manner consistent with their preferred styles of learning.

> The historian does not first think of a problem and then search for evidence bearing on it; it is his possession of evidence bearing on a problem that alone makes the problem a real one" (Winks, 1968, p. 521).

Renzulli's Enrichment Triad uses a dynamic rather than a sequential approach to help gifted students find areas of sincere interest and "real problems" to investigate. Type I Activities (General Exploratory Activities) can lead directly to an investigation, or instead to Type II Activities (Group Training in Thinking and Feeling Processes). Depending on the level of interest and readiness, a student might begin right away with a Type III Activity (Individual and Small Group Investigation of Real Problems). Table 7–2 categorizes the types of activities for social studies.

Through even a simple investigation, students can come to understand and appreciate the difficult task of the social scientist. They may find it necessary to develop information skills, such as locating sources, narrowing the focus of inquiry, organizing snapshots, or using cassettes. To answer their questions, they may have to conduct oral research, observe, interview, or survey. Students can come to view the social sciences as an opportunity for exciting detective work.

The action learning approach usually involves some connection between ideas under exploration and the world outside school. The focus frequently begins with the concrete and accessible rather than the abstract, and requires that students become actively engaged with their topics. The key to successful action learning may be the

Table 7-2   THE ENRICHMENT TRIAD MODEL IN SOCIAL STUDIES

Type I Activities	Type II Activities

Teacher-led discussions
Exciting speakers
Simulation
Field trips
Presentation of old pictures
  and historical memorabilia
Presentation of old news-
  papers
Panel discussions
Films
	Locating information sources
	Interviewing skills
	Affective training in dealing with controversial
	  historical issues
	Advanced research and reference skills
	Photography and media skills
	Organization, cataloguing and preparation of
	  materials
	Advanced writing and editing
	Evaluation of primary vs. secondary sources
	Textbook stereotyping and bias in portraying
	  history

Type III Activities	

A historical walking tour of a city
Oral history interviews with past city
  mayors
Development of a simulation war game
A media presentation of the music of
  the 1940s
Oral history interviews recording a fac-
  tory's influence on a community
A book summarizing local folklore
A family tree: A study of genealogy	

From S.M. Reis, and T. Herbert, Creating practicing professionals in gifted programs: Encouraging students to become young historians. (Article submitted for publication; University of Connecticut, 1983.) Used with permission.

opportunity to reflect on the meaning of the activity and to compare experiences and insights with others (Mehaffy, Atwood, & Nelson, 1981). Personal reflective inquiry may then be an impetus for further application of the tools of a social scientist to a problem.

These booklets from *The Triad Prototype Series: Curriculum Units for the Gifted and Talented Based Upon The Enrichment Triad Model* give examples for implementing the Enrichment Triad Model in areas of social studies.

- Krause, C.S. *Genealogy: Your past revisited.* Mansfield Center, Connecticut: Creative Learning Press, 1980.
- Dutton, N.C. *Civil defense: From town hall to the pentagon.* Mansfield Center, Connecticut: Creative Learning Press, 1980.
- Johnson, J.M. *Victorian house-keeping: A combined study of restoration and photography.* Mansfield Center, Connecticut: Creative Learning Press, 1978.
- Dow, C. *Lunchroom waste: A study of "how much and how come."* Mansfield Center, Connecticut: Creative Learning Press, 1978.

Ward's DEG Model

Ward's (1980) Differential Education for the Gifted (DEG) Model provides a foundation for developing interdisciplinary programs for gifted and talented students. Ward (1981) contends that in preparing gifted students for their anticipated social role of reconstructionists, it is important to introduce them to the theoretical or connected level of ideas as early as the first grade.

The following propositions from Ward's model guide the educator toward an interdisciplinary approach for gifted students:

VI. A. That in the education of the gifted child and youth the scope of the content should extend into the *general* nature of *all* the chief branches of knowledge.

VI. B. That the curriculum for the gifted individual should be introduced and initially explore the concepts extending over broad expanses of knowledge.

VII. A. That instruction in methods of inquiry should be included in the education of the intellectually superior child and youth.

VIII. B. That existing sources of knowledge should be emphasized as a regular part of instruction in any subject matter area.

IX. A. That the history of the various fields of knowledge should be taught as foundational to present concepts within each academic discipline.

IX. B. That classics of the world's literary and educational store should be treated as foundational in the development of the thought of man and that the gifted should be instructed in such great works.[1]

Ward challenges the notion that both a teacher's book and a student's book are necessary, and cites these two books as substantive sources for an integrated approach:

- Bronowski, J. *The ascent of man.* Boston: Little, Brown, 1973.

---

[1] V.S. Ward, Differential Education for the Gifted (Ventura, Calif.: Ventura County Superintendent of Schools, 1980): 144–75.

- Clark, K. *Civilization*. New York: Harper & Row, 1969.

These are other excellent sources for exploring the connectedness of ideas, events, and people:

- Jung, C.G. *Man and his symbols*. Garden City, New York: Doubleday, 1964.
- Sagan, C. *The dragons of Eden: Speculations on the evolution of human intelligence*. New York: Random House, 1977.
- Steichen, E. *The family of man*. New York: Museum of Modern Art, 1955.
- Spier, P. *People*. New York: Doubleday, 1980. (A picture book for all ages illustrating various shapes, sizes, characteristics, habits, homes, holidays, languages, and customs of people.)
- Connections, film series.

Ward's DEG model calls for attention to psychological and developmental needs as well as to the nature of knowledge. He suggests an emphasis on major themes, such as great ideas, great drama, or great poetry.

Ward (1961) says that one should stress the function of meaning in the instruction of gifted students.[2] Bronowski's *Ascent of Man* (1973) illustrates the integrated nature of various subjects. Several ideas from this book can serve as points for discussion about the threads of meaning that run through various disciplines:

- But the Ascent of Man is not made by lovable people. It is made by people who have two qualities: an immense integrity, and at least a little genius. (pp. 144; 148)
- . . . a scientific discovery flows from a personality, and that discovery comes alive as we watch it being made by a person. (p. 141)
- The most powerful drive in the ascent of man is his pleasure in his own skill. He loves to do what he does well and, having done it well, he loves to do it better. You see it in his science. You see it in the magnificence with which he carves and builds, the loving care, the gaiety, the effrontery. The monuments are supposed to commemorate kings and religions, heroes, dogmas, but in the end the man they commemorate is the builder. (p. 116)
- I use the word ascent with a precise meaning. Man is distinguished from other animals by his imaginative gifts. He makes plans, inventions, new discoveries, by putting different talents together; and his discoveries become more subtle and penetrating, as he learns to combine his talents in more complex and intimate ways. So the great discoveries of different ages and different cultures, in technique, in science, in the arts, express in their progression a richer and more intricate conjunction of human faculties, an ascending trellis of his gifts. (p. 20)
- That is the essence of science: ask an impertinent question, and you are on the way to the pertinent answer. (p. 153)
- When a listener asked him what was the practical use of some theorem, Euclid is reported to have said contemptuously to his slave, "He wants to profit from learning—give him a penny." The reproof was probably adapted from a motto of the

---

[2]An excellent aid to dealing with the dimension of meaning in an interdisciplinary approach with gifted students is a model developed by Philip H. Phenix, described in Phenix, P.H., Toward realms of meaning: Curriculum implications for the gifted and talented, in *Curricula for the Gifted: Selected Proceedings of the First National Conference on Curricula for the Gifted/ Talented* (Ventura, Calif.: The National/State Leadership Training Institute on the Gifted and Talented, 1982) and in Phenix, P.H., *Realms of Meaning* (New York: McGraw-Hill, 1964).

Pythagorean brotherhood, which translates roughly as 'A diagram and a step, not a diagram and a penny'—'a step' being a step in knowledge. (p. 162)[3]

Gifted students can also explore the implications of these ideas for their personal meaning, since they may share characteristics mentioned by Bronowski.

The design of the Governor's School of North Carolina (Ward, 1982) as well as the Arkansas Governor's School for the Gifted and Talented (Churchill and Haggard, 1982) illustrate the DEG model at the secondary level. Both are intensive residential summer programs to serve gifted and talented students who have just completed their junior year in high school. The curriculum for the Arkansas Governor's School is composed of three areas:

Area I: Special Aptitude Development

Students spend the largest portion of their time participating in an area of special interest or ability. Students select from Natural Science, Social Science, Mathematics, English/Language Arts, Visual Art, Drama, and Instrumental or Choral Music. This area of study deals primarily with "how theory works in organizing a field of knowledge." (p. 8)

Area II: General Conceptual Development

Area II is conducted with an emphasis on open discourse where students deal with a variety of world views. Students are encouraged to "analyze, criticize, understand, and evaluate the competing or complementary claims such theories make upon our beliefs." (p. 11) They examine a variety of ways of knowing with an aim toward open-mindedness and critical thought.

Area III: Personal and Social Development

The curriculum of this area is designed to deal with personal and social problems faced by gifted and talented young people. Students are exposed to ideas in personality theory and social theory, but most often are involved in directed discussion of personal and social topics.

The three areas are designed to complement one another and to encourage dialogue among faculty members and students. Students often mention the intensive interaction as a stimulus to becoming excited about ideas and as an aid in learning to think more critically and openly.

Taba Model

Although developed for use in the regular classroom, Hilda Taba's (1971) inductive thinking approach to elementary social studies is an excellent resource for teachers of gifted students. Taba's approach is influenced by Piaget's (1973) idea that "to understand is to invent" and Bruner's (1961) concept of the spiral curriculum. She emphasizes the inquiry process for students in forming concepts, interpreting data, and applying principles. Table 7–3 shows how the inquiry process can help students interpret data.

---

[3]Ideas for Discussion: An Interdisciplinary View (From Bronowski, *The ascent of man*. Little, Brown and Company, 1971.)

Table 7–3   APPLICATION OF TABA'S INDUCTIVE THINKING APPROACH*

	Overt activity	Covert mental operations	Eliciting questions
1.	Identifying points	Differentiating	What did you notice? See? Find?
2.	Explaining items of identified information	Relating points to each other. Determining cause and effect relationships.	Why did so-and-so happen?
3.	Making inferences	Going beyond what is given. Finding implications, extrapolating.	What does this mean? What picture does it create in your mind? What would you conclude?

---

*From Hilda Taba, Teacher's *Handbook for Elementary Social Studies,* 1967, Addison-Wesley, Reading, Mass.

The following example illustrates the use of teacher questions to encourage inductive thinking:

> Let us look at two question sequences (one deductive and one inductive) planned by two teachers who wanted their classes to identify some of the characteristics of Cortes and to make general statements about them. One teacher approached the task by asking, "From all that you have read about Cortes, what kind of person do you think he was?" In other words, she asked the students to make inferences in the opening question. Her class identified several characteristics, and she followed up on certain ones by asking "What did he do that makes you think that he was tricky?" "Why do you think that he was courageous?" and so on.
>
> This teacher was using a deductive questioning sequence, asking students to start by making trial inferences or conclusions and then to support them. The second teacher's opening question was, "As you think of Cortes, what were some of the things he did?" She then made a list of a number of Cortes' acts. Next, she moved in and said, "Well, let's look at, for instance, his burning of ships. What kind of person do you think would do this?" And "Let's think of Cortes as he wept on 'The Sad Night.' What kind of person do you think would do this?" She pursued a number of Cortes' actions and then asked, "Now, what kind of person would you say Cortes was?" One child might see him as a man of strong character; another might see him as a man of many different characteristics. The teacher who sought a conclusion in her opening question denied her class the opportunity to examine his actions before judging him. The second teacher planned to have her children see as many sides as they could. (Taba, 1971, pp. 110–11)

Taba's social studies curriculum includes not only academic skills such as listening, notetaking, making charts, constructing time lines, and asking relevant questions, but focuses on social skills as well:

- Planning with others
- Participating in research projects
- Participating productively in group discussions
- Responding courteously to the questions of others
- Leading group discussions
- Acting responsibly
- Helping others

Taba's approach employs carefully-sequenced content and suggested activities, but can also provide an excellent foundation of skills for gifted students who are interested in extending their learning as firsthand inquirers or investigators of real problems.

Williams's Model

Frank Williams's (1970) model, Ideas for Developing Productive Divergent Thinking, offers a wealth of strategy suggestions to aid elementary teachers in helping students use creative thinking skills as they deal with classroom content. The model is indexed by both subject area and thinking skill. The Williams Model best serves the social studies teacher by "triggering ideas" for designing learning experiences, since the model's activity suggestions are not systematically tied to social studies or the other content areas. It does, however, combine the use of thinking skills with a variety of highly usable teaching strategies. These examples* illustrate the use of the Williams Model with various elementary grade levels:

IDEA NO. 31

TO ENCOURAGE: FLEXIBLE THINKING AND IMAGINATION
THROUGH: Social Studies
USING: Strategies No. 5—Provocative questions
                         No. 14—Evaluate situations

The teacher *asked the class to pretend* that "tomorrow a rocket ship will land on the playground and after a few hours it will take off for a new planet. *Imagine that you are* responsible for selecting 100 persons who will board the ship and blast off to build a new world. Because only 100 persons will be allowed to go, you must carefully *decide as many different ways as you can for selecting the most valuable people.* When you make your suggestions, also give the reason for your choice."

The activity was used in order to determine the class's concept of American society and the teacher wanted the children to realize the value of social interdependence. (p. 34)

---

*From F. E. Williams, *Classroom ideas for encouraging thinking and feeling* (Buffalo, N.Y.: D.O.K. Publishers, 1970).

IDEA NO. 103

TO ENCOURAGE: ORIGINAL THINKING AND COMPLEXITY
THROUGH: Social Studies
USING: Strategies No. 8—Organized random search
                           No. 12—Adjustment to development
                           No. 18—Visualization skill

The children had been studying about the history of Indians and reading Indian stories. They had written letters using Indian sign language, and *were asked to write a message communicating in a new and original way. Each child was to hitchhike upon what he had already learned and develop a new and unique set of symbols of communication for expressing a message to the rest of the class.* After all the children had invented their own language symbols, their messages were written and shown to the class. The other class members were *to study what the symbols meant and make attempts to decode each message.* (p. 67)

IDEA NO.197

TO ENCOURAGE: CURIOSITY: COMPLEXITY
THROUGH: Social Studies
USING: Strategies No. 2—Attributes
                           No. 9—Skills of search
                           No. 14—Evaluate situations

Conducting a comparative study of eight cities in the United States was an exciting unit. The class was divided into eight subgroups with each group investigating a different city. *The groups were to explore and try to discover what made each city distinctive, why it grew up where it did, and predict what its future development would likely be.* After library materials, filmstrips, brochures, and other sources obtained from the Chamber of Commerce from each city were examined, each group prepared a presentation for the class about their specific city. The presentations were to be as detailed, informative, and challenging as possible. This type of activity worked best with more mature students, although each student was able to contribute something to each subgroup. (p. 109)

Taylor Model

Calvin Taylor's (1968) Multiple Talent model has been used to provide enrichment for the full range of students in a regular classroom setting, as well as for gifted students in special programs. The multiple talent approach can also help identify gifted students through their responses to talent activities. In the Talents Unlimited research project using the multiple talent model, successes in talent development occurred as often among minority and disadvantaged gifted students as among those from predominantly urban and white middle-class schools. (Schlichter, 1981). The model may thus be useful in talent identification as well as talent development. Taylor's model focuses on six "world of work" talents: academic; productive thinking; planning; communication; forecasting; and decision making.

Taylor's emphasis on activities that parallel skills used in the everyday world of work receives support from recent research in information processing among gifted students (Sternberg, 1981). Learning tasks are more valuable when students have to think in ways that are new for them and have to use thinking processes that are central to a particular discipline. Rather than using them as discrete skills in unrelated exercises, the talent processes can be linked to help bright students "make the connection between their problem-solving activity and problem solving in the world of work" (Schlichter, 1981, p. 149).

The talents have been illustrated by materials developed by the Talents Unlimited Project (1974), in which activities were designed to accompany texts for the Mobile County Public Schools. The following example illustrates the Forecasting Talent.

Always Jungle/Desert
(to accompany the fourth grade unit, "Hot, Wet, Dry Lands," Main Idea VI)

Motivation: Discuss some of the climatic, geographical and natural resource factors your class has been studying about hot, wet lands. Let class members describe a hot, wet land. Ask your class to think carefully about what might happen if the entire land surface of the world were covered with jungle vegetation and the weather was always hot, rainy and humid. For Mobile students who have difficulty visualizing this possibility, remind them of the July and August weather in our own city, which closely resembles tropical climate conditions. Allow individuals to predict many different things that might happen if the world were like this.

After about five minutes, shift to a different situation, telling your class they are going to continue their forecasting as a part of their social studies unit.

Teacher talk: Say, "We have been making predictions about a jungle; now let's make many different predictions about a desert. Suppose that the world were just one big hot Sahara Desert. What would happen? Write your many different predictions on a sheet of paper."

Student response: Encourage students to shift categories as they write their many predictions. Also remind them to continue to work for fluency of categories. These responses can be judged using the guidelines for forecasting.

Reinforcement: Use verbal and nonverbal reinforcement for relevant forecasting efforts of students as they write their many different predictions. (p. F-8)

Selected Strategies for the Gifted and Talented

Examining Role Models

Looking at history through biographies and autobiographies of famous people can help students see the connections between their own experiences and the larger world. As students imaginatively reconstruct the lives of others, they also gain self-understanding through the comparison. "It is through the inward development of personality that individual human beings are able to perform those creative acts, in their outward fields of action, that cause the growth of human societies" (Toynbee, 1933, p. 233). For a fuller understanding, it is important that students study not only the lives of individuals but the social systems in which they lived. As students focus alternately on individuals and social systems, they begin to more effectively pose and rationally test their own hypotheses about how people respond creatively in a crisis and become effective agents of change (Johns, 1983).

Besides studying the lives of heros, heroines, and leaders,[4] it would be helpful for gifted students to study the life of a historian. Theodore White's *In Search of History: A Personal Adventure* (1978) is a rich source of ideas on how history becomes history and on the role of the historian. The teacher might use an activity such as the following to tie together a unit about role models.

Sample Activity

Before showing students the following list of quotes from Theodore White, have them jot down their ideas of at least three factors that might influence the life and thoughts of a historian. Have them compare their predictions with White's words.[5]

Good reporters organize facts in "stories," but good historians organize lives and episodes in "arguments." (p. 14)

This thought had lasted for years, as popular fashion went at the time—the thought that leadership is a quest of men seeking to find themselves and that in so seeking, they shape the lives of other people. (p. 16)

I had become obsessed with force as the engine of history: who gathers the guns together at what point to hammer at the state or the enemy. Fairbank wrote back to my remonstrance a long letter on the causes of human action in man, saying that "force forces them at times, fear of force more often—and ideals still more often." (p. 72)

I remained, as I can see now, still a sightseer but of a different kind—a collector of impressions of whatever could be typed or pasted into a dispatch. I collected sights, sounds, personalities, famous names, episodes. *Time* was then a far less responsible magazine than it is today, and delighted in quips, curiosities, anec-

---

[4]A useful guide in studying the concept of leadership with elementary gifted students is J.J. Gallagher et al., *Leadership unit: The use of teacher-scholar teams to develop units for the gifted.* (New York: Trillium Press, 1982.)

[5]From T. H. White, *In search of history: A personal adventure* (New York: Harper and Row, 1978). Used with permission.

dotes and quotes, whether true or not. If there was a history that framed it all then the editors back in New York decided what the history meant, and reporters simply supplied raw materials. As a purveyor of such raw material, their collector of anecdotes, personalities, episodes, names, in the Far East, I thrived—and left the history to New York. (pp. 140–41)

I could see carts, or files of soldiers, appearing and disappearing in such mists beyond, and their officers on horseback at the head of the column. But in those five days I did not know who was who on the far ridges, so I cannot put this story together correctly, for I was lost in mist myself—political, linguistic, fear-ridden mist. (p. 126)

Making Choices

Some consider the process of decision making not merely a strategy for teaching, but the primary concern of social studies. They believe along with Socrates that "facts from which no conclusion can be drawn are hardly worth knowing." Students need to be aware of both the personal and public nature of their decisions.

Cassidy and Kurfman (1977) point out the need to consider values and feelings along with facts and generalizations in moving through the steps of considering and selecting alternatives. Ochoa (1981) points out the importance of relating goals and alternatives to principles of human dignity as well as to personal values.

Another aid in helping students understand the process of making choices is a mode of valuing developed by Raths, Merrill, and Simon (1978). They describe values as based on the processes of choosing, prizing, and acting. Their book *Values and Teaching* describes and illustrates numerous classroom strategies for helping students

Table 7–4   STEPS IN DECISION MAKING

Facts/ Generalizations	Identify decision occasions and their alternatives: a. Define the decision to be made. b. Identify the goals of the decisionmaker. c. Identify available alternatives. Examine and evaluate decision alternatives: a. Examine the probable outcomes of each alternative. b. Evaluate and rank the alternatives. Decide and reflect on the decision: a. Select an alternative. b. Implement the plan of action. c. Assess the results of action. d. Consider recycling the process.	Values/ Feelings

From E.W. Cassidy and D.G. Kurfman, Decision making as purpose and process. In *Developing decision-making skills*, ed. D. G. Kurfman. Forty-seventh Yearbook of the National Council for the Social Studies. (Washington, D.C.: The Council, 1977.)

examine their values (e.g., rank order, reaction sheets, open-ended sentences, the public interview, role playing, devil's advocates, and the value continuum).

As they examine values within the context of curriculum content, students should be encouraged to discuss and compare with other people, both peers and adults. The following activities lead students to think about and discuss their values as they consider world problems.

A Helping Hand for Pandora[6]

Help Pandora stuff the evils back into her box and cleanse the world.

Pandora is convinced that if she can only catch all the evils, stash them back in the box, and clasp on the lid, everything will be all right again.

Can you help her?

Study the list of evils below. Think about which one causes *you* the most unhappiness. Try to get this one back into the box first by listing it as #1. Then continue down the list the same way—the next worst evil, in your opinion, will be #2, etc. Complete the list and free the world from all its problems and pains.

Some of the evils in the world:

1. Natural disasters like earthquakes, hurricanes, etc.
2. Death
3. Stealing
4. Hunger and starvation
5. Diseases that man hasn't conquered yet, like cancer, heart disease, arthritis, etc.
6. Drugs and man's addiction to them
7. Highway accidents
8. Jealousy
9. Old age and loss of senses and abilities
10. Lying
11. Murder

Put the evils back in Pandora's box in the order they seem most harmful to you.

1.
2.
3.
4.
5.
6.
7.
8.
9.
10.
11.

The Worst of All Possible Evils—An Adult View

How different is an adult's point of view from yours? What kind of experiences over the years have influenced his or her thinking?

Show an adult (not your teacher) the list of evils to put back in Pandora's Box (See ''A Helping Hand for Pandora''). Let the adult suggest the order.

---

[6]From The Acropolis Unit by B. Blair and E. Stewart.

> Compare your first and last choices with the adult's. Are they the same?
>
> | *My choices* | *An adult's choices* |
> |---|---|
> | First | First |
> | Last | Last |
>
> If they are different, think about what might have influenced the adult's decision. (Maybe you'd even like to ask.) Then write your conclusions here. _____
> _____

Developing Future Images

> "Ideas," says W. Macneile Dixon, the English philosopher, in his The Human Situation, "are the most mysterious things in a mysterious world. . . . They are beyond prediction. They appear to have a life of their own, independent of space and time, and to come and go at their own pleasure . . . . They are living, powerful entities of some kind, and as infective as fevers. Some, like flowers, are the creatures of an hour; others are of a prodigious vitality and root themselves, like oaks, in the soil of human nature for a thousand years. Ideas, like individuals, live and die. They flourish, according to their nature, in one soil or climate, and droop in another. They are the vegetation of the mental world." (Cousins, 1981, p. 38)

Morris Stein (1981) contends that "future images" in the minds of students have more influence on eventual productivity than do intellectual or creative ability. Clark (1969), on a broader scale, suggests that the growth and development of an entire civilization may be based on ideas and inspiration. It thus seems particularly important to encourage in students the development of future images.

Sample Activities

Kindergarten Through Grade 3*

I. Subject Area: Art, Social Studies

II. Future studies goal:
To help students develop an awareness of constantly changing social patterns and future trends.

III. Objective:
Students will match a word list with pictures of possible changes in our environment to develop future-focused images.

---

*Sample activities from the Office of the Los Angeles County Superintendent of Schools, Introducing a Futures Perspective into the Career Education Curriculum (Downey, Calif.: Los Angeles County Schools, 1982). Used by permission.

IV. Rationale:
The future has always been of interest to society. People constantly think about what changes the future might bring. We need to actively develop future-focused images that will help us make critical decisions regarding individuals, families, and society.

V. Activity:
Show the students pictures that illustrate possible changes in the environment and that relate to the future. Give the students the list of words below and have them match the pictures to the word list.
Word list:

food	family	home	friendship
energy	art	work	pollution
sports	music	clothes	transportation

Possible Pictures:
Computers, astronauts, robots, rapid transit, protein substitutes, dome houses, jobs, careers, solar heater, nuclear power plant
Ask the students to bring in other pictures to illustrate future images.
Using a large appliance container, construct a Future Box. Make an entrance door on the side of the box and paste all the students' future pictures on the inside and outside. For quiet time, the students can explore the Future Box.

VI. Resources:
1. Magazine pictures
2. Newspaper articles

VII. Evaluation:
Students will match a word list to pictures of possible changes in our environment.

Grade 4 through Grade 6

I. Subject Areas: Social Studies, Mathematics

II. Future studies goal:
To help students realize how anticipated future changes may impinge upon their own life style and aspirations.

III. Objectives:
Students will view change as the natural product of the interaction between people and ideas.

IV. Rationale:
The world around us is constantly changing. Although change is possible for all people, a relationship exists between the kind of person one is today and the kind

of person one will be in the future. Changes in values and goals during the life cycle need to be explored.

V.   Activity:
The students will discuss the following questions:
What do you remember learning in 1st grade, 2nd grade, 3rd grade . . . . ? Is school work getting harder or easier? (Compare math papers from different grade levels.) What has happened in your family since you were five years old? (e.g., vacations, moving, new brothers or sisters) Discuss changing values and goals: family education, money, status, jobs, houses, etc.

VI.   Resources:
1. *Learning for Tomorrow* by Alvin Toffler (Vintage Books, 1974)
2. Mathematics papers from different grade levels

VII.   Evaluation:
The teacher observes student participation in the discussion.

Grade 7 through Grade 9

I.   Subject Areas: Social Studies, English

II.   Future studies goal:
To help students develop an awareness of constantly changing social patterns and future trends.

III.   Objective:
The students will define the phrase "good old days" and relate it to the present and future.

IV.   Rationale:
Many students exposed to the negative aspects of sociocultural change talk about "the good old days." They need to gain a sense of perspective in identifying and evaluating those changes in society that contribute to progress and those that bring new problems.

V.   Activity:
Have students read one or two accounts of everyday life in America between 1900 and 1920. Have them identify what they mean by the term "good old days." What was good about them? What was not so good? In what ways are we better off today? In what ways are we not as well off? Can we have the "good" things without the "bad"? Do you think people fifty years from now will regard our present period as "the good old days"? Will people always look at the past with nostalgia, longing for things to be the way they used to be?

VI.   Resources:
1.   Have students watch TV programs depicting life at an earlier period in history.

2. Have students interview senior citizens and ask them to describe the advantages and disadvantages of life today in comparison to when they were students.
3. *Optimism One* by F.M. Esfandiary (Poplar Library, 1978).
4. *UpWingers* by F.M. Esfandiary, (Poplar Library, 1978).

VII. Evaluation:
Teacher evaluates student's presentation of his/her research comparing quality of life in historical periods.

Grade 10 through Grade 12

I. Subject Areas: Social Studies, Home Economics

II. Future studies goal:
To help students develop an awareness of constantly changing social patterns and future trends.

III. Objective:
Students will be able to distinguish between social and technological innovations and discuss the consequences of social innovations.

IV. Rationale:
There is nearly universal agreement that technology includes physical artifacts, such as power plants, telecommunication systems, and airplanes, as well as the physical activities or actions that alter the environment, such as building construction and the siting of oil refineries.

Sometimes the definition of the term "technology" is expanded to include social tools and techniques. Unquestionably, social technology is a major source of secondary impact on society. Consider, for example, the far-reaching consequences of such social instruments as:
1. The "pay as you go" (withholding) income tax, proposed by Beardsley Rumi during World War II, and now a generally accepted part of the tax system.
2. The Morrill Land Grant College Act of 1862.
3. The invention and application of farm subsidies.
4. The county agent system.
Just as a minor alteration in a physical technology may have profound side effects, so a minor alteration in a nation's social technology can have many important consequences undreamed of by the legislators or others who approve the alteration.

Example: One example of an unintended effect is the impact of the U.S. Social Security System on the living arrangements of elderly persons. Since social security payments are reduced when two people get married, large numbers of elderly couples live together without benefit of clergy.

V. Activity:
Discuss the secondary effects of the following future social technologies:

1. Retirement at age 55.
2. Consequences of a guaranteed income for every family.
3. People admired for buying and consuming as little as possible rather than as much as possible.

VI. Resources:
The Futurist, "Technology Assessment: The Benefits, the Costs, the Consequences" by J.F. Coates (December 1971): pp. 225–231.
Social Innovations by Stuart Conger (Saskatoon, Saskatchewan: Modern Press, Canada, 1970).

VII. Evaluation:
Teacher evaluates student ability to describe orally or in writing the distinction between social and technological innovation and to provide examples of social innovations anticipated in the future and their possible consequences.

Role-Taking

Role-taking is a useful strategy for helping students understand social values and make effective decisions (Shaftel & Shaftel, 1967). Role-taking, or sociodrama, at its best can be described as a group creative problem-solving process (Torrance & Myers, 1970). It allows a group to examine a social problem through a dramatic method—an unrehearsed skit. Torrance (1975) suggests that some students will find it easier to identify with a role if they are given a simple prop, such as a cap, coat, or other gear.

In the direct presentation technique (Moreno & Moreno, 1969), students are asked to act out a conflict situation. In the following example, students assume roles based on the conflict that surrounded the building of the Parthenon in Athens, Greece.

A Press Conference: Please, Mr. Pericles*

Pericles was bombarded with protests from all sides against building the Parthenon. Though they envisioned the temple, when finished, as something that would reflect how great Athens really was, few people shared Pericles' dream at first—even among the Athenians.

For a description of the opposition he faced, read Plutarch's "Quarrel about Building the Parthenon." Then choose a role to play yourself—either Pericles or one of the Greeks who opposed his idea (General, Citizen, or Opposition Party Leader).

Interviewers (General, Islander, Citizen or Opposition Party Leader): After you choose the role you want to play, study the profile sheet of that character. Then make up one relevant question to ask Pericles at the Press Conference.

Pericles: You must be able to answer all of the protests. Before you appear at the Press Conference, read the roles of the interviewers so that you know how to go about answering the questions as the real Pericles would have.

If your performance comes off sounding like a real Press Conference, your teacher may ask you to put it on tape.

---

*From the Acropolis Unit by B. Blair and E. Stewart

Pericles—Profile Sheet

You are calm and cool. However, you try to persuade your interrogators that your action is reasonable and you are completely within your rights as the leader of Athens to try to build something that will not quickly be forgotten through the ages and will reflect how great your city really is.

Your role is clearly outlined in Plutarch's "Quarrel about Building the Parthenon." Remember that despite the quarrel and opposition, you will win if you persist.

General of the Athenian Army—Profile Sheet

You feel that Athens has lost her fine reputation as one of the leading Greek states. Now with money intended for defense, Pericles is gold-plating a 40-foot statue of Athena and building a temple just to house the sculpture.

As a man of military science, this stuff seems silly to you. You think Pericles is decking out your city like a vain proud woman with gold and precious gems.

You protest.

Opposition Party Leader in Athens—Profile Sheet

The Greek states which dot the countryside are now antagonized by Athens. Instead of the small Greek states trying to join together and build a nation, they resist.

You see that Sparta is Athens' greatest threat and you foresee that some day Athens will need the military assistance of the neighboring Greek states. You blame the whole mess on Pericles' removal of the Treasury of the Delian League to Athens and then using the funds to beautify the city. You view the move as extremely ill-timed and foolish.

You protest.

Athenian Citizen—Profile Sheet

You are a Greek citizen and father of three children. Since you yourself are an only child, you also have the responsibility of taking care of your parents and bringing them into your household. This exempts you from military service.

With seven people living under your roof, you find it difficult to make ends meet. If you were only able to go on military expeditions then the state could pay you. Maybe your son will soon be able to join the army. Then he can help alleviate your financial burden.

But now you feel that the money from the Delian League is not going to be saved for the military but instead used to beautify your city. You think your source of financial aid is disappearing in front of your eyes.

You protest.

Islander—Profile Sheet

A great deal of money for Pericles' Building Program which included the Acropolis and several other temples came from money in the treasury of the Delian League donated by the islands such as Aegina (EH-yee-nah), Naxos, Lesvos, Chios (HEE-os) and Samos. They gave this money in exchange for a promise of protection against the Persian fleet.

Now Pericles had chosen to move the treasury from the island of Delos to Athens. You along with the other islanders, thought he moved the money in case the island of Delos was invaded by the Persians. Now you find out Pericles is planning to use the money to make Athens beautiful. It's your money and now Athens is using it.

You protest.

Beyond the direct presentation techniques, other approaches may be even more effective in helping students gain new insights. Torrance (1975) describes the soliloquy technique, in which actors tell the audience thoughts and feelings that are usually hidden; the double technique, in which one of the actors is given a double who interacts with the actor as "himself" or "herself"; and the role reversal technique, in which two actors stop after a short time in the conflict situation and change roles, along with other techniques. Sociodrama provides a natural and absorbing way for students to look at their own values and feelings as well as those of others.

Use of Humor

Humor is a powerful instrument for instructing and intriguing social studies students. Its dimensions of surprise and unusual connections frequently lead students to probe ideas more deeply. The most common example of learning through humor is the political cartoon. Other cartoons are also useful, however, as are books that make use of discrepancies, anachronisms, or alternate points of view, some of which are:

- Bettman, O.L. *The good old days—they were terrible*. New York: Random House, 1974.
- Muir, F. *An irreverent and thoroughly incomplete social history of almost everything*. New York: Stein and Day, 1976.
- Shafer, B. *Can we afford this revolution*? New York: Scholastic Book Services, 1960.
- Seuling, B. *You can't eat peanuts in church and other little-known laws*. Garden City, New York: Doubleday, 1976.

Simulations

Simulations can be intense and highly motivating learning experiences, giving students opportunities for thinking "on their feet" about social studies concepts. A simulation may launch a gifted student into further self-directed inquiry about a particular topic. In *The Guide to Simulations/Games for Education and Training*, Horn and Cleaves (1980) describe more than 50 games and simulations related to social studies. Among them are:

- Bafa' Bafa', a simulation designed to encourage students (grades 7 and up) to experience differences among cultures.
- Dig, a simulated archaeological dig where students (grades 5–college) create hypothetical civilizations and construct artifacts for the dig.
- Baldicer, a simulation designed to allow students (grade 9–adult) to experience issues related to economic interdependence.

Multiple Viewpoints

By trying out multiple viewpoints, the young historian can move toward greater creativity as one who sees with new eyes and a fresh view. Rather than focusing on generals and presidents, a student might look at the day-to-day life of any historical period through the eyes of a peasant or villager, a view of history from the "bottom up" rather than the "top down." Sophisticated statistical techniques for applying the computer to historical analysis now allow projections of future trends based on a comparison of day-to-day newspaper accounts across small towns as well as large cities. (See, for example, *Megatrends* by John Naisbitt.) Students can also gain new insights by asking questions about the kinds of information that have been omitted from historical accounts.

A multidisciplinary approach helps students assume different viewpoints. Just as history is filled with examples of people who invented things outside their specialized fields (de Bono, 1974), so do students assume a more flexible view when they are interested in several areas and attempt to make connections between their various "networks of enterprise."

Responding to authentic documents about local history also helps students assume different points of view. The following document was used with gifted students in grades 4–6 to discuss the history of their hometown. After they read the document, the teacher encouraged students to pose questions and speculate about life in their hometown in 1820.

Social Life at Arkansas Post, 1820*
James Miller was the first governor of the Arkansas Territory. He was appointed because of his military record in the War of 1812, and he accepted because he needed the money. A native of New Hampshire, he came to Arkansas without his family and was generally displeased with what he found. His comments on Arkansas Post society probably exaggerate the influence of the French; American settlers were becoming numerous in the area and they were grazing cattle and growing crops on farms away from the Post in a manner that was characteristically American.

Post Arkansaw March 20th, 1820
My beloved Wife,
This country is very new, and society very uncultivated. They are at this place particularly very fond of Balls and Loo [a card game] parties. Saturday and Sunday nights are the

*From C.F. Williams, S.C. Bolton, C.H. Moneyhon, and L.T. Williams, eds. *A Documentary History of Arkansas* (Fayetteville, Ark.: University of Arkansas Press, 1983). Used with permission.

fashionable nights for their parties to meet, and they never disperse until after daylight. The population was originally French, and the Americans who come in fall into their practice. I wish you could see one of these balls. I refuse to attend on those nights, and they made one or two on other nights, which I did attend. They have one young lady, a Mamselle Don Carol, the rest of the ladies are married, from twenty to seventy-five years of age. The houses generally have two rooms, one room for dancing, the other to play Loo in and beds to lay the young suckling children on, a married woman is almost disqualified to attend a ball without a child, they nurse as unconcerned as at home in their nursery. They have one fiddler who can play one tune they can dance but one figure, which is a kind of reel or cotillion, they commence at dark and hold on until day light, when each of the fair sex saddles her own pony, mounts and trudges home. The men generally hold on longer at the card table. At these card tables I have seen Grandfather, Grandmother, son and daughter, and granddaughter all engaged in gambling as eager to make money as if playing with anyone else. It is not uncommon to lose 150 to 200 dollars in a night, or they may win. This appears to be their principal vice and it is a great one—I have discouraged it since I have been there . . .

Your devoted husband,
James Miller

Documents on a number of social studies topics, as well as facsimiles of letters, newspapers, cartoons, telegrams, and maps, are available through a series of packets called Jackdaws (New York: Grossman Publishers). The packets include such topics as The Making of the Constitution, Women in Revolt, Indian Resistance: The Patriot Chiefs, China: A Cultural Heritage, The Peasant's Revolt (Medieval Times), Children in the Middle East, Life in Africa, and The Conquest of Mexico.

Preschool/Primary Programming

Social studies programming for gifted primary age children has tended to focus on an integrated or interdisciplinary approach. Although a broad-based theme can help organize activities, the questions children initiate themselves guide much of the exploration and discussion. Units of study for young gifted children often emphasize their immediate environment and relationships.

The Astor Program for gifted children attempts to encourage a "joyful response to natural and spontaneous curiosity" (Ehrlich, 1977) in addition to intellectual expansion and exploration, and social responsibility. Interdisciplinary curriculum units developed by the Astor Program include several social studies concepts, such as *Beginnings,* an open-ended unit of study approached through anthropology.

Interaction between people and their environments gives rise to social studies explorations for young gifted children. The *Curriculum Guide for Teaching Gifted Children Social Sciences in Grades One through Three* (California State Department of Education, 1977) uses the theme of interaction to discuss skills, objectives, and teaching techniques for primary gifted students.

Young gifted children's developmental characteristics call for certain adjustments in the social studies learning environment. Primary children require a great deal of free movement in the classroom. They need time and encouragement for conversation, particularly student-to-student interaction. They acquire concepts more effectively by means of concrete props accompanied by explanations and the chance for hands-on exploration. For young gifted children especially, one should use questions they raise as starting points to help them explore possible answers in an environment rich in the raw materials and activities of learning.

Although some special programming for primary gifted and talented students occurs in a regular classroom setting, specialized help and an environment for exploration are best provided through small extended learning groups. Although "pull-out" time for learning in a resource room is less common for primary age students than for those of upper elementary levels, it can be valuable for some primary gifted children. A specialist-teacher is another alternative for guiding an extended learning group in the classroom setting. This approach can be helpful to the regular classroom teacher as well as to students.

Secondary Programming

As gifted students move from primary to elementary to secondary level, their need for a broader and more complex learning environment increases. A variety of delivery systems or administrative designs are available—resource rooms, separate classes, independent study, honors programs, advanced placement classes, internships, mentorship programs, before- and after-school groups, early college courses, and intensive summer programs. Whatever the combination of approaches, teachers should encourage independent thought and exploration as the student develops the understandings and skills of a creative social scientist. Students need maximum opportunities to interact with one another, to test their own ideas, and to assume positions of leadership. Educators should consider evaluation as part of the learning process, with minimal emphasis on grades and maximal emphasis on self-evaluation, and feedback directed toward on-going efforts, to encourage continuing motivation.

Adapting Instructional Materials

Far more money is spent on television productions and media presentations than on developing classroom materials. Major research and development efforts for social studies materials designed especially for gifted and talented students are almost nonexistent. According to the report to the U.S. Secretary of Education from the Commission on Excellence (1983), curriculum materials for the gifted is considered a thin market, less profitable for commercial publishers. Some curriculum projects, however, can be adapted or used as resources for work with students who are gifted in social studies.

The following materials, from the new social studies curriculum project era of the sixties and seventies, although not designed specifically for gifted and talented students, use strategies and materials compatible with the goals of educating the gifted.

Elementary Materials

Man: A Course of Study (Cambridge, Mass.: Education Development Center, 1978).
This curriculum, for grades 5–6, was heavily influenced by Jerome Bruner. It takes a philosophical social science approach and emphasizes inductive teaching. Although there has been controversy as to whether the materials are too realistic for children, they are well-researched, carefully developed, and sensitive materials.

Anthropology Curriculum Project (Athens, Ga.: University of Georgia).
These materials for grades K–1 deal primarily with the concept of culture. They focus on anthropological understandings and stress deductive teaching strategies.

Elementary School Economics Project (Galien, Mich.: The Allied Education Council).
These curriculum materials in economics were developed at the University of Chicago for grades 4–5.

Casebooks on Law in Society (Chicago: Law in American Society Foundation).
These curriculum materials on law in society were develped for grades 4–5.

Geography Curriculum Project (Athens, Ga.: University of Georgia).
This curriculum for grades K–6 emphasizes involvement and inquiry teaching strategies with key concepts from geography.

The Taba Social Studies Curriculum (Menlo Park, Calif.: Addison-Wesley).
The Taba curriculum for grades 1–8 is a spiral program built around key concepts such as conflict, cultural change, and interdependence, using both inductive and deductive teaching strategies.

Secondary Materials

Public Issues Series: Harvard University Social Studies Project (Columbus, Ohio: American Education Publications).
This series of booklets engages secondary students in discussions of controversial topics.

Images of People: Sociological Resources for the Social Studies (Boston: Allyn and Bacon).
These sociology materials focus on testing hypotheses through experiments to help students examine stereotypes.

Studying Societies: Anthropology Curriculum Study Project (New York: Macmillan).
The case study lessons in this curriculum use information written by anthropologists about the Kalahari Bushman. Students formulate questions and test hypotheses while learning the basics of social science research.

Advanced Placement Program in American History and European History (Advanced Placement Program, Box 2899, Princeton, New Jersey 08541).
This program provides college-level studies in American and European history for secondary school students. Students take examinations following the AP courses, and participating colleges grant advanced placement or credit to students who pass the examinations.

Other Sources

Clendening, C.P., and R.A. Davies. Challenging the gifted: Curriculum enrichment and acceleration models. New York: R.R. Bowker, 1983.
This book describes model programs for gifted students grades K–12. Among the programs are Exploring the United States: Its History, Geography, Peoples and Culture—An Enrichment Acceleration Program; The Black Experience (honors mini-course); Exploring World Cultures (honors social studies); and Advanced Placement in American history.

Martin, B.A. *Social studies activities for the gifted student.* Buffalo, N.Y.: D.O.K. Publishers, 1977.

Tiedt, P.L., and I.M. Tiedt. *Multicultural Teaching: A handbook of activities, information, and resources.* Boston: Allyn and Bacon, 1979.

Abruscato, J., and J. Hassard. *The earthpeople activity book: People, places, pleasures and other delights.*

Hasuly, D., ed. Arlington, Virginia Gifted/Talented Program Devleopment Project, Arlington School District, Arlington, Va., 1973.

The Arlington, Virginia Gifted/Talented Program Development Project has designed a series of inter-disciplinary units with broad-based themes such as "Courage" (grades 3–4), "Adaptation" (grade 7), and "Idealism as a Force for Change" (grade 11). The units focus on intertwining of content, process, and products. Tables 7-5, 7-6, and 7-7 give examples of these three units.

Summary

The goals of social studies reformers are remarkably similar to many of the goals of educators of gifted and talented students. Both groups emphasize critical thinking, creative thinking, problem solving, and decision making. Critics have suggested stronger emphasis on the Reflective Inquiry approach to social studies for the general curriculum, while the Social Sciences approach is a natural outgrowth of the characteristics of many gifted students. The social science emphasis provides gifted and talented students with the tools for making original contributions as creative producers in social studies.

Models developed by Ward, Taba, Williams, and Taylor facilitate talent development and identification in the classroom setting. Renzulli's Enrichment Triad is an effective model for specific talent development in young social scientists. Since the creative process is the driving force of the productive social scientists, gifted and talented students need to learn about their own creative strengths while they immerse themselves in content.

Selected strategies for developing creative thinking and talent in the social studies include examining role models, making choices, developing future images, role-taking, humor, simulations, and assuming multiple viewpoints. Although few materials have been designed specifically for gifted and talented social studies students, many curriculum projects created during the 1960s and 1970s use strategies that are appropriate for gifted and talented students.

Should suggestions for social studies programming for gifted and talented students gear toward classroom realities or toward the hopes of reformers and theorists? The energy, interests, motivation, and potential of the gifted and talented should inspire us to set our goals high. We may find, in fact, that students can become their "future images" as we encourage them to question, to test their ideas, to engage in dialogue and discussion, and to respond creatively to real-world problems in the social sciences.

References

Allen, J. A., ed. *Education in the 80s: Social Studies.* Washington, D.C.: National Education Association, 1981.

Barr, R. D., J. L. Barth, and S.S. Shermis. *Defining the social studies.* Washington, D.C.: The National Council for the Social Studies, 1977.

Barron, F. *Creativity and psychological health.* Princeton, N.J.: Van Nostrand, 1963.

Table 7-5 INSTRUCTIONAL PLAN*

Unit: Courage
Grade: 3–4
Component: Interdisciplinary
Learning Experience: After reading various literary forms (fantasy, science fiction, tall tale, folk tales, historical fiction, and/or novels), make inferences about the characteristics of courageous people and groups. Combine these characteristics into an "ideal courageous" individual or group. Describe your ideas in a story, play, poem, or tall tale.

	Areas	Description	Activities	Resources
Process	Combine characteristics	Put two elements together to get a new thing	(1) A box of junk—total group (2) Show total group a stick and a piece of clay. Have group list ways they can be combined to make other things. (3) In small groups, have children come up with three ideas of how to combine a cup and a piece of chalk.	*Invitations to Thinking and Doing* Unit 16 pg. 61–64
	Making Inferences	Finding out by reasoning	(4) Have children read *The House With the Flickering Lights.* (5) Show and discuss movie "Do You Know How to Make a Statement a Fact?"	S.F. Level 12 pg. 36–37
	Making similarities and differences	Discuss how things are alike and different	(6) Have children do worksheet on "Word Families." (7) Have children do worksheet, "What do they have in common."	M 12–113 *New Directions In Creativity* 21a & b
			(8) With a small group, read *Call It Courage* (novel), *Door in the Wall* (Hist. fiction), and *Mrs. Frisby and the Rats of NIMH* (fantasy). a. Have children keep a journal and make a list of words that denote courage. b. Keep a record of situations that called for courage.	*Invitations to Thinking and Doing* Unit 9, p. 33–36 librarian
	Exaggeration	Extension of the truth	(9) Children will participate in Jr. Great Books Read and discuss worksheet on exaggerations Give children simple sentences to make into exaggeration a. The cat ran. b. The children watched T.V.	Beginning Critical Thinking p. 14
Products	Write original story, play, folktale, or poem	Discuss originality	Discuss the process of writing an original: a. story (beginning, middle, end) b. play (how to write dialog) c. folktale (elements involved) d. poem (types of poetry) e. tall tale	Library Poet from Humanities Program

*Used by permission from Arlington Public Schools.

Table 7-6 INSTRUCTIONAL PLAN*

Unit: Adaptation
Grade: 7
Component: English/Social Studies
Learning Experience: Use maps, charts, pictures, graphs, tables, interviews, and at least one primary source to gather information on significant influences on adaptations by individuals, social groups (family) and political organizations to changes in the 1920s and 1930s. Write an essay on what you consider to be the most significant influence. Give evidence from your research to justify your selection.

	Areas	Description	Activities	Resources
Process	Use of primary source Justify importance of changes	Prepare an interview Influence of change on your life	Interview a person who lived in the 1920s or 1930s and find out how they had to adapt to the changes and what was the most significant influence on this adaptation. *Independent Study Options:* -Write a letter or diary as if you were a person living in the 1920s or 1930s to express your ideas on the changes taking place. -Draw political cartoons to depict changes in 1920s and 1930s. -Research the topics of art, music, theater, or literature to learn the changes and influences on adaptations in this era. -Read a novel on this era and prepare a review of this book relating it to events of the time and how the character(s) adapted to changes of this time.	America: *Its People and Value,* Wood, et al., pg. 652–661 *Free and Brave* by Graff, p. 603–644 *Impact of Our Past,* Weisberger, pg. 613–658.
Products	Write an essay	Most significant influences on adaptations	Write an essay on what you consider to be the most significant influence on adaptation to changes in the 1920s or 1930s. Give evidence from your research to justify your selection.	Films: "Boom or Bust" "The Great Depression"

*Used by permission from Arlington Public Schools.

Table 7-7 INSTRUCTIONAL PLAN*

Unit: Idealism as a Force for Change

Grade: 11

Learning Experience: Develop a debate, write an essay, present your ideas orally or write a research paper concerning the value of ideals to the individual and her society. Give supportive evidence for your position.

Related Subject Areas	Descriptions Content	Processes		Product	Suggested Activities	Resources
		Basic Research	Thinking			
Anthropology	The value of ideals and idealism to the individual and his or her society	Research Process —reading for general information —creating hypotheses —taking notes —making an outline —reading for supportive evidence —writing the thesis —using many sources —writing the bibliography —making appendices	Apply theory to new material	Debate	FOCUS ON CONTENT	Wallace, Anthony F. C. *Religion*
History			Judge the value with criteria	Oral presentation	1. Read about the concept of Revitalization Movements and its application to cultural histories. Discuss further the applications of this theory.	Farb, Peter *Man's Rise to Civilization as Shown by the Indians of North America,* Dulton, N.Y. 1968.
Literature			Create criteria to judge success, failure, and influence	Research paper		
Religion	Content areas:		Give supporting evidence	Essay	2. Study different revitalization movements particularly among North American Indian groups and determine if they were successful to their cultures. Determine the influence of these movements even if they failed. Write an essay or a research paper giving your conclusions.	Mooney, James *The Ghost Dance*
Philosophy	1. North American Indian revitalization movements 2. Transcendentalism 3. Reform movements					

3. Listen to lectures on various transcendentalists: Emerson, Thoreau, Alcott and Fuller and take notes.

4. Read about the various transcendental-inspired reform movements and then— prepare notes and outlines for a debate on which transcendentalist made the greatest contribution to American culture and society.

5. Based on your reading and lectures, organize information to support conclusions about the value of idealism to society. Present this orally from an outline.

Bloom, B. S., and L. A. Sosnink. Talent development vs. schooling. *Educational Leadership*. 86–94.

Bloom, B. S. Report on creativity research by the examiner's office of the University of Chicago. In *Scientific creativity: Its recognition and development*. Edited by C.W. Taylor and F. Barron. New York: John Wiley, 1963.

Bronfenbrenner, U. *The ecology of human development: Experiments by nature and design*. Cambridge, Mass.: Harvard University Press, 1979.

Bronowski, J. *The ascent of man*. Boston: Little, Brown, 1973.

Brookover, W. B., J. H. Schweitzer, C. H. Beady, P. K. Flood, and J. M. Wisenbaker. Elementary school climate and school achievement. *American Educational Research Journal* 15 (1978): 301–18.

Bruner, J. *The process of education*. Cambridge, Mass.: Harvard University Press, 1961.

Bruner, J. *The relevance of education*. New York: W.W. Norton, 1971.

Bruner, J. S. *Toward a theory of instruction*. Cambridge, Mass.: Harvard University Press, 1966.

California State Department of Education. *Social sciences: Curriculum guide for teaching gifted children social sciences in grades four through six*. Sacramento, Calif., 1977.

Cassidy, E. W., and D. G. Kurfman. Decision making as purpose and process. In *Developing decision-making skills*. Forty-seventh Yearbook of the National Council for the Social Studies. Edited by D.G. Kurfman. Washington, D.C.: The Council, 1977.

Churchill, J., and B. Haggard. *Governor's school of Arkansas for the gifted and talented*. Unpublished paper, Hendrix College, Conway, Arkansas, 1983.

Clark, K. *Civilization: A personal view*. New York: Harper and Row, 1969.

Cousins, N. *Human options: An autobiographical notebook*. New York: W.W. Norton, 1981.

Cusick, P. A. *Inside high school: The student's world*. New York: Holt, Rinehart and Winston, 1973.

de Bono, E. *Eureka: An illustrated history of inventions from the wheel to the computer*. New York: Holt, Rinehart and Winston, 1974.

Deal, T. E., and A. A. Kennedy. Culture and school performance. *Educational Leadership* 40 (1983): 14–15.

Ehman, L., H. Mehlinger, and J. Patrick. *Toward effective instruction in secondary social studies*. Boston: Houghton Mifflin, 1974.

Ehrlich, V. Z. *The Astor Program for gifted children*. New York: Teachers College and the Board of Education of New York City, 1977.

Ellis, A. K. *Teaching and learning elementary social studies*. Boston: Allyn and Bacon, 1977.

Fancett, U. S., and S. D. Hawke. In *Social studies in the 1980s: A report of project SPAN*. Edited by I. Morrissett. Alexandria, Va.: Association for Supervision and Curriculum Development, 1982.

Fontana, L. A., and H. D. Mehlinger. Querencia, politische bildung, and social studies. In *Education in the 80s: Social studies*. Edited by J. Allen. Washington, D.C.: National Education Association, 1981.

Getzels, J. W., and J. T. Dillon. The nature of giftedness and the education of the gifted. In *Second handbook of research on teaching*. Edited by R. M. W. Travers. Chicago: Rand McNally, 1973.

Goodlad, J. I. A study of schooling: Some findings and hypotheses. *Phi Delta Kappa* 64 (1983): 465–70.

Goodlad, J. I. What some schools and classrooms teach. *Educational Leadership* 40 (1983): 8–19.

Grabe, M. School size and the importance of school activities. *Adolescence* 16 (1981): 21–31.

Guilford, J. P. *Way beyond the IQ.* Buffalo, N.Y.: Creative Education Foundation, 1977.

Hamilton, S. F. Synthesis of research on the social side of schooling. *Educational Leadership* 40 (1983): 65–72.

Hertzberg, H. W. *Social studies reform: 1880–1980. Report of project SPAN.* Boulder, Colo.: Social Science Education Consortium, 1981.

Hertzberg, H. W. Social studies reform: The lessons of history. In *Social studies in the 1980s: A report of project SPAN.* Edited by I. Morrissett. Alexandria, Va.: Association for Supervision and Curriculum Development, 1982.

Horn, R. E., and A. Cleaves, eds. *The guide to simulations/games for education and training.* Beverly Hills, Calif.: Sage, 1980.

Johns, R. W. *Biographical history: Microcosm of meaning and mankind.* Article submitted for publication, University of Arkansas at Little Rock, 1983.

Joyce, B. R. *New strategies for social education.* Chicago: Science Research Associates, 1972.

Joyce, B. R., and W. Weill. *Models of teaching.* Englewood Cliffs, N.J.: Prentice-Hall, 1972.

Kaplan, S. N. Language arts and social studies curriculum in the elementary school. In *The gifted and the talented: Their education and development.* The Seventy-eighth Yearbook of the National Society for the Study of Education. Edited by A.H. Passow. Chicago: The University of Chicago Press, 1979.

Lengel, J. G., and D. P. Superka. Curriculum patterns. In *Social studies in the 1980s: A report of project SPAN.* Edited by I. Morrissett. Alexandria, Va.: Association for Supervision and Curriculum Development, 1982.

MacKinnon, D. W. *In search of human effectiveness: Identifying and developing creativity.* Buffalo, N.Y.: Creative Education Foundation, 1978.

Mehaffy, G., V. R. Atwood, and M. Neloon. Action learning in social studies. In *The social studies: Eightieth Yearbook of the National Society for the Study of Education.* Edited by H. D. Mehlinger and O. L. Davis. Chicago: University of Chicago Press, 1981.

Mitsakos, C. L. The nature and purposes of social studies. In *Education in the 1980s: Social studies.* Edited by J. Allen. Washington, D.C.: National Education Association, 1981.

Moreno, J. L., and Z. T. Moreno. *Psychodrama.* Vol. 3. New York: Beacon House, 1969.

Morrissett, I., and J. D. Haas. Rationales, goals and objectives. In *Social studies in the 1980s: A report of project SPAN.* Edited by I. Morrissett. Alexandria, Va.: Association for Supervision and Curriculum Development, 1982.

Munday, L. A., and J. C. Davis. *Varieties of accomplishments after college: Perspectives on the meaning of academic talent.* Iowa City, Iowa: American College Testing Program Research Report No. 62, 1974.

National Council for the Social Studies. A guide to content in the social studies. In *Crucial issues in the teaching of social studies.* Edited by B.G. Massialas and A.M. Kazamias. Englewood Cliffs, N.J.: Prentice-Hall, 1964.

National Council for the Social Studies. Revision of the NCSS curriculum guidelines. *Social Education* 43 (April, 1979): 261–78.

National Education Association. *Report of the committee on secondary social studies.* Washington, D.C.: Government Printing Office, 1893.

National Education Association. *The social studies in secondary education.* Bulletin 28, Department of the Interior, Bureau of Education. Washington, D.C.: U.S. Government Printing Office, 1916.

Ochoa, A. S. Now more than ever . . . decision-making and related skills. *Education in the 80s:*

Social studies. Edited by J. Allen. Washington, D.C.: National Education Association, 1981.

Patrick, J. J., and S. D. Hawks. Curriculum materials. In *Social studies in the 1980s: A report of project SPAN.* Edited by I. Morrissett. Alexandria, Va.: Association for Supervision and Curriculum Development, 1982.

Peshkin, A. *Growing up American: Schooling and the survival of community.* Chicago: University of Chicago Press, 1978.

Piaget, J. *To understand is to invent: The future of education.* New York: Grossman, 1973.

Plowman, P. D. *Teaching the gifted and talented in the social studies classroom.* Washington, D.C.: National Education Association, 1980.

Ponder, G., and S. A. Hirsh. Social studies education for the gifted: Lessons from other pasts? *Roeper Review: A Journal on Gifted Education* 4 (November 1981): 17–19.

Popham, D. *Teaching gifted students social sciences in grades ten through twelve.* Sacramento, Calif.: California Department of Education, 1971.

Raths, L. E., H. Merrill, and S. B. Simon. *Values and teaching.* Columbus, Ohio: Charles E. Merrill, 1978.

Renzulli, J. S. *The enrichment triad model: A guide for developing defensible programs for the gifted and talented.* Mansfield Center, Conn.: Creative Learning Press, 1977.

Renzulli, J. S., S. M. Reis, and L.H. Smith. *The revolving door identification model.* Mansfield Center, Conn.: Creative Learning Press, 1981.

Renzulli, J. S. What makes giftedness: Reexamining a definition. *Phi Delta Kappa* 60 (1978): 180–84, 261.

Schlichter, C. S. The multiple talent approach in mainstream and gifted programs. *Exceptional Children* 48 (1981): 144–50.

Shaftel, F. R., and G. Shaftel. *Role playing for social values: Decisionmaking in the social studies.* Englewood Cliffs, N.J.: Prentice-Hall, 1967.

Shaver, J. P. A critical view of the social studies profession. *Social Education* 41 (1977): 300–7.

Shermis, S. S., and P. R. Clinkenbeard. History texts for the gifted: A look at the past century. *Roeper Review: A Journal on Gifted Education* 4 (November 1981): 19–21.

Smith, J. A. *Creative teaching of the social studies in the elementary school.* Boston: Allyn and Bacon, 1979.

Stake, R. E., and J. A. Easley, Jr. *Case studies in science education.* Washington, D.C.: National Science Foundation, 1978.

Stein, M. I. *Creativity research with adults and children: A comparison.* Paper presented at Second National Conference on Creativity and the Gifted/Talented, Memphis, Tennessee, March 20, 1981.

Sternberg, R. J. A componential theory of intellectual giftedness. *Gifted Child Quarterly* 25 (1981): 86–93.

Stewart, E. D. Learning styles among gifted/talented students: Instructional techniques preferences. *Exceptional Children* 48 (1981): 134–38.

Superka, D. P., S. Hawks, and I. Morrissett. The current and future status of the social studies. *Social Education* 44 (1980): 362–69.

Taba, H., M. C. Durkin, J. R. Fraenkel, and A. H. McNaughton. *A teacher's handbook to elementary social studies: An inductive approach.* Reading, Mass.: Addison-Wesley, 1971.

Talents Unlimited, *TAP.* Mobile, Ala.: Mobile County Public Schools, 1974.

Taylor, C. W. Be talent developers. *Today's Education: NEA Journal* (December 1968): 67–69.

Torrance, E. P. Foreward. In J. S. Renzulli, S. M. Reis, and L. H. Smith. *The revolving door identification model.* Mansfield Center, Conn.: Creative Learning Press, 1981.

Torrance, E. P. Sociodrama as a creative problem-solving approach to studying the future. *Journal of Creative Behavior* 9 (1975): 192–95.

Torrance, E. P., and R. E. Myers. *Creative learning and teaching*. New York: Harper and Row, 1970.

Toynbee, A. J. *A study of history*. Vol. 3. London: Oxford University Press, 1933.

Wallach, M. A. Tests tell us little about talent. *American Scientists* 64 (1976): 57–63.

Ward, V.S. Differentiating the curriculum: principle, design, and application. In *Curricula for the Gifted*. Ventura, Calif.: Ventura County Superintendent of Schools Office, 1982.

Ward, V. S. *Differential education for the gifted. A Perspective Through Retrospective*. Vol. 2. Ventura, Calif.: Ventura County Superintendent of Schools, 1980.

Ward, V. S. *Differential education for the gifted*. Lecture, University of Connecticut Confratute, August 5, 1981.

Ward, V. S. *Educating the gifted: An axiomatic approach*. Columbus, Ohio: Charles E. Merrill, 1961.

White, T. H. *In search of history: A personal adventure*. New York: Harper and Row, 1978.

Whitehead, A. N. *The aims of education*. New York: Macmillan, 1929.

Wiley, K. B. *The status of pre-college science, mathematics, and social sciences education: 1955–1975*. Vol. 3. Washington, D.C.: National Science Foundation, 1977.

Williams, F. E. *Classroom ideas for encouraging thinking and feeling*. Buffalo, N.Y.: D.O.K. Publishers, 1970.

Weiss, I. R. *National survey of science, mathematics, and social studies education*. Washington, D.C.: National Science Foundation, 1978.

Wronski, S. P. Societal forces in the social studies. In *Education in the 80s: Social studies*. Edited by J. Allen. Washington, D.C.: National Education Association, 1981.

8

Reading and Writing

Walter B. Barbe
Michael M. Milone

Of all the skills a student acquires in school, none are as useful as reading and writing. Reading gives one access to the vast store of knowledge that has accumulated through the ages, and is one of life's most enjoyable pastimes. Writing is an important means of self-expression and the vehicle by which thoughts and emotions are shared in a way that transcends space and time. It is not an exaggeration to say that reading and writing form the cornerstone of personal and academic success.

Educational Emphasis

The emphasis schools give to reading and writing underscores their importance. Schools spend more time on them than on any other cluster of related subjects, and spend far more money on reading and writing textbooks and supplemental materials than for any other discipline. When measuring students' academic progress, reading or writing is invariably taken as the index of performance. And, when the media bring the condition of American education into the public eye, it is reading and writing that are held up for display.

One's social acceptability is also determined in part by the degree to which one has mastered reading and writing. In literate society, it is not enough simply to understand and speak the common language; one must also be able to read and write it fluently. If gifted students are to assume a place of prominence as adults and contribute in a manner consonant with their potential, they must learn to read and write exceptionally well.

Despite the personal and academic significance of reading and writing, students receive only a comparatively small proportion of skills in these areas through direct intervention on the part of the teacher or instructional materials. Most of the reading and writing abilities of gifted students are acquired through socialization, personal effort, and incidental learning.

Applebee (1966) argues that few people teach writing during the first six or eight years of school because teachers are not prepared to teach it. According to Walmsley (1980),

> The typical preparation of an elementary classroom teacher consists merely of a unit or two in a general language arts course, perhaps a college composition course, plus whatever they can pick up from professional reading, fellow teachers, curriculum materials, inservice workshops, and professional meetings . . . they appear to be significantly less well prepared to teach writing than they are to teach reading. (p. 732)

With respect to reading, teachers are certainly better prepared, but they still teach this basic skill only during the first few years of school. By about the fourth grade, reading occupies a much smaller part of the school day (Dearman and Plisko, 1980), and is assigned rather than taught. Only a moderate amount of direct instruction in reading occurs after the primary grades. In contrast, the amount of direct instruction in other subjects, such as mathematics, science, and social studies, increases in the postprimary years.

Reading and writing may not often be taught in the middle and upper grades, but they are the most frequently applied basic skills. Presumably, the degree to which they are applied enhances skill development. Durkin (1981), however, in commenting on the types of instructional activities offered in popular basal series, questions whether numerous application and practice exercises, as opposed to direct, explicit instruction, really help children see the relationship between what they do in school and what they should do when they read on their own.

Another characteristic of reading and writing instruction is that educators are moving toward an integrated approach. In the past, it was believed that the receptive language arts, listening and reading, preceded their expressive counterparts, speaking and writing. Recent thinking is that the receptive and expressive language arts develop almost contemporaneously. This conclusion has had an especially great impact on the teaching of reading and writing, which were previously taught separately; reading instruction preceded writing instruction, and received far greater emphasis. The current perspective is that the two should be introduced at the same time and treated equally:

> In view of children's early interest and experience with imitative writing, the ease of learning manuscript writing, and the close tie between reading and writing, teachers are advised to provide informal writing experiences for children early in the first grade, devoting as much time to writing as to reading in beginning instruction. (Hildreth, 1963, p. 19)

Although reading is in some respects an underdeveloped subject, there is no dearth of instructional materials. In fact, a greater variety of materials is available in reading than any other subject. Basal materials, both consumable and nonconsumable, are found in every classroom; so, too, are supplementary materials, such as games, spirit duplicating masters, computer programs, films and filmstrips, audio cassettes, overhead transparencies, and a host of other paraphernalia. The publishing of reading material is almost an industry in itself, and the sheer quantity of available material is so large that one of the teacher's major tasks is selecting what she considers appropriate instructional tools.

Quite the opposite is true with writing. Although there are many instructional materials at the teacher's disposal, they are fragmented, and reflect the various skills that constitute writing: spelling, handwriting, composition, grammar, and so on. The teacher faces the challenge of selecting materials that are enough alike to provide students with a sense of consistency, and yet cover all the skills the teacher deems necessary.

Underachievement of the Gifted

A common misconception is that gifted children exhibit reading and writing abilities commensurate with their high intelligence. The basis of this misconception is the relative performance of gifted children when compared to their nongifted peers. Certainly, gifted children and youth are better readers and writers than other children of the same age; when contrasted with mental age norms, however, gifted children fare less well (Miles, 1954). Unfortunately, nongifted children achieve reading and writing test scores that are more consistent with their ability than do gifted children.

Table 8-1 summarizes data obtained from seventh grade students in a junior high school. Their intelligence test scores, as measured by the Henmon-Nelson Tests of Mental Ability, ranged upward from 120. Paragraph meaning (PM) and word

Table 8-1 DISTRIBUTIONS OF GRADE EQUIVALENTS ON ACHIEVEMENT TESTS FOR SEVENTH GRADE PUPILS WITH I.Q.s OF AT LEAST 120.

Grade Equivalent	Paragraph Meaning	Word Meaning
11	6	36
10	42	32
9	38	28
8	30	49
7	25	11
6	23	6
5	1	—

From F. Tyler, Intraindividual variability, In *Individualizing Instruction, The Sixty-First Yearbook of the National Society for the Study of Education,* ed. N. B. Henry (Chicago: University of Chicago Press, 1962): p. 167.

meaning (WM) were measured with the Stanford Achievement Tests. As you can see from the table, a sizable number of students were reading at or below grade level; an even larger number were reading below the grade equivalent of their intelligence test scores. These data clearly support Miles's (1954) contention that ". . . contrary to the general trend, many (gifted) individuals have failed to achieve academically at the level of their predicted competence" (p. 1043).

Gifted students also achieve less well in writing than one might suspect, given their high intelligence and advanced language skills. Little research has been done to confirm this belief, but teachers' observations seem to bear it out. Fearn (1981), for example, asks:

> Am I the only person who finds, after reading hundreds of writing samples from gifted children and youth, that one or more of the following statements can be made?
> - A distressing number of the writing samples do not display a skill level substantially beyond that of their non-certified age mates.
> - For all of the romantic attention that gifted learners get for their "creative writing," their writing samples are often not much more clever or insightful than those of their non-certified agemates.
> - There is an enormous difference between their language proficiency as expressed in reading and that expressed in writing.
> - Many gifted learners produce "stories" in some profusion, that, when one objectively applies common standards of excellence regarding short story writing, are not very good.
> - Gifted learners sometimes believe that recording their thoughts, feelings, and observations interferes with their creativity.
> - Gifted learners seem to think that standard conventions for reasonably disciplined writing are somehow beneath their dignity. (p. 26)

Admittedly, most gifted students' reading and writing achievement falls within the acceptable range. There is great room for improvement, however, and in planning reading and writing instruction for gifted students, teachers must bear in mind that it is not enough to maintain current skill levels. Gifted students must improve their reading and writing abilities, not simply to achieve parity with their intelligence scores, but because these abilities permit students to realize their potential in other endeavors, both in and out of school.

Unstructured Curriculum

One factor that may contribute to the poor showing gifted students make in reading and writing is the unstructured curriculum. This practice begins as early as kindergarten and the primary grades, persists through high school, and is usually justified by a statement such as "Gifted children seem to need less structure than other children." Although this may be true (Dunn and Price, 1980), the negligible degree of structure currently imposed on gifted students' reading and writing curricula does not permit them to progress at a satisfactory rate.

A curriculum is a ". . . course of study, the specific content and skills that teachers are expected to teach and that children are expected to master as a direct result of their school experiences" (Savage, 1977, p. 35). The essential questions relating to a curriculum are what to teach; when to teach it; how to teach it; and how to determine if learning has occurred. If these questions cannot be answered, then instruction will be haphazard.

Few of those responsible for programs for the gifted can easily answer the essential curriculum questions as they apply to reading and writing instruction. The most frequent response, that the curriculum designed for the entire student population is used with gifted students, is unsatisfactory because it denies a difference between gifted and nongifted students' abilities and learning styles. Evidence gathered during the past six decades suggests marked differences between gifted and nongifted students, and unless differential instruction is provided to the most able children and youth, they will not learn to read and write as well as they could.

If a program for gifted students has been well designed, there should be no trouble answering the essential curriculum questions, and when the questions have been answered, it should be possible to recognize the qualitative differences between the reading and writing instruction given to gifted students and that given to nongifted students.

Identifying Gifted Students

One problematic area in education of the gifted is identifying the children and youth whose performance or potential is great enough to merit special instruction. With respect to reading and writing, the difficulties associated with identification are compounded by several factors, not the least of which is overreliance on standardized tests of intelligence and achievement.

Educators, psychologists, and parents agree that no single indicator is sufficient to identify gifted children. As suggested by the American Psychological Association's (1974) *Standards for Educational and Psychological Tests*:

> Decisions about individuals should ordinarily be based on assessment of more than one dimension: when feasible, all major dimensions related to the outcome of the decision should be assessed and validated. This is the principle of multivariate prediction; . . . In

any case, care should be taken that assessment procedures focus on important characteristics; decisions are too often based on assessment of only those dimensions that can
be conveniently measured. (p. 62)

Unfortunately, far too many decisions concerning placement of gifted or potentially gifted children are made primarily on the basis of achievement or intelligence
test scores. This overdependence is fraught with shortcomings, particularly if a child
has exceptional talent in writing but only average or slightly above average ability in
reading, mathematics, or science.

As Miller and Price (1981) point out, "The list of universally recognized talented
people whose gifts were not identified by the professionals in their youth is dis-
tressingly long" (p. 6), including such notables as Winston Churchill, Emily Dickinson,
Lincoln Steffens, and Edward Gibbon. It is no coincidence that these four luminaries
made their marks on history through the written or spoken word rather than in
another area of endeavor.

Exceptional ability in the language arts is often accompanied by superiority in
other areas, so the linguistically gifted child is sometimes discovered by means of
standardized tests. This is not always the case, however, because the linear-sequential
abilities that are the basis of most achievement and intelligence tests may be comparatively weak in the gifted writer. When standardized test scores receive more
weight than school performance or parent and teacher recommendations, the exceptional writer will probably be overlooked.

Another problem with identifying children who are gifted in reading or writing
is that the emergence of superior talent in these fields is protracted. The flashes of
brilliance that signal giftedness in mathematics, science, music, and the visual arts are
almost unknown in the language arts. Expressive language and the high-level thinking associated with advanced reading comprehension evolve slowly and are functions
of maturation and experience. Even educators who have been long involved with
children who are gifted in other areas may not recognize the linguistically gifted child
because the signs are so subtle.

Surprisingly, some educators are reluctant to admit that a student may be gifted
in reading or writing, as this school principal tells us:

> When I met with teachers to discuss candidates for the gifted program, they seemed
> unwilling to concede that any child was gifted in poetry, creative writing, or in other
> forms of verbal expression. From their comments, I found that no one in the school felt
> competent to work with these children. They also expressed the belief that if a child were
> identified as a gifted writer, we would be expected to provide an appropriate education.
> Since no one could do that, the problem could be avoided by not recognizing children's
> giftedness in this area.[1]

Finally, one must realize that not all gifted children are superior in the language
arts, and that exceptional ability in one aspect of the language arts does not
necessarily mean that a child is gifted. Those concerned with the education of the
gifted generally recognize the former contention, but not the latter. The child who
uses impeccable grammar may be of average intelligence and academic ability, yet

---

[1] Sue Lyons, Principal, Santa Monica-Malibu Unified School District, 1982.

come from a home that emphasizes proper use of spoken English. Similarly, a school's best speller may excel in no other area. Calling either of these children gifted, even by limiting the extent of giftedness to the language arts, stretches the meaning of the term.

Primary/Elementary Reading

The old saying that "ability begets interest" is nowhere more true than in the case of gifted children and reading. Because of their almost insatiable curiosity, gifted children gravitate naturally toward reading, for the opportunity to satisfy their great desire for knowledge. Terman characterizes the gifted child as an "inveterate reader," and if there is one attribute that is a *sine qua non* of academic giftedness, it is love of the printed word.

Gifted children can be considered superior readers in several ways (Strang, 1955):

1 They learn to read at an earlier age than do other children.
2 Their interest in reading surpasses that of nongifted children.
3 They move into adult literature long before their age-mates.
4 They read intensely in particular fields that interest them.

To these traits, Klemm (1953) adds that gifted children read more widely than their peers, their selection of books is of higher quality, and they choose more difficult material.

As mentioned previously, gifted students' reading superiority is a relative trait that becomes evident only when comparing them to nongifted students. This apparent superiority has been detrimental to gifted students, because they usually receive less instruction and encouragement than they deserve. Gallagher (1975) refers to this instructional deficit by suggesting that the language arts and reading instruction gifted students receive is rarely equal to their ability and usually fails to meet their needs. This problem is particularly evident in, although not limited to, the elementary school.

Goals of A Gifted Elementary Reading Program

A reading program for gifted students should be structured around a set of goals that reflects the children's characteristics and the purposes to which they will put reading. Barbe (1961) notes that the general goals of a reading program for gifted students are to help them learn the skills to become effective readers, instill a respect for good books, and promote a love of the reading process and the results of reading. When educators meet these goals, the exceptionally capable student is likely to come to cherish the act of reading, become a lifelong learner, and develop his gift to the fullest.

Cushenbery and Howell (1974) list a similar set of goals. They say the reading program should help gifted students apply decoding skills; develop comprehension skills beyond mere rote memory; evaluate reading matter for authenticity, validity, and objectivity; differentiate between good and mediocre literature; compile and organize information; think creatively about what they read; and enjoy reading.

There are two purposes to describing the goals of a reading program for the gifted. The first is to make it clear that some degree of organization is necessary in teaching a subject as important as reading to gifted students. Unless a plan of action details what should be taught, how it should be taught, and so on, it is unlikely that learning will take place to the degree it should. The "seat of the pants" philosophy of education may be ideal for teaching divergent thinking, but can lead to disaster when used with reading.

The second purpose is to help educators avoid the "parity" game. The discrepancy between many gifted children's mental age and reading age has prompted some school officials to establish an overriding goal for the reading program of elevating reading scores to the same lofty heights as students' intelligence test scores. Current emphasis on accountability and fiscal austerity fans the fire, and it is more and more necessary to resort to questionable practices to justify special education for gifted students. Establishing equality between students' mental ages and reading ages is a satisfactory incidental outcome of an instructional program, but when reading achievement for its own sake becomes the primary goal, both comprehension and enjoyment will suffer.

Beginning Reading Instruction

Approximately one-third to one-half of the gifted group enters first grade already able to read (Cushenbery and Howell, 1974). Research with early readers suggests that these children come from homes where reading materials have been readily available, have been read to from an early age, and were interested in and enjoyed the printed word (Durkin, 1966). To reteach beginning reading to these children is neither necessary nor recommended, because they will become bored and frustrated if they have to spend time on skills they already have. It is far wiser to assess these children's reading competence and gear instruction to their functioning level, giving them an opportunity to master the preliminary skills they may have passed over and the upcoming skills for which they are prepared.

The remaining gifted children who enter school not knowing how to read are no less able or intelligent than those who can already read. Usually, they have simply not had the opportunity or encouragement to learn to read. When opportunity and encouragement are provided in the school setting, these children take readily to the reading task.

It is surprising how much difference there will be in pre-academic skills in a group as ostensibly homogeneous as the gifted. Some will know the letters of the alphabet, their sounds, the left-to-right progression, and book-use skills. Other gifted children may know none of these, and must be taught even the most basic readiness skills. Before providing prereading instruction to gifted children, one must assess their knowledge with an appropriate individual or group reading test. An instrument that can be administered to a group is timesaving, but an individually administered test provides more accurate information and gives the teacher an opportunity to observe the child functioning in a structured academic situation.

Grouping for Instruction

In general education, teachers most frequently manage reading instruction by grouping, enabling them to reduce the number of students with whom they must work at one time and eliminating some of the average classroom's heterogeneity. Children are usually grouped according to ability, a convenient and traditional practice despite its shortcomings.

Even though gifted children represent a more homogeneous population than do nongifted, grouping is still advisable for reading instruction, although ability is not the recommended basis for classification. More sensible criteria reduce the number of students to manageable size without limiting the degree to which students can progress or giving them the feeling they are less capable than children in other groups.

It is practical to group gifted children according to the specific skills to be taught. For example, the teacher may discover that several children are unsure of the sounds of *gh* when this letter combination appears at the end of a word. The children, who vary in terms of general ability and interest but share this common problem, can be grouped for instruction until they master the skill. The group can then be disbanded and a new group formed to teach the next skill. Skill grouping has a clear purpose that does not reflect negatively on the students' ability or potential, permits interaction among children with varied interests and general ability, and is consistent with the erratic sequence of skill development through which gifted children progress. Grouping for mastery of individual skills permits gifted students to advance at their own pace and gives them the support they need to acquire specific skills that might otherwise be overlooked.

Gifted children can also be grouped for reading instruction according to interests (Cushenbery and Howell, 1974), so they can work with material that will hold their attention. Motivation will be high and resistance low. Verbal interaction among students will promote higher level thinking abilities, but structure will ensure that the necessary skills will be acquired.

The purpose of grouping gifted students for reading instruction is to promote better teaching and learning. Instruction should not be regimented to march students through skill after skill within a fixed amount of time. A "lock step" reading program may be justifiable in some educational situations with nongifted children, since a strong skill basis can enhance instruction. With gifted children, however, the practice will prove suffocating, and do more harm than good.

Evaluating Reading Skills

To provide appropriate beginning reading instruction for gifted children, or to group them later for reading instruction, the teacher must assess their reading ability. Many teachers reject the notion of using standardized assessment procedures with gifted children, reacting more to their potential for abuse than to the possible benefits. Without periodic assessment, gifted children are unlikely to reach their full reading potential. Indeed, it is possible that gifted children's relative underachievement in reading may be a consequence of educators' unwillingness to use appropriate assessment procedures.

Evaluating gifted students' reading status achieves four purposes (Cushenbery and Howell, 1974):

1 Determines students' exact instructional needs
2 Helps group students appropriately
3 Provides information for selecting and using appropriate instructional materials
4 Helps in the study of students' levels of reading competency

We can add a fifth purpose that is usually unstated, but nonetheless important. When evaluation is part of the education process, teachers, students, and parents are more likely to recognize that certain aspects of reading are observable and measurable. Of course, other aspects of reading, such as motivation, are beyond assessment, but awareness that at least some elements can be taught directly and their mastery measured objectively, will probably cause students to progress at a rate more consistent with their potential.

Tests that measure the reading abilities of the general student population are sometimes acceptable for use with gifted students. A criterion-referenced instrument that yields a complete profile of reading skills is more useful than a norm-referenced test that gives a single percentage or grade equivalent score. The more information a test provides, the more it contributes to a sound and motivating program of instruction.

A widely used instrument that has applications with gifted students is the Barbe Reading Skills Checklist (Barbe, 1975). Comprising nine levels, readiness through grade eight, the checklist covers a broad range of reading skills, from simple word recognition through word analysis to creative reading. No norms have been established for the Barbe Reading Skills Checklist, because it is intended to show a single child's various strengths and weaknesses rather than to compare children with each other or a national standard.

Mindell and Stracher (1980) have developed a recording system that can be used with gifted children to assess reading abilities and program planning. These materials are easy to use and present none of the problems associated with norm-referenced tests.

Most publishers now include a skill checklist of some kind with their basal reading materials. With some modifications, these skill listings can be helpful in planning reading instruction for gifted students.

Recent advances in minicomputer hardware and software have resulted in more frequent applications of this technology in the classroom. One promising application is diagnostic testing of reading abilities. Houghton-Mifflin offers a software package called "The Answer'"'that relates to their basal reading materials. The test is administered with a computer that scores student responses and develops a skill profile based on the results. The profile identifies the student's weaknesses and matches them to the portions of the basal materials that can be used to improve these abilities. A more extensive version of this type of program, available through Zweig and Associates, is the *Fountain Valley Program,* which provides diagnostic testing and relates the results to many major reading series. The *Fountain Valley Program* is available as a computer software package and in a printed version.

With gifted students, any diagnostic material can result in an erratic skill profile. In a nongifted child, this kind of skill profile can indicate underlying learning problems, but gifted children, because of their superior cognitive abilities and interest in reading, acquire skills in an idiosyncratic manner. For example, highly developed comprehension abilities may emerge before more fundamental skills such as phonetic analysis. Do not attempt to hinder this seemingly irregular sequence of skill acquisition, because you could thwart the child's motivation and natural curiosity. Instead, promote acquisition of the unlearned skills while you encourage the child to progress at his own pace.

Reading Skill Development

The dispute between the sight-word method and the phonics method has no place in education of the gifted. Children with superior ability must be taught with both methods.

Proponents of the sight-word method contend that:

- The process of reading, from the start, should include not only word recognition, but also comprehension, interpretation, appreciation, and application of what is read.
- The child should start with "meaningful reading" of whole words, sentences, and stories, and silent reading should be stressed from the beginning.
- After the child recognizes "at sight" about fifty words, she should begin to study, through words learned as wholes, the relationship between the sounds in spoken words (phonemes) and the letters that represent them (graphemes); that is, phonics.
- Instruction in phonics and other means of identifying words should be spread over the six years of elementary school.
- Drill or practice on phonics in isolation should be avoided; instead, phonics should be integrated with meaningful connected reading.
- The words in the pupils' readers for grades 1, 2, and 3 should be repeated often.
- The child should have a slow and easy start in the first year.
- Children should be instructed in small groups arranged according to their reading achievement. (Chall, 1967)

Those who favor the phonics approach agree with most of these points, but think phonics should be taught more directly and earlier in the child's school career, and that more ground should be covered (Chall, 1967). The chief critic of the sight-word group and apologist of phonics is Rudolph Flesch, author of *Why Johnny Can't Read*.

Certain aspects of sight-word instruction are not suitable for gifted students. Grouping according to general ability is not recommended; neither is it reasonable to limit gifted children's reading vocabulary to a small number of high frequency words. It is important, however, that gifted children learn a core vocabulary of words they recognize on sight. Many gifted children do this without formal instruction, and as Barbe and Milone (1981) found, they appear to have the visual perception and memory skills that permit acquisition of a large sight vocabulary. Recognizing words on sight is also the first step in rapid reading, and as any teacher of the gifted will attest, rapid reading is one way gifted children satisfy their voracious appetite for information.

Nonetheless, gifted children cannot progress in reading if they cannot extract meaning from the new words they encounter. The word attack skills usually taught as "phonics" permit gifted children to decipher the vast number of unfamiliar words they will come upon in everyday reading.

All gifted students need to learn the phonics and syllabication rules, structural analysis, comprehension, and vocabulary skills taught at each grade level, even if they read above grade level. They may not need grade level skills until a later time, but they need to learn them. A student may progress through the elementary grades by relying on a few important skills, but will falter in the secondary grades when material becomes more difficult. Neither the student nor teachers will be able to discern the problem after the student has so long been considered a superior reader. The few skills the student had mastered are no longer sufficient; he must acquire the skills that were overlooked in the earlier grades before he can progress.

Reading skills, unlike other academic skills, do not emerge in a clear sequence. For example, to learn how to multiply, the child must first master the concept of addition. In reading, there are few instances of such sequence. A gifted child may, for instance, see the parallel between "Chicken Little" and rumors that circulate in school long before she can recall all the sounds of the letter combination *ough.*

In addition to the nonsequential nature of the reading task, one must also consider the manner in which gifted children learn. As Trezise (1978) suggests,

> Closely sequenced reading programs may be quite inappropriate for gifted children, since these students often learn so quickly that they seem to pass right over most of the sequenced objectives, take inexplicable cognitive leaps, and learn best by a series of complex mental associations. (p. 744)

Although some teachers abhor the notion of using workbooks with either gifted or nongifted children, there are circumstances for which workbook assignments are appropriate. Gifted children who need extra practice in a few specific skills can benefit from the structured drill a workbook provides, as long as the workbook does not become the major instructional method. Workbooks also allow gifted children to advance at their own pace, and permit them to learn skills rapidly.

When using workbooks with gifted children, remember that completing an activity depends upon motor as well as cognitive abilities. Because some gifted children's cognitive abilities are far more advanced than their motor abilities, progress in a workbook does not serve as an index of reading skills. For younger children especially, this will result in an underestimation of their ability. If a child seems to be having trouble with workbook activities, it may be helpful to have the child complete the activities orally in a one-on-one situation, or to pair a child who has the appropriate cognitive ability with one whose motor skills are up to the task. Team learning precludes the possibility that motor skills will interfere with reading progress, and teaches children to work cooperatively.

Skill acquisition is an important part of the reading program for gifted students, but it is not the total program. They must also have time to apply reading skills, not as free reading or extra reading, but reading for a purpose, after or during which the teacher participates in some way.

As a rule of thumb, 50 percent of classroom reading time should be spent on skill development and 50 percent on application. This ratio is a reminder to teachers

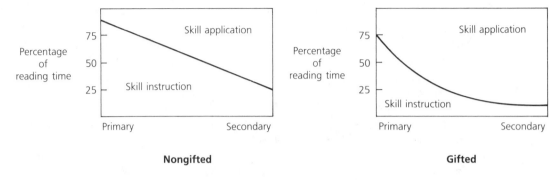

Figure 8–1 VARIATION BETWEEN SKILL INSTRUCTION AND APPLICATION FOR GIFTED AND NONGIFTED ELEMENTARY STUDENTS

that neither skill development nor skill application alone constitutes a complete program of reading instruction. In reality, the proportion of skill instruction to application varies from grade to grade and differs for gifted and nongifted students. Figure 8–1 shows the approximate relationship between skill instruction and application for gifted and nongifted children in the elementary grades.

In the early grades, skill acquisition occupies a larger proportion of instructional time than does application. The proportion gradually decreases as students move through the grades; at the secondary level, skill instruction takes up only a small part of the curriculum.

There is a radical difference between the skill progression of gifted and nongifted children. Gifted youngsters will be ready for certain kinds and levels of instruction earlier, and will undoubtedly be able to move more rapidly through materials (Trezise, 1978).

Enrichment

Enrichment is another important ingredient in a successful reading program for the gifted. Reading enrichment consists of special assignments, projects, free choice activities, demonstrations, released time, hobbies and clubs, special classes, summer school, and the opportunity to take advantage of community and human resources (Cushenbery and Howell, 1974). Enrichment activities do not have to come from the reading textbook itself, although many teachers have gifted students read at least one of the basic texts in their grade level (Barbe, 1961), because basal reading series usually balance reading skills with opportunities to practice these skills.

According to Cushenbery and Howell, enrichment in reading for the gifted does not mean adding projects or extras to the curriculum; it must *be* the regular curriculum. The problem with this assertion is its implication that enrichment activities alone provide children with opportunities to develop all the reading skills they will need. Although enrichment is a good way to refine skills, to satisfy gifted children's curiosity, and a way to instill love for and reliance upon the printed word, it is not a complete curriculum. It is merely one component of a curriculum that must give gifted children the skills they need to benefit from enrichment.

A popular form of reading enrichment is a "Great Books" program. Unfortunately, some professionals believe the "Great Books" constitute an entire reading curriculum. If gifted children's reading instruction is built solely around the "Great Books," they will probably not acquire the reading skills necessary to truly benefit from these books. The "Great Books" certainly have a place in a reading program for the gifted, however, because they add breadth to children's reading experiences, expose them to the universal themes of classic literature, and challenge them with language that is richer and more complex than they will encounter in popular literature. Experience with the "Great Books" gives children an advantage in the later secondary years and in college. To help them benefit from the "Great Books," teachers must establish a set of objectives to accompany their use, encompassing comprehension and critical reading skills, and perhaps structural analysis, vocabulary development, and other similar skills. Cushenbery and Howell (1974, pp. 130–31) describe a sample teaching plan that could easily be applied to the "Great Books," including purposes, materials, procedures, and methods of evaluation.

Objections to imposing structure on a "Great Books" program are certain to arise from some teachers and students, chiefly the objection that "Great Books" are meant to be enjoyed, not dissected. Of course, children should occasionally read a literary classic for enjoyment or for spontaneous discussion, but teachers must remember that enjoying a book and being able to discuss it are only two aspects of reading; other aspects remain untouched unless they receive specific emphasis.

Oral Reading

Few teaching practices are as widespread as oral reading, which, when correctly presented, can be a means of teaching new skills, refining previously acquired skills, or evaluating reading proficiency. Oral reading also gives students who are not reading a chance to think about what is being read, the first step in creative reading.

Oral reading can be a great help in teaching gifted children, but only if they are grouped correctly. Barbe (1961) cautions that gifted students may become bored with oral reading assignments because of the time wasted while less capable students stumble through the material. He believes oral reading is an effective way to develop appreciation for a particular piece of literature only when students can read aloud fluently and expressively. The greatest benefit from oral reading comes during the primary grades and decreases as students begin to prefer to read to themselves. When gifted children reach adolescence, they may resist oral reading primarily because of shyness; boys are likely to resist more than girls.

One valuable kind of oral reading for gifted students of any age is a selection of their own choice that has particular meaning to them. They should read the passage aloud to the class and discuss why it is meaningful to them. Students seem to relish this chance to participate, especially if they have enough time beforehand to practice reading the passage.

The practice of providing students with an advance organizer extends the usefulness of oral reading. Advance organizers range in complexity from a series of simple questions to highly detailed diagrams, and prepare students for the material to come. For example, suppose the final pages of Hemingway's *For Whom the Bell Tolls* have been chosen for oral reading. The expatriate American, Roberto, has been injured too severely to escape by horseback; he decides to stay and hold off the enemy long enough for his comrades to flee. Death is certain as he sits against a tree clutching a machine gun, waiting for the government troops. The teacher can pose several questions to encourage the students who are not reading to think about the passage. What is Roberto thinking? Was leaving his comfortable life in America to fight for freedom worth the price he will pay? Is he considering surrendering to the enemy? Does he have time to hide? What does Roberto see around him? Can he feel the pain in his leg? With these questions as a starting point, students can think about the passage as it is being read to prepare for discussion. They will certainly come up with other questions and discussion points, but the advance organizer gets them started.

Comprehension

The major goal of reading instruction is comprehension, and teaching comprehension to gifted students presents an interesting challenge. The usual comprehension questions that ask "how much" or "how many" will not be appropriate. Whereas the average student may have to think through this type of question and draw on comprehension skills to answer it, the gifted student will rely on his superior memory. Questions that ask "why" or "how" are much better, because they force the gifted student to remember facts, analyze them, and draw conclusions (Barbe, 1961).

Comprehension is not a single skill. It embraces many skills, ranging from the relatively simple (recalling the main idea) to the complex (responding to the author's mood and point of view). In teaching comprehension to gifted students, the teacher must focus on the aspect of comprehension he expects the students to learn and keep them on target. Gifted students' verbal and memory skills are so well developed that they can hide a lack of understanding with a barrage of words that relate closely to the question asked. When the teacher does not have a clear notion of the specific skill being taught, these "near misses" may seem satisfactory, and will lead students to think that "almost" is good enough. They will acquire the habit of browsing through their reading instead of giving it careful thought. Teachers of gifted students must therefore work from an extensive list of comprehension skills, such as the teacher's manual that accompanies most basal series, the *Barbe Reading Skills Checklist*, or the *Fountain Valley Teacher Support System*.

Other aspects of comprehension are creative and critical reading. Critical reading implies the ability to differentiate between fact and opinion, to recognize subtle propaganda techniques (such as name-calling, the band-wagon effect, card-stacking, identification with prestige, and personal endorsement), and to assess the worth of a piece of literature by comparing it to internal or external standards (Cushenbery and Howell, 1974). Creative reading may be described as the process by which the printed page serves as the source for imaginative and original thought (Barbe, 1961). It involves analysis, synthesis, integration, application, and extension of ideas (Boothby,

1980). Critical and creative reading are so closely related that Cushenbery and Howell call them "practically synonymous" (1974, p. 71).

Boothby (1980) recommends several procedures for encouraging creative and critical reading among gifted students, commenting that "Certainly neither intellectual giftedness nor fluent reading ability guarantees that students will apply critical thinking to their reading" (p. 674). These are her recommendations:

1 Stauffer's (1975) directed reading-thinking activity (DRTA) promotes critical thinking through prediction and problem solving, and can be used for either group or individual instruction.

2 Crucial to critical and creative reading is vocabulary development. Often neglected because of the superior decoding and oral language skills possessed by many gifted children, vocabulary development should not be left to chance nor to prodigious reading. The gifted frequently use and decode words but are unsure of meanings.

3 Fundamental to the evaluative process in critical reading is familiarity with the subject and with the writer. At an early age, gifted children are able to benefit from instruction in comparative reading. They should be given many opportunities to read widely on a topic (Boothby, 1980, p. 674–676).

For gifted children to truly comprehend what they read, they must learn both inductive-analytical thinking and deductive-synthetic thinking (Cushenbery and Howell, 1974). Inductive-analytical thinking requires reasoning from the particular to the general; the deductive-synthetic process is the ability to reason from the general to the particular. The latter is more easily taught, but the former results in more divergent thinking.

As an example of how both forms of reasoning can be taught, suppose the author of a novel introduces new characters in the context of their relationship with other family members. Students can learn to recognize this device in two ways: the teacher can explain before they read the novel that the author uses this method to introduce new characters; this is the general instance or "rule." Students can deduce from this "rule" the particular instances where it is used by giving examples of how the various characters are introduced. The second way they can learn to recognize the device is by discovering it for themselves. After they read the novel, the teacher asks how the characters are introduced. If no one answers correctly, the teacher leads the class through the novel again, rereading passages in which characters are introduced. The students will probably derive the rule through discussions of the "particular" ways characters are introduced.

Workbook activities that relate to the content of basal readers and stories can promote deductive-synthetic thinking. Nongifted children often get most of their instruction in reading comprehension through activities that develop this type of thinking. Gifted children, however, must receive more varied instruction that will encourage them to think inductively and analytically. Some workbook activities do this, but the best way to foster this high level of thinking is through questioning and discussion. To ensure that questioning and discussion will be productive, the teacher should have a clear idea of the discussion content and some anticipated outcomes. There should, however, be room for students to engage in divergent thinking if it relates to the topic at hand.

Reading Problems of the Gifted

Some gifted students have demonstrated reading problems for a long time. Thirty years ago, Klemm (1953) surveyed the reading difficulties of gifted students and found that 37 of 41 schools or school systems had special provisions for improving these students' reading. One school, however, stated that children with reading problems were not considered gifted. This response prompted Barbe (1961) to comment that "One cannot help but wonder how many potentially gifted children have been excluded from receiving challenging material and an enriched program because of this rigidity of definition of the gifted" (p. 220).

Gifted students' reading problems are usually easy to correct, because they have high motivation and the necessary skills that underlie reading. The first step in correction is to identify the area of weakness and follow this with individual or small group instruction. These gifted students are often assigned exercises that are meant to give practice in a particular skill, not teach it. They should have direct instruction from the teacher before practicing the skill in a workbook.

The student should then attempt to apply the skill through meaningful reading, and should have the opportunity for further practice in a nonthreatening situation. Gifted students recognize their weaknesses as well as their strengths, and are often reluctant to attempt tasks in which they perceive the threat of failure. When remedial reading work is handled so as to prevent embarrassment, then the student is more likely to cooperate.

Many people believe that students with academic problems engage in disruptive behaviors to mask their shortcoming. Gifted children are not immune to this tendency, so if one or more students misbehave during a lesson, they may be reaching their frustration level. Rather than exacerbate the problem by putting the student on the spot, it is wiser to proceed with the lesson and work with the student individually at another time.

Escapism is another type of reading problem to which some gifted children are prone. Strang, McCullough, and Traxler (1955) suggest that:

> Occasionally a gifted child uses reading as an escape . . . (and) sometimes finds the world of books more satisfying than the real world. Consequently they use reading as an escape from desirable physical activities or developmental tasks. (p. 361)

One of the gifted students who participated in the National Student Symposium on the Education of the Gifted and Talented implied these sentiments. This student had not yet engaged in detrimental behavior, but without the guidance of a peer or an adult, he might easily have slipped into a world of fantasy as a substitute for the real world:

> When your mind feels restrained and boxed in on four sides with superficial teachers, boring school days and no challenge whatsoever, I recommend the world's best antidote. This secret remedy is simply reading. Books truly open up whole new worlds. When your own life becomes dull and monotonous, you can easily delve into someone else's through books. I can throw myself, mind and body, into a good book and watch reality slip away. There is so much to be learned—limitations at school shouldn't stop you. Remember, books are a great place to visit, and you know, sometimes I wouldn't mind living there. (American Association for Gifted Children, 1978)

Reading for Secondary Gifted Students

Less direct emphasis on instruction for gifted students at the secondary level than at the elementary school level is not limited to reading; generally, there are many more elementary programs for gifted students than there are secondary programs (Silverman, 1980). The need for secondary programs is equally great, but efforts to establish them have been comparatively unsuccessful.

When planning a secondary reading program for gifted students, one must remember that the nature of giftedness changes as children grow older. Keating (1976) states:

> Whereas most ability variance seems well accounted for by a single general factor during the primary grades, much of the variance in ability during the adolescent years and subsequently is better accounted for by a number of major group factors such as verbal ability, mathematical ability, logical reasoning, spatial visualization, and so on. (p. 189)

Gifted adolescents, therefore, seem to have developed more specific abilities and their interests have crystallized. In terms of a reading program, more individualization will thus be necessary, and interest will play a more important role in selection of reading material.

Besides student characteristics, the organizational structure of the school itself changes between elementary and secondary school. Elementary schools are smaller, and classes are mostly self-contained. Some subjects, such as physical education or music, are taught separately, but the bulk of the academic curriculum is taught by a single teacher.

This arrangement changes in high school. Each subject is taught by a specialist, who may have six classes and as many as 200 students. In the typical high school organizational structure, managing a general program of instruction for gifted students may be difficult, and organizing a reading program will be even more challenging.

Finally, there is an attitudinal difference between elementary and secondary schools. In the elementary school, instruction is unhurried, because teachers think "there's always next year" to offer what was not taught or learned this year. Gifted students are under relatively little pressure, because they are being prepared for more of the same. In high school, however, there is a greater sense of urgency, because there are fewer "next years," and college is imminent. Extracurricular activities steal precious time from the curriculum, and it seems unlikely that students will have the opportunity to make up the reading skills they missed in the elementary grades, learn the new skills that will prepare them for the college years, and read all the "Great Books" they should.

Reading Skills

By the time gifted students reach secondary school, they should have mastered the more fundamental reading skills such as phonics and structural analysis. Some gifted students, however, particularly those with physical disabilities or whose first language is not standard English, may require remedial instruction in even basic skills. Instruction should aim at completing the skill repertoire to allow students to progress at their own pace to more advanced skills. Teachers' attitudes should not be punitive, as is sometimes the case with students "who have so much potential but just do not want to work." The problems these gifted students face are the result of our inability to teach, not their inability to learn. Had they received the support and instruction they needed early in their school career, they would not need remedial work later.

Vocabulary development, a lifelong learning task, should be part of a secondary reading program. Students should not learn vocabulary in isolation, through repetitious drill or rote memorization, but in context, in reading for pleasure or as an academic assignment, and students should be encouraged to use new words at once.

When working with older gifted students, there is a tendency to promote vocabulary development for its own sake. Some students love this challenge, while others enjoy rooting through a dictionary to discover the source of new words. There comes a point, however, at which amassing vocabulary words loses its value unless students can use the words actively or understand them when they encounter them in reading. It is wise to test gifted students' understanding of vocabulary words periodically, perhaps by having them rewrite sentences that contain the new vocabulary words, substituting synonyms for the target words or writing around them by changing the sentence structure without affecting meaning.

The secondary-age gifted student must learn how to derive the meaning of new words through contextual clues. They will have learned this skill in elementary school, but it is worth refining during the secondary years. Despite their prodigious language skills, gifted students will encounter unfamiliar words in content reading in high school and college. The ability to derive meaning without continually consulting a dictionary will save time, although a dictionary and a thesaurus should still be their major reading and writing aids.

Besides deriving meaning from printed words, gifted children should learn to do the same thing with spoken words, and to pronounce new words correctly. The auditory skills that parallel structural analysis and deriving meaning from contextual clues are almost always acquired incidentally, and receive less emphasis than visual skills. Unfortunately, when gifted students enter college, much of their instruction will take the form of lectures, and if they have not learned to derive meaning from spoken words as they do from written words, they will not get much benefit from lectures that cover new ground.

The ability to understand new information, assimilate it, and correlate a large number of unrelated facts and principles may be the student's most important reading skill (Cushenbery and Howell, 1974). This type of comprehension is rarely taught, because teachers assume gifted students can already do this. Some gifted students acquire this ability without a teacher's intervention, and do so at an early age. Other students with the same general ability may not develop this skill on their own, and will have a more difficult time with content reading in science, social studies, and other subjects.

There is no single "right" way for gifted students to gain meaning from the information they encounter in reading or listening, so teaching this cluster of skills does present something of a problem. A group discussion in which all members of a class have an opportunity to describe how they attack the problem is a good instructional activity. This kind of discussion gives students with weak comprehension skills clues to solving the problem for themselves. Students can summarize the discussion into a set of comprehension strategies or a study guide they put together and edit by themselves.

Developmental Reading

A developmental reading program at the secondary level is normally provided for students who have reading problems, although rarely for gifted students. Conant (1959) recognized the need for a developmental reading program for gifted students, to make better readers out of good readers.

As with elementary reading instruction, a developmental reading program must have clear aims, one of which is teaching students that the range of reading speeds varies according to what is being read and for what purposes. Rapid reading or scanning might be used with an encyclopedia article to ascertain a date, a slower rate for a popular novel, and a very deliberate reading for a literary classic.

A second aim is to increase reading speed. A gifted student can often read at a leisurely pace and still accomplish all her work during the high school years, but the quantity of work in college may prove overwhelming. It is far better to prepare this student for the future by teaching speed reading during the secondary years.

The third aim of a developmental reading program for gifted students relates closely to the second; in addition to reading faster, they must read "better"—that is, their comprehension skills must improve, and they must realize that the major purpose of reading fast is not just to finish a book. The purpose of speed reading is to help students use their reading time more efficiently without lessening their comprehension. Gifted students should be able to deal with great quantities of written material in a reasonable span of time, but they should also be able to recall important details and characters, recognize the sequence of events, understand the book's literary devices, and so on.

Gifted students usually make greater gains in reading ability in a special class than do either average or slow students (Barbe, 1981), suggesting that there is a need for such programs and that they are successful. The major problem with developmental reading programs at the secondary level is finding a teacher with the right training and interest. One possibility is an elementary teacher who has dual certification.

Who Should Teach Reading?

Customarily, the English teacher gives secondary age gifted students the reading instruction they require. Unfortunately, this teacher's effectiveness is diminished because of the vast and varied content he is expected to teach. One teacher often teaches reading, literature appreciation, grammar, spelling, composition, and creative writing in the same course. Consequently, gifted students' reading abilities and related skills often reach a plateau during the secondary school years.

Teachers other than the English teacher should also work to improve gifted students' reading ability. "Every teacher is a teacher of reading" is nowhere more applicable than at the secondary level with gifted students. For probably the first time, reading in the content areas supersedes reading as a general skill, and teachers of individual subjects should help gifted students learn the best ways to assimilate and make sense of content.

Because virtually every teacher will participate in gifted students' reading instruction, someone must assume responsibility for coordinating their efforts—the English teacher, the reading specialist if one is available, or the coordinator of programs for the gifted. Otherwise, school professionals may work at cross-purposes and gifted students may complete high school without all the reading skills they need to succeed in college and beyond.

The individual who coordinates reading instruction for gifted students should evaluate their reading needs as well as monitor their progress. The coordinator may encounter some resistance from students or other teachers, but it is a necessary aspect of reading instruction. Those who object to the notion of reading evaluation for secondary gifted students can sometimes be persuaded otherwise if they can see the parallel between math or science and reading. Curriculum in these two subjects is normally so well organized that when a question arises concerning a specific skill, such as learning the periodic table of elements, one can pinpoint exactly when this skill should have been taught. The same degree of specificity is impossible with reading, but an effort should be made to ensure that secondary-age gifted students have the opportunity to learn the reading skills they will need later.

Another important task for the reading coordinator is to help teachers and students make the most of the relatively short time devoted to reading instruction. To use the time most effectively, someone must determine what skills students already have, what skills they must learn, and how the remaining time can best be managed.

It is not enough for one school professional, whether the English teacher or a reading coordinator, to plan the reading instruction that will be offered to gifted students. All the teachers in the school must work together to develop the program.

Quality instruction will not be as effective if it is fragmented, so it is vital to develop a comprehensive plan that describes the scope and sequence of reading skill instruction for gifted students. The plan should embrace both fundamental reading skills as well as skills associated with content reading, and techniques should be specific enough to show when a skill should be taught and who is responsible for teaching it.

If there will not be enough time to teach all the skills students should learn, gifted students should have opportunities to work on their own with self-instructional materials. Students normally enjoy working independently, particularly when they can arrange their own schedule and select materials that coincide with their learning styles. Independent study should always be considered supplementary, however, and should not be substituted for organized instruction conducted by a trained and dedicated teacher.

Although every teacher should teach reading in his area of specialization, few teachers have received the necessary training to do this, so a resource person should be available to give them instructional assistance. This specialist should have a background in reading and in gifted education, and must be prepared to help other teachers identify important reading skills, select appropriate instructional techniques, evaluate student progress, and motivate gifted students to want to read in the content areas. An arrangement in which the content specialist works with the reading specialist is particularly effective in ensuring that gifted students learn the reading skills they need without sacrificing instruction in the content areas.

Writing

Most gifted students' writing instruction is even less adequate than their reading instruction. This inadequacy is the result of several circumstances, not the least of which is that far less is known about writing than reading. Educators and psychologists have been interested in reading for more than a century, but concern about writing has appeared only in the past decade. Moreover, teachers of the gifted are better trained to teach reading than writing, and are themselves better readers than writers. Considering these factors, it is no wonder that the writing curriculum is perhaps the weakest aspect of gifted education.

Change is in the offing, however, because both general and gifted education are beginning to put greater emphasis on writing. Commenting on the change in general education, Graves (1978) suggests that the growing attention to the composing process will cause the traditional emphasis on reading skills to give way to a better balance between reading and writing instruction. Putting reading and writing on an equal footing in gifted programs would improve the quality of education of our most able children and youth, since, as Thomas Middleton states, "If they can't read, they can't write; if they can't write, they can't reason far beyond mere scheming."

Presently, gifted students are less capable writers than many suspect. From the primary through the secondary school years, their compositions and creative writing are not much better than those of their nongifted peers. The rich vocabulary and advanced thinking skills that characterize gifted students have given rise to the notion that gifted learners are uniquely equipped for writing well, which, according to Fearn (1981), is a ". . . widely disseminated generalization that enjoys not a shred of evidence" (p. 26).

Primary/Elementary Writing

Gifted children may not write well, but with proper instruction and encouragement, they can develop writing skills commensurate with their other abilities. Instruction and encouragement must begin at an early age:

> The critical period of initial language acquisition and development is the preschool and elementary years, and we have used a term in relation to reading that reflects this insight, reading readiness. It is time that we realize that there is also a readiness to write that overlaps the language, perceptual, and cognitive skills that constitute reading readiness. (Stallard, 1977, p. 776)

By the time gifted children enter school, they will probably have passed through several stages of writing development that their nongifted classmates will just be entering. The gifted child will have a substantial active vocabulary, will probably know the relationship between oral and written language, and will either know the rudiments of handwriting or take to it quickly. Given this relatively advanced stage of development and the increasing evidence supporting contemporaneous teaching of reading and writing, we can see the benefits of beginning writing instruction at the same time we begin reading instruction, and the need to emphasize them equally. When gifted children realize early that reading and writing are opposite sides of the same coin, the enthusiasm they show toward reading will tend to carry over to writing as well.

From the time gifted children start school, they should spend a portion of each day developing their writing abilities to help them acquire the habit of writing. Writing activities should vary to cover all aspects of the composing process and the mechanics of writing.

Writing comprises a series of related skills: handwriting, spelling, composition, grammar, and so on. We sometimes teach these skills separately to children of average ability, to give them a focus for learning: when they know what skill is being taught, they are more likely to know what is expected of them. Teaching writing-related skills to gifted children in isolation is not usually recommended, however. This practice can lead to boredom, and is usually unnecessary, because gifted students are usually well aware of the purpose of a lesson and of what they are to do. As a rule, gifted students should be taught the process of writing—prewriting, drafting, revising, and polishing. Specific skills for each stage of the process should be taught and practiced as they are needed. It is also helpful to keep in mind that writing is similar to other abilities, and emerges gradually. As Searle and Dillon (1980) state,

> Learning the mechanics of writing is a developmental process—like learning to walk, talk, or draw—which occurs as a continuing refinement of the whole process of composing and which should occur as part of an environment focused on meaning. (p. 776)

Written language has its basis in spoken language, so dictation is a good first step for teaching the composing process. Gifted children should have a chance to describe stories or personal experiences while the teacher records what the child says. Dictating stories demonstrates to children the correspondence between written and spoken language, indirectly teaches some of the mechanical aspects of writing, and makes them feel that their thoughts are valuable, and worthy of an adult's attention.

Children's dictation will reflect their backgrounds, abilities, and interests, but are most dependent on the child's home environment. As with reading, it is incorrect to judge a child's ability on the basis of early dictation, since children from enriched environments will have larger vocabularies and more varied experiences than children from less advantaged homes. Providing the latter children with interesting field trips and visitations, reading to them, and fostering verbal interaction with other gifted children will generally give them a broader base from which to derive their dictations.

The teacher will not have enough time to record as many stories as she would like, so she may need to use a tape recorder, or have older gifted children act as recorders. Cross-age recording has been successful with nongifted children, and appears to be a good way to promote the writing skills of all the children involved.

Revising and editing should be part of the dictation process. These abilities are usually taught to older children, but there is no reason gifted children cannot learn to improve their self-expression from the start. If the child's dictation has been recorded in writing, the teacher should read back to the child what has been written, and give the child a chance to change the story. If the story has been recorded on tape, the child can re-tape portions that need improvement or revision.

At this stage, editing should be directed at content rather than at grammar, syntax, or other aspects of spoken and written language. Questions such as "Is this what happened?" or "Is there anything else you want to say about that?" will help the child decide if changes are necessary.

Children need encouragement rather than criticism when they are first learning to compose their thoughts to share with others. Gifted children will recognize when they have displeased a parent or teacher, and there is no faster way to break the writing habit than through criticism. The teacher's comments should convey the message that "What you have written is fine. Is it what you wanted to say, or is there more you want to add?"

In a well designed educational program, gifted children will learn all the language arts simultaneously. They will have many opportunities to practice speaking and listening skills, will read abundantly, will compose through dictation, and will learn the developmentally appropriate aspects of writing mechanics, such as penmanship, spelling, and grammar. The mechanical skills must be introduced in such a way that the child sees them as part of the language process, rather than as tedious jobs to get through before one can read or use the tape recorder. Integrating all the language arts at an early age can help gifted children avoid later difficulties with the mechanics of writing.

Whether gifted or not, beginning writers produce at letter, word, and sentence levels; they do not follow a sequence of writing letters before words or words before sentences (Clay, 1975). In effect, gifted children will begin to write in the same way they speak. Their mechanical abilities, however, will lag far behind their expressive abilities, giving rise to a period of possible frustration. Lettering and spelling will

> Still consume their attention. Writing is making letters. It is slow. At this stage, children cannot see beyond the phrases at their pencil point. Just as word-by-word reading prevents children from understanding the main point of their reading passage, word by word writing also prevents children from seeing their writing as a whole piece. They are not able to think ahead, to plan a single main point. (Calkins, 1979, p. 748)

During this period, children should still have opportunities to dictate to the teacher, an older student, or a tape recorder. They should, however, make the transition to more structured expression through writing. The teacher can promote this transition in several ways. One is to establish a fixed period of time during each day when writing, not dictation, is to be done; another block of time should be reserved for oral expression. A second step is to provide many types of reinforcement for writing. Reading is intrinsically rewarding for gifted children, whereas writing's rewards must be learned. After the child has attained a sense of craft, writing also becomes its own reinforcement; in the early grades, however, external reinforcement will be needed. Social reinforcement is excellent, so children's papers should be posted around the room, they should be praised for good work, their papers should be sent to other teachers or home to parents, and published in a class or school paper.

Third, establish a writing center where there are many kinds of writing stimuli, as well as writing instruments and different writing surfaces. Writing center activities should be based on students' interests, skills that need reinforcement, different learning styles, and ease of implementation. Open-ended activities such as story starters, writing headlines, building a book, and diaries are all appropriate for writing centers.

Froese (1978) describes four stages through which children pass in becoming competent writers. The first two stages, writing readiness and dictating, occur during the primary grades. The third stage, independent writing, takes place during the later elementary years, and leads to the fourth stage, language experimentation.

Independent writing should stress content rather than mechanics. Over-emphasizing correct spelling, handwriting, and grammar during the time set aside for composing will not improve the mechanical aspects and will interfere with the composing process. When children are attempting to keep daily logs, record their feelings, or relate significant events, they should not be burdened with the need for precision. They should concentrate on mechanics during a time specifically set aside for this purpose or during the revision process.

Gifted children will find language experimentation challenging and enjoyable, because it capitalizes on their language facility and extensive vocabularies. They should be encouraged to expand vocabulary through reading, dictionary usage, and reliance upon a thesaurus, and to attempt to use their newly expanded vocabularies in everyday writing.

Teachers often post lists of synonyms around the room so that children can vary their usage of descriptive words. This writing aid should be used only sparingly with gifted children; it is better to teach them how to use a thesaurus or dictionary, since they have the ability to do so and should not be encouraged to rely on an artificial writing aid that will not play a role in their later writing. Mature writers use the thesaurus and dictionary, and the sooner gifted children learn how, the better.

As part of the language experimentation stage, Froese (1978) suggests that children learn to adopt different points of view. For example, they might be asked to describe a school event (assembly, field trip, or the like) as seen through the eyes of another person: a friend, the teacher, or the principal. This exercise forces children to think divergently, helps them view a familiar event from a different perspective, and has both academic and personal benefits.

As gifted children progress through the elementary grades, they must learn to structure their writing through the conventional devices accomplished writers use. Model stories help introduce these conventions (Jett-Simpson, 1981). First, select an interesting story written in a form children can imitate, then have the children read the story and discuss it until they are familiar with it. Explain the author's literary devices and conventions, and when the children understand what they are to do, have them write a similar story in the same style but with different characters, settings, and events. Some teachers object to this practice on the grounds that it is mimicry, but experienced authors know that writing from an accepted format or model is a good way to begin an assignment. Jett-Simpson (1981) describes how using model stories overcomes some of the problems children encounter in their writing:

> For many children, writing a story presents several obstacles. They are often uncertain about how to plan and organize the writing. Actual classroom time to develop a story is minimal, the physical act of moving the pencil seems overwhelming when more than several pages are expected, and the pressure to spell, to punctuate, and to be grammatical is inhibiting. (p. 293)

Model stories should be used such that gifted children recognize them as means to an end, not ends in themselves. They must understand that writing a story based on a model is practice for helping them develop better writing skills. Introducing model stories without sufficient explanation or using them too frequently can confuse children about their purpose, and they may try to make all their writing conform to the model. If they fall into this pattern, their composing will become stilted and they will lose interest in writing altogether.

Writing is a new and exciting experience during the early elementary years, so there is little difficulty motivating gifted children to write. As they move through the grades, however, the initial excitement often fades. Dinan (1977) suggests a reason for teachers' lack of success in motivating students to write creatively and enthusiastically:

> The distance between the language model and the student language-user is not bridged. As a result, our students do not move beyond the passive ''consuming'' of language to become confident, inspired, active language-users. (p. 750)

Requiring students to write daily and tying their writing to their reading can help avoid this problem. Gifted students' affinity for reading can be used to promote writing by having them write about their thoughts or feelings toward what they are reading. This writing usually should not assume the form of a book report; rather, students can keep a log or diary of their thoughts while reading. This will encourage the writing habit, ensure that there is some substance to students' writing, and help them understand that the essence of writing is realistic communication. Writing informally about their reading is ''real'' writing, and gifted students will often express themselves more efficiently through this form of writing than any other.

Secondary Writing

The central theme that should pervade writing instruction for secondary-age gifted students is that ''Writing is something you will be doing for the rest of your life, and will be one means of judging your accomplishments. Master the craft of writing now, and your success later will be more certain.'' Gifted students should evaluate their writing against more rigorous standards than when they were younger, and should begin to develop a preference for one kind of writing over another.

Gifted secondary students will have different elementary backgrounds, so the writing instruction they have received and their writing skills will vary. It is wise, therefore, to use early writing assignments to provide developmental writing instruction. The teacher can group students for instruction on specific writing skills, and when they have been brought to a common skill level, can conduct large group instruction.

Direct instruction on composition skills is necessary at the secondary level as well as at the elementary level. It may be even more important, since there is less time remaining to teach the skills students must learn for success in college. Unfortunately, the amount of direct instruction most secondary age gifted students receive in composition is far less than they need. As Stallard (1977) comments:

> As a high school student with ambitions to write, I was often frustrated by teachers who didn't know that I needed to be told or shown how to go about writing a composition. To be sure, I also needed to know something about the conventions of writing and of

Students' writing should tie in to their reading, and assignments should give them opportunities to try different kinds of writing.

> language generally, but I especially needed to know something about how to compose a piece of writing. The only advice I had received was to make an outline. That was first suggested in the sixth grade and repeated each year thereafter. (p. 775)

Stallard goes on to say that when a group of good student writers was asked how they produced required outlines, they said they wrote the paper first and then made the outline.

Deciding what they want to write about can be difficult for gifted students because they are able to see so many possible directions. And while they may be able to verbalize what they want to say, they may be unable to put their words on paper. Using a tape recorder can help overcome both difficulties. Students can dictate their ideas into the recorder, select those that are closest to their intended meaning, revise them, and transcribe the revised ideas. After several sessions with the tape recorder, students will probably be able to put their thoughts directly onto paper. If they still cannot write their thoughts directly after a period of time, they should be permitted to use the tape recorder as the first step in composing initial drafts of papers. Many professional writers find it easier to compose with a tape recorder, and there is no reason that gifted students should be discouraged from doing so if they find this practice helpful.

Whether dictating or writing, the gifted student needs a clear picture of what he wants to communicate to others. This key to mature writing provides a focus for initial expression and revising. Haley-James (1981) stresses the importance of the first draft:

> Drafting and a redrafting type of revising can profitably take place only when there is enough raw material on paper that interests the writer to allow the writer to focus on content and meaning that fit a felt or emerging purpose for writing. Finding this usable information helps the writer drown out unfocused noise in the mind. (p. 564)

After discovering what they want to say, gifted students must learn to say it better. They must work their way through convoluted sentences, double negatives, and awkward constructions until a product emerges that communicates the writer's meaning and keeps the reader's interest. There are no shortcuts between first drafts and polished prose, and gifted students must come to see that excellence in writing requires as much effort as does excellence in any other endeavor.

Secondary students should also acquire a sense of writing style. They do this most easily through extensive reading and directed discussion of what they have read. At first the teacher will lead these discussions, but within a few sessions, students will probably interact without the need for continual adult intervention. The teacher's major role at this time is to help students apply the stylistic elements they identify in their discussions to their own writing.

Vocabulary development also has a place in the secondary school. Gifted students will almost always have rich speaking and reading vocabularies, but less extensive writing vocabularies. Use of a dictionary or thesaurus remedies this problem; rather than promote dependence, use of these resources increases students' writing vocabularies to the point that their reliance on them diminishes.

As students' writing abilities improve, so must their critical abilities. Students learn critical evaluation by reading professional book reviews and plays and following the interaction among contributors to newspaper op-ed pages. Reviews and written commentaries demonstrate the aspects of writing that are susceptible to criticism, and the approaches to criticism different individuals take. Reading critical reactions of professionals gives students insight as to how to improve their own work, shows them that criticism is an accepted aspect of the writing process, and perhaps makes them less reluctant to seek criticism of their own work.

Teacher conferences also help diminish the fear of criticism. Gifted adolescents may be overly sensitive to criticism, and may react defensively to comments about their written work, especially when it is public. They may take the same comments more positively when delivered privately. After students become accustomed to having their work critiqued by one person with whom they are comfortable, the teacher may be able to comment on students' writing in front of the whole class. Teacher conferences are also a good forerunner to peer conferences.

As does reading, writing in the content areas assumes greater importance in the secondary years. Some writing instruction for gifted students should be directed toward the kinds of reports they will have to write in both high school and college. They should learn how to collect information from reference sources, organize the material into a logical sequence, synthesize several ideas into a consistent format, and express conclusions clearly and precisely.

The Sense of Craft

To write in a way that reflects their capabilities, gifted students must be confident about their writing skills and must perceive the writing act as a process that results in a worthwhile product. They must:

> Attain a sense of craft, not to satisfy the teacher, but to keep pace with their developing critical perception. If the disparity becomes too great, if the written product falls far short of the student's sense of what writing should be, the product will be viewed as "distressingly wanting." At this point, students may conclude that "they are not writers" and avoid writing just as they avoid drawing. The race has been lost. (Wilde and Newkirk, 1981, p. 292)

Because gifted students are such avid readers and have such formidable thinking abilities, they are harsh critics when it comes to differentiating between good and poor writing. They recognize the deficiencies in their own work, and often prefer not to write at all rather than to fail in their own eyes. It is important, therefore, to help them understand that writing develops slowly over a long period of time, and that even the most capable writers have many false starts and revise their work often before they produce a satisfactory manuscript. Encouraging gifted students to write often, to revise, and to set reasonable standards for themselves will do much to help them attain the sense of craft that will keep them writing.

Revising and Rewriting

Sager (1977) distinguishes between writing in the early grades and that done later.

> The chief writing problem in the intermediate grades is different from that of the primary: to clarify the children's writing and make it better without taking away the joy. In the primary grades we write; in the intermediate grades we improve writing. (p. 86)

Young children, then, must learn the writing habit; the emphasis of instruction should be to get them to write often and naturally. In contrast, older gifted students must acquire the rewriting habit, and should strive to make their writing better through revising.

It is critical to their progress that gifted students perceive rewriting in a positive light. These students are accustomed to success, and may misinterpret the need to rewrite as an indication of failure. With teachers' encouragement, gifted students must come to believe what experienced writers know:

> Right the first time means discovering what you want to say, but not, necessarily, in complete sentences, correctly spelled and neatly written.
>
> Rewriting is not just recopying neatly, minus a few punctuation errors. It is not just fixing what is wrong. Rewriting is finding the best way to give your newly-discovered ideas to others; it's a finishing, a polishing up, and it should be creative and satisfying as any job well done. (Schwartz, 1977, p. 756)

As important as rewriting is for gifted students, they are not well prepared to do it. More often than not, they are asked merely to "write this over again;" they never learn the principles of rewriting nor how to edit systematically. To rewrite, students need a purpose for writing. As Wilde and Newkirk (1981) say,

> To revise, a writer must be able to move back from the text and test what he or she has written against some internalized standard. If the standard does not exist, the writer is swimming in a cloudy pool indeed. If anything can follow anything, it is impossible for the writer to detect a wrong turn. There are no wrong turns. (p. 286)

Gifted students, even more than their nongifted classmates, need to see a purpose in their writing. Students with superior ability know when a task is only busywork, and will resist wasting their time on meaningless writing. Perhaps the teacher's most vital task is to design writing assignments that give gifted students the opportunity to express themselves in a way that means something to them.

Another principle of rewriting is that students must know for whom they are writing; they must develop a sense of audience. To do so, they can contrast several familiar writing forms (the local newspaper, a national news magazine, a Shakespeare play, a popular novel, and a technical book) according to length, sentence length, vocabulary, illustrations, literary devices, and so on.

Students also need an understanding of the factors that contribute to effective written communication: vocabulary, organization, elaboration, and structure (Applegate, 1963). Few students learn how to apply these factors incidentally, and probably only hear about them when their writing is being criticized. They may be told, for example, that their choice of words is poor, without having been taught how to choose more appropriate words. Before students revise their writing, they must receive direct instruction on the elements of composition on which criticism and revision will be based.

Creativity and Writing

The writing program for gifted children and youth should "balance practical utilitarian writing and personal subjective expression" (Strang, 1961, p. 189). Creative writing should not dominate the curriculum, as it often does, nor should it substitute for report writing or other more structured forms of composition.

Although creativity has a special place in the hearts of teachers of the gifted, and creativity is a necessary condition for giftedness, creative writing should not be the only form of written expression gifted students produce.

Creative thinkers are problem finders, and their mistrust of easy answers and quick solutions leads them into a pattern of divergent thinking. This process is fundamental to the scientific method, and manifests itself in the creation of the written word (Getzels and Csizszentmihalyi, 1979). Creative thought need not be fanciful, and for writing, can be rooted in reality in a variety of forms.

Kantor and Perron (1977) argue that writing in the linguistically more difficult modes of argumentation and exposition are just as challenging as discourse, description, and narration, and should be stressed equally in the writing curriculum. They add:

> To many teachers, creative writing means writing that is "cute" or "clever"—or simply "nice." . . . But creativity involves social sensitivity and problem-solving ability as well as aesthetic appreciation. . . . In a discourse sense, creative writing cannot be limited to stories, poems, or descriptions; an explanation or an argument also require the creative generation of ideas. (p. 745)

Gifted students, whether elementary or secondary, should enjoy a balanced writing curriculum. They should have the opportunity to express thoughts and feelings in a unique way, where novelty and innovation are encouraged, but they should also learn to use writing to support positions they adopt. Because they will find a use for both kinds of writing as adults, gifted students should be trained to write effectively both ways.

Instructional Strategies

Sample lesson: Primary Reading

Primary purpose: To teach pupils the difference between reality and fantasy.

Secondary purpose: To teach pupils the comparative and superlative forms of adjectives.

Materials: Captioned filmstrip of "Goldilocks and The Three Bears"; similar objects of different sizes, such as balls, chairs, shoes, and bowls.

Method: Introduce the story of "Goldilocks and The Three Bears" by asking if any of the children know the story and can summarize it. Show the filmstrip and have the children read along using the captions. Provide help where necessary in sounding out words or explaining the meaning of new words. Each time objects of different sizes appear in the story, bring them to the pupils' attention, stressing how the objects differ. After showing the filmstrip, discuss with the children what parts of the story were true and what parts could not be true. Ask them to think about how the story could be made true, and see if they can think of different endings. Ask the children to think of other fairy tales or nursery rhymes in which comparisons are important (Three Little Pigs, Jack Sprat, Billy Goats Gruff). Have the children discuss which parts of these stories are real and which parts are imaginary.

After the discussion, show the children the different sized objects, and have them label the objects as larger and largest, smaller and smallest, and so on. See if they can come up with other characteristics on which the objects differ in terms of degree. Have them identify other objects in the classroom or school that differ in degree.

To combine the two purposes of the lesson, have the pupils describe an imaginary animal. Write the description on the board, and see if the children can draw the animal. Have them describe the animal using comparative and superlative adjectives: it is larger than a lion, but smaller than a whale; it is the fastest animal in the forest; it can fly higher than any bird; and so on.

Sample lesson: Secondary reading

Purpose: To teach students to recognize various kinds of imagery different authors use.

Method: Have each student select a passage of several hundred words from books they are currently reading. Divide the class into small groups, and have them discuss how the passages differ in terms of descriptions, which passage they prefer, and why. Ask the students to name other authors or works and classify them according to types of imagery—visual, auditory, or kinesthetic.

Bring the entire class together, and see if the students can organize themselves into groups who prefer visual, auditory, or kinesthetic descriptions. Have each group create a passage of its own describing a common event or place (a school assembly, football game, local park, or historical site). Compare the descriptions to see if they are consistent with each group's modality preference.

Sample Lesson: Primary writing

Purpose: To teach pupils the prewriting skill of identifying and ordering ideas they wish to include in a composition.

Materials: Poster board or other heavy stock cut into 4" × 12" strips; tape.

Method: Discuss with the children a recent class experience such as a field trip or assembly. Have them describe each aspect of the experience, and as they do so, write the descriptions on a card. When they have thoroughly described the experience, arrange the cards in a manner that could be used as an outline for a composition. Tape the cards to the chalkboard so the pupils can see the flow of events. Be sure to point out that some events preceded others, and that there are instances when several things happen at the same time. Have the children each write a brief description of the event using the outline on the board.

To promote divergent thinking, have the class repeat the activity but invent a happening, such as a trip into space, a safari, travel to a past or future time, or an adventure such as Alice in Wonderland's. The pupils should develop an outline and use it as the basis of a composition describing the "fantastic voyage."

Sample lesson: Secondary writing

Primary Purpose: To show how layout influences the effectiveness of prose.

Secondary Purpose: To demonstrate some of the finer points of text editing.

Method: Select a text passage of approximately 1,000 words from one of the class's current readings. Have a local typesetter reset the text in several different formats, including various line lengths, right-justified versus unjustified, and various styles and sizes of type. Photocopy the text for every student, and discuss the characteristics of each version of the passage. Show how syllabication is important for word breaks on right-justified text, how line length affects readability, and how text changes are sometimes necessary to eliminate "widows," in which the last word in a paragraph falls on a line by itself. Have the students choose the version of the passage they think is best and explain why.

Consult the school librarian for references on the typesetting process. It would also be advantageous if the students could interact with the typesetter to discuss stylistic considerations such as line length, justification, and type sizes and styles. If the students could contact a local author, he or she could explain the editorial changes that are sometimes necessary to solve typesetting problems.

Adapting Instructional Materials

The comparatively small number of gifted students makes it unprofitable for publishers to develop reading and writing materials specifically for this population. Many print and nonprint materials, however, can be adapted for students of exceptional ability. The necessary adaptations usually do not involve the materials themselves; rather, they entail changes in how the materials are applied or in developing supplements.

The primary adaptation of any reading or writing material is to ensure that it requires active involvement on the part of the gifted student, and that it reflects a clear educational purpose. A gifted student who sits through a ten-minute instructional computer program or completes six pages in a workbook should be able to answer the question "What did you learn?" and demonstrate a new or improved skill; if not, then he has not really been involved in the activity.

The teacher should compile a set of questions to accompany each instructional material, consistent with the purpose of the material but also promoting development of higher level cognitive skills, including analysis, synthesis, and evaluation; questions can require either oral or written answers. Burmeister's *Reading Strategies for Middle and Secondary School Teachers* and Lamberg and Lamb's *Reading Instruction in The Content Area* both discuss strategies for generating questions that require higher level thinking.

The teacher can also adapt materials by organizing them so that gifted students can work independently. Reading and writing centers allow students to move ahead at their own pace and in a direction that reflects their interests. Reading and writing centers offer one solution to the curriculum differentiation problem. With sufficient materials and opportunities to work independently, gifted students usually differentiate their own curricula.

Gifted students should also have access to a wide variety of materials reflecting both depth and breadth of content, again to give them opportunities to differentiate their curricula. Rather than simply assemble a hodgepodge of instructional materials, the teacher needs to organize and cross-reference them so that when students have finished one set of materials, they can go on to additional materials that provide continuation in either breadth or depth. Cross-referencing enables students to move beyond the limitations of any single material. For example, many gifted students are interested in biographies, and rather than read a series of unrelated biographies, they would probably enjoy seeing how the lives of famous people often intertwine. After a student reads a biography of Thomas Jefferson, she can gain another perspective on both Jefferson and his times by reading about Benjamin Franklin or John Adams to see how their lives interrelated.

To make the most of instructional materials, gifted students should discuss with one another and the teacher the purpose of the materials, their format, and their strengths and weaknesses. The criticism should be constructive, to help students take advantage of the materials.

Perhaps the most effective adaptation the teacher of gifted students can undertake is to revise the teacher's manual that accompanies instructional materials. Revision should include:

- Modification of the scope and sequence chart to reflect gifted students' abilities.
- Deletion of redundant material intended to give average students practice with basic skills. Gifted students do not usually need as much practice.
- Inclusion of enrichment materials to permit gifted students to progress beyond the minimum competency levels that are normally the goal of instructional materials.
- Development of activities that promote integration of reading and writing skills.
- Development of activities that promote healthy competition among students as well as a sense of internal competition.

Summary

Reading and writing are perhaps the most useful school subjects, and account for more instructional time than any other group of related subjects. To a degree, skill in these areas determines a person's social acceptability. But despite their importance, gifted students acquire most of their reading and writing skills through socialization, personal effort, and incidental learning, rather than through direct instruction.

Gifted students' reading and writing achievement is often below what we would expect of their general intellectual abilities. On the other hand, students who do have exceptional ability in reading and writing often remain unidentified. And, while gifted students gravitate naturally toward reading to satisfy their curiosity, they still require direct instruction.

Initial reading instruction should focus on skill acquisition, with emphasis in the later grades on application. Gifted students make the transition from skill acquisition to application earlier than do their nongifted peers. Two ways to group gifted students for reading instruction are according to individual skills and according to interests. Gifted students should learn a core vocabulary of sight words as well as phonetic word attack skills. Their erratic acquisition of reading skills reflects their atypical cognitive development.

Reading comprehension for gifted students should involve more than simply "how much" or "how many" questions. They should be encouraged from an early age to read creatively and critically, and comprehension should involve inductive-analytical and deductive-synthetic thinking.

Reading instruction for secondary gifted students differs from that of primary students because the nature of giftedness changes along with the nature of the school. Emphasis in the secondary school should be on reading skills that prepare one for the academic challenge of college. At the secondary level, one person should be responsible for managing reading instruction so that important skills are not overlooked. Most gifted students receive inadequate writing instruction, although this situation is beginning to change. Rather than teaching a series of fragmented skills, it is better to teach gifted students the writing process—prewriting, drafting, revising, and polishing, emphasizing spelling, handwriting, and grammar at different stages of the process. Whereas elementary writing instruction should emphasize prewriting and drafting, secondary instruction should focus on revising and polishing.

Resources for Reading and Writing Instruction

There are many reading and writing resources available to the teacher of gifted students, but unfortunately, few of them are identified as such, so teachers must sort through an enormous number of references to find those that are appropriate. To reduce this task, the teacher should first consult the *Handbook* of *Instructional Resources and References for Teaching the Gifted* by Frances Karnes and Emily Collins (Allyn and Bacon, 1980). This invaluable reference brings together information on a wide range of materials suitable for use with gifted students, and includes a general discussion of the practical aspects of educating the gifted and adapting instructional materials.

Journals devoted to education of the gifted are also important sources of information about reading and writing instruction. They include *G/C/T* (Gifted/Creative/Talented), the *Journal for the Education of the Gifted*, and the *Gifted Child Quarterly*. Special education journals such as *Exceptional Children*, *Teaching Exceptional Children*, and *Exceptional Parent*, and the *Journal of Special Education* sometimes feature articles on reading and writing for gifted students. The teacher can also consult the *Current Index to Journals in Education* and the annual index of each of these publications for a quick overview of the contents.

The *Reading Teacher, Reading Research Quarterly,* the *Journal of Reading, Language Arts,* the *Elementary School Journal,* the *English Journal,* the *Journal of Reading Behavior,* and *Reading Improvement* offer the most current opinion and research on reading and writing instruction. The popular education magazines, including *Instructor, Learning,* and *Early Years* provide practical tips on general reading and writing instruction and occasional articles on teaching these subjects to gifted students. Each year's research on reading, including that which is devoted to gifted students, is reviewed in the *Annual Summary of Investigations Relating to Reading,* published by the International Reading Association. The IRA also has a special interest group that focuses on reading for gifted and creative students.

Publishers annually issue hundreds of textbooks and student materials that teachers of the gifted can use for reading and writing instruction. The reviews of these materials that appear each month in professional journals and magazines are generally more useful and less biased than the publishers' promotional materials, and save the teacher the trouble and expense of ordering an unsatisfactory product. Materials are also reviewed in *Curriculum Product Review, Educational Dealer,* and *Media and Methods.*

Another source of information on reading and writing instruction for gifted students often overlooked is the program book for annual conventions of the Council for Exceptional Children, the International Reading Association, the National Council of Teachers of English, and other professional associations. Teachers, administrators, and researchers who present papers at national conventions are usually willing to provide copies to interested parties. The information in these papers is even more current than that in journal articles, as there can be a time lag of a year or more between presentation of a paper and its eventual appearance in print.

One of the most recent trends in education is the use of microcomputers for reading and writing instruction. Most of the educational courseware has been designed for children of average ability, but can be used with gifted students. The most comprehensive sources of information on courseware are the *Apple Blue Book,* published by Visual Materials, Inc., (Gurnee, Illinois) and the *TRS-80 Applications Software Sourcebook,* available at any Radio Shack store. *Classroom Computer News, Electronic Learning,* and many of the periodicals mentioned review educational software.

References

American Association for Gifted Children. *On being gifted.* New York: Walker, 1978.

American Psychological Association. *Standards for educational psychological tests.* Washington, D.C.: American Psychological Association, 1974.

Applebee, R. "National study of high school English programs: A record of English education today." *English Journal* 55 (1966): 273–81.

Applegate, M. *Freeing children to write.* Evanston, Ill.: Harper and Row, 1963.

Barbe, W. "Reading aspects." In *Curriculum planning for the gifted.* Edited by L. Fliegler. Englewood Cliffs, N.J.: Prentice-Hall, 1961.

Barbe, W., and M. Milone. *Modality characteristics of gifted students*. Paper delivered at the Annual Convention of the Council for Exceptional Children, April, 1981.

Boothby, P. "Creative and critical reading for the gifted." *Reading Teacher* 33 (1980): 674–76.

Calkins, L. "Learning to throw away." *Language Arts* 56 (1979): 747–52.

Chall, J. *Learning to read*. New York: McGraw-Hill, 1967.

Clay, M. *What did I write?* London: Heinemann, 1975.

Conant, J. *The American high school today*. New York: McGraw-Hill, 1959.

Cushenbery, D., and H. Howell. *Reading and the gifted child: A guide for teachers*. Springfield, Ill.: Thomas, 1974.

Dearman, N., and V. Plisko. *The condition of education*. Washington, D.C.: National Center for Educational Statistics, 1980.

Dinan, L. "By the time I'm ten, I'll probably be famous!" *Language Arts* 54 (1977): 750–55.

Dunn, R., and G. Price. "The learning style characteristics of gifted students." *Gifted Child Quarterly* 24 (1980): 33–36.

Durkin, D. *Children who read early*. New York: Teachers College Press, 1966.

Durkin, D. "Reading comprehension instruction." *Reading Research Quarterly* 16 (1981): 515–44.

Fearn, L. "Writing: A basic and developmental skill for gifted learners." *Gifted/Creative/Talented* 17 (1981): 26–27.

Froese, V. "Understanding writing." *Language Arts* 55 (1978): 811–15.

Gallagher, J. *Teaching the gifted child*. 2nd ed. Boston: Allyn and Bacon, 1975.

Getzels, J., and M. Csikszentmihalyi. *The creative vision: A longitudinal study of problem finding in art*. New York: John Wiley, 1979.

Graves, D. *Balance the basics: Let them write*. New York: Ford Foundation, 1978.

Haley-James, S. "Revising writing in the upper grades." *Language Arts* 58 (1981): 562–66.

Hildreth, G. "Early writing as an aid to reading." *Elementary English* 40 (1963): 15–20.

Jett-Simpson, M. "Writing stories using model structures: The circle story." *Language Arts* 58 (1981): 293–300.

Kantor, K., and J. Perron. "Thinking and writing: Creativity in the modes of discourse." *Language Arts* 54 (1977): 742–49.

Keating, D. *Intellectual talent: Research and development*. Baltimore, Md.: Johns Hopkins University Press, 1976.

Klemm, E. *Reading instruction for gifted children in the elementary grades*. Doctoral dissertation, Northwestern University, 1953.

Miles, S. "Gifted children." In *Manual of child psychology*. 2nd ed. Edited by L. Carmichael. New York: John Wiley, 1954.

Miller, B., and M. Price, eds. *The gifted child, the family, and the community*. New York: Walker, 1981.

Mindell, P., and D. Stracher. "Assessing reading and writing of the gifted: The warp and woof of the language program." *Gifted Child Quarterly* 24 (1980): 72–80.

Renzulli, J. "What makes giftedness? Re-examining a definition." *Phi Delta Kappa* 60 (1978): 180–84.

Sager, C. "Improving the quality of written composition in the middle grades." *Language Arts* 54 (1977): 760–62.

Savage, J. *Effective communication*. Chicago: Science Research Associates, 1977.

Schwartz, M. "Rewriting or recopying: What are we teaching?" *Language Arts* 54 (1977): 756–59.

Searle, D., and D. Dillon. "Responding to student writing: What is said or how it is said." *Language Arts* 57 (1980): 773–81.

Silverman, L. "Secondary programs for gifted students." *Journal of Education for the Gifted* 4 (1980): 30–42.

Stallard, C. "Writing readiness: A developmental view." *Language Arts* 54 (1977): 775–79.

Stauffer, R. *Directing the reading-thinking process.* New York: Harper and Row, 1975.

Strang, R. "Psychology of gifted children and youth." In *Psychology of exceptional children and youth.* Edited by W. Cruickshank. Englewood Cliffs, N.J.: Prentice-Hall, 1955.

Strang, R. "Creative writing." In *Curriculum planning for the gifted.* Edited by L. Fliegler. Englewood Cliffs, N.J.: Prentice-Hall, 1961.

Strang, R., C. McCullough, and A. Traxler. *Problems in the improvement of reading.* New York: McGraw-Hill, 1955.

Trezise, R. "What about a reading program for the gifted?" *Reading Teacher* 31 (1978): 742–46.

Walmsley, S. "What elementary teachers know about writing." *Language Arts* 57 (1980): 732–34.

Wilde, J., and T. Newkirk. "Writing detective stories." *Language Arts* 58 (1981): 286–92.

Part Three

Extended Experiences

art Three examines important additional educational experiences, particularly those that project education into areas uniquely suited to the gifted and talented. Computers, creativity, and career education have to be considered in light of the children's potentials. These areas offer unique opportunities for schools to revitalize and expand their learning environments into the community, and take advantage of the businesses, museums, research opportunities, and cultural experiences. Computers and mentorships may be found in all of these places.

Four themes run through Part Three. The first is that of problem solving. The microcomputer brings to education an entirely new medium for developing and expanding problem identification and problem solving. Logical systems are needed to move from problem statement to solution, and creative problem solving is needed for creative solutions.

The second theme is that of measuring learning outcomes, evident in chapters 9 and 12. By definition, the gifted and talented exceed the normative expectations of the curriculum, and the usual measures of learning provide little information about them. Alternative strategies must be developed.

The third theme involves computers and career education. Youngsters beginning school today are going to enter a world of information processing. Computer literacy and "computing teachers" are musts for moving today's children into tomorrow's careers.

The fourth major theme is that of the interaction of mind and machine. How the human intellect interacts with artificial intelligence is an intriguing facet of computers and of brain performance research. Research offers exciting new paths for future utilization of artificial intelligence. Music, art, and medical diagnosis are but three diverse uses of today's tabletop microcomputers.

Chapter 12 offers an alternative to the usual methods of examining learning outcomes. In addition, it offers some frequently unmentioned issues in initiating and establishing programs. The assistance of state level education personnel is, in particular, an unexamined resource for program support and guidance. Part Three extends basic curriculum concerns to the exciting "unknowns" of tomorrow's professionals.

9

Using Computers to Teach the Gifted

John J. Trifiletti

The computer offers a highly interactive, intelligent learning environment. For education, the computer represents long-needed measurement technology, and will probably replace pen and paper. The computer is a general-purpose tool for solving problems, a window to a world of information, a simulator of complex events and processes, a displayer of graphics and visual information, a microcosm of languages for precise thought and logic, and a trusted companion in an increasingly technological society.

Computers help people solve problems. They also help people learn. The computer can be anything it is programmed to be, and the applications in education are limited only by the imagination. The power and appeal of computers with children or adults is their ability to form a responsive environment. They talk back, smile back, and generally communicate to learners.

Like any new tool, the computer requires initial learning to use it properly. One communicates with a computer through a programming language composed of statements the computer can understand. Computer systems are composed of hardware (physical components), software (sets of instructions), and people who understand and use them. Generally, people who understand computer language can use computer systems more effectively and efficiently, and anyone who can learn 20 to 60 new words can learn a programming language.

The use of computers with gifted children is an exciting development in education. Computers provide a challenging learning environment for preschool levels through adulthood. Programming computers requires planning, organization, problem solving, logic, and a level of attention to detail usually not present in the curriculum. Gifted children who program computers must teach the computer how to think and solve problems; in doing so, they gain valuable insights into their own thought processes.

This chapter outlines seven examples of computer use with gifted children:
1 Programming languages as structures for logical thought
2 LOGO computer language for gifted children
3 Word processing and composition
4 Computer simulations and modeling
5 Computer art and imaging
6 Information and communication networks
7 Problem solving with computers

Programming Languages as Structures for Logical Thought

We live in an increasingly technological society. It is estimated that over forty percent of today's graduating high school seniors will have daily contact with computers or computer terminals in their vocations. In a computer-rich world, computer languages simultaneously provide a means of control and communication with the computer and offer new and powerful descriptive languages for thinking (Papert, 1980).

The key to successful communication with a computer is programming. Programming involves creating a set of sequential instructions for the computer to interpret and execute. The instructions must be syntactically correct commands that the computer can understand and must also be logically intact to accomplish the task at hand. The programming commands, their syntax, and their inherent logical structure (that is, the ways the commands can combine) comprise a computer language. The language itself is nothing more than a collection of short programs that reside in an area of the computer's memory called Read Only Memory (ROM). The language interprets commands from the keyboard or a collection of commands (a program) and transforms them into signals the computer can understand.

The major higher-level programming languages are BASIC, FORTRAN, COBOL, PASCAL, and to some extent PL/I, PLC, APL, RPG, and WATFIV. These languages were developed by computer manufacturers, universities, and committees to make the computer more available to users (Spencer, 1981) and permit students to learn programming in a short time.

Learning a computer language greatly enriches the child's interaction with the computer.

BASIC (Beginners All-purpose Symbolic Instruction Code), the primary language of microcomputers, can be successfully taught to students as early as third or fourth grade. BASIC consists of about twenty single-word commands that can be combined in about ten different basic structures. It is an interactive language that can communicate immediately with a computer terminal or computer. These are some of the advantages of teaching BASIC language to gifted students:

- The majority of inexpensive computers are supplied with BASIC resident in the computer or available on magnetic disk.
- BASIC at its most difficult levels requires mastery of concepts frequently learned in elementary algebra courses.
- BASIC is user-friendly—its commands look like English words. For instance, when you wish to print something on the screen, the command is PRINT.
- BASIC language is one of the easiest of all computer languages to learn; it can be mastered in a few weeks of systematic instruction.

There are, however, some disadvantages of teaching BASIC to gifted children:

- Although BASIC programming can be structured and organized clearly with notations to facilitate clear descriptions of data flow and logic structure, the ability to branch the flow of the program to different areas of the code can lead to unstructured or difficult-to-understand programming.
- Since variable names in BASIC are limited to one or two characters, programs that use many variables are difficult to interpret and change.
- Successful use of BASIC with very young children has not been demonstrated, although whether this is due to the language structure of BASIC or the present models for teaching BASIC has not been determined. Logo language has had demonstrated utility with preschool age children and has simple language structures.

The rationale for teaching one or more computer languages to gifted students is that the child can control the computer only through the language. As computers proliferate throughout the educational and home environments, those children who master a computer language will be able to control the computer, while those who do not will be controlled by the computer. This phenomenon is happening today in schools. Schools with limited financial resources use the computer to deliver and prescribe instruction; schools with adequate financial resources use the computer to teach programming languages, problem solving with computers, and inquiry learning methods.

Issues and Concerns

In the last few years, great emphasis has been put on promoting computer literacy among educators, administrators, and students. The focus has been knowledge of computers, their potential use in education, and a limited mastery of computer terminology. No attempt has been made to systematically teach computer languages. Although it is not necessary to master a computer language to use or interact with a computer, mastery allows communication with the computer in such a way that the computer becomes an extension of one's thought processes. The real utility of a computer programming language is as a tool for extending thought and solving problems. Using a computer language facilitates logical thinking and attention to detail, the seeds of scientific inquiry and formal thinking. Inevitably, using a computer language will enrich and increase gifted children's ability to acquire knowledge and act on their environment.

Logo Computer Language for Gifted Children

Originally developed for use on the Texas Instruments T199/4A computer, Logo has been refined and tested with children over a twelve-year period by Dr. Seymour Papert and the staff of the Artificial Intelligence Laboratory at the Massachusetts Institute of Technology. Logo is designed for discovery-oriented learning in which children learn through exploration, trial and error, and discovery. The intent is to actively involve children in their own learning and thought processes. Programming in Logo is defined as teaching the computer how to think (Papert, 1980). In teaching the computer how to think, children must explore how they themselves think.

With Logo, very young children can draw geometric figures and designs on the screen, experiment with lines and proportions, and program animated shapes such as a moving plane, truck, rocket, ball, and box. Students can create their own shapes and give them attributes of color, speed, and direction.

Logo was extensively tested at the Lamplighter School in Dallas, Texas and in New York City public schools through a program of the New York Academy of Science. Three-year-old children demonstrated proficiency with the language, including familiarity with issuing keyboard commands to make columns, shapes, and sizes. At this level, it is possible to introduce number and spatial relationships, decision-making processes, and logical problem-solving strategies. These skills are building blocks for increasingly complex thought processes. As such, Logo use by gifted students is an introduction to formal thinking.

The manual for the Logo language is written at a fourth-grade reading level. It instructs the beginner on the basic steps of using the language structures. Intrinsic to the language is Turtle graphics. A turtle is visualized which can move in any direction. The Turtle can have a directional heading of 0 to 360 degrees and can move any distance along that heading. Children can identify with the Turtle and easily learn the Turtle Talk commands to make it move. Powerful ideas available to children through Turtle graphics include the concept of symbolic naming through a variable, geometric concepts, heuristic strategy, differential instructions, and laws of motion.

In addition to Turtle graphics, Logo includes a MAKESHAPE command for making shapes, and a MAKECHAR command for redefining keyboard characters. Logo also has thirty-two SPRITES, invisible 16 by 16 character spaces that cannot be seen until they are given visible attributes including shape, position on the screen, color, heading, and speed.

Logo opens a new world for young children to explore. Although the full implications for discovery learning at early ages are yet to be determined, young children's enthusiastic response to the Logo language is obvious. They are not intimidated by the computer and gain command of the language in a very short time.

Word Processing and Composition

The word processor is the most powerful tool for teaching composition. In a typical application, a student works with a keyboard, computer screen, and printer to create a typed document—paragraph, essay, short story, letter, newspaper article, or any textual material—on the screen. The length of the document can vary from a partial page to hundreds of pages. Change to the text, or editing, is accomplished through single key or two-key commands from a keyboard. When the student finishes entering and editing the text, a copy of the document is saved in a magnetic storage medium such as cassette tape or magnetic disk and a printed copy of the document is then obtained through the printer.

The three advantages of word processing over writing for compositions are (1) the student learns to type, a valuable skill since typed compositions are quicker to prepare and easier to read than written compositions; (2) editing compositions is easier with a word processor, because students can use simple key strokes to move a word, sentence, paragraph, or block of text. They can use global commands to search the entire text and replace a word or phrase. Other commands will right-justify text, left-justify text, or both. It is possible to format the text into newsprint columns. Insertion and deletion at any point in the document is easily accomplished. With such powerful editing capability, rewriting becomes a simple matter of shifting things around on the screen, inserting, and deleting. And (3), the student learns to compose at the computer. The computer screen becomes an extension of the student's thought process. Thoughts appear and are tentatively displayed, then the student fits the thought into the composition to best advantage. Thoughts can easily be expanded or modified.

With a word processor, writing takes on a new dimension of flexibility. Since typing and editing are so easy, students produce greater detail in their compositions, and their works take on a better quality. They submit clear, typed copy, that is easier for both student and instructor to read and evaluate. Writing is more fluent, thoughts more completely developed, and prose clearer.

The teacher can demand much more of students who use a word processor. They have no excuse for submitting anything less than their very best effort. The instructor can insist on revision when it is necessary, since the student can display copy on the screen, make the recommended changes, and resubmit a greatly improved paper.

The advantage of using word processors for composition with gifted students is that their writing will become easier, faster, and a function of their quality of thought. Word processing is not a substitute for hard, rigorous thinking, but an exciting new way to facilitate composition of thoughts.

Issues and Concerns

The ability to type is a prerequisite for full utilization of word processing. Children who have difficulty typing are too absorbed in searching the keyboard to follow a train of thought in composing text at the computer.

An additional concern is whether to allow students to use dictionary software in conjunction with word processing software. With dictionary software, a computer will check the spelling of each word in a document against the proper spelling of 60,000 to 100,000 common words. If the dictionary program encounters a questionable spelling, it flashes the word and gives the student an opportunity to exchange the words. Some educators contend that spelling programs will diminish spelling ability by increasing the student's reliance on the computer; however, it is possible that spelling programs will increase the visibility of frequently misspelled words and thus allow the student to become more proficient at spelling. Obviously, the dictionary option improves the quality of a composition and may incidently teach spelling.

Word Processors and Formal Thinking

Seymour Papert (1980) believes computers will fundamentally affect children's thinking. In his vision, children actively build their own intellectual structures, appropriating for their use the models and metaphors in the surrounding culture. Papert suggests that a computer-rich environment can shift the onset of "formal" thinking from approximately twelve years, as suggested by Piaget, to an earlier age. The mechanism for this accomplishment is the computer's ability to make the formal concrete and personal. Word processors can make a child's experience of writing more like that of a real writer. Using the computer as a writing instrument, the child begins to think and act as an adult and acquires further mastery of language. In the complex interplay of developing cognitive structures and cultural models, the computer as a writing instrument presents an enriched intellectual environment for the child. A gifted student can use a word processor for: creative writing, plays and dialogue, essays, poetry, outlining skills, newspaper articles, short stories, business contracts, biographical writing, song lyrics, scripts for debate, scripts for public speaking, recipes, tour guides, round robin writings, directions for new games, research papers, letters, technical writing, and classified advertisements.

Computer Simulations and Modeling

A computer simulation is a system for reproducing essential aspects of reality to find ways to manage, control, solve, and/or ultimately agree upon the best solution for a problem (Noonan, 1981). Computer simulations allow active and repeated investigation within time and resource constraints and without risk. Presently, the wide range of computer simulations fall into four broad categories:

- Simulation of experiments
- Simulation of complex processes
- Simulation of complex events
- Simulation games

Students can work with simulations alone or in groups or teams, but most simulation games are designed for more than one student or team of students to work competitively.

The strength of the computer simulation as an instructional tool lies in the student's ability to control essential variables that affect the result. Simulations challenge students to try different methods to solve a problem, control a process, or manage events. They study the results, then apply what they have learned to create new and better solutions.

Interaction with computer simulations involves students with a number of significant intellectual processes, including discovering cause and effect relationships, acquiring technical information, making judgment decisions, working cooperatively in groups, and developing creative problem-solving strategies. All these processes stimulate creativity. Simulations are usually complex, drawing on many contributing variables. A simulation has no single correct solution; instead, the student forms patterns of cause and effect relationships through a process of trial and error learning. The student synthesizes what he learns to create a tentative solution and observes the immediate result of the decision.

Situations that use graphics are most exciting because they allow visual examination of the results. In SCRAM, a nuclear power plant simulation for the Atari computer, the student observes a graphic display of the reactor, coolant tanks, control valves, pumps, temperature readings, and a moving flow of fluids throughout the system. The objective of SCRAM is to bring the nuclear reactor from cold start to full operating capacity and keep it operative despite random mechanical breakdowns and natural disasters including earthquakes. The student must control a great number of variables, including levels of coolant in tanks, control rods that extend into the reactor core, valves, and pumps.

With the SCRAM simulation, students gradually conceptualize the workings of the nuclear power plant as three subsystems: a primary loop consisting of the reactor coolant system, a secondary loop of the main feedwater system, and a tertiary loop of the circulating water system. Two additional systems, the high pressure injection system and auxiliary feedwater system, are backups for the reactor coolant system. Sections of the SCRAM manual introduce students to principles of thermodynamics and power station indicators. Obviously, students who work with SCRAM become knowledgeable about control of nuclear energy, at the same time they gain a healthy perspective of randomness and probability. Eventually they develop a number of data-gathering and problem-solving strategies to use when breakdowns occur. SCRAM develops the abilities to think logically and objectively, to see patterns in complex systems, to see cause and effect relationships, and to analyze and solve problems.

Simulations such as SCRAM are excellent supplements to standard educational tools and techniques. Besides providing access to topics not normally covered or covered only briefly, simulation models encourage active acquisition of knowledge and development of inquiry strategies. Simulations allow students to deal with many variations of critical elements in processes, events, or experiments.

These are some of the advantages of using computer simulations with gifted students:

- Feedback on the effects of decisions appears quickly, making cause and effect relationships more visible.

- The computer can easily simulate situations that involve complex calculations while keeping outward appearances very simple.
- Computer simulations can slow down or speed up experiments for easy observation of results and processes.
- A computer can simulate experiments that would normally be too dangerous, complex, or expensive to perform in the classroom.
- Simulations educate students in specific problems or areas and impart technical knowledge and new vocabulary.
- Students are initiated in the art of building and using models.
- Students learn to recognize and vary assumptions on which models are based, and thus vary the results of the model and its approximation to events in the real world.
- Students develop and refine the ability to systematically investigate problems, processes, and events.

Computer simulations can be applied in virtually any content area: ecology, history, politics, finance, population, nuclear energy, flight, combat, strategy games, scientific experiments, intelligence, architecture, energy, manufacturing, business, organic chemistry, music, astronomy, motion, marketing, medicine, biology, and genetics.

Computer Art and Imaging

Computers can produce art with plotters, with printers, and with visual displays. A plotter produces a pen-and-ink drawing of lines and points. Multicolor plotters are popular and relatively inexpensive. Plotters have been used to produce graphs, charts, and maps, but are finding new uses in computer art and imaging. Printers produce art by printing rows of characters. The Snoopy printouts that decorate most computer facilities are an example of printer art. One can shade areas of the image by using dense characters or by overstriking characters.

Graphic displays on computer screens are the most flexible and versatile type of computer art. Techniques for creating computer art include special programs for drawing points, lines, and shapes. Light pens and graphics tablets are also used.

Computers can also produce special effects scenes and animated scenes. Computer animation involves computer-generated moving pictures. In a typical animation project, a student creates a three-dimensional space vehicle by defining points on a three-dimensional coordinate grid. After he defines the space vehicle on graph paper, he loads a special graphics program into the computer. The points that define the space vehicle are entered into the computer as pairs of coordinates (X, Y, Z). Next, commands will be given from the keyboard for lines to connect the points. The outline of the space vehicle will now be visible on the computer screen. Editing adds or deletes points or lines. When the space vehicle is fully defined and outlined on the computer screen, the student can give additional commands from the keyboard to color all or parts of the space vehicle. He can give the vehicle a variable name and use a computer program to move the vehicle along the X, Y, or Z planes, rotate along the planes, and scale the space vehicle to various sizes.

Projects such as this three-dimensional animated shape are fascinating exercises for gifted students of all ages. But computer art and imaging are more important as the basis for a number of diverse technologies, including special effects movie production, computerized surveillance, scientific imaging, computer assisted design and manufacture, computer assisted architecture, and building design. Microcomputers make possible the computer art and imaging generic to each of these technologies.

The rationale for computer art and imaging in the classroom is that graphic representation is a form of human communication. People perceive information visually and aurally. Just as distortions occur in spoken communications because of intonation and differences in background, so do similar distortions occur in visual information. The problem of visual distortion is especially relevant to graphics that organize or reduce large bodies of information, such as charts and graphs. When presenting information visually with a chart or graph, changing the scale of either axis will distort the visual relationships and possibly mask important patterns and relationships. We see this problem in the published findings of educational researchers who attempt to demonstrate changes in learning. The literature of educational research is filled with charts and graphs of behavioral change that have been scaled or distorted to amplify change, regardless of whether the amount of change is qualitatively significant. Attempts to standardize reporting of change, such as Lindsley's Standard Behavior Chart, (1968) have led to significant improvements in the science of human behavior and learning.

Measurement technology and visually graphic representations are important tools in many professional disciplines. To the engineer, a mechanical drawing is a far more effective means of communication than the spoken or written word; to the businessman, graphic representation is an intermediate step to making appropriate decisions; to the soldier, a contour map of surrounding terrain is critical to the success of a mission; to the astronomer, computer-assisted imaging and enhancement are new ways to look at the universe. Computer graphics are thus a form of communication as well as a tool of many professions and technologies. Students must learn to use computer graphics not merely to convey information, but to organize and convey information with minimal distortion. Effective communication through graphic representation is the desired skill.

Issues and Concerns

Computers vary widely in their ability to create and animate graphics. Most computers are capable of low resolution graphics that are easy to learn and program. The high resolution necessary for observation of small detail in images is possible with some computers, but usually requires mastery of difficult machine language programming or assembly language programming. Recently, several programs have become available that allow easy access to high resolution graphics without learning a new computer language. These programs allow input of points and lines through game paddles, light pens, graphics tablets, or keyboards for definition of shapes and images. The obvious advantage of these graphics programs is the easier interface between computer and student. With graphics programs, it is possible to reach a younger population of students, as in the case of the Logo language. BASIC and PASCAL are other computer languages with graphics capabilities. The singular absence of graphics as a form of communication in today's curriculum is an example of how we infantize children by depriving them of adult models and tools. These are only some of the ways we can use computer art and imaging projects with students:

- Represent a body of data using a bar graph, line graph, and pie charts. Experiment with changing the scales of the graphs and size of the pie chart.
- Create a two-dimensional shape and experiment with changing its color and the background color.
- Create a three-dimensional geometric object and experiment with rotating it along the X, Y, and Z axes.
- Create a three-dimensional representation of a building that can be observed from different perspectives.
- Plot mathematical equations and observe the results when values of the variables are changed.
- Experiment with docking two objects traveling in different orbits.
- Find the shortest path through a network of lines and points where distances are assigned to the lines.
- Using Logo language, define two Sprites to have shape, color, direction, and velocity. Create boundaries for movement.
- Using BASIC language, assemble a shape with character string graphics and identify the shape with a variable name. Animate the shape by changing the position of the printed shape within a loop.

Information and Communication Networks

The computer is used increasingly as a communications terminal for accessing a broad range of information. In a typical application, a classroom computer can access information in large regional computers through the telephone. The regional computer networks house an incredible amount of information organized into data bases or continually updated subject areas. Communication with the regional network is interactive—both computers send and receive messages. The user simply dials the telephone number of the network and waits for the sound of the carrier signal. When he hears the carrier signal, the user enters a password for billing purposes and pages through menus or gives direct commands to search and select information. After reaching the desired information, the user can read it on the computer screen, send it to a printer for hard copy, or store it on a disk for later use. The user is charged for actual connect time with the network. Charges vary with each regional network and are more expensive during the business day.

One advantage of an electronic medium over a traditional print medium is that it can be updated immediately; information can be accurate to within the hour. Primary methods of information retrieval are the computer, communications software, a modem, the telephone line, and membership in one or more of the commercial networks. A modem is a hardware unit that can convert an outgoing computer signal into audible tones for transmission over telephone lines. It also converts an incoming telephone signal into the binary information the computer requires.

Presently, there are four major commercial networks in the United States: the Dow Jones Retrieval Service, CompuServe, Tymnet (a commercial data base that currently uses telephone lines, but has announced plans to use microwave or satellite transmission in the future), and in Canada, the Telidon videotext system. American Telephone and Telegraph (AT&T) has adopted a videotext standard based on Canada's Telidon system and announced plans to test it in the United States. These commercial networks offer hundreds of subject listings of interest to the average citizen or businessman. In addition to the commercial networks, professional networks are available in many technical professions, including medicine, law, and science.

The computer as a communications device opens the information revolution to the average person and brings the outside world into the classroom. The rationale for teaching computer communication and information retrieval skills to gifted students is similar to the rationale for teaching library research skills. The library has been the primary resource of information and knowledge; as our resources shift to an electronic medium, students must be able to apply research skills there, as well. To fully utilize computer communications, one must know what kinds of information are available through the commercial networks. The following topics are only a sampling from literally hundreds of subject listings.

Education

CompuServe offers The College Board, a guide to planning for college that includes how to select a college, obtain funding, apply for admission, and prepare for the S.A.T. examination. The Source offers foreign language courses in Esperanto, French, German, Greek, Italian, Latin, and Spanish. Courses in geography and mathematics are also offered.

News and Information News summaries in over 80 categories from over 6000 companies can be accessed. CompuServe receives news from Associated Press, and has menus with story titles for locating news. The Source provides access to United Press International's wire service news reports. The Source requires the user to enter a keyword, then searches all stories in a category for the keyword. Subjects can be referenced over several days, so that any story that mentions the Space Shuttle, for example, can be displayed.

Reference Library CompuServe has a diverse reference library including U.S. Government publications, reports from the Aviation Safety Institute, and The Future File. Documents include Consumer Safety Reports and other hard-to-find information.

Weather CompuServe reads up-to-the-hour weather data directly from the National Oceanic and Atmospheric Administration (NOAA) computers, providing forecasts and warnings, including forecasts for major sporting events.

Travel and Dining The Source provides Data Travel and USREST for travelers' information on accommodations, restaurants, and flight schedules. With this information, users can function as their own travel service. The Source lists the entire domestic and foreign airlines schedules for flights originating in North America (direct flights only), with departure times, arrival times, and meals available for all airlines.

The Source also contains the Citycon data base with listings for all direct destinations from any given airport.

Entertainment   The Source contains a weekly best-sellers book list as well as reviews of current movies taken from major daily newspapers, such as The New York Times. Information on TV programs and soap operas is available.

Communications   Electronic bulletin boards allow messages to be sent and stored, even if the receiver is away from the computer or busy. If interactive dialogue is required, users can communicate directly with each other and obtain a printed copy of the conversation. CompuServe offers a CB radio simulator with 40 channels. Electronic mail service is available for sending memos, letters, visual information, and computer programs. A group or club can establish an electronic bulletin board in place of a newsletter.

Other services available through the commercial networks include agricultural data bases, job hunting services, "how-to" courses on everything from foreign languages to home repair, catalogue shopping, banking, and bartering exchanges. The next few years will see even greater use of computer information networks and a rapidly increasing selection of data bases. Microwave and satellite communications links will play an important role in this technology. With a little initiative, it is possible for the classroom to come on-line with the rest of the world.

Problem Solving With Computers

A principal responsibility of education is to help students learn to cope with a complex present and future world. Current changes in curriculum emphasize problem-solving skills, strategies, and processes. The National Council of Teachers of Mathematics (1980) issued recommendations regarding the teaching of problem solving.

All problems can be divided into two categories. The first category, called *primitives,* consists of problems to which a solution is immediately evident. Generally, these are problems that have been previously encountered, or are similar to problems previously encountered. The second category of problems includes those that are not immediately solvable. We know little about nonroutine or novel problem solving, except what we can summarize in a few short statements:

- Novel problem-solving skills improve through study and practice.
- Novel problem solving builds upon the work of others.
- Appropriate measurement technology helps in novel problem solving.
- The intellectual ability to move from concrete to abstract and from abstract to concrete can facilitate novel problem solving.
- Accumulated knowledge of the human race is stored in its tools, which allow access to problems and facilitate their solution.

A computer is a general-purpose tool for problem solving. The fact that it can be programmed to follow step-by-step instructions, make logical decisions, analyze and summarize information, store and recall information, and display information in predetermined formats make it an extremely powerful tool for problem solving.

Every professional discipline can use the computer to work with problems. The computer is like many tools that require some practice before they can be used. Computer scientists list these essential steps to writing computer programs for solving problems:

1 Understand the problem.
2 Select or develop a solution strategy.
3 Write the program.
4 Enter, debug, and verify the program.
5 Write documentation for the program.

Understanding the Problem

Understanding the problem is the most difficult step, because most problems are not clearly defined. It helps to identify input (what information the computer will need to start with), output (what will be the result from the computer), and allowable procedures. Often, a thorough understanding of the problem suggests a solution strategy. It helps to clearly define all the vocabulary associated with the problem and to look at the problem from several different points of view.

Select or Develop a Solution Strategy

A solution strategy is a primative or series of primatives, a model, or a pattern for solving a problem. Increasing students' repertoire of primatives and models gives them basic building blocks for problem solving, as does increasing general knowledge through reading and experiential activities. Breaking the overall problem down into small, discrete solvable units (stepwise refinement), then solving them with subprograms or subroutines is often an effective strategy. The goal of stepwise refinement is to divide the original problem into manageable units.

When stepwise refinement is not possible, redefining the original problem sometimes helps. Another successful tactic is to shift emphasis to different elements of the problem.

At this point, it is necessary to decide on the programming language and computer hardware that will best solve the problem. Computer languages have strengths and weaknesses; some are best suited to business problems (COBOL, PLC, PL-1), while others are more efficient for mathematical or statistical solutions (FORTRAN, APL), and some languages are better at artificial intelligence problems (FOURTH, ADA). Computers themselves have various strengths and weaknesses; some are better for color graphics (APPLE, ATARI), while others are better for textual display (RADIO SHACK, COMMODORE).

Write the Program

Most programmers write from indented outlines that sequentially identify the steps or procedures for entering into the computer. Beginning programmers should not be allowed to compose programs at the computer, because it consumes valuable computer time and often results in wasting time later in revision. The teacher should check the student's outline for a program for logic and completeness before allowing the student to work at the computer.

Enter, Debug, and Verify the Program

Because typing is a prerequisite skill for programming, it is essential that we alter curricula to include typing at the elementary school level. Allowing students to "hunt and peck" at keyboards interferes with later acquisition of typing skills.

When keying in the program, a reference manual for the language should be nearby for looking up exact syntax, ASCII code numbers, and other information the student has not memorized. It is good practice to periodically save the partially completed program or cassette or disk in the event of a power failure or disturbance which can destroy the program in memory.

Elements of good programming style include minimizing branching, labeling each section of the program, and identifying all variables. It is also good practice initially to use spaces to make statements easier to read. Spaces can be deleted after the program is debugged through a CRUNCH utility. Novice programmers should avoid multiple statements on a line so the logic is easier to follow. Numbering lines by increments of ten (10, 20, 30, etc.) allows room to insert program lines during debugging or subsequent modification.

Debugging involves identifying and correcting errors, both program errors and logic errors. Program errors are easy to detect by running the program. Programming languages have precise rules for constructing and punctuating statements. A program will stop when it encounters a program error, and usually indicates the line number in which the error occurs. Logic errors are much more difficult, and usually do not interrupt the program, but cause it to behave in unexpected ways and fail to correctly solve the problem. Logic errors are corrected by testing the program against known or predicted results. It may be necessary to insert statements that print the values of variables at critical points in the program. Building the program in modular units allows individual testing of each unit.

Debugging often takes as long or longer than entering the program, and must be approached with ample determination, perseverance, and attention to detail.

Verifying the program requires testing it with all possible ranges of input. It is often difficult to determine whether all parts of a program are working; a change or correction at one point may interfere with another part of the program. Some parts of a program may be seldom used and will have to be verified with an artificial situation. Verification of data usually requires painstaking visual inspection.

Program Documentation

Proper program documentation includes a statement of the problem, an outline of procedures, a printout of the program code, sample computer runs or actual sets of data, and directions on how to use the program. If the program is self-documenting (instructions produced on the computer screen), the instructions should be repeated in the paper documentation. The program listing should have all variables and all procedures properly labeled and commented. A listing to a programmer is like a schematic to an electrician. It should be written to facilitate later modifications. The directions should be comprehensible to someone who has never used the program and is not familiar with the computer. A glossary of terms is helpful.

Program documentation is an excellent opportunity to teach technical writing skills. Many individuals judge the quality of a program by the quality of the documentation, and in many cases, documentation time is more extensive than all other phases of problem solving combined.

Problem-Solving Process

The movement toward the use of problem-solving processes is not confined to any single discipline—all disciplines can benefit from development of problem-solving skills. These are five areas in which the computer can be used to develop problem-solving skills:

1 Constructing models of a problem situation with programming solutions
2 Participating in computer simulations of events, processes, and experiments
3 Securing information through computer networks and making decisions based on the information
4 Exploring computer-controlled environments, such as remote manipulators, sensors, and robotics

Gifted students should learn to use computers as part of their problem-solving skills.

5　Studying and using computer languages and language structures related to problem solving

The intellectual needs of our technological society require development of problem-solving skills. Although we cannot possibly teach the technology that will predominate in the future, we can teach children the tools and strategies for future problem solving.

Microcomputers in Schools: An Example*

The two major goals of using microcomputers in the London Gifted Program are to provide opportunities for students to use their knowledge of programming in BASIC and LOGO to develop and apply upper-level thinking skills, and to provide resources (reference books and packaged programs) for independent study in more difficult commands and for enrichment. More specific objectives include:

- Experimenting with commands to modify existing program listings and exercises
- Applying programming knowledge to solve extension questions
- Using programming skills to share information or display results of studies
- Synthesizing programming knowledge to design original programs
- Independent study of use of commands not presented in class (graphics, sound, animation)

Our computer lab, housing four microcomputers (Apple and Franklin), serves as a learning center; software is provided in the form of the students' personal disks, reference materials in book and manual form, and tutorial and simulation programs to enrich as well as to develop upper-level thinking skills. The motivation to use this center approach has been through challenges to program something that has not been attempted before and to design game format programs using graphics and text modes, sound, animation, and joysticks.

Evaluation of these experiences is a three-part process. First, individually—the student's program will simply not run if written improperly. Second, as a team—comparing solutions to problems allows students to analyze different solutions, synthesizing parts of each to create the "best" group solution available. A third evaluation approach is provided through independent study presentations. Seventh and eighth graders who choose programming as their study present their products to interested students and teachers, answering their questions, and reworking parts that need modification.

The Spelling Program

Mike McAdow is a fourteen-year-old eighth grader at London Middle School; he participates in the gifted program through a special algebra offering as well as through the pull-out program. His independent study developed into a group study to write a spelling program for the seventh-grade language arts teacher.

Mike began talking with Sue Nichols about a program she needed for drilling

---

*This section was contributed by Patricia Jones Holcomb, coordinator/teacher in the London (Ohio) City Schools Gifted Program.

her students on weekly spelling words. Mike wrote a skeleton program and met with Mrs. Nichols to modify the program to her specifications. Features of his program include data statements that can be changed to accommodate each weekly spelling list; a random statement that will give these words in a different order for each student who uses the drill; a formula to determine the percent answered correctly; and a list of the words the student spells incorrectly.

This program was such a success that Mrs. Nichols wanted all the lessons saved on her disk; this became a group project for five seventh graders. They had to type in the data statements for each lesson, including three incorrect spellings for each word and its correct spelling. This project benefited the school and helped the seventh graders understand how the DATA statement could work in programming.

Mike presented this program at our Teacher Inservice Day in January. He has ideas for programming lessons in other areas using other DATA commands.

The Flag Program

Jeff Loudon is also fourteen years old and in the eighth grade. He also participates in the special algebra program as well as in the resource room pull-out class. His independent study began with evaluation, ran into a snag, then culminated in a wonderful product that can be useful to our Middle School.

Jeff's first decision was to study high resolution graphics; low resolution was too primary, dividing the screen only into 40 by 40 blocks. His resolution had much more to offer, dividing the screen into 280 lines across and 160 lines down. The only problem was that our Apple offered limited color options, especially for what Jeff had in mind.

Flags of the world intrigued Jeff; he had researched this topic and wanted to put the information into a program that would display the information for each country and generate a graphics representation of the flag. Apple high res colors had only three shades in its palette, besides white and black.

Jeff's family owns an IBM computer for use in their business, and he quickly evaluated the available middle resolution colors as superior. He then spent countless hours designing his program to draw and print the information he had found.

After completing his work and saving it on his disk, he tried to run his program; it wouldn't boot. This was a mystery to both Jeff and his parents, but the conclusion was the same—he'd have to type the information in once more. This is testimony to Jeff's incredible task commitment; it would have been so easy to give up!

Our department is currently checking into the possibility of expanding our high res palette to provide the colors necessary to program this design on our Apple. This would be an excellent resource for our Middle School Social Studies Department; its best feature would be that it had been designed by one of the school's own gifted students.

Training the Computing Educator

It is fair to say that the computer caught us by surprise in education. Few realized its potential in the classroom. Early uses of computers in education were administrative. Model instructional demonstration projects were considered expensive, experimental, and unsuitable for the mainstream of education. Now, of course, educators have taken another look at the computer.

Advances in circuit technology have made computers more powerful and at the same time less expensive. The ability to network computers together, inexpensively, in a laboratory design has further increased their desirability in the educational setting. The unexpected explosion of computerized game centers has stimulated a great deal of thought about the interactive nature of computers. And, gradually, a growing body of educational software is demonstrating that significant and measurable learning can be accomplished through computers.

In addition, the computer is increasingly seen as the long-awaited measurement device for a technology of learning. With the ability to continuously measure students' speed and accuracy in learning situations, and to deliver a majority of the instruction, computers are facilitating a shift in the educator's role to that of a manager of learning.

Any new technology, however, requires trained people who understand the technology and can help it grow. Barriers to technological change in education include the shortage of training sites and trainers, the absence of planned inservice programs for computer educators, and the absence of university-based certification programs for entry-level computer educators. Its technical vocabulary even prevents many educators from reading the journals in the computer field.

Despite these problems, it is possible to outline some of the competencies educators will need to increase their effectiveness in a computerized environment. The educator should be able to:

- Design and manage an instructional computer lab, including selection of hardware and software, curriculum design, and scheduling students
- Describe the history of computer technology and outline present and future trends
- Demonstrate familiarity and proficiency with computer terminology and language
- Demonstrate mastery of one or more programming languages
- Demonstrate familiarity with software directories
- Be a member of and participate in local, regional, or national computer users' groups
- Subscribe to and read computer journals
- Demonstrate familiarity with one or more teacher authoring languages
- Participate in computer curriculum design as an integrated part of the general curriculum
- Use computers and software to individualize instruction
- Use computers and software to teach problem-solving skills
- Use computers and software to teach programming skills
- Use computers and software to teach graphics techniques
- Demonstrate knowledge of local and regional networks
- Secure information from commercial networks
- Communicate with students, teachers, parents, and administrators about computerized education

- Demonstrate familiarity with computer simulations and modeling techniques
- Exercise grant-writing skills to secure funding for computerized instruction
- Make data-based decisions on students' learning through computerized instruction
- Evaluate software and hardware
- Type and teach students to type

This list of skills is by no means exhaustive; it refers to an entry-level computer educator. Most computer educators are self-taught; many have personal computers that inspired them to learn more about educational applications. An exciting recent development is the appearance of several computer journals for educators, among them, *The Computing Teacher, Classroom Computer News, Electronic Education, Classroom Computing,* and *Electronic Learning.*

Computer users' groups and organizations, such as the Florida Educational Computer Users Group, are ways for educators to help each other learn about computers. School districts that are serious about computers in education hire a district-level trainer to facilitate training.

Computer technology will inevitably cause fundamental changes in the traditional curriculum. It is important that these changes be initiated and carried out by educators who are trained and familiar with instructional uses of computers. To use computers for maximum benefit, they must be integrated into the curriculum at all levels and in all subjects.

Periodicals For Computer Education

- Classroom Computer News
  51 Spring Street
  Watertown, MA 02172
- Educational Technology
  140 Sylvan Avenue
  Englewood Cliffs, NJ 07632
- Electronic Education
  1311 Executive Center Drive, Suite 220
  Tallahassee, FL 32301
- Electronic Learning
  902 Sylvan Avenue
  Englewood Cliffs, NJ 07632
- The Computing Teacher
  ICCE, Dept. of Computer and Information Services
  University of Oregon
  Eugene, OR 97403
- T.H.E. (Technological Horizons in Education) Journal
  Post Office Box 992
  Acton, MA 01730

Glossary of Computer Terminology

Analog Computer A computer that translates physical variables such as temperature or voltage into computer language in a continuous manner, producing graphs as output.

Application The system or problem the computer has to solve.

Arithmetic Unit The part of the computer system that performs all arithmetic operations.

ASCII American Standard Code for Information Interchange; a data alphabet that gives meaning to strings of 0's and 1's

BASIC Beginners All-Purpose Symbolic Instruction Code; a general-purpose computer language

Baud A measure of data transmission speed in terms of bits per second; three hundred baud (approximately 30 characters per second) is the most commonly used speed of data transmission over telephone lines.

Bit A binary number 0 or 1; eight bits (a byte) are required to represent each alphanumeric character.

Bulletin Board Data bases (usually general or conversational) that can be set up and accessed by anyone with a computer and a modem; a videotext terminal is not necessary to access a bulletin board.

Cathode-Ray-Tube (CRT) A device like a TV screen in which a cathode-ray (electron beam) impinges upon a phosphorescent screen for the display of information.

COBOL Common Business Oriented Language; a computer language commonly used for business applications.

Central Processing Unit (CPU) The unit of a computer system containing the circuits that control and perform instructions; it contains the main storage (memory), arithmetic, and control units.

Coding The act of preparing in programming language a list of successive computer operations required to solve a specific problem.

Computer A device capable of accepting information, processing information according to a set of instructions (program), and supplying the results of these processes; it usually consists of input and output devices, memory, arithmetic, and control units.

Control Unit The part of a computer system that directs the sequence of operations, interpets programmed instructions, and initiates commands to execute instructions.

Data A general term used to denote facts, numbers, and symbols that refer to or describe an object, idea, condition, situation, or factor; data are the basic elements of information that can be processed by a computer.

Data Base An information source, stored in the host computer memory, accessed by a videotext terminal or microcomputer.

Data Processing The rearrangement and refinement of raw data into a form suitable for further use.

Data Terminal A device for communicating data from one location to a remote computer system.

Debug To search for and correct errors in a computer program.

Digital Computer A computer that uses numbers to solve problems by performing arithmetic and logical processes on discrete alphanumeric data.

Dumb Terminal A terminal or terminal software that can only send and receive data, with no ability for onboard computing.

Duplex Capable of transmitting and receiving at the same time; in full duplex, a host computer system echoes characters back to the remote terminal. In half duplex, the terminal displays its own transmitted characters on the screen. Full duplex is the standard operating mode.

Electronic Mail Sending letters and other mail electronically from one computer terminal to another.

Flowchart A graphic representation to help organize the solution of a program.

FORTRAN Formula Translator; a computer language commonly used for science and engineering applications.

General Purpose Computer A computer designed to solve a wide variety of problems.

Hardware The physical equipment or devices that form a computer and its peripheral equipment.

Input The data to be processed; the act of transferring data from an external source to an internal storage medium.

Input Device A mechanical unit designed to bring data into a computer for processing; commonly used input devices are card readers, keyboards, cassette recorders, and disk drives.

Instructions A set of symbols used to communicate with and control a computer.

Keyboard A set of labeled keys to permit entry of information into a computer.

Language Instructions that convey information between people and computers.

Light Pen A device used to select numbers or letters on a cathode ray tube (CRT).

Line Printer An output device that prints an entire line of information at one time.

LOGO A computer language developed by Seymour Papert and the staff of the Artificial Intelligence Laboratory at the Massachusetts Institute of Technology.

Memory A device capable of storing information.

Modem A device mediating between the telephone line and a computer or terminal; it can make direct electrical connection or be an acoustic coupler.

Output Data that has been processed; the act of transferring data from an internal storage medium to an external device.

Parity A method of error detection used in data communications; parity is seldom used in microcomputer communications; it is usually set to "off."

PASCAL A general-purpose computer language developed in 1968 by Niklaus Wirth in Zurich, Switzerland, and formally defined in 1971.

Port A computer location through which data can pass.

Printer A device for printing of output.

Program A set of instructions or statements designed to solve a problem on a computer.

Programmer A person who writes and verifies computer programs.

Report Printed output from analysis of data by a computer.

RS-232c A standard method of voltage signaling, voltage range between plus and minus 12 volts; a voltage change indicates a digital 0 or 1. These digits are used to encode data according to ASCII standards.

Serial Transmission of data in a serial stream as opposed to parallel stream.

Simulation A computer system or program designed to reproduce essential aspects of reality for purposes of finding ways to manage, control, solve, or agree upon the best solution for a problem.

Smart Terminal   A terminal or software capable of onboard computing as well as accessing data bases.

Software   Programs required for computers to process data and solve problems.

Storage Device   A device into which data can be entered and retrieved.

System   An organization of hardware and software to accomplish a data processing function or solve a problem.

Terminal   A device that can process the input and output of data.

User   An individual who requires the services of a data processing center or computing system.

Variable   An entity that can assume a value, as in algebra, *x, y*, etc.

Videotext   A generic term for interactive electronic communications using computers or videotext terminals.

References

Atari. *Scram: A nuclear power plant simulation.* Sunnyvale, Calif.: Atari, 1981.

Beard, M. *Computer assisted instruction: The best of ERIC 1973–May 1976.* Stanford, Calif.: Stanford Center for Research and Development in Teaching, School of Education, Stanford University, 1976.

Blechman, F. Adventures in modemland. *80 Microcomputing* (October 1981): 264–68.

Corrigan, A. STERL: Computer simulation of pest control methods. *Creative Computing* 5 (1979): 42–45.

Dahmke, M. Home services on the Source and CompuServe. *Popular Computing* (August): 107–8.

D'Angelo, J. Logo: Discovering the language is quite simple, really. *Electronic Education* (January 1982): 12–14.

Derfler, F. Data Communication—TRS–80 style. *80 Microcomputing* (June/July 1982): 82–92.

Frank, M. *Discovering computers.* London: Trewin Copplestone Books, 1981.

Gula, R. Beyond the typewriter. *Classroom Computer News* (May/June 1982): 31–32.

Hall, K. *Computer-based education: The best of ERIC June 1976–August 1980.* New York: ERIC Clearinghouse on Information Resources, 1980.

James, D. Coming on-line with the world. *Personal Computing* (April 1982): 36–44.

Kleiman, G., M. Humphrey, and T. VanBuskirk. Evaluating educational software. *Creative Computing* (1981): 84–90.

Krutch, J. *Experiments in artificial intelligence for small computers.* Indianapolis, Ind.: Howard W. Sams, 1981.

Horn, C., and J. Poirot. *Computer literacy: Problem solving with computers.* Austin, Tex.: Stirling Swift, 1981.

Lawler, R. Logo ideas. *Creative Computing* 8 (1982).

Lindsley, O. Standard daily behavior chart. *Journal of Applied Behavior Analysis* 1 (1968): 97.

Mathes, S. Using microcomputer graphics to train teachers. *Creative Computing* 8 (1982): 88–94.

Morusund, D. *An introduction to computers and computing.* Eugene, Ore.: International Council for Computers in Education, Department of Computer and Information Science, University of Oregon, 1979.

Morusund, D. *Basic programming for computer literacy.* New York: McGraw-Hill, 1982.

Morusund, D. Introduction to computers in education for elementary and middle school teachers. *The Computing Teacher* 9 (1981): 15–24.

Morusund, D. *School administrator's introduction to instructional use of computers.* Eugene, Ore.: International Council for Computers in Education, Dept. of Computer and Information Science, University of Oregon, 1979.

Morusund, D. *Teacher's guide to computers in the elementary school.* Eugene, Ore.: International Council for Computers in Education, Dept. of Computer and Information Science, University of Oregon, 1979.

Nadeau, M. Videotext for the masses. *80 Microcomputing* (January 1982): 60–64.

Nazzaro, J. *Computer connection for gifted children and youth.* Reston, Va.: Council for Exceptional Children, 1981.

Noonan, L. Computer simulations in the classroom. *Creative Computing* 7 (1981): 132–38.

Orwig, G., and W. Hodges. *The computer tutor: Learning activities for homes and schools.* Cambridge, Mass.: Winthrop, 1982.

Pattis, R. *Karel the robot: A gentle introduction to the art of programming.* New York: John Wiley, 1981.

Papert, S. *Mindstorms: Children, computers, and powerful ideas.* New York: Basic Books, 1980.

Poirot, J. and K. Swigger. *Computer literacy.* Austin, Tex.: Sterling Swift, 1981.

Spencer, D. *Introduction to information processing.* 3rd ed. Columbus, Ohio: Charles E. Merrill, 1981.

Spencer, D. *The illustrated computer dictionary.* New ed. Columbus, Ohio: Charles E. Merrill, 1983.

Taylor, R. *The computer in the schools: Tutor, tool, tutee.* New York: Teachers College Press, 1980.

Thornburg, D. *Picture this! Pilot turtle geometry, an introduction to computer graphics for kids of all ages.* Reading, Mass.: Addison-Wesley, 1982.

10

Career Preparation

E. S. Fleming

Any adequate consideration of the educational needs of the gifted and talented must include attention to their living enriched and enriching lives after their years of formal schooling. The importance of career education is apparent when seen as an integrated effort to help the gifted and talented create the most satisfying match between talents and abilities and work and play. We can hope that each gifted and talented individual will become aware of his talents, abilities, interests, values, become aware of the many possibilities and opportunities available to him, explore those prospects, learn about required and available resources, know how to set goals, make appropriate decisions, and be prepared to face the challenges of rewarding work, renewing leisure, and societal participation with confidence and competence.

Herr (1982) summarizes the role of the schools for career education in the 80s:

> If much of career behavior is learned, then it can also be relearned or unlearned. Education can neutralize a lack of information as well as a lack of encouragement to explore, to plan, to choose. Indeed, most career development theorists now advocate the systematic development of programs that can be organized to facilitate positive career behavior for young people. (p. 124)

Earlier beliefs regarding responsibilities toward career development of the gifted were quite different. They were grounded in the assumption that able students would, when properly educated in the classic mode, find their appropriate station in life. The schools, therefore, had only to provide quality academic instruction and college admissions guidance to insure that gifted students would find the right career niche. Longitudinal research tracked career patterns of the academically able to find the degree of life success they experienced after completing schooling (Terman & Oden 1959; Rothney, 1972; Flanigan, Tiedeman, Willis, & McLaughlin, 1973). To the extent that career guidance was offered at all, it fell to postsecondary institutions to provide the academic counseling necessary to create compatible matches between able individuals and career possibilities. Secondary counselors concentrated on academic counseling for scheduling and meeting college requirements (Bish, 1958). But assumption of the inevitability of harmonious career selection is totally unfounded in the complex and contradictory era of the 1980s. Changes in what we know about the gifted, their needs, and our responsibilities to them force a wholly different perspective on the matter of career education.

Today, a broadened definition of what constitutes gifts and talents creates the necessity of considering careers in ways far different from what was demanded of the verbally precocious. As giftedness encompasses distinguished skills in leadership, creativity, the visual and performing arts, and special academic abilities, we must find ways to contribute to the career development of these new groups of gifted for whom old practices are inappropriate. And, just as definitions have changed, so has our view of where we will find individuals with these gifts or the potential for them. Thus, the reservoir of talent, tapped and untapped, among the culturally different, those in rural areas, females, the handicapped, and underachievers create very different issues for the educator of the gifted and talented interested in helping students with career education.

The radically changing nature of our universe, our world, and our nation along with the anticipation of even greater change in the immediate future make old answers about career choices useless. Those choices also have the potential for damage when irreversible decisions are made by default rather than through careful, informed planning. Such a changed world and our perceptions of its limits and opportunities carry significantly altered messages for the future careers of gifted and talented youngsters (Cetron & O'Toole, 1982; Toffler, 1981; Torrance, 1976a).

Relationships between schools and the communities they serve show changed expectations and interactions, with both greater fluidity and greater watchfulness on the part of the citizenry. Gifted education can benefit from such resources, but will also be scrutinized in new ways because of economic exigencies.

Because social scientists have taken a different view of the nature of the life cycle, greater emphasis on the developmental sweep of human behavior from birth through death characterizes the psychologies of our time. For gifted education, this means directing attention to needs from earliest childhood through adulthood.

Because our refocus on the gifted and talented is so recent, as is the linkage with the relatively new area of career education, there is a disappointing lack of data and validated programs to use as guideposts. For example, a recent computer search of the literature on career education for the gifted and talented student yielded a scant 126 citations, or slightly more than one percent of a pool of over 10,000 items in career education and guidance. The area is new and relatively uncharted; the potential contribution to the lives of children enormous.

A Brief History: From Terman to Marland

Terman's view (1954), based upon extensive study of a group of California gifted, was that they could be readily identified through intelligence tests and classroom performance. He believed constraints on their advancement were imposed by the lockstep curriculum that kept them in school when accelerated progress might have allowed them to get on with additional training toward establishing adult careers. Terman's target group was primarily white, affluent males with superior academic abilities, so the assumption was that once comfortably situated in college, their potential would be fulfilled through appropriate selection of a field of study and associated career choice. Emphasis on academic excellence as the key to career decision making prevailed through the Sputnik era, as individuals such as James Conant (1958) and Brandwein (1955) advocated improving the quality and rigor of secondary education for the academically gifted and talented for entry into scientific careers.

One individual provided the impetus for concern with both the gifted and the career education movements. Sidney Marland, U.S. Commissioner of Education in the early 1970s, defined the gifted and talented in an entirely new way. Marland's (1972) viewpoint represented a dramatic break with the past in terms of delineating areas of excellence formerly excluded and in opening the door for identifying those who had the potential for excellence. In response to accusations that career education promoted excessive vocationalism, Kenneth Hoyt (Hoyt & Hebeler, 1973) linked the two areas: "Career education, especially for the gifted and the talented, must provide the insights necessary not only for economic independence but for cultural interdependence—the ability to live a personally satisfying as well as socially useful life within a variety of alternative lifestyles" (p. 19).

Justification: Career Choices by Design Or Default

Career choices have repeatedly been shown to be random events, that is, arrived at through haphazard and accidental processes whereby individuals awaken in adulthood to find themselves trapped in disagreeable and unrewarding occupations (Fredrickson & Rothney, 1972). Many believe that worker alienation is a direct result of the incompatible match between talent and occupation. The career education movement itself grew up around the assumption that early attention to work choices would reduce worker dissatisfaction, which is particularly tragic in the case of gifted and talented for whom identity and career are so inextricably bound.

Thus, early efforts concentrated on secondary programs. In specialized high schools around the country, primarily in major cities where gifted students attended in concentrated numbers, career education became an accepted part of the curriculum (Hoyt & Hebeler, 1973). Opportunities at the elementary level appeared more slowly. It has now become apparent that career education cannot be left to chance, but needs thoughtful preparation from the earliest entry of gifted and talented into the schools. The need becomes even more urgent with the broadening of the definition to include children with little or no exposure to the enormous range of career possibilities beyond their restricted environments. The notion of systematically building career awareness in early childhood and offering opportunities for career exploration in later childhood and adolescence is a more recent recommendation, based on the assumption that pervasive and continued exposure will provide gifted and talented students with the requisite skills to make informed decisions. No educator should foreclose possibilities by design or default.

What Early Research Tells Us

Wolfie (1954) was among the first to document the magnitude of talent loss accruing from the failure of the gifted to attend college, and identified socioeconomic status as the reason for the denial of opportunity. Documentation of talent loss was also one of the cornerstones of Marland's (1972) plea on behalf of the gifted nearly two decades later. The current concern is with talent loss among minorities and females.

To the extent that failure to attend college, underemployment, and job dissatisfaction are evidence of the failure of schools to meet children's career education needs, some of the older longitudinal data provide information about the inadequacies of career education for gifted and talented students particularly.

The career patterns of the Terman group represent a society and values system very different from our own time. For example, even among his group of highly selected women with a minimum IQ of 135, the constraints imposed by stereotypic expectations were clearly evident, with only 66 percent reported as having attended college (Sears & Barbee, 1977).

In a more recent longitudinal study of gifted and talented in Wisconsin (Sanborn, 1979), a differential was observed in the number of women going on to graduate and professional education. Although the disparity in undergraduate college attendance had virtually disappeared, with 98 percent and 97 percent college attendance reported for males and females respectively, the disparity at the graduate level may have the equivalent meaning of an undergraduate degree during the Terman era.

More evidence is available in Project Talent data, which revealed (Marland, 1972) that "information from grades, from curriculum choices, and from composite grade point averages shows that significant numbers of the most gifted high school students are failing to achieve, and are curtailing or eliminating their opportunities for meaningful achievement as adults. This waste of human resources is a serious national problem" (p. 202). In fact, 13 percent of the gifted in Project Talent did not have plans to enroll in a college program, and in the first year follow-up, almost 20 percent had not entered college. Nonattendance was highest among the high ability students in the bottom socioeconomic quartile: only 48 percent of these students attended college, whereas 87 percent of their high socioeconomic counterparts with the same ability attended college (Flanigan & Cooley, 1966). The five-year follow-up documented the magnitude of underemployment and job dissatisfaction, which were dramatic among the women—25 percent were employed as secretary-typists, 90 percent of whom planning to leave their clerical employment.

Current Status of Special Groups

The information gap is particularly troublesome in documenting the need and program requirements for gifted and talented minorities, females, rural residents, and the handicapped. Because of the paucity of data regarding career education for these subgroups, we must piece together information from older longitudinal studies, expert judgments on their affective and cognitive needs, and U.S. Government Labor Bureau statistics. From this, we can infer where we stand and where we need to be.

Although some resources describe the characteristics of gifted minority students and women, much of the writing focuses on the college age population (Watley, 1972; Astin & Myint, 1971). On the other hand, information tells us that special groups of gifted are still failing to fulfill potential in proportion to their numbers. If gifted and talented individuals should have access to professions that draw on such talents, then the uneven representation of minorities and women in intellectually demanding professions suggests that access is still limited.

Table 10-1 illustrates the percent of the total numbers employed in selected occupations where women and minority members are dramatically over- and underrepresented. In those areas where gifted and talented students should be heavily involved, unequal balance with white males sharpens the talent loss occurring for women and minorities. The assumption is that, all other factors being equal, women

Table 10-1   SEX AND RACIAL CHARACTERISTICS OF PERSONS IN SELECTED OCCUPA-
TIONS IN 1981

Occupations	1981		
	Total Employed	Percent of Total	
		Female	Black and Other
Computer specialists	613*	26.9	8.6
Engineers	1,497	4.3	6.0
Lawyers and judges	570	14.0	4.4
Librarians, archivists and curators	190	83.2	5.3
Life and physical scientists	303	21.8	9.6
Dentists	127	4.7	5.5
Economists	157	24.8	5.7
Social workers	383	64.0	20.4
Recreation workers	119	58.0	16.8
Prekindergarten and kindergarten teachers	239	98.3	15.5
Managers and administrators, except farm	11,315	27.4	5.4

*Numbers in thousands
Adapted from *Employment and Unemployment During 1981: An Analysis*, Special Labor Force Report 234, U.S. Department of Labor Bureau of Labor Statistics, January, 1982.

should be represented by upwards of 50 percent and minorities by 14 percent within particular career fields. In the legal profession, including lawyers and judges, there are only 14 percent women and 4.4 percent minorities represented. Engineering and computer systems analysis, areas with excellent future prospects, show significantly depressed representation for minorities and women, that is, underrepresentation of particular categories of gifted who have the capacity for competing successfully in these developing areas. Table 10-2 makes the point even more forcefully with a more select population, where there is little doubt regarding ability to meet the definition of giftedness. Here, the significant disparities in doctoral degrees for all fields, particularly engineering, mathematics, and the physical sciences, is obvious—only 2.2 percent of doctorates in engineering have been awarded to women, 1.4 percent to blacks, .5 percent to American Indians, and 3.2 percent to Hispanics. Overrepresentation of Asians results from the awarding of 45 percent of the doctorates awarded in these fields to non-U.S. citizens.

While we do not claim that appropriate attention to career education for the gifted and talented will totally eradicate the disparities in representation of certain

Table 10-2 DOCTORAL DEGREE RECIPIENTS BY FIELDS OF STUDY, RACE, AND SEX

Item	All fields	Edu-cation	Engi-neering	Humani-ties	Life sciences	Mathe-matics	Physical sciences	Professional fields	Social sciences
1	2	3	4	5	6	7	8	9	10
Doctor's degrees conferred	30,850	7,190	2,423	4,235	4,887	838	3,234	1,454	6,453
Sex (percents):									
Men	73.1	60.3	97.8	62.3	77.9	85.7	90.4	77.3	69.8
Women	26.9	39.7	2.2	37.7	22.1	14.3	9.6	22.7	30.2
Racial/ethnic group (percents):									
American Indian	.6	.8	.5	.5	.7	(*)	.5*	.4	.4
Asian	7.8	2.8	26.3	2.2	10.5	(*)	13.8*	6.2	4.2
Black	4.5	9.5	1.4	2.6	2.7	(*)	1.8*	5.0	4.2
Hispanic	2.7	2.7	3.2	3.3	2.7	(*)	2.2*	2.5	2.6
White	76.3	77.3	60.0	83.5	75.8	(*)	73.0*	77.9	78.5
Other and unknown	8.2	7.1	7.4	8.2	7.8	(*)	38.6*	7.0	10.0

Field of Study

*Mathematics and Computer Sciences combined with Physical Sciences.
Adapted from National Academy of Sciences, National Research Council, Summary Report—1978, Doctorate Recipients from United States Universities.

groups within occupational categories, there is little doubt that, along with conscientious efforts at identification and quality educational programming, some of the imbalances can be alleviated.

Essential Concepts

Major Concepts Defined

Few subspecialties in the field of education have generated the volume of research and writing that we find in the investigation of career-related issues. Consequently, confusion arises about the similar-sounding terms used to characterize individual behavior about career choice, so we need to make distinctions in the vocabulary.

According to Donald Super, *Career* is "the sequence of positions occupied by a person during the course of a lifetime . . . with its recognition of the life stages of growth, exploration, establishment, maintenance, and decline" (Super & Hall, 1978, p. 334). This notion of a life-span developmental perspective is particularly relevant to the kinds of career decisions the gifted and talented must make, in light of their multipotentiality, the multiple demands upon them, and the complexities of the life cycle for active participants in an ever-changing society.

Several other definitions help focus the present concern more sharply. Hoyt and Hebeler (1973) spell them out:

- *Vocation* is one's primary work role at any point in time.
- *Occupation* is one's primary work role in the world of paid employment.
- *Leisure* is those activities which an individual pursues when not engaged in his or her vocation. (pp. 44–45)
- *Work* has been defined by Hoyt (1978) as "conscious effort, other than that whose primary purpose is either coping or relaxation, aimed at producing benefits for oneself and others."(p. 9)

With these basic definitions in mind, we can look at the meaning of career education itself, although no definition finds universal agreement. Various writers emphasize different aspects; in fact, Hoyt and Hebeler (1973) provide more than a dozen different definitions of career education, with varying emphasis on educational, psychological, or societal responsibility.

Hoyt (1978) says:

Basically, career education can be defined as a joint effort of the education system and the broader community aimed at helping individuals acquire and utilize the knowledge, skills, and attitudes necessary for each to make work a meaningful, productive, and satisfying part of his or her way of living. (p. 9)

Hoyt emphasizes the importance of infusing career education into all aspects and levels of education. Career education skill development encompasses a wide range of behaviors, including "(a) basic academic skills; (b) good work habits; (c) personally meaningful work values; (d) understanding and appreciation of the private enterprise system; (e) self-understanding and understanding of education/work relationships; (f) career decision-making skills; (g) skills in productive use of leisure time;

(h) job seeking/setting/holding skills; (i) skills in reducing stereotyping as deterrents to full freedom of career choice; and (j) skills in humanizing the workplace for oneself and others'' (Hoyt, 1978, p. 9).

Career Development Theory and the Gifted

While there is no specific model for describing the career development of the gifted and talented, most early theorizing in the area is built upon samples of white, gifted males.

Thus, what we know today about patterns of career development originated in small-scale studies of highly selected students, so that in attempting to characterize career development life-span patterns, we find ourselves returning to the beginnings of the field when gifted, white, and largely affluent males were the focus for inquiry. Major theories from the fifties and sixties, whose influence continues largely unabated, include Roe's retrospective analyses of physical, biological, and social scientists; Holland's research with National Merit Scholarship samples; and Ginsburg's upper and middle class Anglo-Saxon white boys of above average intelligence and Columbia University male undergraduate and graduate students (Osipow, 1973). Missing even from broader socioeconomic representation, as in Super's Career Pattern Study (Super & Overstreet, 1957), were (1) adequate treatment of females and minorities and (2) inclusion of groups with diverse talents not necessarily tapped by the highly verbal intelligence measures.

Unique Needs of the Gifted and Talented

Numerous writers have dealt with issues that differentiate career development needs of the gifted and talented from their peers. Since the gifted and talented themselves represent such diversity, one must be cautious about applying generalizations across the full gifted and talented range. Nonetheless, particular attributes many gifted individuals share need to be factored into their career education requirements.

Figure 10–1 illustrates one way to organize consideration of the unique career education needs of the gifted. Influences on career choice, such as self, family, peers, and society, are a shared function of the human condition, at least in our culture, and are not unique to the gifted, but how these factors operate separately and collectively in the lives of the gifted requires our attention.

Self

Among the unique determinants of career choice for gifted and talented individuals is their particular set of talents and abilities. Obviously, extraordinary talent in the arts or in sports can shape one's destiny (Bloom, 1981). Less obviously, the multipotentiality of the gifted can create serious problems. To illustrate, one young person with a multitude of talents—mathematical, musical, verbal, and leadership abilities—was troubled and confused over which career direction to pursue, so he sought vocational

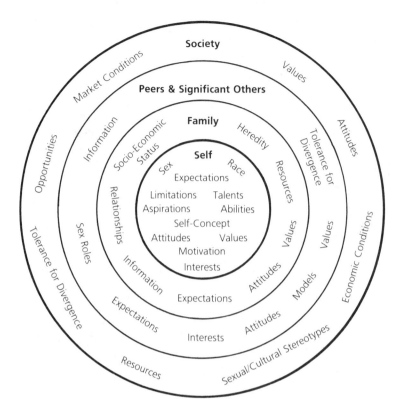

Figure 10-1 INFLUENCES ON CAREER CHOICE FOR THE GIFTED AND TALENTED

counseling to help solve the dilemma. After hours of testing with extensive batteries of instruments, a process that costs hundreds of dollars, the counselor pronounced: "You can be anything you want to be!" The young man's problem remained unresolved and, as Perrone, Karshner, & Male (1979) observe, the admonition carries the perjorative message of negation and denial of what and who the person is *now*.

The other side of the "you-can-be-anything" message is that the gifted individual fails to develop a realistic sense of limitations and deficiencies (Perrone et al., 1979). An unrealistic view of self can have devastating consequences when the unprepared individual must compete with equally or more capable peers in demanding postsecondary programs. Failure to acquire requisite study skills and intellectual discipline can result in "self-concept shock."

Considerable research supports the notion that many gifted suffer an embarrassment of riches in interests and competencies. Through data from the Wisconsin Research and Guidance Laboratory for Superior Students Hebeler and Hoyt (1973) document uniform excellence across ability areas for many gifted. Another set of data from a study of 281 gifted and talented high school women identified four young women with as many as nine outstanding abilities, nine with eight such talents, and 50 with seven, when judged on seventeen different indices (Fleming and Hollinger,

1981). As Margaret Mead (1928) observed long ago, with a multiplicity of choices, the potential for conflict increases proportionately.

Several writers point out that one implication of multipotentiality is that values and interest dimensions are more important as determinants of career choices than are aptitudes (Hoyt, 1978; Perrone et al., 1979). One's personality may determine which possibilities will be identified or overlooked, which directions chosen or not chosen, and whether one will show a pattern of success or failure. If career is the principal means of self-expression for the gifted and talented (Perrone et al., 1979), then career issues are inextricably and profoundly tied to personality. Thus, one must assess a number of motivational variables to understand the career patterns of the gifted and talented, such as needs for mastery and achievement, fears of failure and success, and willingness to take risks. Many case studies describe people's failure to fulfill their promise because of unresolved motivational conflicts.

Yet another important personality area has to do with the expectations and aspirations the gifted hold for themselves that have obviously been shaped by significant others. The gifted person may feel pressures to achieve what he perceives as impossibly high aspirations, or may lower his expectations for fear of rejection if he fails to measure up.

Building self-awareness about one's talents and abilities as a function of what one's environment accepts or rejects is one key to responsive program development. Many gifted have real problems in identity formation that Erikson (1950) long ago pointed out as crucial to vocational decisions. Forming a clear sense of self and one's values as distinct from others is a key developmental task. Inability to resolve identity issues can manifest itself in protracted dependency, failure to achieve closure by making choices, or premature closure. The gifted may latch on to the first area in which competence has produced recognition and success, or delay decision making indefinitely (Hoyt, 1976). Another escape may be frenzied participation in a multitude of activities through which the multitalented can avoid dealing with questions of "Who am I?" and "What do I wish to become?" Among the 281 gifted and talented young women of Project Choice, many showed clearly that it was often easier to submerge oneself in a flurry of club memberships, community activities, sports, and academic endeavors than to come to grips with one's goals and formulating future plans.

For purposes of organization, attributes of race and sex have been classified under "self." Obviously, their importance resides less in their direct biological influence on career choice than on the meaning they hold for the individual, which is shaped by significant others and society. Controversy abounds as to whether or not sex and race directly account for individual differences in ability. The recent debate spurred by Benbow and Stanley's (1980) conclusions that deficiencies in mathematical abilities of females are a function of biological factors is a case in point. Controversy over the origins of racial differences in intelligence recurs in the literature. The assumption here is that race and sex influence career development through socialization of the individual, that is, the internalization of messages society communicates and reinforces by subtle and direct barriers to free opportunity. In any event, the interactions are so complex that efforts to sort out specific constitutional bases for specific talents remain unconvincing.

Gottfredson's (1978) evidence suggests that sex differences loom larger than racial differences in determining career outcomes. He concludes: "Differences in what the races and sexes want to do, even before they look for jobs, limit the range of jobs they seek; differences in the jobs they get then amplify the initial differences in preferences for field of work" (1978, p. 19). Differences between the sexes in attitudes and expectations about work have been documented within racial groups, even among the gifted. For example, Schab (1978) reports that black males wanted greater autonomy on the job, were less willing to tolerate poor working conditions, and desired to surpass their parents' successes more than did their gifted female counterparts. That the vocational aspirations of black gifted females are higher than males has also been documented (Watley, 1972).

Gifted women encounter special kinds of conflict around career decision making. Rodenstein, Pfleger, and Colangelo (1977) describe the mixed messages that confuse gifted females. They are socialized to behave in one way as women, but their giftedness demands diametrically opposed behaviors: selflessness vs. energetic development of talent; passivity vs. activity; marriage ahead or instead of career vs. career success; femininity vs. nontraditional career aspirations in science, mathematics, and business.

Family

Any list of important career choice determinants underscores the many direct and indirect roles family members play in influencing vocational decisions. Hereditary factors help determine one's talent and ability potential; recent research convincingly establishes the hereditary contribution to mental ability (Bouchard & McGue, 1981). While it is difficult to separate hereditary and environmental contributions to extraordinary talent, the family, first by setting the genetic heritage and then by creating the environment in which talents and abilities develop or fail to develop, exercises multiplicative influence (Bloom, 1981). The literature contains numerous references to the ways families contribute to decisions about types and levels of occupational choice, including psychoanalytic interpretations of choice based on early interfamilial relationships and other more eclectic views of the ways early experience in the family shapes personality, attitudes, and interests (Fredrickson & Rothney, 1972).

Family socioeconomic status indicates many influences beyond the issue of financial and informational resources for supporting the gifted and talented child in fulfilling her potential. The aspirations and expectations the family holds and transmits become critical to the limits and opportunities that children perceive (Hoyt and Hebeler, 1973); Herr and Watanabe, 1979; Sanborn, 1979). Recent research suggests that socioeconomic factors may be more powerful determinants of the educational aspirations and expectations of boys than they are for girls (Marini and Greenberger, 1978), although such influences may be exerted on females and minority members where the family reinforces cultural stereotypes to the gifted child's detriment. One talented young woman who wished to explore the legal profession as a possible field of study was told by her lawyer father to think about becoming a legal secretary, a more suitable occupation for a woman.

A recent longitudinal study of gifted young women identifies socioeconomic status as a critical factor in predicting career choice and describes how paternal education and higher status occupations interact to determine nontraditional job entry. Surprisingly, daughters of better educated parents chose final careers in medicine while those with parents with some college training chose math and engineering. Young women choosing to become nurses and teachers came from families with little education, who were engaged in low status occupations, and resided in rural areas, small towns, or very large cities (Vidulich, Sachs, & Christman, 1978).

A great deal of research has centered on the differential effects parents have on same-sex and different-sex children. Viernstein and Hogan (1975) report on their study of highly gifted seventh and eighth grade participants in the Johns Hopkins verbal talent search:

> In summary, achievement motivation in boys may be explained in terms of exposure to dynamic, ambitious, achievement-oriented mothers, to an acceptable paternal model, and to parents with similar values. In contrast, achievement motivation in girls may arise from exposure to parental conflict, and from modeling after the parent of opposite sex. In both cases, achievement motivation may be a function of modeling rather than experience with a particular set of child-rearing practices designed to foster independence and self-esteem. It follows that unambitious, disaffected, anergic parents may have considerable difficulty producing upwardly mobile children. (p. 189)

Peers

Peers and significant others also exert the values, expectations, pressures and demands for conformity or tolerance for divergency that characterize family influences. Sociologists (Coleman, 1961) document the powerful influence of the adolescent subculture, including often anti-intellectual values that discourage academic achievement. Such messages from the peer culture can result in either capitulation to peer values on the one hand, or social isolation on the other (Herr & Watanabe, 1979). In either case, the conflict aroused requires the support and assistance of caring teachers and counselors. Vidulich et al. (1978) found that for gifted girls, the size of the high school they attended was important relative to decisions about entry into the fields of science and medicine. One assumes, of course, that a number of factors contributed to this conclusion, including values of the peer group as well as roles played by influential adults in suburbs and smaller cities where there was encouragement for nontraditional careers.

Presence or absence of role models is another determinant. Biographies of creative individuals document the importance of these influences in shaping their lives. For many gifted and talented, no such role models exist; they have no adult with whom to share ideas in stimulating exchanges (Herr & Watanabe, 1979). Much of Torrance's work (1979) has been devoted to publicizing the vital need of gifted, talented, and creative individuals for sponsors or patrons for support, encouragement, and validation. Torrance believes such sponsorship is particularly essential for those from culturally different and/or economically disadvantaged backgrounds.

Society

As Figure 10–1 illustrates, gifted and talented children, their families, and their peers function within a sociopolitical context that influences career choices in many significant ways. Cultures and subcultures set the stage regarding which areas are esteemed during any given historical era; for example, musical precocity was highly esteemed in the 18th century, as is athletic prowess in our own time (Newland, 1976). Messages the gifted child, family, and peers receive help to shape career directions by ordering the importance assigned to various occupational alternatives. Nowhere is this more evident than in the sex-role stereotyping that forecloses options for girls talented in math and science and boys with special performing arts abilities. The slow change of these societal values is evident in the new study, *High School and Beyond*: seniors graduating in 1980 continued to make traditional choices, although some progress was noted in the increase, from 1972 to 1980, of women choosing engineering, from 2 percent to 15 percent (Peng, Fetters, and Kolstad, 1981).

Societal influences appear in the kinds of public and private support, both financial and informational, made available to gifted and talented children. For example, during the Sputnik era, support for the arts and social sciences was considerably less than for science and math (Tannenbaum, 1979). The gifted and talented tended initially to elect sciences, only to drop out later and shift toward occupations involving greater social concern. Similarly, economic conditions and realities of the marketplace also exert pressure on choices, as we see in the current flight toward careers in business and finance and away from social service enterprises.

Advocates for the gifted and talented must confront the implicit assumption that the gifted, by virtue of their gifts, have a responsibility to repay society for its largesse, and that this obligation transcends their personal needs and wishes. Both Hoyt (1978) and Frederickson (1979) decry placing demands on the gifted that restrict their freedom of choice. The emphasis is more properly placed on fulfillment of individual potential, whether or not society will benefit either directly or indirectly.

Lastly, we need to mention the importance of prevailing attitudes toward individual differences. What are the prevailing attitudes toward diversity, whether racial, ethnic, sexual, or socioeconomic differences, or for the acceptance of new and bold ideas? These attitudes will influence the futures of special groups of gifted and talented students. In the face of prevailing societal attitudes, psychological support from significant others can often mean the difference between a creative individual's success and failure.

In sum, one must factor into the overall career education programming for gifted and talented students each of the concentric circles of influence, singly and in combination, so as to build and strengthen positive influences and confront and overcome barriers to fulfillment. A diagnostic-prescriptive approach would inventory the various factors in a young person's life and then design a program responsive to the individual's developmental needs. For example, a profile for a young black woman aspiring to be a bassoonist with a symphony orchestra who has low self-esteem, parental resistance to nontraditional occupational interests, lack of peer support, and faces a depressed labor market would require quite a different intervention strategy than that for a confident male from a middle class environment who, along with his friends, aspires to a career in engineering. Each of the approaches we will describe must be evaluated in terms of its provisions for such individual differences.

Models of Career Education and the Gifted

The U.S. Office of Education tested four general career education models, two of which are relevant for gifted and talented students in the elementary through secondary age range: the school-based comprehensive career education model (CCEM) and the experience-based career education model (EBCE). Herr (1974) provides an organizational scheme for relating the elements of a school-based career education to intended student outcomes, as we see in Table 10–3. The framework may provide a way to relate content from fifteen career clusters or occupational families, such as agribusiness, communication, environmental science, fine arts and humanities, and marine science, to desired outcomes.

Milne (1979) provides one example of a structure around which program development specifically designed for the gifted could be built. His educational-occupational interaction model specifies ways in which the individual's unique cognitive and affective attributes interact with educational training and experience to create possibilities for a satisfying life. The model in Figure 10–1 can also be seen as an effort to insure that program building is responsive to the unique needs of the gifted and talented. It places greater emphasis than does Milne on the impact of society and significant others in determining career development patterns.

Torrance (1978b) suggests four kinds of help that homes and schools can offer gifted and talented children, offering another perspective for program design. Torrance says the gifted and talented need:

- To see clear relationships between what they are expected to learn and their potential *future* careers.

Table 10–3 SCHOOL-BASED CAREER EDUCATION AND INTENDED OUTCOMES*

Element	Outcome
Career awareness	Career identity
Self-awareness	Self-identity
Appreciations, attitudes	Self-social fulfillment
Decision-making skills	Career decision skills
Economic awareness	Economic understanding
Skill awareness and beginning competence	
Employability skills	Career placement
Educational awareness	Educational identity

*Herr, 1974, p. 50.

- To develop and use problem-solving and decision-making skills in coping with daily problems and *future* careers.
- To learn about the *future* world of work.
- To discover personal characteristics (What am I like?), reasons for these characteristics (Why am I that way?), see ways in which these characteristics can be changed and enhanced, and see how these characteristics are related to their *future* careers. (p. 28)

Programming

Herr and Watanabe (1979) caution against overlooking the needs of special groups. Programs must thus avoid both overgeneralization and overindividualization.

Comprehensive programs need to provide systematic attention to career education needs of the gifted and talented from their earliest contact with the schools. As the needs of the gifted and as society's alternatives change, so must career education, neither duplicating experiences nor ignoring the special requirements of the developing person. Unfortunately most career education programs for the gifted and talented presently focus on the adolescent stage and fail to consider the developmental sweep included in, for example, the nine exemplary programs designed for the normal spectrum of children Kindergarten through the 12th grade as described in the U.S. Office of Education publication, *Career Programs That Work* (1979).

An important component of any program is to help the gifted come to know who they are through awareness of self: their talents, abilities, attitudes, interests, values, strengths, and weaknesses (Herr and Watanabe, 1979). Many gifted are unaware of their capacities and potential, either because they have never been informed, or because their low self-esteem bars a positive view of self. An exercise in self-evaluation can point out discrepancies between the individual's perception of self and reality.

The school has a vital function to perform in providing informational resources through people and materials. Although the gifted are assumed to be sophisticated regarding the larger world, for many, resources are limited to their very restricted surroundings, and erroneous assumptions are often made regarding the gifted's informational backgrounds.

There is no reason to believe the gifted and talented do not travel the same developmental course as the general population in formulating decisions about careers: awareness, exploration, and preparation as described by Super and Hall (1978). The timing and emphasis may vary among the gifted, so the responsibility falls to educators to provide appropriate individual experiences, whether that takes the form of an early mentorship or availability of an updated library on ophthalmology.

The gifted need to learn that particular gifts and talents do not necessarily need to be directed into specific career choices, but that such talents can find expression in use of leisure time (Milne, 1979).

Career education needs to be an integral part of the total curriculum throughout the entire school experience (Sellin and Birch, 1980). Making the linkages to careers explicit enriches academic content, as exemplified by Tobin and Fox's (1980) effort to encourage middle school-aged children to enter math/science careers through the introduction of career materials into an accelerated mathematics program. There is also the potential for reciprocal skill building, as when computer interest is developed through the utilization of increasingly available computer-based career development programs.

All communities have extraordinary resources that can be tapped for creation of long-term internship opportunities. Such experiences can make a lasting impact on the lives of the gifted and talented. The key is identifying, cultivating, and actively maintaining such relationships as linked to the ongoing school career education program. Building these bridges to the community will benefit all the individuals and institutions involved.

Involving students' families is critical to any career education program's success. Many parents are overwhelmed by a sense of inadequacy as to the support they can offer their children. They often respond eagerly with information about financial aid, exposure to program objectives and outcomes, and sharing in the spirit of cooperative planning. Helping parents help children is surely one of the most meaningful activities educators of the gifted and talented can have. Interpreting the nature of gifts and talents and their implications and possibilities must be a significant aspect of any worthwhile career education program.

For the gifted, acquiring skills in the processes of making decisions and setting goals can be of lifetime importance. These skills help one learn to adapt to change, and apply to all aspects of daily living.

The Teacher and the Learning Environment

For a career education program and for all educational interventions to succeed, careful attention must be paid to the learning environment the teacher creates. Maker (1982) suggests that, while environmental dimensions exist on a continuum, the context for the gifted should be more student-centered than teacher-centered, more independent than dependent, more open than closed, more accepting than judgmental, more complex than simple, and more mobile than passive. These objectives are perhaps more easily met in the career education area than in other curricular areas because of the nature of the subject matter, its exploratory and inquiry-based requirements and the necessary fluidity between the physical boundaries of the school and the community at large. Content, process, and product in career education center around flexible interchanges among students, teachers, and community. The notion of career education as a didactic, teacher-dominated, formal course is ludicrous. While individual learning styles may dictate a variety of approaches to deriving content-related activities, the discovery mode is clearly the method of choice. Similarly, group processes will prove a most effective medium for learning about self, existing and future careers, and societal interdependence. Sociodrama (Torrance, 1976c) provides a good illustration of ways the teacher can encourage flexible, active, and interactive learning about careers. Above all, as Fox (1976) observes, "the most crucial aspect of the learning environment is the development of an atmosphere of mutual trust and respect among individuals and a commitment to self-improvement" (p. 109).

The Teacher and the Content

While Hoyt (1978) and others argue persuasively that concepts of career education should be infused throughout curriculum, it does not appear that the message has been heeded. As we will see shortly, even among programs developed with a clear gifted and talented focus, the "add-on" rather than the infusion principle seems to prevail. It therefore remains the teacher's responsibility to plan for infusion on a subject-by-subject basis at the elementary level or for the particular discipline at the secondary level. The inventive teacher, after thought and practice, will soon automatically draw career implications with each unit of study. Almost all content areas lend themselves to career-related activities or to bridges between the two. Tobin and Fox (1980) demonstrate this in the math and science fields, and Turner (1979) provides useful suggestions in creative writing and composition which, while intended for regular education, can be adapted for the gifted and talented. He suggests, for example, writing parodies, poems, and song lyrics with work ethic themes; job competency test questions; a year-by-year diary of one's career projected into the future; skits or a "yesterday" show illustrating how careers have changed; designing "wanted posters" for particular career roles; making up crossword puzzles with answers related to careers or career clusters; fantasizing a new career and describing the necessary preparation for it; compiling principles for starting your own business; and forming your own corporation. His suggestions for letter-writing activities would challenge gifted and talented learners: writing letters of resignation, investigative letters, letters of complaint, letters requesting promotion or transfer, and letters seeking legal or other advice. Additional topics can include tall tales relating to a modern career, or themes like My Dream Job, The Job I Would Have Had in Julius Caesar's Day, If I Were Boss of . . . , The Magical, Mystical, Magnificent Career Machine, How the Animal Lost Its Job, Careers on a Distant Planet, King or Queen Wanted: Only Experienced Individual Should Apply, and How I Made My First Million. The point is that teachers can draw career implications in each discipline that will help gifted and talented learners explore related occupations as they acquire the basic skills, sound work habits and values, self-understanding, and skills in the use of leisure time.

Primary-Elementary Concepts

In 1973 Hoyt and Hebeler observed that most programs in career education for the gifted were targeted at the secondary level. Where younger children were involved, music appeared as the most prevalent programmatic theme. Of the 18 exemplary programs they described, only five appeared to include elementary age children: the Interlochen Center for the Arts, which accepted children eight years of age and above; the District of Columbia Youth Orchestra Program, beginning at the fourth grade level; the California Project TALENT Demonstration Centers, including fourth through sixth graders; the Children's Theatre in Quincy, Illinois; and the Middle Grades Exploration Institute for Teaching Children with Exceptional Ability in the Charlotte, North Carolina Schools. Hoyt and Hebeler said in 1973: "Evidently very little has actually been accomplished which could be described as permeating career education focus for the gifted and talented, which could accompany general education from kindergarten through the twelfth grade" (p. 210). The same statement is true today.

Few references described any programs at all developed specifically for primary and elementary gifted and talented children, and none described comprehensive programs that sequentially infused concepts of career education into the gifted and talented curriculum. Of the 126 references identified in the ERIC data base, only three focused on the elementary age child; none had exclusive applicability to the primary grades. This is the case, despite the assertion of Sellin and Birch (1980) that career development has its strong beginnings in the preschool and elementary years where the regular teacher and the curriculum itself provide information and educational experience. Sellin and Birch identify three themes that should characterize career education for the gifted and talented during the early school years: (1) awareness and exposure to information; (2) exploration and examination of careers; and (3) pupil understanding of the interdependence of all people. Expanding awareness of self and the world of work, exploration of broadly-based career alternatives, and the beginnings of reality tests of knowledge of self against accumulated information circumscribe the objectives for building responsive programs for gifted and talented primary and elementary age children.

This delineation suggests that the areas of concern are quite similar to primary and elementary programs developed for the regular curriculum. It is through alteration of content, level, and pace, however, that differentiation can take place. For example, the program developed by the Akron Public Schools (*Programs That Work*, 1979) has as its goals for the K–6 levels ". . . helping students to develop positive self-concepts, an awareness and appreciation of many different careers, positive attitudes toward work, and an appreciation of the dignity of all work" (p. 10). In the absence of contrary data, these appear to be appropriate goals for the gifted if placed in the context of differentiated content. For example, one might use the kinds of experiences described in programs specifically developed for the gifted such as the future problem-solving experiences described by Torrance and Kaufman (1977); Operation DISCO (Designation of Inter-Space Community Occupations) developed by OrRico (OrRico & Feldhusen, 1979); the mentorship program of the Springfield, Massachusetts Schools (Sweet, 1980), and a language arts program related to business administration described by Cidis (1980).

In its preservice Career Education Project, the University of Georgia has established four generic competencies for teachers that specify appropriate applications at the primary, intermediate, middle, and high school levels (Torrance, 1976b). The competencies, although not exclusively for the gifted, are elaborated with increasing sophistication during the successive developmental periods, providing a model of sequential planning and clear transitions. These are the four competencies with examples of emphasis at primary, intermediate, and middle school levels:

1 "Assist students to see and develop clear relationships between what they are being asked to learn in school and potential future careers." Focus ranges from building positive learning attitudes at the primary level, to examining the instrumental value of subject matter in home, community, and with workers at the intermediate level, to becoming aware of relation-

ships between educational alternatives and potential careers at the middle school level.

2 "Assist students to utilize problem-solving skills in making career decisions." Children at the primary level learn about gathering information while practicing basic problem-solving skills; intermediate children apply the techniques to decisons that relate the process to career choices, and middle school youngsters increase skills and are introduced to various career alternatives.

3 "Assist students to develop career-related personal and interpersonal skills." Children at the primary level develop work skills and look at the rewards of various careers; intermediate children look at societal and personal implications of careers; middle school children gain firsthand knowledge and begin some career planning.

4 "Assist students to discover their characteristics (what am I like?), to understand reasons for these characteristics (why am I that way?), to see ways in which these characteristics can be changed (how can I change?), and to see ways in which these characteristics are career-related."

Primary age children are helped toward a developing awareness of self vis à vis others; intermediate level children are helped to develop a good self-concept and see its relationship to life style; middle school children test their self-concepts against real-world vocational settings.

Torrance (1976c) has written extensively about applying the educational methodology of sociodrama to career education. Useful across the age spectrum, sociodrama is particularly effective in the early years of schooling as a way to help young children become involved in creative group problem solving, focusing on career-related issues. Torrance gives teachers detailed guidance for adapting multiple sociodramatic production techniques to career education by applying new knowledge, skills, and attitudes to career issues, doubts, conflicts, and future possibilities. An interested teacher can elaborate on the customary role-playing strategy of direct presentation and become skillful in the Soliloquy technique, in which students can express hidden feelings and thoughts, brainstorm problem solutions, and evaluate alternatives. Other strategies include the Double technique or Multiple Double technique in which the individual acts out a conflict with an "alter ego" or "alter egos" to encourage expansion of states of consciousness. Torrance (1976c) recommends variations such as the Double and Contrary Double techniques to promote "applying information to career problems, asking pertinent new questions, examining both positive and negative predictions, examining both positive and negative aspects of proposed decisions or plans of action, examining alternative work values, and positive and negative evaluations of potentialities" (p. 20).

The Mirror technique can also help children examine role requirements of various careers, as can Role Reversals and the Future Projection technique, in which young children with limited writing skills can do the scenario forecasting aspect of futurology through sociodrama instead of in writing. Other possibilities Torrance suggests include approaches such as the Auxiliary World technique, to examine future life style demands of various careers; the Magic Shop technique for working through dilemmas; the High Chair and Empty Chair techniques for learning how people can change according to their career needs; the Therapeutic Community

Technique to learn about societal interdependence; the Magic Net technique for fantasizing career changes the future might bring; and Reality Level sociodrama to enhance occupational awareness while reinforcing primary children's basic skills, as, for example, in construction of a city community within the classroom. These approaches can be used in combination and to involve all class members in one way or another in career education activities.

Despite the usefulness of these techniques, many tend to be short-term additions to the curriculum rather than part of a total comprehensive program. Some excellent sequences of experiences in the arts, for example, developed by the Allegheny Intermediate Unit in Pittsburgh (1978), are conducted on Saturdays apart from the regular instructional program. These experiences are, of course, extremely valuable, but one wonders if their importance might not be enhanced by inclusion in the day-to-day gifted and talented offerings. Emphasizing greater use of mentoring experiences and introducing career possibilities in the study of the disciplines characterize career education components at the primary and elementary levels. Although this is an advancement from Hoyt and Hebeler's 1973 assessment of the state of the art, the gifted are not yet receiving the planned career education that their nongifted peers are.

As for all children, career education for the gifted must include instruction in basic job-seeking skills, as well as general career planning.

Secondary Concepts

Career education for adolescent gifted and talented has shown more encouraging signs of growth during the past seven or eight years. Torrance (1978b) describes the need for help during the early adolescent years in these areas: (1) seeing the connection between school work and future careers; (2) relating interests and abilities to educational and career possibilities; (3) having opportunities to use academic and interpersonal skills in simulated and real work; and (4) evaluating options given present abilities and interests. For the middle and later adolescent period, he suggests that, "GCT children need continued help in finding opportunities for making reality tests of their future plans in educational and work settings and in evaluating discrepancies between their present achievements and their future expectations and aspirations" (p. 28). To meet the needs Torrance identifies, programs must include assessment for diagnosis and prescription, career information sources, mentorships, role models, or internships, skill development, and futurism.

Assessment for Diagnosis and Prescription

The first step in career education must provide the opportunity, materials, and interpretation to promote self-assessment of abilities, interests, and values. Assessment is an ongoing component of a comprehensive program, to help students remain aware of where they are in relation to where they want to be in the future. This does not mean we should assault gifted and talented students with a barrage of standardized tests at every turn. Some school systems routinely administer such instruments, and students may at best be uninformed and at worst, misinformed, about their test performance. Information derived from instruments such as the DAT (Differential Aptitude Test) or the GATB (General Aptitude Battery) provide a profile against which descriptions of characteristics of occupational group members can be compared. Use of such standard measures as the Strong-Campbell Interest Inventory, the Ohio Vocational Interest Survey (OVIS), Holland's Self-Directed Search (SDS), and Crite's Career Maturity Inventory (CMI) are examples of measures that purport to tap interests, personality dimensions related to career choice, and level of career development. Although there is justifiable criticism regarding the assumptions that underlie such measurements, particularly their potential for cultural and sexual bias (Diamond, 1975), they can, when judiciously interpreted in combination with other relevant data, help students in the self-assessment process. More informal instruments can be used with or developed specifically for a given target population. Thus, data about abilities, interests, and values can be brought together for the student. Project Choice (Fleming & Hollinger, 1979) developed forms for self-assessment that introduced data from standardized tests and academic performance, including grades and achievement test scores. Students judged the instrument extremely helpful for making self-perceptions more congruent with reality. This diagnostic-prescriptive approach, beginning with determining where the individual is, ascertaining self-perceptions, then helping to make connections to the future, provide a promising starting point for designing appropriate experiences in career education. It also suggests possible special interventions for the individual. This is particualry so in the personality domain, where particular barriers may seriously impair an underachieving gifted student's level of functioning.

Career Information Sources: Print and Computers

There is nearly an overwhelming abundance of material available to gifted and talented students in their career exploration activities. Much is available from U.S. Government agencies, such as the Bureau of Labor, professional societies and organizations within the career guidance profession (for example, the National Vocational Guidance Association), and individual professional societies. These groups are eager to educate others regarding their roles and functions, and often distribute materials at little or no cost.

The Occupational Outlook Handbook, now available in its 1980-81 edition, is an important source of information, particularly with its addition of more esoteric occupations of interest to the gifted—for example, climatologic geographers and geomorphologists. The *Dictionary of Occupational Titles* (DOT) is a companion volume with classificatory information, as is the *Occupational Outlook Quarterly*; all are U.S. government publications.

The availability of computer systems for the delivery of career information is a relatively new development. For those gifted who are somewhat fearful of math, exposure to the new technology while engaged in another absorbing activity has the potential for helping them overcome apprehension about its use. As schools and libraries increasingly make available such systems as SIGI (System of Interactive Guidance and Information) and DISCOVER, and as individual states adopt computer-based career information systems, the opportunity will spread for using computer systems as yet another avenue for information gathering. Unfortunately, issues of quality control remain troublesome for much of the field, because advances in hardware have far outstripped software capability.

Mentorships, Role Models, and Internships

Mentorship is the one area in career education for the gifted that has enjoyed substantial growth, either as a distinct program entity or as a component of more inclusive offerings. Mentorship takes a number of different forms, ranging in practice from the one large-group lecture by a plasma physicist to a group of gifted, to a year-long (or more) ongoing intense professional association of a gifted student acting as research assistant to a hematologist. In each instance, the label "mentorship" applies. Bruce Boston (1975) says of this relationship:

> The central issue here is that in order for the mentor-pupil relationship to work, to do what it is supposed to do, a commitment is necessary. Interest, curiosity, eagerness, and earnestness are all important, but not sufficient, either singly or together. What seems to count in the last analysis is the risk, the commitment. (p. 10)

Boston points out that the mentor's responsibilities include advocacy, modeling, a sense of timing, the use of planned, guided experiences, realistic appraisal of progress, training toward the predisposition of the student, maintaining creative tension, and teaching by indirection. Many educators are uneasy at the prospect of creating a mentorship program. Usually, however, there is enthusiastic response from the community, for as Runion (1980) points out, "mentoring is the gifted and talented tutoring the gifted and talented."

Project Choice had an extensive mentorship segment as one of its major components. Students were placed, according to their wishes following program exposure, with professional women who represented some sixty occupations. Some experiences were relatively short-term, for example, shadowing a biochemist in an industrial setting; others resulted in long-term paid employment with a security analyst in one case and a marine biologist in another. Program evaluation ratings showed the mentorship experience to be considered the single most valuable feature of the entire program (Fleming & Hollinger, 1979). Subsequent informal follow-up suggested that the mentorship experiences provided a critical link in career development. The young woman in the marine biology placement said this opportunity in high school confirmed her earlier fantasized career, gave her psychological and informational resources for realizing her goal, and resulted in her present paid college assistantship in the field of her choice.

Networking school personnel, parents, and interested community representatives produces many potential mentors. Creating matches between students and mentors requires creative oversight, but suggestions in the literature will help order the procedures, organize mentor pools, and monitor the relationships. Sweet (1980) describes a successful program in the Springfield, Massachusetts schools and shows forms for managing and evaluating a mentorship program. The Executive High School Internship program, begun in 1971 and subsequently expanded (Hirsch, 1976), explains released time internships for learning about management in government, business, and other organizations. While direct empirical support is limited, the contribution of mentorship programs to cognitive and personal growth has been extremely valuable in terms of content and process, particularly among minority group members, those who are geographically isolated, and young women, many of whom have had little or no direct personal exposure to individuals like themselves who have attained high levels of professional accomplishment in adulthood.

Skill Development: Goal Setting and Decision Making

In the preparation phase of career education programming, it is traditional to try to build planning skills. Students should learn to set reasonable goals, knowing when they have attained them, and adjust them when appropriate. They need to learn to make informed decisions by gathering information, examining alternatives, and weighing consequences. Although we could enumerate other important skills that are often included as part of group procedures in career development programs, such as preparing resumes and interviewing, we highlight goal setting and decision making because they are transferable across time and situations and because useful materials can be adapted to a wide range of gifted and talented settings. (The reader is referred to the College Examination Board publication, *Decisions and Outcomes* [Gelatt et al., 1973].)

Futurism

Torrance (1976a,b; 1978a,b) argues the importance of emphasizing futurism studies with the gifted. He believes their vision of what the future will be helps the gifted decide what to learn, how to cope and what to strive for in a volatile world, how to search for identity and help determine what the world will be like for all of us. He reports that gifted students are increasingly attracted to thinking about the future, with 95 percent of gifted and talented senior high school students reporting this absorption and 86 percent of gifted and talented elementary children. Because of this affinity and the role the gifted will play in creating societal advancement Torrance developed his Future Problem Solving Program to help the gifted improve their problem-solving skills, improve teamwork, and enlarge and enrich their view of the future through interdisciplinary study. The program has met with considerable success. The logical connection between study of the future and career education is summed up by Torrance's (1976a) challenge to educators:

> We need to develop better procedures for helping gifted students learn about the future. We need to help them invent alternative futures, evaluate these alternative futures, improve these alternatives, and make the choices about them that will make a difference in the kind of world we shall have. (p. 143)

Instructional Strategies

The criterion for selecting the particular programs we will discuss is their availability in the ERIC data base or the periodical literature that would enable the interested teacher or counselor access to examining the program for possible adaptation. An advantage of the federally-funded programs is that they tend to contain instruments for assessment and evaluation as well as recommendations for possible modifications. We will look at programs across content areas and by level in the arts and humanities, mathematics, science, business, career guidance and mentorships, and programs designed for special target groups such as minorities, rural isolates, and women.

Arts and Humanities

The Pittsburgh, Pennsylvania Allegheny Intermediate Unit (1978), with federal funding, developed a Career Education program conducted on Saturdays. It brought students in grades four through nine in contact with professionals in art, creative writing, dance, drama, media, and music. Structured experiences that enabled the children to engage in the same processes as the professionals combined acquisition of knowledge about careers, skill development in the area, and affective understandings in an interdisciplinary context. Their specification of objectives, activities, materials, and resources is useful information for adaptation either as a curricular or extracurricular effort.

At the secondary level, the Rhode Island State Council on the Arts (1977) has made extensive information available on an alternative program funded by the U.S. Office of Career Education, designed to develop understanding of self, knowledge of careers in the arts, and the relationship between the two. It includes a component for developing parental knowledge about careers in the arts. The program as offered carried academic credit, with students spending three afternoons in a selected art form, another afternoon taking electives, and the remaining half day in career education activities. The availability of detail on student selection, objectives, activities, procedures, and resources necessary for implementation, along with a positive external evaluation, suggest that the program could be successfully adapted.

Mathematics, Science, and Business

Business Related to Industry to Develop Gifted Education or BRIDGE (1979), is another program sponsored by the Office of Career Education for gifted high school juniors and seniors. One of its purposes was to involve business and industry with the schools to help the gifted increase their knowledge of careers, learn decision-making skills, increase self-confidence in career planning, improve written and oral communication skills, and improve work-related habits. Seminars were held to examine career options, learn how to make decisions, and clarify values. More than sixty businesses, industries, cultural, and educational institutions participated in the internship phase. Evaluation, based upon a field trial with 200 students, suggests that the major objectives were attained. Written materials are available detailing the project, its procedures, and evaluation instruments which would help in developing a comparable program at the local level.

Pinellie (1973) details a six-week Career Exploration program arranged with NASA personnel to allow the gifted and talented to work on a one-to-one basis in a variety of scientific areas: acoustics, computers, electronics, and aerospace technology. Research opportunities, field trips, and lectures broadened the total experience. Informal evaluation supports the effectiveness of this model, which could be transferred to other communities with the cooperation of universities and other research institutions and industries.

Career Guidance and Mentorships

Texas A & M University developed a program with funding from the Office of Career Education seeking to combine several elements of career development for the gifted and talented secondary learner (Borman, et al., 1977; Colson, 1980). The triadic community-based model incorporates a guidance laboratory experience in the first phase, combining educational, career, and self-awareness counseling with skill development in planning and decision making. The second phase calls for shadowing a university professor in a specified career area; the third phase is a working internship experience pairing the student with a mentor from business, industry, labor, or the professions. The effects of the year-long program were evaluated through a posttest control group design, documenting the advantages to program participants compared to untreated peers. The availability of methods, materials, and measures makes this a useful package for replication.

Another packet available through the ERIC system has been prepared by the Eugene, Oregon, school district (1978). It details the 12- to 18-week unpaid internships developed for gifted and talented 11th and 12th graders. This program also includes career counseling.

We should also mention the Mentor Academy Program (MAP) developed by Runion (1980), which has three components: (1) Basic Workshops, directed at creative problem solving, research skills, mentorship contract skills, and futuristics; (2) Synergistic Seminars which are content-based; and (3) the Mentor Exchange, wherein mentors, community members, and students come together under student leadership to share ideas. The elaborate program differs from other approaches in its focus on a closer relationship between intellectual inquiry within a community of scholars rather than on the guidance and counseling function.

Special Groups

Minority/Low Income

We found only one program describing a special career development program for minority, economically disadvantaged gifted. Moore (1978) reports on Professional Career Exploration Program for Minority and/or Low Income Gifted and Talented Tenth Graders (PCEP). This is a federally funded program out of Purdue University, implemented in Elkhart, Indiana, and Columbus, Ohio. After creating an advisory committee and hiring coordinators, the program identified students gifted in leadership, art, and in the intellectual domain, and located community placement sites. Students attended seminars for four weeks before being assigned one day per week for the next nine weeks to three different professions. The seminars continued twice weekly during the community exploration experience and thereafter, and included self-concept development, values clarification, lifestyles examination, career planning, discussion of the professional work ethic, and occupational and educational information. Students also kept logs describing the experience of shadowing the three individuals to whom they were matched. Group and individual career counseling was to have been included in the total program. Results of the evaluation, including measures of self-concept and career maturity as well as project-designed instruments, were not available at the time the project was reported. The program conforms to the elements typically believed appropriate for gifted and talented. If the program is truly tailored to the special needs of the target group, it appears to have promise for attaining the specified objectives.

Rural Gifted

We were unable to find many programs designed for gifted students isolated in rural areas. Rask (1980) reports a small-scale federally-funded project undertaken in rural Colorado which favored the six participants over the control group with respect to gains in career development skills and attitudes toward work. Similarly, Milne (1976) provides guidelines for working with special groups in the sponsored manual he and his co-workers prepared.

Females

Once again there is a paucity of materials specifically designed to deal with the career development needs of gifted girls and young women. Fox and her associates (Fox, 1976; Fox & Tobin, 1978; Tobin & Fox, 1980) report on the evolution of a career awareness model originally developed with elementary age children, but later refined for use with seventh grade girls selected from top scorers on the math talent search of the Johns Hopkins Study of Mathematically Precocious Youth. With the objective of persuading girls about the instrumental value of mathematics in their lives and the myriad opportunities that can be opened through the study of mathematics, the five-week summer program combined mathematics-related content with skill development in scientific reading, use of role models, and community research resources. Activities included field trips and lectures. Evaluative data suggests there were favorable responses from students, parents, and staff, at least over the short term. Ultimately, outcomes will have to be measured according to whether or not the program influences later mathematics course enrollments and career choices.

Project Choice (Fleming and Hollinger, 1979), funded under the Women's Educational Equity Act, was a fourteen-week career development program designed to help remove internal and external barriers to fulfillment of potential in gifted and talented high school young women. The diagnostic-prescriptive career development program was field-tested with 281 gifted and talented young women from six public, private, and parochial high schools. With special attention to the needs of ethnic and minority young women, the program was based on a model that included dealing with issues in women's socialization, acquiring career information, testing career alternatives against reality, and developing skills in goal setting and decision making. Special interventions elaborating on the general theme of planning life work, for those diagnosed as having low social self-esteem, fear of success, lack of assertiveness, or low achievement motivation, were implemented for half the young women so diagnosed. Career information workshops and mentorship experiences with over 100 women professionals representing traditional and nontraditional careers were important program components. Evaluation data suggests that participants with high attendance rates, with or without diagnosed internal barriers, showed increased career maturity. Progress in overcoming internal barriers was greater for high participants in the homogenous groups. The project manual contains all necessary materials for duplication, including identification procedures, exercises, project instruments, resource bibliographies, and sample scripts for conducting the 14 sessions.

Making It Work

The success of any educational program is largely determined by the care given to each of its parts. Career development programs for the gifted are no different. Attention to specific steps in planning, implementing, administering, providing resources for support, and evaluating make the difference between successful programs and those that fail. There are no shortcuts for reducing the process or eliminating bothersome elements without sacrificing quality and effectiveness.

Planning

To plan effectively, one needs a conception of the overall design. In the absence of elaborated models for program design, starting points would be an inventory of the gifted's special needs (Hoyt and Hebeler [1973]; Milne [1979]), and determination of the specific characteristics of the target population. The overall design exemplified in the comprehensive programs described in *Programs That Work* (1979) provides a useful framework for setting forth what needs to be done and for whom. It is important to be careful in articulation among and between levels, system constraints, and the time dimension. One should attend to sequential mapping of objectives, intended activities, and desired outcomes early in the process.

Implementation and Administration

Giving overall management responsibility to one individual can reduce headaches for everyone else. Diluting authority often accounts for negative program evaluations. No matter how inspired the plan, a problem in one area can contaminate or jeopardize all others; for example, an identification plan that selects a category of gifted different from those originally intended, or a book purchase order never sent.

Identifying Resources

An inventory of necessary resources—people, places, and things—is more crucial to career education than to general gifted and talented curriculum development, both because of the need to draw heavily on individuals outside the school and because of the scattered nature of materials that lend themselves to adaptation. As Karnes (1980) points out,

> Instructional materials in career education that are parallel with the interest and abilities of the gifted are presently unavailable. There is a paucity of instructional activities that are expressly designed to teach the processes of group dynamics. Relatively few instructional aids in futuristic problem solving are obtainable, especially for young students. (p. 222)

Nonetheless, some commercially available materials, for example, simulations in solving problems in jurisprudence, ecology, international conflict, space exploration, and financial markets, can supplement planned activities. Similarly, the creative teacher or counselor can adapt materials for achievement motivation, values clarification, and group dynamics. An increasing number of firms publish catalogues of resources for the gifted and talented, and Karnes and Collins's compendia (1980, 1981) identify potential sources.

We have already discussed the creation of networks to identify individuals and organizations to assist in a variety of roles in direct instruction, as mentors, and to provide internships. The effort to establish personal contact with potential contributors in the community is time-consuming, demanding, and requires conscientious bookkeeping. Parent groups can often help manage the pool, thus enhancing the school-community partnership and reducing the burden on the gifted specialist.

Assessing Outcomes

Program developers are often unenthusiastic about evaluation. Its role in the program is nonetheless increasingly important in the face of mounting pressures for accountability. Indeed, motivation for program evaluation ought to receive greater impetus from internal rather than external demand; gifted educators should feel the need to determine whether or not what they do makes a difference in the lives of children.

Evaluation has become more sophisticated; *Standards for Evaluations* of *Educational Programs, Projects, and Materials*, recently published by the Joint Committee on Standards for Educational Evaluation (1981), can go a long way, if followed, toward controlling quality. Central to evaluation is the selection of appropriate instruments to assess program outcomes and student growth. Unfortunately, the psychometric properties of many instruments developed at the local level are frequently unknown, or irrelevant to the program's central purposes. While not specifically developed for gifted and talented, the Career Education Measurement Series, five handbooks for evaluating career education programs developed by the National Center for Research in Vocational Education (1979), provides guidelines, references to existing measures, and assistance in construction of project-developed measures and plans to improve the quality of evaluation (Adams,1981;McCaslin,1981). Instruments are available that purport to measure career awareness, career planning and decision making, self-concept, and experience-based education. As has been the case throughout, however, most are designed for advanced secondary level use (McCaslin, 1981). Each of the federally-funded career education programs we described includes an evaluation component; additional guidance is available through reviewing project experience with instrumentation and evaluative approaches described in the reports. Assessment and evaluation are keys to program refinement and to overall determination of outcome. The need for long-term evaluation is equally true, but not ordinarily funded by external agencies. Thus, we may learn that a program has been beneficial immediately or shortly after it concludes, but the crucial test as to whether or not it effectively enhances career development over five or ten years into the future is never known.

Summary

We can summarize the status of career education for the gifted and talented in the early 1980s by looking at needs for the future. A great deal of research will be needed to chart the career development of diverse groups of gifted and talented as it unfolds for them into the next century. Much of what we now know is based on older studies that exclude women, minorities, rural, and handicapped gifted and talented youth. Nor do we understand the patterns of career development of those whose gifts and talents lie outside the traditional academic areas. Construction of appropriate models requires information about the patterns, needs, and characteristics of subclassifications of gifted growing up in a highly complex world of vast changes amid multiple forces. Information gathering must take the long view, that is, following career development histories through longitudinal studies, to show us the meaning of careers in the lives of gifted and talented individuals during particular life stages.

We must construct and test alternative models for career education of the gifted based on sound theoretical principles and empirical research findings. These models must be comprehensive in scope and articulated from level to level to permit individualization for special needs. Programs presently focus on a limited age range and often encompass only a brief summer experience or a one- or two-semester exposure during the secondary school years, and preschool and primary gifted are virtually ignored.

Content specialists who develop curriculum for the gifted need to look at the career implications of all disciplines. Making the career connections explicit is particularly important to special-needs gifted, for whom options may be forever closed unless they are informed about the consequences of their present planning decisions to future career choices. Mathematics is the most conspicuous example of a critical filter that eliminates many minorities and women from challenging and lucrative occupations.

We need to channel people and funds into development of materials and procedures, and undertake more developmental activity as to what to do with whom, how to do it, and what resources to use. We also need to learn more about what we accomplish in our our program development activities—what works, what does not, and for whom. Only long-term follow-up evaluation provides the answers to these questions. We must scrutinize individual components as well as the total program.

Finally, community involvement, particularly of parents of the gifted and talented, is vital to any real progress. Educators have an obligation to make parents full partners in planning for their children's futures. Without collaboration, no program is likely to result in great success. Parents, other adults in the community, and existing institutions can contribute substantially to material and informational resources. Parents and community members can provide support, nurturance, and encouragement to help all gifted and talented realize the bright and challenging futures to which they are entitled.

References

Adams, K. A. *Improving accountability of career education programs: Evaluation guidelines and checklists.* Paper presented at the meeting of the American Education Research Association, Los Angeles, April 1981.

Allegheny Intermediate Unit. *Career education program for the talented.* Pittsburgh, Pa.: 1978. (ERIC Document Reproduction Service No. ED 177 778)

Astin, H. S., and T. Myint. "Career development of young women during the post-high school years." *Journal of Counseling Psychology* 18 (1971): 369–93.

Benbow, C. P., and J. C. Stanley. "Sex differences in mathematical ability: Fact or artifact?" *Science* 210 (December 1980): 1262–64.

Bish, C. E. "Can we provide a better program for the able students?" *Bulletin of the National Association of Secondary School Principals* 42 (1958): 13–21.

Bloom, B. S. *The limits of learning: Studies of selected areas of talent development.* Paper presented at the meeting of the American Education Research Association, Los Angeles, April 1981.

Borman, C. *A unique opportunity for gifted and talented high school seniors.* Final report of the development of an exemplary career education model for the gifted and talented. College Station, Texas: Texas A and M University, June 1977. (ERIC Document Reproduction Service No. ED 165 382)

Boston, B. O. *The sorcerer's apprentice: A case study in the role of the mentor.* Reston, Va.: The Council for Exceptional Children, 1975.

Bouchard, T. J., Jr., and M. McGue. "Familial studies of intelligence: A review." *Science* 212 (May 1981): 1055–59.

Brandwein, P. F. *The gifted student as future scientist*. New York: Harcourt, Brace, 1955.

Cetron, M., and T. O'Toole. "Careers with a future: Where the jobs will be in the 1990s." *The Futurist* (June 1982).

Cidis, E. F. *Career education: An exceptional addition to a gifted curriculum* (ERIC Document Reproduction Service No. ED 189 781)

Coleman, J. S. *The adolescent society*. New York: Free Press, 1961.

Colson, S. "The evaluation of a community-based career education program for gifted and talented students as an administrative model for an alternative program." *Gifted Child Quarterly* 24 (1980): 101–6.

Conant, J. B. *The identification and education of the academically talented student in the American secondary school*. Washington, D.C.: National Education Association, 1958.

Diamond, E. E. *Issues of sex bias and sex fairness in career interest measurement*. Washington, D.C.: National Institute of Education, U.S. Government Printing Office, 1975.

Erikson, E. H. *Childhood and society*. New York: Norton, 1950.

Eugene School District 4J, Oregon. *High school internship project dissemination packet*. 1978. (ERIC Document Reproduction Service No. ED 168 225)

Flanigan, J. C., and W. W. Cooley. *Project TALENT: One-year follow-up studies*. Cooperative Research Project Number 2333. Pittsburgh, Pa.: School of Education, University of Pittsburgh, 1966.

Flanigan, J. C., D. V. Tiedeman, M. B. Willis, and D. H. McLaughlin. *The career data books: Results from Project Talent's five-year follow-up study*. Palo Alto, Calif.: American Institutes for Research, 1973.

Fleming, E. S., and C. L. Hollinger. "The multidimensionality of talent in adolescent young women." *Journal for the education of the gifted* 4 (1981): 188–98.

Fleming, E. S., and C. L. Hollinger. *Project choice: Creating her options in career exploration*. Newton, Mass.: Education Development Center, 1979.

Fox, L. H. "Career education for gifted pre-adolescents." *Gifted Child Quarterly* 20 (1976): 262–73.

Fox, L. H. "Programs for the gifted and talented." In *The gifted and the talented: Their growth and education*. Seventy-eighth yearbook of the National Society for the Study of Education: Part I. Edited by A.H. Passow. Chicago: The University of Chicago Press, 1979.

Fox, L. H., and D. Tobin. "Broadening career horizons for gifted girls." *G/C/T* 4 (September/October 1978): 18–22.

Fredrikson, R. H. "Career development and the gifted." In *New voices in counseling the gifted*. Edited by N. Colangelo and R.T. Zaffrann. Dubuque, Iowa: Kendall/Hunt, 1979.

Fredrickson, R. H., and J. W. M. Rothney, eds. *Recognizing and assisting multipotential youth*. Columbus, Ohio: Charles E. Merrill, 1972.

Gelatt, H. B., B. Varenhorts, R. Carey, and G. Miller. *Decisions and outcomes: A leader's guide*. New York: College Entrance Examination Board, 1973.

Gottfredson, L. S. *Race and sex differences in occupational aspirations: Their development and consequences for occupational segregation*. Baltimore, Md.: Center for Social Organization of Schools, Johns Hopkins University, 1978. (ERIC Document Reproduction Service No. ED 159 456)

Herr, E. L. "Career development and vocational guidance." In *Education and work*. Eighty-first yearbook of the National Society for the Study of Education: Part II. Edited by H.F. Silberman. Chicago: University of Chicago Press, 1982.

Herr, E. L. "Manpower policies, vocational guidance, and career development." In *Vocational guidance and human development*. Edited by E.L. Herr. Boston: Houghton Mifflin, 1974.

Herr, E. L., and A. Watanabe. "Counseling the gifted about career development." In *New voices in counseling the gifted*. Edited by N. Colangelo and R. T. Zaffrann. Dubuque, Iowa: Kendall/Hunt, 1979.

Hirsch, S. P. "Executive high school internships: A boon for the gifted and talented." *Teaching Exceptional Children* 9 (1976): 22–23.

Hoyt, K. B. *Career education for special populations. Monographs on career education*. Washington, D.C.: Office of Career Education, 1976.

Hoyt, K. B. "Career education for gifted and talented persons." *Roeper Review* 1 (1978): 9–11.

Hoyt, K. B., and J. R. Hebeler. *Career education for gifted and talented persons*. College Park, Md.: University of Maryland, 1973.

Joint Committee on Standards for Educational Evaluation. *Standards for evaluations of educational programs, projects, and materials*. New York: McGraw-Hill, 1981.

Jordaan, J. P., and M. B. Heyde. *Vocational development during the high school years*. New York: Teachers College Press, 1978.

Karnes, F. A., and E. C. Collins. *Assessment in gifted education*. Springfield, Ill.: Charles C. Thomas, 1981.

Karnes, F. A., and E. C. Collins. *Handbook of instructional resources and references for teaching the gifted*. Boston: Allyn and Bacon, 1980.

Maker, C. J. *Curriculum development for the gifted*. Rockville, Md.: Aspen, 1982.

Marini, M. M., and E. Greenberger. "Sex differences in educational aspirations and expectations." *American Educational Research Journal* 15 (1978): 67–79.

Marland, S. P., Jr. *Education of the gifted and talented*. Washington, D.C.: U.S. Government Printing Office, 1972.

McCaslin, N. L. *Using paper and pencil tests in evaluating career education*. Paper presented at the meeting of the American Educational Research Association, Los Angeles, April 1981.

Mead, M. *Coming of age in Samoa*. New York: William Morrow, 1928.

Milne, B. G., and K. J. Lindekugel. *Vocational education: An opportunity for the gifted and talented students*. Vermillion, S. Dak.: South Dakota University, 1976. (ERIC Document Reproduction Service No. ED 146 454)

Milne, B. G. "Career education." *The gifted and the talented: Their education and development*. Seventy-eighth yearbook of the National Society for the Study of Education: Part I. Edited by A. H. Passow. Chicago: The University of Chicago Press, 1979.

Moore, B. A. "Career education for disadvantaged, gifted high school students." *Gifted Child Quarterly* 22 (1978): 332–37.

National Academy of Sciences. *Doctorate recipients from United States Universities*, 1978.

National Center for Research in Vocational Education. *The career education measurement series*. Columbus, Ohio: Ohio State University, 1979.

Newland, T. E. *The gifted in socioeducational perspective*. Englewood Cliffs, N.J.: Prentice-Hall, 1976.

Office of Career Education, Office of Education, U.S. Department of Health, Education, and Welfare. *Career education programs that work*. Washington, D.C.: U.S. Government Printing Office, 1979.

OrRico, M. J., and J. F. Feldhusen. "Career education for the gifted, creative and talented." *G/C/T* 10 (November/December 1979): 37–40.

Osipow, S. H. *Theories of career development.* 2nd ed. Englewood Cliffs, N.J.: Prentice-Hall, 1973.

Peng, S. S., W. B. Fetters, and A. J. Kolstad. *High school and beyond: A national longitudinal study for the 1980s: A capsule description of high school students.* Washington, D.C.: National Center for Education Statisitics, U.S. Government Printing Office, 1981.

Perrone, P. A., W. Karshner, and R. Male. *The career development needs of talented students: A perspective for counselors.* Madison, Wisc.: University of Wisconsin, 1979. (ERIC Document Reproduction Service No. ED 185 731)

Pinellie, T. E. "Utilizing community resources in programming for the gifted." *Gifted Child Quarterly* 17 (1973): 199–202.

Rask, G. *A career education program for the gifted and talented in rural Colorado. (Rural internship program.)* Pueblo, Colo.: South Central Board of Cooperative Educational Services, 1980. (ERIC Document Reproduction Service No. ED 190 798)

Rhode Island State Council on the Arts. *A curriculum for career education in the arts.* Providence, Rhode Island, 1977. (ERIC Document Reproduction Service No. ED 172 005)

Rodenstein, J., L. R. Pfleger, and N. Colangelo. "Career development of gifted women." *Gifted Child Quarterly* 21 (1977): 340–58.

Rothney, J. W. M. "Longitudinal evidence of multipotentiality." In *Recognizing and assisting multipotential youth.* Edited by R.H. Fredrickson and J.W.M. Rothney. Columbus, Ohio: Charles E. Merrill, 1972.

Runions, T. "The mentor academy program: Educating the gifted/talented for the 80s." *Gifted Child Quarterly* 24 (1980): 152–57.

Sanborn, M. P. "Career development: Problems of gifted and talented students." In *New voices in counseling the gifted.* Edited by N. Colangelo and R. T. Zaffrann. Dubuque, Iowa: Kendall/Hunt, 1979.

Schab, F. "Work ethic of gifted black adolescents." *Journal of Youth and Adolescence* 7 (1978): 295–99.

Sears, P. S., and A.H. Barbee. "Career and life satisfactions among Terman's gifted women." In *The gifted and the creative: A 50 year perspective.* Edited by J. C. Stanley, W. C. George, and C. H. Solano. Baltimore, Md.: The Johns Hopkins University Press, 1977.

Sellin, D. F., and J. W. Birch. *Educating gifted and talented learners.* Rockville, Md.: Aspen, 1980.

Super, D. E., and P. L. Overstreet. *The vocational maturity of ninth grade boys.* New York: Teachers College Press, 1957.

Super, D. E., and D. T. Hall. "Career development: Exploration and planning." In *Annual Review of Psychology*, vol. 29. Edited by M.R. Rosenzweig and L. W. Porter. Palo Alto, Calif.: Annual Reviews, 1978.

Sweet, H. D. "A mentor program—Possibilities unlimited." *G/C/T* 15 (November/December 1980): 40–43.

Tannenbaum, A. J. "Pre-Sputnik to post-Watergate concern about the gifted." In *The gifted and the talented: Their education and development.* Seventy-eighth yearbook of the National Society for the Study of Education: Part I. Edited by A. H. Passow. Chicago: The University of Chicago Press, 1979.

Terman, L. M. "The discovery and encouragement of exceptional talent." *American Psychologist* 9 (1954): 221–30.

Terman, L. M., and M. H. Oden. *The gifted group at mid-life: Genetic studies of genius*, vol. 5. Stanford, Calif.: Stanford University Press, 1959.

Tobin, D., and L. H. Fox. "Career interests and career education: A key to change." In *Women and the mathematical mystique*. Edited by L. H. Fox, L. Brody, and D. Tobin. Baltimore, Md.: Johns Hopkins University Press, 1980.

Toffler, A. *Third wave*. New York: Bantam, 1981.

Torrance, E. P. "Future careers for gifted and talented students." *Gifted Child Quarterly* 20 (1976a): 142–56.

Torrance, E. P. *Future problem solving and career education*. Athens, Ga.: College of Education, University of Georgia, 1976b.

Torrance, E. P. "Giftedness in solving future problems." *Journal of Creative Behavior* 12 (1978a): 75–86.

Torrance, E. P. "Helping your G/C/T child learn about the future." *G/C/T* 1 (January/February 1978b): 28–29.

Torrance, E. P. *Sociodrama and career education*. Athens, Ga.: College of Education, University of Georgia, 1976c.

Torrance, E. P. "Unique needs of the creative child and adult." In *The gifted and the talented: Their education and development*. Seventy-eighth yearbook of the National Society for the Study of Education: Part I. Edited by A. H. Passow. Chicago: The University of Chicago Press, 1979.

Torrance, E. P., and F. Kaufman. "Teacher education for career education of the gifted and talented." *Gifted Child Quarterly* 21 (1977): 176–85.

Turner, T. N. "A stylish wedding: Infusing career education into creative writing and composition." *English Journal* (October 1979): 59–62.

U.S. Department of Labor Bureau of Labor Statistics. *Employment and unemployment during 1981: An analysis*. Special Labor Force Report No. 234. Washington, D.C.: U.S. Government Printing Office, 1982.

Vidulich, R. N., D. G. Sachs, and J.F. Christman. *Career choice and change in high-ability young women*. Paper presented at the Annual Convention of the Southeastern Psychological Association, Atlanta, Ga., March 1978.

Viernstein, M. C., and R. Hogan. "Parental personality factors and achievement motivation in talented adolescents." *Journal of Youth and Adolescence* 4 (1975): 183–90.

Watley, D. J. "Multipotentiality among bright black youth." In *Recognizing and assisting multipotential youth*. Edited by R. H. Fredrickson and J. W. M. Rothney. Columbus, Ohio: Charles E. Merrill, 1972.

Wolfe, D. *America's resources of specialized talent*. New York: Harper and Row, 1954.

Yonkers City School District. *BRIDGE: Business relating to industry to develop gifted education—A career education for the gifted and talented*. Yonkers, New York, 1979. (ERIC Document Reproduction Service No. ED 189 297)

11

Methods of Developing Creativity

Beverly N. Parke

During the past twenty years, few topics have received as much attention in research, textbooks, and popular educational magazines as has creativity. It seems that everywhere you look, you find a new game, curricular strategy, or workbook designed to ensure that students meet their creative potential. Everything from needlepoint kits to chemistry sets are sold with the promise of building creativity. Teachers have been deluged with information on creativity through the educational media and professional development activities.

It would seem that with all the interest the topic has aroused, we would by now have clearer notions as to what it is, how it is encouraged, and how it is maintained. But such is not the case. Creativity remains an elusive concept, the focus of a great deal of debate as to its origin, characteristics, prevalence, processes, and its place in education.

While creativity did receive mention in educational literature early in this century, the work of J.P. Guilford in the late 1950s initiated the heightened interest of the past two decades. Guilford's Structure of the Intellect (SI) Model (Guilford, 1967) presented an expanded concept of human intelligence from previous theories. His model (see Figure 1.5), derived through factor analysis, outlined 120 factors he believed to comprise intelligence, and showed how they interrelate. This model categorizes thinking processes according to content area, complexity of the product produced, and the mental operation involved. Among the more significant impacts of the SI model was its contribution to the area of creativity. Along with factors traditionally thought to be part of intelligence, such as memory, convergent production, and awareness, Guilford gave equal attention to the areas of divergent production and evaluation in classifying the operations, or processes, involved in the intellect. This departure legitimized the place of creative thinking functions within the framework of the mind. Divergent production, the ability to produce various responses to a given task or question, is the primary operation involved in creativity. Fluency, flexibility, originality, and elaboration, the basic factors of divergent production as outlined by Guilford, are guideposts for development of creative abilities. The factors associated with evaluation, the ability to make judgments about the worth or value of a response according to some criteria, complement divergent production by providing the mechanism for judging responses or products on set criteria or by new criteria established by the producer. Thus, unique divergent responses are not only generated within the intellectual structure of the model, but are also evaluated, allowing for the growth and development of individual thought.

The SI model's recognition of creative thinking operations encouraged others to continue explorations into this area. Two particularly significant ideas have since emerged: the expanded notion of intelligence and multiple talents, and the concept of encouraging creativity through planned experience. The appropriateness of teaching creativity in the classroom is based on these two premises.

Guilford's model expanded the traditional concepts about intelligence and paved the way for the multiple talent concepts of human potential and giftedness that emerged in the 1960s. One such model developed by Taylor (1964), "Taylor's Talent Totem Poles," grouped abilities based on practical needs derived from the workplace. He listed six talents—academic, creative (and productive), evaluative decision making, planning, forecasting, and communication—upon which students could be rank-ordered to establish a profile of abilities. Taylor thought that by assessing more areas of talent, more students would fall above the average on at least one talent area. He believed that thirty percent of the students would fall in the upper ten percent on at least one of the specified talent areas. This multiple talent approach again highlighted the notion that intelligence is a combination of many factors and that performance may vary across ability levels. He saw creativity as one of the talent areas to consider when assessing and developing abilities.

Research studies indicate that factors commonly associated with creativity, such as fluency, flexibility, originality, and elaboration, can be encouraged, contrary to the once popular belief that "either you have it or you don't." Over the past thirty years, studies have consistently shown that training has a measurable positive effect on creative production. Researchers have studied methods to increase originality; in one study, Ridley and Birney (1967) considered the effects of training procedures on originality scores on Guilford's Unusual Uses Test. They found that when instructed to produce original responses, subjects scored higher on the test's originality index, indicating an increase in original responses. A creative problem-solving course offered through the University of Buffalo has been studied extensively since 1959. Results of these studies (Meadow and Parnes, 1959; Meadow et al., 1959; Parnes, 1967; Reese et al., 1976) point out that a course designed to train creative problem solving can result in increased performance on tests of creative thinking and that the gains may last across time and be transferred to other situations.

There appears to be consensus that creativity is among the multiple abilities involved in intelligence and that its various factors can be encouraged to develop, but there are still varying opinions concerning the nature of creativity and how it can best be nurtured. The controversies, however, do not overshadow the one underlying goal of educators, researchers, psychologists, and philosophers who deal with creativity in the educational systems—to provide the best possible instructional experience for educating the whole child.

Essential Concepts in Creativity

To provide appropriate educational programs for students that take into account the creative elements of their intellect, one must understand what creativity is, the nature of the creative individual, the role the school and community play in developing a student's creative potential. These concepts are the background for developing curricular practices to enhance creativity.

Creativity—An Integrated Concept

Definitions of creativity are plentiful, with each reflecting a particular approach to a complex intellectual function. Some definitions are based on primarily cognitive processes; others stress affective and emotional approaches. Still others define creativity in terms of higher states of awareness beyond the conscious mind. What is the true nature of creativity?

Clark's (1979) integrated model of creativity synthesizes past definitions into a Creativity Circle, as shown in Figure 11-1. Based on Jung's unity circle (Jung, 1964), it categorizes creativity into "(a) rational thinking; (b) high levels of emotional develop-

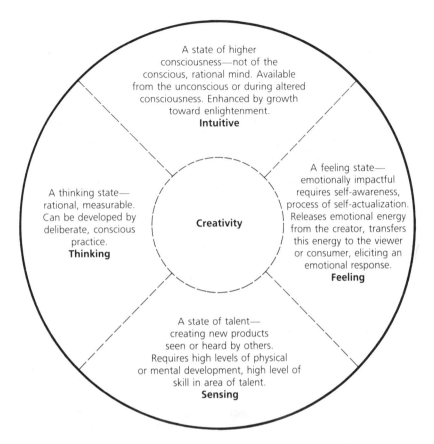

Figure 11-1 THE CREATIVITY CIRCLE

From B. Clark, *Growing Up Gifted* (Columbus, Ohio: Charles E. Merrill, 1979).

ment or feeling; (c) talent and high levels of mental and physical development; and (d) higher levels of consciousness, resulting in use of imagery, fantasy, and break-throughs to the preconscious or unconscious states" (Clark, 1979, p. 245). Clark believes the integration of these four functions releases creativity, and that restriction of any one function reduces creativity. Besides this synthesized functioning, creativity "includes a spark from another dimension" (p. 244):

> When viewed from this common base, instead of describing different phenomena or even different types of creativity, all of these perceptions may be only fragments of the total; creativity includes all of these ideas and more. Thinking, feeling, sensing, and intuiting unify to become creativity. Any one function operating alone could not create. Only as the functions combine and interact, drawing from and giving to each other, can creativity occur. (Clark, 1979, p. 246).

Most of the literature on creativity falls into the *rational thinking function* of Clark's Creativity Circle. She categorizes the works of experts on creativity such as Torrance (1977) and Guilford (1950) in this area. Each considers creativity a thinking skill that can be developed through training, as we see in these definitions of creativity and creative individuals:

- " . . . Process of sensing problems or gaps in information, forming ideas or hypotheses, testing and modifying these hypotheses, and communicating the results" (Torrance, 1977, p. 6)

- " . . . Those patterns of traits that are characteristic of creative persons. A creative pattern is manifest in creative behavior, which includes such activities as inventing, designing, contriving, composing, and planning. People who exhibit these types of behaviors to a marked degree are recognized as being creative" (Guilford, 1950, p. 444)

- " . . . Forming of associative elements into new combinations which either meet specified requirements or are in some way useful" (Mednick, 1962, p. 221)

- " . . . Combination of flexibility, originality, and sensitivity to ideas which enables the learner to break away from usual sequences of thought into different and productive sequences, the result of which gives satisfaction to himself and possibly others" (Jones, 1972, p. 7)

Each definition relies on manipulation of ideas in a new and different way and implies or states that the result of this process is in some way productive, useful, or acceptable in a more generalizable sense. Growth in the rational thinking function can be assessed with instruments such as the Torrance Test of Creative Thinking, the Remote Associates Test, and the Minnesota Test of Creative Thinking.

Clark says those who adhere to the *feeling function* of creativity "focus on the emotional well-being and self-actualizing qualities of the human being. For them, creativity forms more of an attitude or belief system that permeates all the life choices and activities of the creative person. It is a concept of health, naturalness, intunedness, and development of unique potentials" (p. 252).

The researchers most closely associated with this view are Maslow (1968), Rogers (1962), and May (1959): They describe creativity as:

- "Fundamental characteristic, inherent in human nature, a potentiality given to all or most human beings at birth (p. 138) . . . seem(s) to be an epiphenomenon of . . . greater wholeness and integration (p. 141) . . . almost synonymous with . . . essential humanness." (Maslow, 1968, p. 145)
- "The mainspring of creativity . . . man's tendency to actualize himself, to become his potentialities." (Rogers, 1959, p. 72)
- "The encounter of the intensively conscious human being with his or her world." (May, 1975, p. 56)

These definitions cast the ability to function creatively on the individual's healthy physiological and psychological development. Maslow (1968) associates creative abilities with a person's development toward self-actualization. The freer people are to draw on their potentialities, the more likely they will function creatively. The rational thinking function relies more heavily on ideas and tests as evidence of creativity; the feeling function finds its evidence in one's interaction with the environment; but neither function is totally separate from the other. Rather, they join with the remaining functions to make an integrated holistic response.

The *talent sensing function* of the Creativity Circle involves creation of products in skill areas. Creation of the new forms calls on a high level of physical and mental development, and products are evaluated according to "how original, inventive, or imaginative the product is" (Clark, 1979; p. 256). Renzulli (1973) is among those defining creativity in these terms: "Creativity is the production of an idea or product that is new, original, or satisfying to the creator or to someone else . . . " (Renzulli, 1973, p. 3)

The final function, the *intuitive higher levels of consciousness function*, has had the least research. Clark cautions, "as we examine the higher levels of consciousness aspect of creativity, we must be aware that much of what happens can only be understood experientially and that rational, verbal explanations dilute the events, for the essence of the experience may be changed by its description" (p. 257). Others mention:

- "There is reason to think that much of the creative process is intuitive in nature and that it entails a work of the mind prior to its arising to the conscious level and certainly also prior to its being in expressible form. It is most likely preconscious, nonverbal or preverbal . . . " (Taylor, 1963, p. 4)
- "Creativity is a dawning of the psychedelic powers of man which can transform him from a rational being into a super-rational one through the use of psychedelia, hypnosis, religious or meditational exercises, mysticism, and what have you." (Gowan, 1972, p. 6)

To fully function creatively in this area, one must have all levels of consciousness readily available and be able to switch from one to another.

Creative Process

The four quadrants of the Creativity Circle are highly developed and interacting in the creative individual. Process, product, intuition, and skill development combine as the process takes place. Wallas (1926) introduced evidence of the interaction of functions in the four distinct but overlapping stages of thought involved in creative production. They are *preparation*, during which one defines the problem, gathers information, and generates an approach to finding the solution; *incubation*, during which time one puts the problem out of the conscious mind; *illumination*, where the solution comes without effort; and *verification*, in which one tests and revises the product or solution as it evolves into its final form. Although the four functions are interactive, each stage in process clearly relies more heavily on certain functions. Preparation involves development of each quadrant; incubation relies most directly on the intuitive area, as does illumination; and verification draws on the functions of the rational, emotional, and skill development functions.

The Creative Individual

Most research into the personality of the creative individual has been conducted on adults (Barron, 1963; Barron, 1971; Crutchfield, 1962; MacKinnon, 1966; Roe, 1952). Inferences to early childhood years are often retrospective. We do have a profile of the creative individual, however, perhaps best represented in MacKinnon's

(1966) studies. He studied a group of eminent architects, nominated by their colleagues as representing distinctly different levels of creative achievement. They were given a battery of tests that resulted in this list of traits:

1 High level of effective intelligence
2 Openness to experience
3 Freedom from crippling restraints and impoverishing inhibitions
4 Esthetic sensitivity
5 Cognitive flexibility
6 Independence in thought and action
7 High level of creative energy
8 Unquestioning commitment to creative endeavor
9 Unceasing striving for solutions to the even more difficult problems [they] constantly set for [themselves]. (p. 156)

Recent studies of the brain add even more insight into the creative individual. From the research, it appears that the brain has laterality, and that each side specializes in different abilities. Studies of epileptic patients in whom the communication pathway between the two lobes has been severed, conclude that each hemisphere perceives its own reality in its own way. It appears therefore, that human brain functions develop asymmetrically, with each side specializing in certain functions. The nature of the task to be accomplished determines which side will be used. In most people, the left hemisphere is involved with the verbal-analytic processes and is responsible for the language base. Spatial-global processes take place in the right hemisphere. The two modes of thinking are complex, yet complementary. Edwards (1979, p. 40) lists the following traits for each hemisphere:

Left	Right
verbal	nonverbal
analytic	synthetic
symbolic	concrete
abstract	analogic
temporal	nontemporal
rational	nonrational
digital	spatial
logical	intuitive
linear	holistic

The creative person has the ability to make the cognitive switch from one hemisphere to the other. Most creative functions seem to be associated with the processes of the right hemisphere; however, abilities associated with the left hemisphere also enter into the process. The holistic, intuitive mode that relies heavily on images and visualizations can be explicated through use of the verbal, rational skills of the other side. The creative person appears to have ready access to both hemispheres and can use them jointly in the process of creative production.

Creativity and Giftedness

A number of researchers (Getzels and Jackson, 1962; Wallach and Kogan, 1965; Welsh, 1977) have studied the relationship between intelligence and creativity. These and other studies have sought to determine how the functions interrelate, if they are distinct from each other, and the personality correlates of those who fall into either group. Research is ongoing, with many questions yet to be answered. Getzels and Jackson administered five creativity tests and traditional measures of intelligence to identify four groups of students—high intelligence/high creative, high intelligence/low creative, low intelligence/high creative, and low intelligence/low creative. Yet the creativity tests they used correlated significantly with the intelligence measures, presenting a question as to whether or not they actually measured two distinct abilities.

A second problem lies in defining either term—intelligence or creativity. There is no consensus as to the components or dimensions of either, so it is difficult to compare them. Do IQ tests actually measure intelligence? Do creativity tests measure the totality of the ability? Probably not, and without adequate instrumentation to measure these phenomena, making the distinctions becomes increasingly complex.

Gowan (1981) views creativity as a "threshold variable," which can, however, be viewed in relation to intelligence. Using traditional measures such as IQ tests and creativity measures, intelligence and creativity correlate highly below 120 IQ and are virtually independent above that level. Yamamoto (1965) estimates the true correlation at approximately .88, a very high association. He says this correlation diminishes as the IQ factor increases. Guilford reports similar results, after studying eight hundred ninth grade students using measures of verbal intelligence tests and verbal divergent-production tests. He concludes from the range of test scores that "below an IQ of 120 in the population the correlation is higher and above an IQ of 120 it is lower" (p. 1).

These results seem to indicate that when identifying giftedness solely on traditional IQ measures, many highly creative students may be missed. The multiple-talent approaches to intelligence and giftedness necessitate identification through multiple measures. From the Yamamoto and Guilford studies, we see that broad definitions of giftedness, inclusive of creativity, must be followed with broad, multifaceted assessment procedures.

Guilford's SI Model (see Figure 1.4) depicted creativity as a component of intelligence rather than a separate ability. Integration appears to be a much more meaningful approach than continuing an artificial dichotomy. While there appears to be a threshold at which the factors as they are traditionally defined become independent from each other, they are still highly intertwined. It could very well be that demonstrated giftedness is really intellectual functioning at its height—the ultimate creative function.

Encouraging Creativity Through Opportunity and Training

Creativity, then, is an encompassing concept, but its appearance must be encouraged. Schools and community have a role in ensuring that this happens. Both arenas have the means and ability to provide both opportunity for creative expression and training for its development. As Hudgins (1977) states, "creativity demands continuing emphasis upon divergent thinking, coupled with discipline" (p. 290).

Schools are in the unique position of seeing students almost daily during most of their formative years, and their opportunity to make an impact is obvious. Many school programs assume they can make a person creative with a thirty-minute "creativity period" twice a week, but this is not the case. Hudgins says, "the intention of programs is not to build creative people, but to nurture the creativity in each person" (p. 289). This is not accomplished through "creativity periods," but through entwining opportunities for creative expression throughout the curriculum and the school day. Torrance (1977) lists these guidelines for the school (p. 24):

1   Provide opportunity for creative expression
2   Develop skills for creative learning
3   Reward creative achievement
4   Establish creative relationships with the children

By combining opportunity and skill development in the curricular approach and learning strategies, schools will begin to enhance student's creativity. Specific guidelines are found later in this chapter.

The community also has a role to play in developing individual creativity. Rogers (1962) states that psychological freedom and safety are necessary to the emergence of creativity. Unless communities accept creativity as a valuable ability, schools will not have the necessary support to integrate its development into the curriculum. Krippner (1967) says that to nurture creativity, we must avoid stating or implying these notions:

- Everything you do must be useful.
- Everything you do must be successful.
- Everything you do must be perfect.
- Everyone you know must like you.
- You must not prefer solitude to togetherness.
- Remember concentrated attention and keep it holy.
- You must not diverge from culturally-imposed sex norms.
- You must not express excessive emotional feeling.
- You must not be ambiguous.
- You must not rock the cultural boat.

The community is in a position to provide resources for its youth to help them enhance their abilities; among other things, this requires support of the artistic community. Students need to see creative productions to help them develop and evaluate their own work, and must speak with practicing artists and creative producers to exchange ideas and grow. Through its nurturance and acceptance of artistic and creative resources and institutions, the community assures its young that it values creativity and excellence and that those qualities play an important role in society.

Preschool and Elementary Concepts in Creativity

Creativity begins to emerge in young children's play and exploration. As they start to interact with their environment, they are constantly probing, testing, and discovering. During the early years, the imaginaton develops through play as children learn about their world. Shockingly, we find that creative imagination seems to peak at between four and four-and-one-half years. In many children, a drop is apparent by age five (Andrews, 1930). Whether this is a function of development or of societal and cultural influences is not certain; however, Torrance (1977) reports that growth in creative thinking, as measured by the Torrance Test of Creative Thinking, grows from first to third grades and drops sharply in fourth-grade children. His cross-cultural studies suggest that this is a societal, not biological, phenomenon. If this is the case, how can we reverse these situations to encourage creativity in preschool and elementary aged children?

Torrance (1977) states that "people fundamentally prefer to learn in creative ways—by exploring, manipulating, questioning, experimenting, risking, testing, and modifying ideas . . . [and] recent research suggests that many things, though not all, can be learned more effectively and economically in creative ways" (p. 22). The teacher can encourage creative expression and development by integrating opportunities for growth in this area throughout the curriculum and school day.

First, create an atmosphere that allows creative expression. The fear of being wrong may be students' greatest deterrent to attempting originality and new ideas (DeBono, 1969). A nonthreatening, psychologically safe environment is crucial to the development of creative abilities. The teacher must respect each child's uniqueness and the child must feel free to exhibit and explore that uniqueness. Toward this end, Torrance (1965) offers guidelines for teachers:

- Be respectful of unusual questions.
- Be respectful of imaginative, unusual ideas.
- Show your pupils that their ideas have value.
- Occasionally have pupils do something "for practice" without threat of evaluation.
- Tie in evaluation with causes and consequences. (p. 43)

Besides providing psychological safety, the classroom environment should offer sensory stimulation. An abundance of various types of materials should be available for students to manipulate, explore and utilize. Visual, auditory, and tactile experience and expression should be encouraged as students dabble in their thoughts and imaginations. The environment must facilitate students' growth as they seek to extend themselves and their creativity. A psychologically safe and at the same time stimulating environment is the basis for building opportunities for creative expression.

Second, focus primarily on the processes of creative production, rather than the products. Young children naturally engage in the processes we associate with creativity. In their play, they actively imagine and act out situations, explore their physical and emotional limitations, manipulate sounds in attempts to communicate in new and different ways, and so on. The natural extension of this developmental pattern is to encourage this divergent thinking and expression. With young children, we should emphasize process, not product. This is the time to develop abilities to predict possible outcomes, generate possible solutions to a problem, develop new and exciting ideas and applications of ideas, embellish ideas and see their implications, and explore new media and modes of expression. Opportunities to do these things must be present in an atmosphere that assures the student he can take risks without fear of punishment; at this stage, students should learn to enjoy taking risks and extending themselves to find new modes of expression. Creativity is playful; capitalizing on students' playfulness makes training the processes of creativity a delightful experience.

Third, initiate the process of training. As mentioned previously, evidence indicates that training can result in increased creative production. Greater attention to technique appears to be one means of unlocking creative talents. Callahan (1978) reports a study by Maltzman, Bogartz, and Breger in which subjects were asked to make repeated associations to a word list. Over five presentations, subjects' responses became statistically more original. It appears that when we ask students to extend their creative abilities, they are quite able to do so.

One approach to training technique deals with the fluency, flexibility, originality, and elaboration processes of creativity. Many programs and materials are available for helping teachers present these skills. One technique, brainstorming, has received considerable attention. Gallagher (1975) cautions that wholesale use of such techniques to train process may turn into simply a game unless they are made meaningful. The popular flexibility exercise, "How many uses can you think of for a brick?" can build the ability to approach problems from many different angles; this application of training is essential for learning to identify a variety of solutions for problems.

Teachers must also be alert to opportunities for training both hemispheres of the brain. Chosen tasks or activities are more likely to activate one side than the other. Edwards's *Drawing on the Right Side of the Brain* presents a unique approach for teaching drawing with activities geared to assessing the right hemisphere. Edwards's premise is that students can be trained to know how to tap into the right brain and will dramatically improve their drawing by making this transition.

The second approach to training technique deals less with rational processes and more with talent and sensory functions of creativity. Talented students should begin the process of training technique in their area of talent at an early age. A student with talent in art should begin to explore and manipulate color, line, tone, and composition; a dancer can begin to learn movement techniques; a writer can initiate manipulation of words, phrases, and expressions to see how they relate in communication.

Patrick (1937) asked a group of poets to draw a landscape picture based on a poem, and asked a comparison group of untrained amateurs to do the same. Comparing their products, Patrick noted that the trained professionals were able to draw on the discipline and conventions of the craft and produced products with a greater variation of expression. Hudgins (1977) comments on the study, "What comes through is the increased precision and opportunity to express oneself in intended ways that is made possible by the mastery of the art. Teachers who are afraid that providing standards of excellence for children and giving them basic skills and techniques may rob them of creative spontaneity should take heart from these findings" (pp. 278–79).

Fourth, help children explore the full range of their creative potential. Creative products are not limited to creative writing, art, or dance; the range of creative expression is endless, and we must help elementary and preschool children explore their range of creative potential. Multiple outlets for creative expression can accomplish this. Providing areas for art, music, and movement is a beginning, but we must go beyond those conventional approaches to seek new ways to experience and communicate. Provocative questions, exploring the unknown, and solving problems in unique new ways can initiate the process of self-discovery. Students with a particular talent in one area often prefer to deal solely with that medium; for example, a student who is good at art may prefer only to draw. We must encourage that child to try to express the same ideas and emotions in a different way—perhaps through dance.

This exploration involves trial and error; students will experience some successes and some failures. What becomes important is the quest, the discovery, and the adventure of learning and trying new things in a new way. As students begin this process, they open up a new set of responses and outlets to their abilities and can begin to draw clearer notions of what they are and what they are capable of producing.

Next, bring the child into contact with people who are actively engaged in creative production. In biographies of eminent people, we find a consistency: there is nearly always one person who provided the guidance or inspiration that changed their lives. Mentors can be extremely influential in a child's life, and increasingly important as the child grows older. At an early age, it is not as important to find one person with whom the child can develop a special relationship as it is to provide exposure to many talented people. They should have a chance to talk to these people about their lives and their work, to give them a frame of reference for looking at their own work and lives. It also helps them explore their potential through exposure to options they may not know about. A renowned jazz musician tells how he studied classical music for years, until a teacher saw his interest in jazz and introduced him to a local jazz musician. This exposure and the encouragement that followed resulted in his current pursuit of composing and performing jazz.

Also, begin to provide outlets, public and private, for creative products. While preschool and elementary students will primarily engage in developing the processes and techniques of creativity, their products are still important. Creative products provide the means of training the processes in context, and give them meaning and purpose. Not all products are for public viewing; most are for instructional purposes. Even young children, however, should have the opportunity to share products publicly. Students may wish to submit writings to journals that publish children's writing, or publish their own journal, hold an art show or auction, assemble a talent review, or participate in activities such as the Future Problem Solving Bowl.

Whatever the outlet, these activities help students begin the process of evaluation. They receive feedback from their audience, which may be classmates, a friend, parents, or an assembly of people. Whatever the audience, the exposure and public response helps them begin to mold their perceptions of their abilities and the results of their creative endeavors.

Last, begin to teach mechanisms for self-evaluation. As mentioned, evaluation is an important part of the creative process. Early on, students should begin to evaluate their own work. This skill does not come naturally; rather, you must build specific provisions for evaluation into the process. As students learn the techniques of their craft, these can be used as criteria for measuring. Personal feelings also enter into evaluation; students may wish to comment publicly on their work, or they may wish to keep their assessments to themselves. In that case, keeping a journal of reactions can be a useful personal evaluation tool. How the evaluation is expressed is not as important as the fact that it is done in some form.

The Creative Problem Solving method employs strategies for evaluating ideas (Gillespie, 1972), including developing criteria for evaluation, weighing factors that have an impact on the criteria, developing an evaluation grid on which to rate the factors, and then taking final action. This type of planned evaluation process provides a model for other types of evaluative activities. Even at an early age, students should learn to reflect critically on their work and themselves to enhance growth and development.

Helping preschool and elementary students develop their creative potential is a matter of continuing the natural processes in their development and growth. For the teacher, the task is to continue to open up new horizons to the students and guide their exploration with care and understanding.

Nurturing the Secondary Student

As students begin to develop their creative potential and become more adept at using the creative functions, the role of the educator begins to change. With younger students, one first helps them explore the range of their abilities. As the student matures, one helps to fine-tune those abilities.

First, although process is still important, focus more on product. At this stage in the students' development, they should begin to be more concerned with the products they generate. If they have been properly instructed up to this point, they should be in touch with their creative processes and know how to best harness their abilities. With this insight, they are now in the position to make the most of their talents.

The new focus on product does not minimize the importance of continuing to train process; rather, the emphasis shifts. For the more advanced student, process alone is not enough. Students must be concerned with types of products, quality of the products, and how best to express creativity through what they choose to produce.

Second, encourage students to continue exploring the range of their creative potential. They should feel free to test new approaches to their art and ideas, try new media in new environments, and new audiences through new means of communication. Teachers should feel free to explore their abilities with the students, modeling risk-taking behavior. Interdisciplinary courses are a natural forum for exploration. Blending ideas from different curricular areas, looking for similarities and generalities, elucidates common areas of interest for further study. Students who study in this type of approach are in a position to probe beyond one topic, and the expansion gives them experiences with the transformations of thought inherent in the pursuit of extending oneself.

Students should also continue to familiarize themselves with talent areas outside their areas of expertise. The unique combinations that evolve help the student create a unique style and approach and give him greater insight into his creative processes.

Third, we will find that mentors and role models become more important. As in the younger grades, the mentor provides the secondary student with an understanding of the creative process from the expert's point of view. The opportunity for personal contact and interchange can be extremely valuable as new talent develops. The school can help by allowing flexibility in the student's schedule for regular work with the mentor. Some school districts bring professionals into the school to work with students; others encourage students to go into the community to work alongside their mentor. Either way, the mentor provides a frame of reference for the student to experience the world of the creative adult, as well as outlets for products and student self-evaluation.

Fourth, the teacher must offer outlets for creative works. Advanced students should display some of their products. As they become more skilled in their technique, they should seek ways to share it with others. As with elementary students, art fairs, expositions, talent reviews, literary journals, debates, and science fairs are a few of the possible forums. Displaying their work helps students learn to review their work critically as they gauge others' reactions to it. They must also prepare for these events carefully, as does the professional.

The teacher or mentor should help students select their best products for public display, while still allowing them to produce mostly for themselves and to choose the products they feel most comfortable sharing with the public.

Lastly, we must continue to encourage self-evaluation. A mentor helps the student learn to ask the right questions about his work, and publicly displaying products also yields valuable information. Whatever the means, it is essential that students regularly assess their progress. The goal of evaluation is for students to develop their abilities to the greatest extent. They should recognize excellence and work toward achieving it. Students should learn to look at themselves and their accomplishments critically and objectively, although they need not always share their self-evaluations. A teacher's or an expert's evaluation is also important, to help students learn to take suggestions profitably.

Helping secondary students develop creative ability is primarily a matter of facilitating their advancing skills and encouraging them in the pursuit of excellence by moving them toward a greater concern with the products of creative expression, self-evaluation, and refined technique. The school's role becomes one of putting the student in touch with local professionals, arranging schedules so they have time to explore their crafts with these experts, helping identify outlets for student works, and continued training of the creative processes, techniques, and self-evaluation.

Instructional Strategies

Instructional strategies do not teach a student to be creative; they give students the chance to develop the creative potential they already have. We have seen that creative production drops at about the fourth grade; obviously, then, the educational community must take steps in the early grades to foster this ability. Most of the specific methods derive from the rational thinking quadrant of the Creativity Circle (Clark, 1979), but teachers should feel free and be encouraged to develop their own methods. They know what best enhances their teaching style. As Torrance (1977) says, ''No matter how much we learn from this research, the individual teacher's way of teaching must be his or her unique invention. Teachers must arrive at this personal invention through their own creative process in trying to accomplish their teaching goals'' (p. 34). Teachers can consider the following strategies as a basis for developing more personal techniques and methods.

Creative Problem Solving

Creative Problem Solving (CPS) is a method of finding solutions to a problem, developed and refined by the Creative Education Foundation at the State University of New York at Buffalo (Parnes, 1972). The strategy for tackling problems evolves systematically after perceiving a problem. CPS involves five steps: fact-finding, problem-finding, idea-finding, solution-finding, and acceptance-finding. According to Treffinger and Huber (1975), training in the method enables students to:

- Be sensitive to problems
- Define problems
- Break away from habit-bound thinking
- Defer judgments
- See new relationships
- Evaluate the consequences of one's actions
- Plan for implementation of ideas
- Observe carefully and discover facts
- Use effective techniques for discovering new ideas
- Refine strange ideas to usefulness
- Decribe and use a systematic approach
- Describe the influences of interpersonal relationships on problem solving and illustrate problems associated with interpersonal relationships

The steps in creative problem solving are designed to take the students through a systematic process yet allow them to deal with a problem or situation creatively. The procedure begins when someone has a feeling that something is incomplete, wrong, or missing. There may also be a feeling of anxiety or restlessness as one looks for a reason for this uneasiness. This is referred to in CPS as "The Mess": Some sort of fuzzy problem exists, although it may not be clear what the problem or concern is.

Fact-finding is the first step and serves primarily an organizational function. At this time, the student determines what is already known about the problem or mess, and decides what additional information or resources are necessary to make sense of the mess.

Problem-finding requires sorting through the known facts for potential problems. Usually, a number of problems are discovered. The student looks at the "messy situation" from all angles, considering as many sides to the problem as possible. The culmination of this step involves generating problem statements and possible sub-problems, using the phrase, "In what ways might I . . . . "

Idea-finding begins with selecting one problem for consideration and stating it in proper form. The student then tries to produce as many alternative solutions to the problem as possible, for which brainstorming can be useful. Brainstorming, a technique associated with Alex Osborn (1963), results in the generation of new ideas, usually in a group of five to ten people coordinated by a leader, although it can be done individually. The goal is to list as many alternative ideas as possible in relation to the stated problem. It functions on four rules: no criticism; quantity is desirable; "freewheeling," generating wild ideas, is welcomed; and "hitchhiking," building on others' ideas to seek new combinations.

Solution-finding is the evaluation phase during which specific criteria for assessing ideas generated during idea-finding are established. Criteria may vary according to the characteristics of the problem. During solution-finding, participants brainstorm possible criteria and choose those most significant to the problem as a basis for the evaluation. A grid can be established to rate each solution according to the chosen criteria to determine the most likely solution. The strength of alternative solutions is also assessed along with their potential as possible alternative strategies.

The final step, *acceptance-finding* follows selection of a possible solution to the problem. As described by Treffinger and Parnes (1980), this step "involves creating many alternatives or strategies, and then weaving the best of them into a plan for creative action" (p. 31). One must determine a plan of action after considering variables such as where support will come from, where the opposition will be, what steps must be taken, and who needs to be involved to ensure success.

Treffinger and Parnes suggest one further step in the process, called "New Problems and Challenges." They speak of creativity as an ongoing process, saying that CPS is not complete without consideration of the new challenges that arise from solving the old.

The applications for CPS seem endless. It provides a mechanism for structuring creative action, and the discipline for progressing through use of the creative processes. Families, administrators, business people, and students have used the process effectively.

Future Problem Solving

The Future Problem Solving Program began in 1974 under the direction of E. Paul Torrance. It "has emerged as a national program of interscholastic competition and as a curriculum project in creative problem solving and future studies" (Torrance & Torrance, 1978). School teams compete in local and statewide contests to generate solutions to problems written especially for the competition. State contest winners meet yearly in three divisions (junior, grades 4–6; intermediate, grades 7–9; and senior, grades 10–12) for the national competition.

The steps students follow in Future Problem Solving parallel those found in CPS:
1   List subproblems
2   Recognize and state important problem
3   Produce alternative solutions
4   Evaluate alternative solutions
5   Plan and implement solutions
6   Sell the idea

Torrance and Torrance state that "the necessary ingredients [for success in the program] are a few creative students, a good teacher, much study of future problems, and practice in problem solving" (p. 88).

Synectics

Synectics, a form of problem solving associated primarily with Gordon (1971), brings together various individuals for problem-stating and problem-solving exercises. The Synectics method generally deals with real-life problems, as a creative process to problem solving. Gordon lists these premises for the Synectics theory:

- Creative efficiency can be markedly increased if people understand the psychological process by which they operate
- In creative process, the emotional component is more important than the intellectual, the irrational more important than the rational
- These emotional, irrational elements can and must be understood to increase the probability of success in a problem-solving situation (p. 17-18).

The Synectics process is designed to make the strange familiar, through understanding the problem at hand; and to make the familiar strange through a conscious effort to look at the world in a new light, thus making new solutions more apparent. Four metaphorical mechanisms—personal analogy, direct analogy, symbolic analogy, and fantasy analogy make the familiar strange.

Personal analogy requires the individual to take the role of an element of the problem, to see the problem from a new perspective. For example, if you want to determine how a person might retrieve a set of keys locked in a car, you could imagine yourself as the car keys and consider the situation from that perspective.

Direct analogy involves making direct comparisons between two situations to determine where similarities exist. Gordon suggests making direct analogies between elements of the problem and areas vastly different from the problem, forcing a statement of the problem from a different perspective. With the car keys, for example, one might look for similarities between the keys and an amoeba or a sunset, to help clarify the dynamics of the problem.

Symbolic analogy is ususally a short phrase describing the problem abstractly with ideas or phrases that are not usually combined. Symbolic analogy presents a paradox in words, and the attempt to understand the paradox can result in insight into the problem. A symbolic analogy might characterize the car keys as "captured mobility."

Fantasy analogy is based on Freud's wish-fulfillment theory: creative work, especially art, is the fulfillment of a wish through a depersonalized avenue. In Synectics, fantasy analogy is another link to the irrational and subconscious mind. A fantasy analogy question might ask, "In your wildest imagination, how might you get the keys out of the car?"

By combining these four mechanisms, the leader guides group members toward a unique solution to the problem. As an approach to problem solving, Synectics requires a great deal of intellectual and creative energy and a leader with insight. The results are manifested in increased creative fluency and flexibility for the students.

Structure of the Intellect

Guilford's Structure of the Intellect model (see Figure 1.5) has been adapted by Meeker (1969) for use in designing curricular strategies. Her work, referred to as S.O.I. training, involves instructional strategies for training the 120 mental abilities defined in Guilford's three-dimensional cube representing the *content* of thought, the *operations* or kind of thinking performed upon the content, and the *product* of that procedure.

The factors of creative thinking have been outlined within that framework. The divergent thinking operation accounts for much of creative thinking. Meeker defines divergent thinking as the "generation of information from given information, where emphasis is upon variety and quality of output from the same source, likely to involve what has been called transfer" (p. 20). She goes on to state, however, what while divergent thinking is probably necessary for creative development, it is not sufficient by itself. Other factors enter the process, such as:

- Sensitivity to problems (associated with the evaluation operation)
- Fluency of thinking (ability to generate a large quantity of ideas)
- Flexibility of thinking (ability to develop a great variety of ideas—spontaneous flexibility—or unusual solutions to problems—adaptive flexibility)
- Originality (ability to produce unusual responses)
- Redefinition (using familiar objects or ideas in a different way)
- Elaboration (ability to embellish on an idea or object to make it more complex)

Through Meeker's work at the S.O.I. Institue in El Segundo, California, tests and curricular materials are now available to assess and train the various intellectual abilities. Other curricular programs, such as *New Directions in Creativity* (Renzulli, 1973), are also based on the Structure of Intellect Model operations.

A teacher interested in developing creative abilities under the SI Model would use the model as a frame of reference, making sure to offer instruction in the different divergent production areas. Opportunities to develop the abilities represented by the various boxes is important in training the entire operation. By categorizing activities into the various ability boxes, the teacher can determine if she is addressing a wide range of divergent abilities or only a few. The goal is to provide experiences across the broad range of potential abilities.

Throughout the curriculum, then, the teacher provides students with opportunities to express their sensitivity to problems and develop their skills of fluency, flexibility, originality, redefinition, and elaboration. Table 11-1 presents an activity for helping to develop adaptive flexibility of thought in the areas of science and current events, and Figure 11–2 describes an elaboration activity.

Table 11-1   ACTIVITY TO ENCOURAGE FLEXIBLE THINKING

Explore with students the importance water has in the ecology and maintenance of our planet. Discuss the amount of water present on the planet and how it is endangered through such phenomena as drought, pollution and acid rain. When students have an understanding of the role water plays in life and the threats currently present to the planet's water supply, introduce the following activity:

You have been appointed to serve as a delegate to the United Nations' Commission on Water Conservation. As a member of that Commission, it is your responsibility to develop plans for preserving the planet's water supply. List as many different strategies as you can for encouraging worldwide water preservation.

_____   _____
_____   _____
_____   _____

On the blackboard, draw the basic form of an automobile. In turn, have each student add a new feature to the basic outline of the automobile.

Students may add such features as license plates, doors, rearview mirrors, hood ornaments, antennae, etc. Continue the activity as long as the students have new ideas. Make sure the car outline is sufficiently large enough to handle all the improvements!

Figure 11-2 ACTIVITY TO ENCOURAGE ELABORATIVE THINKING

The Structure of the Intellect gives teachers a basis for planning instructional activities. It assures that a range of activities are provided to reflect the various facets of the functions associated with creative thinking and production and facilitates inclusion of the divergent thought processes across curricular and behavioral areas.

Model for Implementing Cognitive-Affective Behaviors in the Classroom

Williams' (1970) Model for Implementing Cognitive Affective Behaviors in the Classroom is a three-dimensional model that "characterizes an interrelationship between strategies employed by the teacher (Dimension 2) across the various subject matter areas of an ongoing elementary school curriculum (Dimension 1) in order to elicit a set of four cognitive and four affective pupil behaviors (Dimension 3)" (Williams, 1970, p. 2).

This model gives teachers an integrated structure for planning instruction. Not only does it include the curricular areas, but the relationship to teacher and student behaviors as well. This shows the teacher a way to plan instruction so as to provide experiences across the entire curriculum and the cognitive and affective domains. Williams believes the feeling processes operate with the thinking processes, not as two separate entities. A combination of the two domains of response leads to effective use of intelligence and ultimately of the creative processes.

To use Williams's model, the teacher selects at least one factor from each of the three dimensions. For example, an activity might be based on the three factors of

Science, Organized Random Search, and Curiosity. An activity for combining these three dimensions might ask students to keep track of the weather for one month on a calendar. At the end of the month, students could graph the frequency of weather types. To extend the activity, students might compare the weather from this year to the previous year, predict the weather during the following month, or attempt to determine trends in the weather over a number of months or years.

Or, for example, one might combine the areas of imagination, social studies, and creative writing skill and ask: "Describe what the United States would be like if it had been settled from the West rather than the East. How would it be the same? How would it be different?" This activity requires students to draw on their knowledge about history as written, and to make judgments about how history would change if one factor were different, drawing on the known to make predictions about the unknown. Creative responses will come from an understanding of the discipline of history as well as from the ability to look at the event from a new perspective.

Using the Williams Model, teachers can balance curricular strategies to include all the areas depicted in the model. This holistic approach infuses creative processes and abilities throughout the curriculum. The creative factors of Dimension 3 (pupil behaviors) are integral to curricular planning. Including them this way will result in a well-rounded program characterized by integration of creativity, curriculum, and broad-based teaching strategies.

Questioning to Encourage Creativity

Few techniques or instructional strategies can infuse creative abilities throughout the curriculum as easily or effectively as appropriate questioning, and it is one skill teachers always have at their disposal for large group situations, small group meetings, or when working with individual students. Appropriate questions develop creative thinking. Teachers must begin by attending to the types of questions they habitually ask. By tape recording a lesson or having a colleague observe a class, the teacher can generate a list of questions asked during a period of time. These should be classified as either divergent or convergent; convergent questions usually have a known answer and responses are either right or wrong: "What is the chemical symbol for water? On what date was the Magna Carta signed? Where did Bobby go after he left the store? How many eggs are in a dozen?" Divergent questions have many possible answers: "How might you dispose of 500 pounds of jelly beans? If Shakespeare lived today, how might his plays be different? Where could you take a Martian on a picnic? Why should we be concerned about acid rain?" A teacher who wishes to enhance creativity will need a command of both types of questions; a balance between divergent and convergent queries is the goal.

As mentioned, the first step in developing good questioning technique is to assess the range of questions the teacher uses naturally. If they are primarily of the convergent type, the teacher may wish to begin the process of introducing more open-ended questions into the lesson plans. Initially, the teacher may wish to plan questions in advance; as she develops greater skill, good questioning technique will become second nature. Various schema help in designing questions. In *Creative Questioning and Sensitive Listening Techniques*, Carin and Sund (1978) present a plan based on fluency, flexibility, originality, elaboration, and sensitivity. By considering each of these dimensions, teachers can develop questions that will focus on this range of creative abilities and require answers in and across these areas. Another simple guide focuses on the higher levels of thinking: analysis, synthesis, and evaluation. Classifying questions in these areas should also lead the teacher to begin to ask a range of questions. The aim is to require students to employ multiple cognitive processes with ease. Without practice functioning in various areas, students cannot be expected to do so with the necessary facility for engaging in creative thinking and production.

By following a guide to questions, teachers can begin to free students from the constraints of looking for the "one right answer" and begin to play with ideas, thoughts, and emotions, drawing on their experiences and expertise in new and unusual ways. Breaking from the traditional convergent approach to the more stimulating divergent techniques opens exciting intellectual avenues for students.

Adapting Instructional Materials

A wide range of instructional materials is available on creativity; however, a teacher need not rely solely on such materials and books to encourage creative expression. There are many ways to adapt materials for developing creative abilities.

The teacher can begin to consider alternative uses of materials, especially as they relate to divergent thinking. Rather than ask questions with only one answer, intersperse questions that can be answered in many ways; for example, besides asking "When did Columbus discover America?" you might also ask, "What might have happened if Queen Isabella had refused to give Columbus the money he needed to make his voyage?" This question has no right or wrong answers, but you can gauge the quality of the response by how well students support their opinions. Along with divergent questions, open-ended activities also have a place in the classroom. A learning center might include opportunities to design a spacesuit for an astronaut, explaining why you have designed it this way; create a poster for nutrition week to put on the bulletin board; or suggest an ad campaign to promote the class prom. Examination items should also reflect divergence. If teachers engage in training creative responses, they should also assess students' abilities in this area. Essay and application items are more likely to elicit creative, synthesized responses that draw on students' divergent thinking.

One must extend opportunities for creative thinking throughout all disciplines. The nurturance of creativity does not belong only in "creativity time." To encourage students to fully develop as creative adults, they must be led to see the implications the creative processes have throughout the phases of their lives. The teacher's role is to help students identify these applications, such as using CPS to solve the problem of not having enough lockers for each student; discovering the multiple ways to solve one math problem; or the endless implications a scientific discovery, such as a computer chip, can have on their lives. One may have to make a conscious effort to bring creativity to bear throughout the curriculum, but the rewards will be evident when students begin to integrate and synthesize the creative functions with more convergent functions.

Creative expression must include the opportunity for new approaches to traditional assignments. This student, for example, is drawing on her talent for photography.

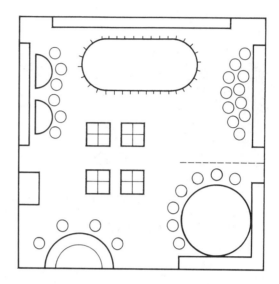

Figure 11-3 AN ENVIRONMENT TO ENCOURAGE CREATIVE EXPRESSION

Teachers also need to increase the range of opportunity and available materials. When assessing the types of materials available in the classroom, we must consider the range as well as the amount. Creative production requires one to draw from many resources and combine information, attitudes, and emotions in unique ways. It is therefore necessary for students to have opportunities and materials that extend their experience or current knowledge. With the broad range of materials available, teachers should look especially for those that propose new ideas or approaches in quality ways or old ideas in clear and concise ways, enhancing the possibility that a student will merge old and new in a creative way. Flexibility and understanding are imperative for the teacher who is asked to accept the uncertainty of creative production and the creative process, but facilitating creative experiences is in the hands of the teacher, who opens up the world of resources to the student.

We must arrange the environment to encourage creative production. Materials alone do not provide the necessary impetus for creative functioning. Students must have an atmosphere that accepts the production of new ideas and allows uncertainty and experimentation. The classroom can be physically arranged to help the creative process, with places for quiet activity and noisier activity. When students engage in the creative process, they may need to draw on various resources throughout the production, and the environment must anticipate the need for materials, assistance, solitude, and collaboration. Figure 11-3 shows one floor plan based on student needs.

Summary

Creativity is a complex process involving integration of many cerebral functions, both known and unknown. It appears that all individuals have the potential to be creative adults to varying degrees. Young children engage in creative explorations almost from birth. Their environmental probings give them the basis for interactions with life experiences. Clark (1979) proposes a model that integrates various conceptions of creativity, combining the mental functions of rational thinking, feeling, intuiting, and sensing. Through research, we find that the creative functions can be encouraged and taught, resulting in increased creative production. The school and the community have a role in its development. Various instructional strategies present mechanisms for training creative production in the classroom. It is evident, however, that the teacher is the crucial component of any program dealing with the creative processes. Teachers must be encouraged to draw on their own creative abilities, and to provide an atmosphere in which students feel psychologically safe to express and explore their creative abilities.

References

Barron, F. *Creativity and psychological health*. New York: Van Nostrand, 1963.

Barron, F. "An eye more fantastical." In *Training creative thinking*. Edited by Gary A. Davis and Joseph A. Scott. New York: Holt, Rinehart and Winston, 1971.

Callahan, C. *Developing creativity in the gifted and talented*. Reston, Va.: Council for Exceptional Children, 1978.

Carin, A., and R. Sund. *Creative questioning and sensitive listening techniques: A self-concept approach*. 2nd ed. Columbus, Ohio: Charles E. Merrill, 1978.

Clark, B. *Growing up gifted*. Columbus, Ohio: Charles E. Merrill, 1979.

Crutchfield, R. "Conformity and creative thinking." In *Contemporary approaches to creative thinking*. Edited by H. Gruber, G. Terrell, and M. Wertheimer. New York: Atherton Press, 1962.

DeBono, E. "Information processing and new ideas—lateral and vertical thinking." *Journal of Creative Behavior* 3 (1969): 151–71.

Edwards, B. *Drawing on the right side of the brain*. Los Angeles: J. P. Tarcher, 1979.

Gallagher, J. *Teaching the gifted child*. 2nd ed. Boston: Allyn and Bacon, 1975.

Getzels, J., and P. Jackson. *Creativity and intelligence*. New York: John Wiley, 1962.

Gillespie, R. "A creative approach to evaluating ideas." In *The Creative Process*. Edited by A. Biondi. Buffalo, N.Y.: D.O.K. Publishers, 1972.

Gordon, W. "Synectics." In *Training creative thinking*. Edited by G. Davis and J. Scott. New York: Holt, Rinehart and Winston, 1971.

Gordon, W., and T. Poze. "SES synectics and gifted education today." *Gifted Child Quarterly* 24 (1980): 147–51.

Gowan, J. *Development of the creative individual*. San Diego, Calif.: Robert R. Knapp, 1972.

Gowan, J., J. Khatena, and E. Torrance. *Creativity: Its educational implications*. 2nd ed. Dubuque, Iowa: Kendall/Hunt, 1981.

Guilford, J. "Creativity." *American Psychologist* 5 (1950): 444–54.

Guilford, J. *The nature of human intelligence*. New York: McGraw-Hill, 1967.

Guilford, J. "Potentiality for creativity." In *Creativity: Its educational implications*. 2nd ed. Edited by J. Gowan, G. Demos, and E. Torrance. Dubuque, Iowa: Kendall/Hunt, 1981.

Hudgins, B. *Learning and thinking: A primer for teachers*. Itasca, Ill.: F. E. Peacock, 1977.

Jones, T. *Creative learning in perspective*. New York: John Wiley, 1972.

Jung, C., ed. *Man and his symbols*. New York: Dell, 1964.

Krippner, S. "The ten commandments that block creativity." *The Gifted Child Quarterly* 11 (1967): 144–51.

MacKinnon, D. "What makes a person creative?" *Theory into Practice* 5 (1966): 152–56.

Maslow, A. *Toward a psychology of being*. New York: Van Nostrand, 1968.

May, R. *The courage to create*. New York: W. W. Norton, 1975.

Meadow, A., and S. Parnes. "Evaluation of training in creative problem solving." *Journal of Applied Psychology* 43 (1959): 189–94.

Meadow, A., S. Parnes, and H. Reese. "Influence of brainstorming instructions and problem sequence on a creative problem solving test." *Journal of Applied Psychology* 43 (1959): 413–16.

Mednick, S. "The associative basis of the creative process." *Psychological Review* 69 (1962): 220–32.

Meeker, M. *The structure of intellect: Its interpretation and uses*. Columbus, Ohio: Charles E. Merrill, 1969.

Osborn, A. *Applied imagination*. 3rd ed. New York: Scribners, 1963.

Parnes, S. "Education in creativity." In *Creativity: Its education implications*. Edited by J. Gowan, G. Demos, and E. Torrance. New York: John Wiley, 1967.

Parnes, S. *Creativity: Unlocking human potential*. Buffalo, N.Y.: D.O.K. Publishers, 1972.

Patrick, C. "Creative thought in poets." *Archives of Psychology* 178 (1935): 1–74.

Reese, H., et al. "Effects of a creative studies program on structure of intellect factors." *Journal of Educational Psychology* 68 (1976): 401–10.

Renzulli, J. *New directions in creativity: Mark I*. New York: Harper and Row, 1973.

Ridley, D., and R. Birney. "Effects of training procedures on creativity test scores." *Journal of Educational Psychology* 58 (1967): 158–64.

Roe, A. "A psychologist examines sixty-four eminent scientists." *Scientific American* 187 (1952): 1–25.

Rogers, C. "Toward a theory of creativity." In *A sourcebook for creative thinking*. Edited by S. Parnes and H. Harding. New York: Scribner's, 1962.

Taylor, C. "Clues to creative teaching: The creative process and education." *Instructor* 73 (1963): 4–5.

Taylor, C., ed. *Creativity: Progress and potential*. New York: McGraw-Hill, 1964.

Torrance, E. *Creativity in the classroom*. Washington, D.C.: National Education Association, 1977.

Torrance, E., and P. Torrance. "Future problem solving: National interscholastic competition and curriculum project." *Journal of Creative Behavior* 12 (1978): 87–89.

Treffinger, D., and J. Huber. "Designing instruction in creative problem solving: Preliminary objectives and learning hierarchies." *Journal of Creative Behavior* 9 (1975): 260–66.

Treffinger, D., and S. Parnes. "Creative problem solving for gifted and talented students." *Roeper Review* 2 (1980): 31–32.

Wallach, M., and N. Kogan. "A new look at the creativity-intelligence distinction." In *Creativity*. Edited by P. Veron. New York: Penguin Books, 1970.

Wallas, G. *The art of thought*. New York: Harcourt, 1926.

Welsh, G. "Personality correlates of intelligence and creativity in gifted adolescents." In *The gifted: A fifty-year perspective*. Edited by J. Stanley et al. Baltimore, Md.: Johns Hopkins University Press, 1977.

Williams, F. *Classroom ideas for encouraging thinking and feeling*. Buffalo, N.Y.: D.O.K. Publishers, 1970.

Yamamoto, K. "Effects of restriction of range and test unreliability on correlation between measures of intelligence and creative thinking." *British Journal of Educational Psychology* 35 (1965): 300–5.

12

Program Implementation and Evaluation

G. Fichter
R. H. Swassing

W̶e have known about and used the conditions necessary for nurturing exceptional abilities for some time. Olympic athletes, for example, are identified early and receive the best instruction, lots of practice, and appropriate recognition for their performance. Musicians are also nurtured this way. Pressey (1955) identified five major points in the careers of talented individuals:

1 Excellent early opportunities for the ability to develop and encouragement from family and friends
2 Superior early and continuing individual guidance and instruction
3 The opportunity frequently and continually to practice and extend their special ability and to progress as they were able
4 Close association with others in the field, which greatly fostered the abilities of all concerned
5 Many opportunities for real accomplishment, within his possibilities but of increasing challenge, the precocious musician or athlete has had the stimulation of many and increasingly strong success experiences—and his world acclaimed these successes (Pressey, 1955, p. 124).

The preceding chapters have dealt with many concerns in educating the gifted and talented, with the primary focus on curricular and instructional issues in relation to the children's characteristics and needs, and a secondary focus on the environmental conditions that nurture exceptional potential. Gallagher (1975) and Maker (1982) emphasize environment as a major component of educational planning. This chapter will focus on establishing the positive, or nurturing, environment by examining program implementation from two points of view, program and classroom.

Program Implementation

State Level

At the apex of a state's educational delivery system is the State Education Agency (SEA) that includes the State Board of Education and the State Department of Education. Roles and responsibilities of the SEAs differ according to legislative authority, rules and regulations of the State Board of Education, and the structure of the SEA. Some state department personnel take an active role in statewide coordination and planning; others take a more reactive or monitoring stance.

Because of their range of duties—fiscal management, personnel certification, curriculum areas, litigation, special programs—SEAs are often organized into specialized groups with personnel who address the activities defined by the organizational structure. The gifted and talented are one such concern of SEAs and the state level consultant (SC) for programs for the gifted.

As of 1977, only three states had no SC for the gifted and talented (Zettel, 1979). Of the personnel in the remaining 47 states, 27 states had one or more SCs devoting 100 percent of their time to the gifted and talented. The Council of State Directors of Programs for the Gifted (CSDPG) is the nationwide organization of SCs. In the decade ahead, this group will become a major unifying force as educational responsibilities shift from the federal level to the states. The CSDPG has 44 full-time active members and a total of 62 members.

The SC brings three major resources to local districts that are considering program implementation or revision:

- Administrative experience
- Curriculum knowledge
- Human resources

In the area of administrative expertise, the state consultant has observed organizational and administrative structures in numerous districts and can share these experiences with local personnel. The SC is aware of the advantages and pitfalls of various arrangements as they relate to the state, its fiscal and educational policies, and as they relate to district and school circumstances.

Given the array of experiences among various populations and age groups, the SC can provide advice and guidance about curricular adaptations that have local potential and those that are likely to cause serious problems.

Finally, the state consultant as a human resource is frequently overlooked in program development and implementation. He or she will know what various programs exist around the state and can guide site visitation teams to programs that are appropriate for a particular district. The SC can visit with parent groups, make presentations at teachers meetings, and offer alternatives to administrators that local personnel cannot. The SC can act as sounding board and interpreter of state rules and regulations concerning program requirements and as an "outside" resource for local groups.

Constituent groups and "publics" with whom SCs may interact vary from state to state as does the extent of the interaction. In some states, an SC may have direct input to legislative activities; in other states, direct participation is outside the job description and antithetical to the overall role of the state education agency and its employees. Generally, SCs must interact with:

- Local program coordinators and teachers
- Local administrative officers
- Local and statewide parent groups
- Local and statewide superintendent groups
- College and university personnel
- Other specialized groups such as school psychologists or fine and performing art educators

These groups are important to the growth and maintenance of programs, and the state consultant's relationship to these groups must be positive. Public relations is a vital link among the programs, the gifted movement, and the taxpayer. It is important that the various publics view education positively, and education of the gifted and talented as an integral part of the statewide educational system.

All the groups with whom the state consultant interacts constitute the basis of a "network" for the advancement of gifted education. In Ohio, for example, three major groups relate directly to programming: the statewide parents' group, the Ohio Association for Gifted Children (OAGC); the Consortium of Coordinators for the Gifted (COCG), composed of coordinators at the local, county, and regional levels; and the Interuniversity Council for the Gifted and Talented (IUC-G/T). Each organization has leadership personnel, and there is overlap among membership, yet each serves a particular function and meets specific needs. The network is both the formal and informal interaction among the groups with the result that information can be quickly spread across the state. Information may relate to statewide legislative efforts, and will usually concern inservice training, parent sessions, certification, state support, and a wide range of other issues.

Second-order networking involves interaction with other educational groups, such as statewide board of education groups, superintendency groups, elementary and secondary principals' organizations, teachers' organizations, school psychologists and counselors, and others. It is vital to build and maintain communication with these organizations.

It is difficult to establish a single principle role of the state education agency in the delivery system of education for the gifted and talented, since the premises under which it operates vary from state to state. The SEA may serve as a monitoring compliance-seeking agency, while in other states there is considerable latitude in guiding programmatic thrusts. All SEAs engage in certain key activities at varying levels of involvement:

- Public relations
- Policy making
- Policy management
- Fiscal policy
- Personnel preparation
- Program evaluation
- Program funding
- Legislative activities
- Parent information and parent groups

Local Level

If a program for gifted and talented is based on a sound curriculum for all children in the school, it becomes the natural extension of overall effective education for all children (Barbe, 1962). Such programming then serves as a possible source of rejuvenation for regular school instructional activities (Barbe, 1962).

Conceptualization and planning become important in answering these questions:

1 Why is a program necessary?
2 What does a program provide?
3 When and where will provisions for the program be available?
4 How will these provisions be put into operation?
5 Who will be responsible for implementing these programs? (Kaplan, 1974, p. 7).

We must add a sixth question: "How will we know if the objectives of the program are being met?" The plan becomes operational as the organization, personnel, and environments emerge.

"If we are to meet the needs of gifted learners, we must have a planned, coordinated, continuous program. This program must be open and responsive to the changing individual while providing continuous challenge and an adequate diversity of content and process. While we may draw from more traditional gifted education models, our own community, our parents, students and staff must make the decisions of structure and intent. While some goals can be generalized, others must be specifically set by the teacher, the student and the parent in a cooperative effort." (Clark, 1979, p. 159)

To achieve this program, we must give attention to certain elements, each in concert with others (Fox, 1979), including:

- An operational definition of giftedness including identification and eligibility of the target population
- A needs assessment of the target population, including geographic and administrative considerations, population characteristics and program scope
- Establishment of goals, objectives, and operational strategies
- Development of timelines, personnel, and inservice training needs
- Specific steps for screening students
- Procedures for matching students and program alternatives
- Plans for counseling students and parents (Fox, 1979, p. 105)
- Methods of evaluation, types of information gathered and by whom, and on which elements or variables

It is important to distinguish between administrative goals and objectives, and instructional, curricular, and student goals and objectives (Clark, 1979; Fox, 1979).

Administrative and organizational goals and objectives define the delivery system, or the arrangement of instructional components. Acceleration, resource rooms, and special classes are models of administrative organization. Content and student goals refer to the course of instruction and the strategies for bringing student and content together for the learning process.

Although separate components, the delivery system does not operate in isolation from curriculum content; there will be strong interaction. The resource room model is an example of the framework for providing learning; what is learned is a separate question. Resource rooms may vary in effectiveness depending on the learners, the content, and teaching methods.

Implementing a program for the gifted must first and foremost be justifiable (Barbe, 1962). There must be a clear reason, clearly stated, for starting such a program. The needs statement should prove that there are gifted youngsters in the schools and that the common curriculum is inappropriate for them.

Special opportunities for the gifted can be justified in terms of benefits for the other children (Barbe, 1962). We have to answer questions such as "What happens to the others in the class if these children are taken out?" and "What about various groups, particularly the next highest performers?" Justification must also be based on the children's needs and the fact that their experiences in the program will differ from those in the regular classroom. The final argument must rest in "differential" experiences (Barbe, 1962). Renzulli (1975) asked a panel of 21 judges to rank features according to their contribution to quality; the highest-ranked features were designated "key features": (1) the teacher, (2) the curriculum, (3) student selection, (4) philosophy and objectives, (5) staff orientation, and (6) evaluation (p. 327). These elements were considered central to differentiated education for the gifted and talented. Other issues that have a direct impact on implementation are: communications, critical publics, parents and community, school personnel, and the teacher.

Communication   Sharing the purposes and objectives of the program with others and communicating progress is particularly important, and we must communicate as effectively as possible.

Written messages should be brief and to the point. Construct sentences to provide one piece of information in one concise sentence. Several short sentences on an otherwise clear field are most effective. Headline the page so the reader will know what is to follow. If the message runs on two or more pages, mark the bottom of the page with "more" or some other expression to tell the reader to go on.

Second, know your audience. Informing parents about the program is one thing; giving superintendents information they may use at a board meeting is another. Parents want to know what will happen to their children; superintendents want to answer questions about cost-benefits and how this program is more appropriate than the regular curriculum.

Remember, too, that much of the communication in our culture is visual. Communications must, then, have "eye appeal." A picture of six children sitting at desks doing calculus may show a great moment in learning, but it will not be visually exciting. The same six children studying physics using playground equipment will be more attractive because it has "action." If action pictures are unavailable, use short phrases in large print to convey a message and attract attention (for example, Swing-A-Pendulum in Action). Communications should be informative, concise, attractive, and directed toward the appropriate audience.

Parent/Community Involvement   Parent organizations, members of business and industry, legislative groups, other personnel at the school and district level, and taxpayers who no longer have children in the schools also have an impact on program implementation and growth. Each of these groups may have different expectations for the schools and different degrees of willingness to support the schools with tax dollars. For the most part, however, people like to hear about things that reflect well on the community and its children. And, we already know that parents and parent groups can offer substantial resources and support for programs for the gifted and talented. Speaker's bureaus, artists, musicians, and local businesses and industries are important resources to supplement the expertise of school personnel.

How parent/community members perceive the program is also important.

> Those educators who have extensively and genuinely involved parents in school efforts contend that when things go wrong or when goals are not met, parents are the most articulate spokesmen in explaining to others, particularly on issues of controversy or high emotion. (Rioux, 1978, p. 12)

This involvement places parents in copartnership with the schools rather than in an adversarial role. Where parents and schools work together, the outcome is likely to be higher quality education. With the child as direct benefactor, adversarial roles are "unconscionable" (Rioux, 1978, p. 12). Parent/community participation in the program results in three benefits:

1   Improved quality of education
2   Community advocates
3   In-school and extramural resources and learning opportunities

Involving parents begins at the earliest stages of program planning, and they should be invited to the initial planning meetings. Most teachers, principals, and other school staff know well-informed, articulate parents who will be willing to serve on committees.

Inviting business and industry participation in planning creates strong bonds of support and resources for the program. Industries may have Executive Clubs or other organizations whose membership seeks community involvement consistent with their organization's goals. Activities may include children's programs and interactions, financial support, or offering mentorships to high school students. These groups are frequently looking for ideas of activities and are eager to participate. Bringing them into the planning stage will garner support of the program and facilitate access to community opportunities.

School Personnel   The principal, teachers, counselors, and school psychologists in any building or district are vital to successful program implementation. When these professionals are positive and supportive, the program tends to move forward rapidly and positively. Without strong administrative support, a program may be doomed to mediocrity.

Schools and school districts have both formal and informal structures. The formal structure is the district's Table of Organization (T.O.), moving from the school board down to the superintendent, central office personnel, principals, and teachers. There are both "line" and "staff" positions, with line positions in a specific authoritative relationship to the superintendent and a staff position as a consultative function. A staff person may recommend and suggest, but is not in a position of authority. Effective use of the formal structure expedites decision making and program growth.

A school or district's informal structure is much more difficult to grasp, because it is unwritten, based on personal interactions, and changes frequently and without notice. Influential teachers will have an impact on other teacher's attitudes toward gifted children, a particular gifted child, the program, or the teachers in the program.

The more amorphous informal structures are those involving nonschool organizations and church and community activities. For example, do principals meet socially from time to time? Does the superintendent play racquetball with the head of a large, local corporation who never graduated from high school? Or who graduated *cum laude* from Yale? In these ways attitudes are passed from one to another. Decisions are made within the formal structure, but attitudes are shaped by a variety of external factors.

Teacher's organizations and unions often directly influence program implementation. Contracts that call for certain numbers and ranges of children in classrooms and delineate teacher's rights, responsibilities, and workloads are integral to planning and can set limits to any program. Efforts at implementation usually must involve a teacher representative or knowledge of the positions of the teacher's organization on program issues. Failure to consider formal and informal structures and the teacher's organization can lead to failure to implement a gifted program.

The teacher is central to program effectiveness. Bishop (1975) studied 109 teachers nominated by one or more students in the First Governor's Honors Program as his "most successful" teacher. Thirty of the 109 were selected for intensive study and interviews (Interview Sample). Bishop reached these conclusions:

- Teachers judged effective did not differ from a group not identified as effective on such variables as sex, marital status, undergraduate institution major, highest degree held, or extent of association with professional organizations
- The successful teachers were mature and experienced
- The mean IQ (WAIS) score of the 30 teachers was 128, or in the upper three percent of the adult population
- They pursued "intellectual" avocational interests
- They held high achievement needs
- They were advised by a teacher to become a teacher and they aspired to intellectual growth
- They took a personal interest in the students, and attempted to see things from the student's point of view
- They were student-centered
- They were orderly and businesslike in the classroom
- They were stimulating and imaginative
- They supported special provisions for gifted students

The question frequently arises, "Should the teacher of the gifted be gifted?" Wirick (1962) suggests that the teacher of the gifted be as "bright" as the students in at least one area, although it would be impossible to be as "bright" in all areas. Above-average intellectual ability is desirable (Bishop, 1975; Lindsey, 1980) but we do not know to what extent.

Lindsey (1980) summarized the personal characteristics of teachers of the gifted:

- Outstanding ego strength
- Sensitivity to others
- Flexible in thinking
- Literary and cultural interests
- Desire to learn
- Enthusiastic
- Intuitive
- Committed to excellence
- Accepts responsibility for one's behavior and its consequences

It is generally accepted that teachers of the gifted need special preparation, although it is difficult to find agreement as to the nature and extent of that preparation. Currently, only ten states have some form of certification for teachers of the gifted (Karnes & Collins, 1981), which include these elements:

- Curriculum strategies
- Education and psychology of the gifted and talented
- Testing and measurement of individual children
- Guidance and counseling of the gifted
- Research on the gifted
- History and philosophy of programming for the gifted (pp. 123–29)

It is also recommended that the teacher have at least two years of teaching experience, some graduate study, and practicum requirements. (Lindsey, 1980; Karnes and Collins, 1981).

Seeley, Jenkins, and Holtgen (1981) suggest including these areas in the training curriculum:

- Identification
- Curriculum models
- Teaching strategies
- Program development, implementation, maintenance, and evaluation, National Council for Accreditation of Teacher Education, and
- Cognitive and affective development (social and emotional)

Skills and knowledge should be demonstrated through supervised practica, and research and comprehensive examination (p. 166).

Maker (1975), after extensive examination of "the state of the art" in teacher qualification and training, advocated different skills for different programs, although so far, little attention has been given to this crucial point. Management skills in self-contained classes differ from the skills required for resource room programming.

Maker (1975) also advocates careful examination of the necessary characteristics and training for teachers who work with special gifted populations. Characteristics of gifted learners who are physically handicapped or emotionally disturbed are quite different from those who do not have handicaps. The highly gifted (above 140–145 IQ) also present educationally relevant differences. We must examine as well, the personal, social, and educational needs of gifted girls and women.

Teaching in a gifted program thus requires more than general training; there must also be training and experience in relevant dimensions of the educational process. For work with the handicapped gifted, skills in those areas are necessary. The resource room teacher must have experience and/or training in organizing and managing such programs. On the other hand, specialized programs can lead to many subspecialties that are not meaningful given the present state of the art.

There can be little doubt about the role of the teacher in programming for the gifted. Teachers' attributes reflect both personal and professional components, but desire to teach the gifted is paramount, followed by love and excitement for learning.

Classroom Level

We mentioned at the beginning of this chapter certain minimal conditions that nurture high level performance (Pressey, 1955). The preceding chapters have stressed curriculum, strategies, and the proper conditions for encouraging children's performance consistent with their abilities. In terms of Maker's (1982) formulation, we have emphasized content, process, and product, and given less importance to environment. So far in this chapter we have discussed programs for the gifted and talented in light of the environment in which they are developed. At the classroom level, a positive, nurturing climate will help to maximize potential.

Maker (1982) translates some of the characteristics and needs of the gifted into specific classroom elements.

1. It should be student-centered, where teacher and students share authority, discussion, and interaction patterns.
2. It should encourage independent student activities, and decision making.
3. It should be open, imposing few restrictions on problem solutions, and accepting divergence.
4. There should be nonjudgmental acceptance.
5. It should emphasize complex ideas, materials that encourage exchange of ideas, and equipment that fosters generalizations and relationships.
6. It should offer high mobility with students allowed to move in and out of the classroom, change groups for different tasks, and select alternative physical areas for study (Maker, 1982).

The elements of classroom environments are, as one would expect, interactive. The classroom is an interactive psychosocial system where the people as well as the elements affect the dynamics of the environment. Interactions among students and between students and teachers are as integral to learning as the interactions of students to the curriculum, the learning tasks, and the modes of presentation. The supportive interaction techniques are interpersonal and communication skills, including attending, responding, personalizing, and initiating (Carkhuff, Berenson & Pierce, 1973). Appropriate use of these skills conveys a "valuing" message—"I value you and this interaction is important to me."

Attending involves visual, physical, and auditory actions. We demonstrate attending with eye contact and with posture or body language. We turn toward the person, seek proximity, or reach out and touch them. A child readily notices visual attending. For example, if I am talking to a teacher who is looking around the top of the desk, and shuffling papers and books, it is easy to get the impression that the teacher's attention is divided. If, on the other hand, the teacher is looking at me, my paper, or my project, I get the impression that this is important. Visual attention does not guarantee intellectual attention, but it goes a long way to assure others that we are trying to attend.

Another aspect of attending is physical, through posture and proximity. When we are attending to someone, we position ourselves so as to receive as much of the message as possible. We turn our heads or bodies toward the person. Our body posture is open to receive the message, not closed to ward it off. We may lean toward the person with our upper torso or step closer to them. We may reach out with a hand to touch the arm or hand of the other person.

Auditory aspects of attending are more difficult to observe. They involve positioning ourselves so we can hear, nodding the head, and using facial expressions. Our expressions indicate that we hear or see the object of attention. We also provide feedback in short, "minimal" vocalizations: "Um huh!" "Oh!" "Yes!" "No" are examples of brief attention indicators. Auditory attention overlaps somewhat with physical attention and the next interpersonal skill, responding. Head nodding and facial expressions are physical indicators of listening. They are also responses, and along with minimal vocalizations, are a form of feedback.

Responding is also a supportive interaction. An individual has initiated some interaction and we respond to it. Responses are generally physical or verbal. Physical responses are facial, gestural, or postural, such as a raised eyebrow, a wave of the hand, or leaning slightly forward. Other physical responses include head nodding, folding or unfolding the arms, shuffling feet, and moving away from the person. Physical responses are often subtle, and we frequently forget to check our responses to see if they correspond to our intention.

Three aspects of verbal response are paraphrasing, acknowledging, and perception checking (Jones, 1980). Paraphrasing is the technique of restating the sender's message in your own words; for example, "You think (or feel) that _____," "Your position is _____," or "If you only could _____, it would be better." In paraphrasing, we do not simply repeat the message, we process it and describe what we are hearing. Paraphrasing can restate a message chronologically or by specific points or facts, but it does not add to or subtract from the sender's message. The process simply demonstrates to the sender what was received by the listener.

The skill of acknowledging requires simply that the listener give evidence of attending through eye contact, and positive and minimal vocalizations; there is no effort to paraphrase or interpret. Head nodding, facial expressions, and verbalizations such as "Oh," "Um huh," "Okay," "Yes, I see," are simple acknowledgements. They do not interrupt the message, but give evidence of attending and of active involvement in the dialogue.

In perception checking, the receiver restates the message and asks the sender if the message was correctly received. The receiver may interpret a message, seek agreement about its accuracy, or ask that it be repeated. The sender may also ask the listener to repeat the message, as when we ask children to repeat instructions to see if they have been accurately received. Examples of perception checks might include "Oh, you're upset by having to make up the work you missed"; "You say it's boring; is that because you can already do the problems?"; "Do you feel childish when you read from this book?" or "You seem happy, was your exhibit accepted for the fair?"

The skills of paraphrasing, acknowledging, and perception checking combine into a series of communications that express positive regard and valuing, and help clarify and improve interactions among children and between children and teachers.

The third supportive interaction skill is that of personalizing, of which the two aspects are personalizing your experiences and personalizing others' experiences. Since we are here emphasizing the supportive aspects of classroom environments, we will concentrate on the personal and positive effects of behavior. Gordon's (1974) "I message" is used to express one's position, feelings, or thoughts.

The "I message" usually takes this form: when (some behavior or outcome of the other person) happens, I feel (some feeling) because (my interpretation, or how I am affected). For example:

- "When I see your ceramic display at the bank, I feel good because I see that your work is recognized."
- "When I see you looking for a file in your desk while I'm talking to you, I feel miffed because I don't think you're giving me your full attention."
- "When I see you putting off assignments until the very last, I feel dismayed because the product may not reflect your best effort."

It is important to remember who "owns the problem." In "I messages," the speaker owns the feelings, and does not make judgments about the other person. The emphasis is on me, how I am affected, and how I react. They are my feelings. I am responsible for them, but here is how the event or behavior affects me. Again, no judgments or value statements are made.

Personalizing others' experiences means recognizing their feelings, accomplishments, and qualities. Positive "I messages" are one important skill; other skills are positive feedback, emphasizing the present, attending, and being courteous.

Positive feedback might be social recognition or acknowledgment of a contribution. The acknowledgment should be specific, honest, and supportive. Simply to look at a project and say "good job" is inadequate. Why is it a good job? Was it the color combinations, the precision, the difficulty of the task? Products should be critiqued but not criticized. An informative critique can be most rewarding. It says, "I cared enough to value your effort, I know that you wish to develop an important skill or ability." Positive feedback can be a pat on the back, a touch on the arm, a nod, or a step toward the person—or a standing ovation, public acclaim, an Academy Award, or a Pulitzer Prize. Feedback should be consistent with the level of performance, and should increase in power as the quality of the product or performance grows.

Emphasizing the present helps us to avoid dwelling on past, now unchangeable events, and forestalls predictions about the future. Staying with events that are happening now keeps the focus on how I am responding to you and what I am feeling right now. Bringing up the past only increases the intensity of negative situations.

Personalizing others' experiences involves attending and courtesy. Courtesy makes a value statement to others. Courteous behavior is positive, and values both the receiver and the sender. Courteous people express self-regard as well as positive regard for others.

The fourth interaction technique, initiating, is essentially defining a plan of action and setting it into motion. Initiating includes establishing a goal, defining the steps to achieve the goal, combining the steps into a series of events, proceeding through the events, and achieving the outcome.

Establishing the goal or goals requires numerous exchanges among teachers and students to answer questions such as:

- Who is or will be involved?
- What actions are needed?
- How should the actions be undertaken?
- Why is this important to the learner? (Carkhuff, Berenson, and Pierce, 1973)

Goals such as better attending, listening, or responding skills may be important to some children. Others may wish to improve "I messages" or the ability to personalize without imposing one's values on others.

The specified steps leading to the goal are sources of feedback to the children. Checking off each step as they complete it is evidence of their own personal growth. Others—teachers, parents, and fellow students—also provide feedback as interactions improve, because the experiences will be positive and more encouraging.

One simple approach to helping children become more responsive to each other is the "Compliment Box." When the children notice someone doing something worthy of recognition, they write the child's name and actions on a sheet of paper and drop it in the decorated box. At frequent intervals, daily or two or three times weekly, the teacher opens the box and reads the compliments.

Van Tassel-Baska (1983) emphasizes the counseling functions of teachers of the gifted in the early school years, particularly as to values clarification and modeling. Modeling the skills of supportive interaction is probably the most significant single method of personalizing the psychosocial environment of the classroom (see chapter 3). Modeling the behaviors of attending, positive responding, "I messages," problem ownership, and personalizing demonstrates the worth of the techniques and shows the children how to use them. Van Tassel-Baska (1983) also encourages bibliotherapy (Wolf and Penrod, 1980). *The Bookfinder*, Volumes I and II (Dreyer, 1977, 1981) is an excellent source of reading selections for ages two through fifteen.

Supportive environments emphasize personal responsibility, positive, supportive feedback, modeling, and supportive interaction techniques. Feedback is consistent with the quality of the product or performance—"I care about you and what you have just done, both are important."—but an individual's worth should not be confused with the worth of the performance or product.

Critical Issues in Evaluation

Some see evaluation as an opportunity to tell others about positive achievements. They consider the process of evaluation an opportunity for identifying points for making changes, a series of checkpoints along a route. Those who view evaluation positively seem far outnumbered, however, by those to whom evaluation sounds ominous. But the real purpose of evaluation is to guide change, and is an integral part of program implementation.

It is common to find that a project, program, or activity has been planned and implemented long before anyone raises the issue of evaluation. It is preferable to consider evaluation measures early in the planning stage, from three perspectives: purposes of evaluation, types of designs, and reporting results.

Purposes of Evaluation

The purposes of evaluation may be considered from two points of view: first, as it serves constituent and consumer groups, and second, as it reveals whether or not goals and objectives are being met.

Accountability has been a key word in education for the past several years. Those who "buy" education, that is, the consumers, have become increasingly resistant to upgrading their investment in the schools. As more and more programs compete for scarce dollars, and as educational decisions are forced by fiscal demands, programs that cannot demonstrate reasonable cost benefit ratios may have to be sacrificed. It is almost axiomatic that the last program to arrive is the first to go, and programs for the gifted and talented are often among the most recent additions in many school districts.

It is one thing to recognize and express the philosophical basis for programs for the gifted and talented, but quite another to convince taxpayers, school boards, and legislators that the programs are worthwhile and have a reasonable cost benefit ratio. Each school board must set priorities as to which educational opportunities it will offer within its budgetary limitations.

What is evaluation? From among several available definitions, we will use Brinkerhoff's: evaluation is "a function that determines the extent to which the program's standards have become manifest in reality . . . evaluation compares the actual performance of the program to the standards set for the program's operation" (Brinkerhoff, 1979, p. 355). Evaluation is the process of comparing actual program outcomes to the goals and objectives defined at the program's inception. Through evaluation, we attempt to answer the question, "Did we do what we set out to do?"

Corollary questions are, "If the program did not achieve the intended outcomes, why not?" and "What elements of the program were inappropriate?" The answers allow us to make necessary revisions and identify and retain effective elements.

One important subquestion relates to the appropriateness of the intended outcomes. "Were the intended outcomes achieved appropriate? Was this goal or set of goals worth spending the resources (teacher's and student's time and money) on?" Given the characteristics of the program, can we say this set of goals should be continued, revised, or deleted in future efforts?

When outcomes have not been achieved, we should examine the question of appropriateness. If raising creativity scores a certain number of points was an intended outcome that did not happen, both the criterion and the goal should be questioned. Was the criterion faulty, was the goal faulty, or was it some combination of the two? If the criterion was faulty, it should be revised; if the goal was faulty, it should be revised or discarded. If the fault lies in the combination of the goal and criterion, then a revision can be made. Examining the value of unmet expectations makes it possible to retain important elements and develop more reasonable goals and criteria.

There are more purposes to evaluation than answering the question, "Did the program do what it was intended?" Evaluation should give us information about the worth of the goals, where we should make revisions, and what elements we should drop from future efforts. Evaluation should also guide us in defining revisions.

Up to this point, we have focused on evaluations that tell about the outcomes of a program, project, or activity. Evaluations that detail the strengths and weaknesses of programs after completion are referred to as "summative" evaluations (Howell, Kaplan, & O'Connell, 1974). Evaluations can also pinpoint the need for change early in the course of ongoing efforts; continuous evaluations are sometimes called "formative" evaluations (Howell, Kaplan, & O'Connell, 1974), since they monitor the progress of the program. Continuous evaluation permits adjustments during the course of the program by addressing these questions:

- Are we doing what we intended to do?
- Is what we intended to do appropriate?
- If we are not doing what we intended to do, why not?
- What needs to be changed?

Continuous evaluation provides constant feedback for comparing progress with the original design, goals, and objectives. It also provides immediate feedback about the effects of any revisions to the original plans. The net effect of continuous evaluation is that we can quickly revise faulty elements rather than carrying them through to the end.

Evaluation Designs

Renzulli's work (Renzulli, 1975; Renzulli & Smith, 1979) over the past decade has guided many evaluation efforts, and his Key Features Evaluation System (Renzulli, 1975) has been widely used.

Evaluation designs, or systems, may be grouped as traditional (group) designs or as single system designs. Much of traditional evaluation has taken place from a group research design framework (Provus, 1971; Reynolds, 1966), in which important variables, such as reading and math achievement, are measured at the start of a program, and some treatment is implemented. Following the treatment, another measure (test) is administered, and initial and final test results (the pre/post design) are statistically compared. Based on the statistical comparisons, a judgment is made about the value of the treatment procedures. If the comparisons show significant differences, the treatment may be judged to be of value; in the absence of statistically significant differences, the treatment may be judged inappropriate or of no value.

Posttest only, control groups, and comparison groups with differing treatments are three possible designs (Campbell & Stanley, 1963). The traditional framework somewhat restrict the design of programs, the course of daily operation, and making final judgments about the outcomes of the treatment.

First, the pre/post design does not identify points where changes should be made during the course of the program. One must wait until the end of the program to judge total effect. Second, it is questionable to change procedures during the course of the program because the end treatment may be different from the initial treatment and the outcome may differ. If program changes are made, one must temper the conclusions accordingly.

Second, in ongoing classroom settings, it is extremely difficult to control all the important variables that influence the course of a program. Individual teacher interpretation and implementation of the program processes and techniques, alterations in schedules, and more subtle changes in the classroom environment put important restrictions on judging the worth of a program.

Traditional research or group designs emphasize the average, or mean, and the extent to which scores tend to cluster around the mean. Grouping of scores around the mean is referred to as *variability*, frequently expressed as the standard deviation.

Statistical procedures have become highly sophisticated over the years; nonetheless, comparisons are still based on means and indices of variability. Individual performance is judged on the basis of means and variability; that is, the standard for an individual's performance is based on the average performance of all the children to whom the measure was administered, or the norming population, as with intelligence and achievement tests.

Using average performance for comparison does have value in some circumstances. For example, one may want to know whether fourth graders learn to read better using one or another textbook. The question becomes "on the average, did a group of children achieve a higher reading score using textbook A or textbook B?'' This is a question of the general efficiency of one text over another, a reasonable, data-based solution to textbook selection.

Gifted and talented children are, however, by definition, above average. If an average is derived from the data obtained from gifted children, some will be above that average and others will be below it. To use that average as the standard puts some children at the disadvantage of lowered expectations for performance, while others will appear below average.

From an evaluation point of view, children who are below the standard will contribute positively to the final evaluation data. Those who are above average at the start of a program have little to gain, since they have already exceeded the standard. Their performance will increase little, if at all. In fact, if some of the children have obtained very high scores on the pretest, their posttest scores can change little in a positive way, and may decrease. Obviously, if a score of 100 percent were obtained on the pretest, the only change will be a decreased score on the posttest. Two designs that offer alternatives to the traditional are the Discrepancy Evaluation Model (Provus, 1971) and the Key Features System (Renzulli, 1975). Both, however, are in the group design category.

An alternative to group or traditional design is the single system (Bloom & Fischer, 1982) or single case (Herson & Barlow, 1976). The single system is less restrictive and includes reference to both the learner and the environment. We then have a ''learner/system'' rather than learner (see Bloom & Fischer, 1982, p. 8, who referred to *client/system* rather than client).

> Single system designs basically refer to the repeated collection of information on a *single system* over time. This ''system'' can be an individual, family, group, organization, community, or other collectivity. Each is treated as a single unit for this type of analysis . . . the *design* part of the term refers to a systematic plan for collection of data. (Bloom & Fischer, 1982, p. 8)

So far, we have seen little use of single system designs in gifted education. Just as factor analysis is a general title for numerous procedures, there are several single system designs, each of which has useful points, including:

- Withdrawal (with variations)
- Reversal (with variations)
- Multiple baseline (with variations)
- Multiple probe baseline
- Changing criterion
- Multielement

For each design, we must understand the term *baseline*. Baseline refers to the amount or rate of a behavior before introducing some instructional strategy or intervention and predicting what the behavior would be without intervention (Herson & Barlow, 1976). Baselines are the visual effects of graphing three or more data points or observations. Baselines tell us what is happening before we do anything to change a behavior. For example, in a verbal fluency task (giving different names for a multidimensional object), a child gave the following number of names during three separate observations:

Observation 1:   5
Observation 2:   6
Observation 3:   4

Graphically, the results would look like Figure 12–1.

There is no set number of observations for a baseline. Convention indicates that the baseline contain at least three data points, but the line should be stable. A stable baseline is consistent, but not necessarily flat. It *may* be flat, or it may show a gradual increase or decrease, or some consistent variability. The key is consistency. In fact, a flat baseline is less common than in increasing, decreasing, or variable baseline, since human behavior is more likely to be variable.

One must also understand the differences between statistical and educational significance. Statistical significance refers to a numerical expression of the probability that some phenomenon will or will not happen by chance alone. If nothing at all were done by way of intervention, would we obtain the same or similar results?

Educational significance, however, refers to the importance of the behavior change for the individual's effective functioning in educational settings. It is entirely possible, on some learning task, to have a statistically significant change with little educational significance. Statistics enable us to make statements about the effects of instruction in cases where changes are not obvious. If the effects of instruction are not obvious, effectiveness has probably not been demonstrated (Herson & Barlow, 1976).

There are several unique features of single system designs. They offer:

1   *Clear definitions of both the problem and the intervention.* The practitioner must be able to specify both the problem and the intervention in such a way and with such precision that two or more persons agree on the behavior under study.

2   *Systematic measurement.* Central to single system designs is the systematic collection of data. This necessitates finding ways and means of observing performance directly through actual observations in many settings. The emphasis is on systematic measurement of overt behaviors.

Figure 12–1   BASELINE DESIGN

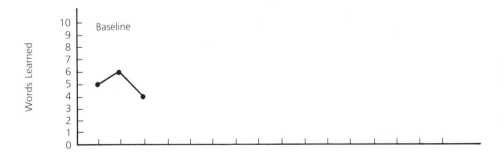

3   *Baseline.* Baseline information is gathered prior to any treatment or intervention.

4   *Design.* The design refers to the arrangements for collecting data. The data are collected in phases, each leading to "different expectations about the nature of the data to be collected" (Bloom & Fischer, 1982, p. 9).

5   *Analysis of data.* Data analysis relies heavily on the visual, as presented on graphs or charts. Statistical treatment is held to a minimum, if used at all (Bloom & Fischer, 1982).

6   *Systematic changes in experimental conditions.* Systematic changes in experimental conditions require that no more than one change be made to an intervention at a time, and that the effects of the changes be observed (Lovitt, 1970).

When considering the various single system designs, of which the reversal and withdrawal designs are the most powerful, one must remember the continuous observation and the systematic changes of experimental conditions requirements. Understanding the designs makes implementing them more meaningful.

The withdrawal design occurs when one takes a baseline, implements intervention, and then withdraws the experimental conditions. That is, the experimenter reinstates the baseline conditions (no treatment at all). For example, a child is sarcastic with his peers, thus causing arguments on the playground. The child says things like "good job" when a peer drops a ball or strikes out. The teacher decides to do something about it. First, she records the number of occurrences of sarcastic verbalizations to form a baseline. Then she puts the treatment into place; in this instance, she makes a positive comment to the child when he passes up opportunities for sarcasm. Intervention continues until there is a clear trend in the line connecting the data points. After the trend has been established, the teacher stops making positive comments but continues to observe the child's rate of sarcastic remarks. If the rate of sarcastic remarks returns to conditions similar to baseline, the teacher may tentatively conclude that reinforcement had a positive effect. The conclusion is tentative because it is difficult to control all classroom influences on the child. Repeating the treatment and observing the effects will add considerable strength to the conclusion if similar effects are observed. This design is also referred to as the A-B-A-B design (A = baseline, B = intervention). The learner/system includes the child, the teacher, the other children, and the playground, all of which are necessary prerequisites for the learner's sarcastic behavior.

The reversal design is similar in many ways to the withdrawal design, with one very important difference. During the second intervention phase, instead of withholding any treatment, the teacher would reinforce some behavior other than the behavior under treatment. In the example, instead of making positive comments about passed opportunities for sarcasm, the teacher could reinforce the child for giving compliments to other children.

For experimental purposes, the A-B-A-B design demonstrates the effects of an intervention. The treatment and its effects can be clearly examined and extraneous variables can be studied and/or eliminated systematically by extending the number of A and B phases.

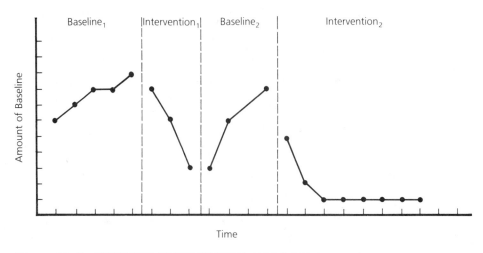

Figure 12-2 PROTOTYPE OF THE REVERSAL (ABAB) DESIGN

From J. O. Cooper, *Measuring Behavior*, 2nd ed. (Columbus, Ohio: Charles E. Merrill, 1981.) Reprinted with permission.

In educational and other settings, the A-B-A-B design has two major drawbacks. First, it makes little sense to reinstate an undesirable behavior. If the youngster in our example has greatly reduced the number of sarcastic statements he makes, we would not want him to return to his initial rate. Second, many educational behaviors do not return to baseline rate (Herson & Barlow, 1976). For example, once children learn multiplication facts, they do not forget them in a five- to eight-day baseline phase. The performance of gifted and talented children in most areas of educational concern fits this category.

The multiple baseline is proabably the most commonly used design in educational settings. The experimenter begins by collecting baseline data on three or more behaviors at the same time. After a stable baseline emerges, an instructional program is initiated on only one of the behaviors. Observations continue on all the identified behaviors, including the first treatment behavior. When the rate of the first behavior becomes stable, intervention is initiated for the second behavior. Now two behaviors are receiving treatment, and the third is still in baseline. Finally, the third behavior is treated. The strengths of this design are that a return to baseline conditions (reducing the rate of a desirable behavior) is not required, and that the relationship between instruction (cause) and the student's behavior (effect) is demonstrated by the effects of instruction on the baseline rate. If instruction has an effect, the intervention rate changes. Further, evidence of the effects of intervention are demonstrated as strategies are initiated on the untreated behaviors, strengthening the evidence of a cause and effect relationship.

Brown (1979) used this design to examine the effects of instruction on questioning skills of fourth grade gifted children, as we see in Figure 12-3. She considered IQ above 125 on a group test, reading class performance, and teacher recommendation. The purpose was to examine the effects of instruction, praise, and graphing on

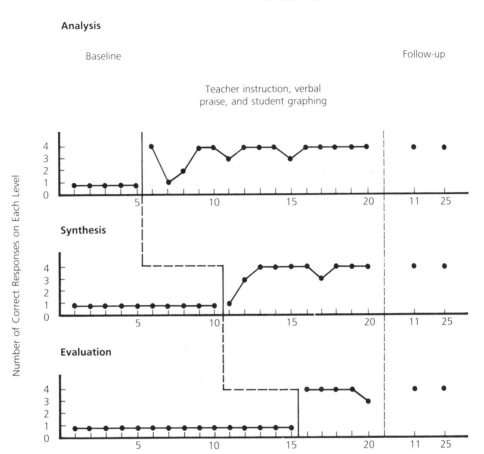

Figure 12-3 A MULTIPLE BASELINE DESIGN

From S. D. Brown, *Effects of Teacher Instruction and Positive Reinforcement on the Questioning Techniques of Gifted Students* (Columbus, Ohio: The Ohio State University, Unpublished Master's Thesis, 1979).

the children's abilities to write questions at the analysis, synthesis, and evaluation levels of Bloom's taxonomy (Bloom, 1956).

During the baseline phase, Brown asked the children to read a story and then write four questions each at the analysis, synthesis, and evaluation levels. The experimenter and another trained observer rated the questions. The subject whose data are shown in 12-3 wrote no such questions during baseline. After five days, Brown implemented a training program relating to analysis questions while baseline was continued for synthesis and evaluation. Following five days of instruction and observation on analysis questions, an instructional program was initiated for synthesis questions, while the baseline continued for evaluation. Five days later, instruction began for evaluation. The total study took 20 days. Follow-up checks, to assess generalization of questioning, were conducted 11 days and 25 days after the last day of instruction.

Examining the data in Figure 12–3, we can see a functional relationship (cause and effect) between the treatment (instruction, praise, and graphing) and the students' ability to write questions that meet the criteria for higher order thinking. Moving from "no questions" prior to instruction to "four questions" after instruction during each of three interventions is educationally significant for the student. The follow-up checks on the 11th and 25th days after instruction show that the levels of questioning were maintained for this student for a 25-day period.

The Brown study demonstrates one type of multiple baseline design, multiple baseline across behaviors. In this case, the behaviors were three types of questioning. Multiple baselines may also be across groups or across settings. Continuing with the Brown example, had the experimenter grouped the children into three groups and initiated instruction on one of the three levels of questioning for each group, one at a time, it would have been an "across groups" design. Had the experimenter initiated instruction in three separate locations, such as a classroom, a school library, and a study hall, and had instruction been sequential, it would have been an "across settings" design. Choice of design depends on its efficiency to examine the cause-effect relationship.

Another aspect of the multiple baseline design is the multiple probe. Instead of continuous observations during the baseline phase, the experimenter "probes" or tests for the behavior on several occasions. After intervention begins, however, observations are continuous. The multiple probe design reduces the necessity for daily observations and is particularly useful where there is little likelihood of the desired behavior before intervention (Cooper, 1981). The multiple probe design may be used across behaviors, groups, or settings.

Another single system strategy is the changing criterion design, illustrated in

Figure 12–4 PROTOTYPE OF THE CHANGING CRITERION DESIGN

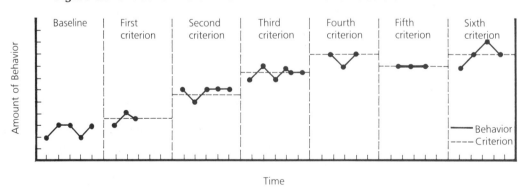

From J. O. Cooper, *Measuring Behavior*, 2nd ed. (Columbus, Ohio: Charles E. Merrill, 1981). Reprinted with permission.

Figure 12–4. This system is suitable for behaviors that can be increased in a stepwise manner, such as learning a foreign language vocabulary. We determine during baseline how many words a child learns during each daily study period, using whatever approach the child chooses. Taking the average rate of five baseline days, the child must reach or surpass that criterion by two words so as to be able to work on a class mural during the first criterion phase. During the second criterion phase, the rate increases by two (or four); the size of the increment depends on progress during the preceding phase. The phases can continue until some maximum is reached.

The changing criterion design is particularly useful for basic skill learning. It obviates the need to return to some baseline condition, since each phase serves as the baseline for the next phase and learning can continue, becoming more involved or demanding.

The final design, and the one considered appropriate for complex behaviors (Sulzer-Azaroff & Mayer, 1977), is the multielement design shown in Figure 12–5. O'Brien (1978) used the multielement design to examine the paired associate learning ratio of five gifted second graders when tasks were presented auditorily, visually, or kinesthetically. The sequence of auditory, visual, or kinesthetic instructional strategies was established randomly. Each day the children were given six trials to learn 10 stimulus-response pairs, and each day the mode of presentation was different. The strength of the design rests in allowing for comparison of more than one independent variable and sensitivity to rapid changes of learner behavior (Sulzer-Azaroff & Mayer, 1977).

By now, you may have detected two problems with single system research. First,

Figure 12–5 MULTIELEMENT DESIGN

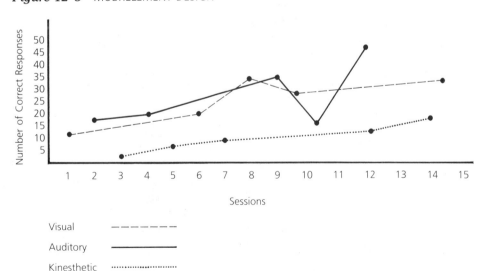

From D. E. O'Brien, *A Functional Analysis of the Learning Modalities of Gifted Children* (Columbus, Ohio: The Ohio State University, Unpublished Master's Thesis, 1978).

one may argue that the sample sizes may be too small to generalize to a population. Second, there appears to be no control, or comparison groups. Both points are correct, although they require some clarification.

As with any science, two basic issues in behavioral science are variability and generality of findings (Herson & Barlow, 1976, p. 34). Intersubject variability is a recognized human phenomenon. Large group designs assume that uncontrolled variables somehow sum to zero; that is, some individuals would exhibit more and others less of the variables. The uncontrolled variables would affect some individuals in one way, and others in another way, effectively canceling them. The "average" would be the individual upon whom the variables had no influence (Sidman, 1960). Single system designs do the opposite, highlighting the effects of intersubject variability and making it possible to isolate and examine the influences of the variables, thus adding precision to the study of human behavior.

Generality answers the questions: "To what extent can we generalize these findings to other subjects, settings, and/or conditions? Will the findings apply in my study? Are my students similar, and can we anticipate (assume) similar results?" Kerlinger (1973) mentions that we can control extraneous independent variables by randomizing. The more truly random the sample, however, the less relevant the findings will be for individuals (Herson & Barlow, 1977).

Randomization of groups and treatments presents a particular problem for studies of children or individuals who function in the top .01 percent of the population. Other variables, for example, age and areas of ability would further reduce the available population, and there may simply not be enough individuals to form a group to study.

The single system researcher's response to generality is through systematic replication. Using several studies of individuals with similar characteristics where treatment is also similar, one can make a case for the generality of findings across individuals, settings, or groups, depending, of course, on the research question. The outcome is several studies of $N = 1$, versus one study of $N = 10, 20, \ldots N$.

So far, we have treated group and single system designs as if there were a clear-cut dichotomy regarding their use. In practice, the evaluation question should control the design. To paraphrase Kerlinger (1973), one should design evaluation to answer evaluation questions.

Dershimer (1968) points out that evaluations help decision making depending upon how valuable the data are. He identifies five sources of data that vary in degree of sophistication and empirical deviation.

1 Folklore—any widely held but untested assumption about the relationship between an educational program and an educational outcome
2 Anecdotes—especially dramatic ones
3 Expert opinion or outside consultants
4 Descriptive data—describes current conditions
5 Research data—refers also to the methodologies (Dershimer, 1968, p. 12–13)

The levels of sophistication are important in the use and acquisition of data. It is not necessarily wrong to use "folklore," but one must know what it is and treat it accordingly. Dershimer (1968) goes on to point out that several sources of information are preferable. Renzulli (1975) and Van Tassell (1980) give numerous examples of instruments, and the work of Link and Kosecoff (1978) can be helpful in examining the processes of evaluation.

Van Tassell (1980) offers suggestions for evaluation. First, consider the timing of data collection. In particular, try to avoid the first and last weeks of the school year because of the organizational and administrative activities that go on.

Second, provide clear, written instructions for those who must gather the data. At least one inservice session per year should be devoted to data collection procedures (Van Tassell, 1980) to insure that they are consistent and the data well organized.

Instruments and formats of data collection should be efficient and effective. One should be able to gather sufficient data without taking too much of the teacher's instructional or planning time. Careful attention to form selection and/or development helps assure that the correct information will be collected and that those who provide the data will understand the importance of the task.

Clark (1979) and Van Tassel (1980) remind us that the results should be usable to laymen. Information should be condensed; charts and graphs will help convey the information concisely. A well-developed evaluation report is an important information and advocacy source for the public and other educators. Folklore and anecdotes are effective examples of what the program does; anecdotes can be quite dramatic, and therefore, influential, but should not be substituted for "hard data."

Selected Evaluation and Research Questions

At the heart of curricular decisions and the processes of differentiation are the questions of what to teach, when to teach it, how to teach it, and measuring the outcomes. The answers tell us what is special about programs for the gifted.

One of the most exciting events of recent years is the advent of the the microcomputer. The silicone chip and miniaturization have revamped the concept of instructional aids and teaching machines. It is not difficult to see how tabletop computers could be novel and motivating "electronic flashcards." For the gifted and talented, this is certainly useful at the lowest level. Research and demonstration are essential for maximizing the effectiveness of the technology in education, and the technology can itself aid the development and conduct of research. The interaction of mind and machine has all the earmarks of a "new frontier."

Understanding of gifted children's growth and development is far from complete. Socialization and learning studies would round out our knowledge of child development and enhance the foundations of educational practice during children's earliest years. Piaget's work and Terman's longitudinal approach would contribute to the methodological aspects of such studies.

During the school years, there are many possible avenues for investigations. The administrative costs of programs for the gifted and talented would give program planners a solid argument for research, along with the opposite question, "What is the cost of not providing special programs to the gifted?" (Gallagher, 1979, p. 13). This question, while much more difficult to resolve, should not be ignored. It goes to the center of philosophical and personal arguments for programming for the gifted and talented.

In addition to the costs of programming, the discourse between acceleration and enrichment proponents continues. Currently, most research points to acceleration, partly because the variables for study are well defined and the goals and objectives of acceleration programs are easy to identify and make public.

The acceleration-enrichment issue seems to be perennial. Stephens (1962) identified 10 points for which we needed answers:

1 What are the best methods for evaluating gifted students when they are placed in special groups?
2 What instructional and curricular activities actually occur in classes for the gifted?
3 The confusion between academic success and potential ability continues to prevail.
4 Are the educational needs of the highly gifted not within a program for gifted students of lesser ability?
5 What are the actual advantages of early identification of the gifted?
6 Follow-up studies are needed of students who are permitted to enter school early.
7 An evaluation of specific enrichment provisions is needed.
8 What costs are essential to a sound program for the gifted?
9 How special are programs for the academically gifted?
10 How should programs for the gifted be administered? (pp. 40–41)

These questions are equally germane today.

Possibly the most neglected area of research in gifted and talented education is that of learning. There is little research to draw upon for decision making, and what is available is often ignored. Investigation in certain areas would add substantially to the bases for both data and advocacy:

- What are the qualitative differences in learning that distinguish the gifted from their normal peers?
- What are the characteristics of the learning curves of the gifted?
- Do the learning curves of the gifted differ from those of normal and below average children?
- Do the gifted naturally acquire some key thought processes that distinguish their learning from the learning of average and below average children?
- What is the role of symbol system manipulation in the thinking of the gifted and talented?
- What is the role of the newer concepts of intelligence in curriculum planning for the gifted?
- Will the Kaufman Assessment Battery for Children be an appropriate instrument for measuring abilities of the gifted and talented?

Certainly, studies across the broad spectrum of giftedness are needed. Under conditions of inexhaustible resources, any study of quality would add to the knowledge base; however, we are economically limited. The most pressing studies must be undertaken at the outset, in the areas of career choices, creative processes, economics of education, educational strategies, growth and development, individualization processes, interaction of mind and machine, learning processes, socialization processes, and teacher qualification and training.

Summary

Throughout this book, we have emphasized the relationships among the characteristics of the gifted and talented and their educational, curricular, and instructional needs. In Part I, we examined the foundations of gifted education; in Part II, the essential concepts and instructional strategies in four basic content areas; and in Part III, educational extensions pertinent to the gifted and talented—microcomputers, career education, and creativity. In this chapter, we have addressed issues of implementation and evaluation. The justification for programs for the gifted must rest on sound educational policy across the spectrum of children the system serves. The gifted program can be either a natural extension of the regular curriculum or a source for curricular rejuvenation. The first is clearly preferable.

When planning to initiate a program, it is essential to define the population and the program that will be offered. The remaining issues evolve from these two points:

- Screening and identification
- Program offerings
- Program delivery models
- Teacher selection
- Evaluation of programs, students, and teachers

The program and the personnel interact with several "publics." Communicating with these publics is an essential activity of the program's teachers and coordinators. Each of the publics has unique information needs, and the best communications serve those needs by providing the most appropriate information in the most efficient way. One communication format does not serve all those who seek information.

The state education agency consultant for the gifted can serve as a valuable human resource for program implementation, because he oversees a group of programs across the state that operate under the same rules and regulations as your system. He is familiar with programs in areas that are similar to yours in social, cultural and economic characteristics. With this information, he can provide information that bears directly on your local needs and can explain state rules and regulations and describe possible funding sources. The consultant's services are available from the state at no expense to the district.

An essential feature of evaluation is communicating program effectiveness to school district officers and to the taxpayers, but the major purpose of evaluation is program involvement. It is essential to the ongoing processes of education (formative) and for making public the final outcomes of the program (summative). Evaluation can be conducted from a traditional point of view (group approach) or from the single system approach; the choice of strategy depends on the nature of the questions asked.

In the history of gifted education, some problems remain from one era to another. Success cannot be left to chance meetings of learners and facilitators, of creators and creative moments. The goal is to prepare for those moments.

References

Aliotti, N. C. Intelligence, handedness, and cerebral hemispheric preference in gifted adolescents. *Gifted Child Quarterly* 25 (1981): 36–41.

Barbe, W. B. Administrative aspects of gifted programs. In *Attention to the gifted—A decade later*. Edited by W. B. Barbe and T. M. Stephens. Columbus, Ohio: Ohio Department of Education, 1962.

Bishop, W. E. Characteristics of teachers judged successful by intellectually gifted, high achieving high school students. In *Psychology and education of the gifted*. 2nd ed. Edited by W. B. Barbe and J. S. Renzulli. New York: Irvington, 1975.

Bloom, B. S., ed. Taxonomy of educational objectives: The cognitive domain. New York: David McKay, 1956.

Bloom, M., and J. Fischer. *Evaluating practice: Guidelines for the accountable professional*. Englewood Cliffs, N. J.: Prentice-Hall, 1982.

Brinkerhoff, R. O. Evaluating full service special education programs. In *Instructional planning for exceptional children*. Edited by E. L. Meyen, G. A. Vergason, and R. J. Shelan. Denver: Love, 1979.

Brown, S. D. *Effects of teacher instruction and positive reinforcement on the questioning techniques of gifted students*. Unpublished Master's Thesis, The Ohio State University, 1979.

Campbell, D. T., and J. C. Stanley. *Experimental and quasi-experimental designs for research*. Chicago: Rand McNally, 1963.

Carkhuff, R. R., D. H. Berenson, and R. M. Pierce. *The skills of teaching: Interpersonal skills*. Amherst, Mass.: Human Resource Development Press, 1973.

Clark, B. *Growing up gifted*. Columbus, Ohio: Charles E. Merrill, 1979.

Cooper, J. O. *Measuring behavior*. 2nd ed. Columbus, Ohio: Charles E. Merrill, 1981.

Dreyer, S. S. *The Bookfinder: A guide to children's literature about needs and problems of youth aged 2–15*. Circle Pines, Minn.: American Guidance Service, 1977. (Vol. 2, 1981.)

Feldman, D. The mysterious case of extreme giftedness. In *The gifted and talented: Their education and development*. Seventy-eighth yearbook of the National Society for the Study of Education. Edited by A. H. Passow. Chicago: University of Chicago Press, 1979.

Fink, A., and J. Kosecoff. *An evaluation primer*. Beverly Hills, Calif.: Sage, 1978.

Fink, A., and J. Kosecoff. *An evaluation primer workbook: Practical exercises for education*. Beverly Hills, Calif.: Sage, 1978.

Fox, L. H. Programs for the gifted and talented: An overview. In *The gifted and the talented: Their education and development*. Seventy-eighth yearbook of the National Society for the Study of Education. Edited by A. H. Passow. Chicago: University of Chicago Press, 1979.

Gallagher, J. J. Issues in education for the gifted. In *The gifted and talented: Their education and development*. Seventy-eighth yearbook of the National Society for the Study of Education. Edited by A. H. Passow. Chicago: University of Chicago Press, 1979.

Gallagher, J. J. *Teaching the gifted child*. 2nd ed. Boston: Allyn and Bacon, 1975.

Galyean, B. C. The brain, intelligence, and education: Implications for gifted programs. *Roeper Review* 6 (1981): 6–9.

Gordon, T. *Teacher effectiveness training.* New York: Wyden, 1974.

Harlow, H. F. The formation of learning sets. *Psychological Review* 56 (1949): 51–56.

Herson, M., and D. H. Barlow. *Single-case experimental designs: Strategies for studying behavior change.* New York: Pergammon Press, 1976.

Howell, K. W., J. S. Kaplan, and C. Y. O'Connell. *Evaluating exceptional children: A task analysis approach.* Columbus, Ohio: Charles E. Merrill, 1979.

Jones, V. F. *Adolescents with behavior problems: Strategies for teaching, counseling, and parent involvement.* Boston: Allyn and Bacon, 1980.

Kaplan, S. N. *Providing programs for the gifted and talented: A handbook.* Ventura, Calif.: Office of the Ventura County Superintendent of Schools, 1974.

Karnes, F. A., and E. C. Collins. Teacher certification in the education of the gifted. *Journal for the Education of the Gifted* 4 (1981): 123–31.

Kerlinger, F. N. *Foundations of behavioral research.* 2nd ed. New York: Holt, Rinehart and Winston, 1973.

Lindsey, M. *Training teachers of the gifted and talented.* New York: Teachers College, Columbia University, 1980.

Lovitt, T. Behavior modification: The current scene. *Exceptional Children* 37 (1970): 85–91.

Maker, C. J. *Curriculum development for the gifted.* Rockville, Md.: Aspen, 1982.

Maker, C. J. *Training teachers for the gifted and talented: A comparison of models.* Reston, Va.: The Council for Exceptional Children, 1975.

O'Brien, D. E. *A functional analysis of the learning modalities of gifted children.* Unpublished Master's Thesis, The Ohio State University, 1978.

Pressey, S. L. Concerning the nature and nurture of genius. *Scientific Monthly* 80 (1955): 123–29.

Provus, M. M. *Discrepancy evaluation.* Berkeley, Calif.: McCutchen, 1971.

Renzulli, J. S. Identifying key features in programs for the gifted. In *Psychology and education of the gifted.* 2nd ed. Edited by W. B. Barbe and J. S. Renzulli. New York: Irvington, 1975.

Renzulli, J. S. *A guidebook for evaluating programs for the gifted and talented: Working draft.* Ventura, Calif.: Office of the Ventura County Superintendent of Schools, 1975.

Renzulli, J. S., and L. H. Smith. Issues and procedures in evaluating programs. In *The gifted and the talented: Their education and development.* Seventy-eighth yearbook of the National Society for the Study of Education: Part I. Edited by A. H. Passow. Chicago: University of Chicago Press, 1979.

Reynolds, M. C. A crisis in evaluation. *Exceptional Children* (1966): 585–92.

Rioux, J. W. Parents and educators—A forced or natural partnership? *The Directive Teacher* 1 (1978): 12.

Roeper Review 4 (1981).

Seeley, K., R. Jenkins, and H. Hultgren. Professional standards for training programs in gifted education. *Journal for the education of the gifted* 4 (1981): 165–76.

Shane, H. G. The silicon age and education. *Phi Beta Kappa* 63 (1982): 303–8.

Sidman, M. *Tactics of scientific research: Evaluating experimental data in psychology.* New York: Basic Books, 1960.

Stanley, J. C. Rationale of the study of mathematically precocious youth (SMPY) during its first five years of promoting educational acceleration. In *The gifted and creative: a fifty-year perspective*. Edited by J. C. Stanley, W. C. George, and C. H. Solano. Baltimore, Md.: Johns Hopkins University, 1977.

Stephens, T. M. *A look at Ohio's gifted: Status study*. Columbus, Ohio: Ohio Department of Education, 1962.

Sulzer-Azaroff, B., and G. R. Mayer. *Applying behavior analysis techniques with children and youth*. New York: Holt, Rinehart and Winston, 1977.

Swassing, R. H. Parameters of the classroom environment for the beginning teacher. *Education and training of the mentally retarded* 9 (1974): 89–92.

Van Tassel-Baska, J. The teacher as counselor for the gifted. *Teaching Exceptional Children* 15 (1983): 145–50.

Van Tassel, J. Evaluation of gifted programs. In *Administration handbook on designing programs for the gifted and talented*, no. 215. Edited by J. B. Jordan and J. A. Grossi. Reston, Va.: The Council for Exceptional Children, 1980.

Winkel, L. W., and W. M. Mathews. Computer equity comes of age. *Phi Delta Kappa* 63 (1982): 314–15.

Wirick, M. E. The teacher of academically gifted children. In *Attention to the gifted—A decade later*. Edited by W. B. Barbe and T. M. Stephens. Columbus, Ohio: Ohio Department of Education, 1962.

Wolf, S., and D. Penrod. Bibliotherapy: A classroom approach to sensitive problems. *G/C/T* 15 (1980): 53–54.

Zettel, J. J. Gifted and talented education over a half decade of change. *Journal for the Education of the Gifted* 3 (1979): 14–37.

Appendix A

Selected Educational Reference Sources

T hese references have been compiled with the understanding that children will
have ready access to abridged and unabridged dictionaries and to thesauruses
as prerequisite classroom resources. Some of these items are specific and others
are relatively common; all are reasonably available from libraries.

Biographies

Biography Index: A Quarterly Index to Biographical Material in Books and Magazines. Bronx, N.Y.: H. W. Wilson.

Debus, A. G., ed. *World Who's Who in Science: A Biographical Dictionary of Notable Scientists from Antiquity to the Present.* Chicago: A. N. Marquis, 1968.

Jaques Cattell Press, ed. *American Men and Women of Science: Social and Behavioral Sciences.* 13th ed. New York: R. R. Bowker, 1978.

Locher, F. C., ed. *Contemporary Authors.* Vol. 1–96, Index and Revision Series. Detroit, Mich.: Gale Research.

Moritz, C., ed. *Current Biography Yearbook, 1981.* 42nd ed. New York: H. W. Wilson, 1981.

The Blue Book: Leaders of the English-speaking World: Vol. 1, A–K; Vol. 2, L–Z. Detroit, Mich.: Gale Research, 1976.

The International Who's Who: 1980–81. 44th ed. London: Europa Publications, 1980.

Who's Who in America: 1980–1981. 41st ed. 2 vols. Chicago, Ill.: Marquis Who's Who, 1980.

Children's Books and Magazines

Cavanagh, G. *Subject Index to Children's Magazines.* 34 vols. Madison, Wisc.: 1982.

Children's books in print: 1981–82. Author Index, Title Index, Illustrator Index. New York: R. R. Bowker, 1980.

Dreyer, S. S. *The Bookfinder. Volume 2: Annotations of Books Published 1975 through 1978: A Guide to Children's Literature about the Needs and Problems of Youth Aged 2–15.* Circle Pines, Minn.: American Guidance Service, 1981.

Dreyer, S. S. *The Bookfinder: A Guide to Children's Literature about the Needs and Problems of Youth.* Circle Pines, Minn.: American Guidance Service, 1977.

Ireland, N. O. *Index to Fairy Tales, 1949–1972: Including Folklore, Legends and Myths in Collections.* Westwood, Mass.: F. W. Faxon, 1973.

Kirkpatrick, D. L., ed. *Twentieth-century Children's Writers.* New York: St. Martin's Press, 1978.

Subject Guide to Children's Books in Print: 1981–82. New York: R. R. Bowker, 1981.

Colleges and Universities

Aitken, D. J., ed. *International Handbook of Universities and Other Institutions of Higher Education.* 8th ed. New York: International Association of Universities, 1981.

Barron's Educational Series. *Barron's Guide to the Best, Most Popular, and Most Exciting Colleges*. Woodbury, N.Y.: Barron's Educational Series, 1981.

International Handbook of Universities and Other Institutions of Higher Education. 8th ed. New York: DeGruyer, 1981.

Lovejoy, C. E. *Lovejoy's College Guide*. New York: Simon and Schuster, 1981.

The College Blue Book. 18th ed. 5 vols. Narrative Descriptions; Tabular Data; Degrees Offered by College and Subject; Scholarships, Fellowships, Grants, and Loans; Occupational Education. New York: Macmillan, 1981.

UNESCO. *Study Abroad: International Scholarships, International Courses*. Vol. 23. Paris, France: United Nations Educational Scientific and Cultural Organization, 1980.

Dictionaries

Asimov, A. *Words of Science and the History Behind Them*. New York: New American Library, 1959.

Bauer, A., comp. *The Hawthorn Dictionary of Pseudonyms*. New York: Hawthorn, 1971.

Concise Dictionary of American Biography. New York: Scribner's, 1964.

Crosbie, J. S. *Crosbie's Dictionary of Puns*. New York: Harmony Books, 1977.

Lapedes, D. A., ed. *McGraw-Hill Dictionary of Scientific and Technical Terms*. 2nd ed. New York: McGraw-Hill, 1978.

Malone, D., ed. *Dictionary of American Biography*. New York: Scribner's, 1934.

Partridge, E. *A Dictionary of Clichés*. 5th ed. Boston: Routledge and Kegan Paul, 1978.

Sippl, C. J., & R. J. Sippl. *Computer Dictionary and Handbook*. 3rd ed. Indianapolis, Ind.: Howard W. Sams, 1980.

Spencer, D. D. *The Illustrated Computer Dictionary*. 2nd ed. Columbus, Ohio: Charles E. Merrill, 1983.

Urdang, L., ed. *The Random House Basic Dictionary of Synonyms and Antonyms*. New York: Random House, 1960.

Wood, C., ed. *The Complete Rhyming Dictionary*. Garden City, N.Y.: Doubleday, 1939.

Miscellaneous

Books in Series. 3rd ed. 4 vols. Original reprinted, in-print, and out-of-print books, published or distributed in the U.S. in popular, scholarly, and professional series. New York: R. R. Bowker, 1980.

Keenan, L. K., ed. *Educators' Index of Free Materials*. 90th ed., annotated. Randolf, Wisc.: Educators' Progress Service, 1981.

Kuhlthau, C. C. *School Librarian's Grade-by-Grade Activities Program: A Complete Sequential Skills Plan for Grades K–8*. West Nyack, N.Y.: Center for Applied Research in Education, 1981.

Nehmer, K. S., ed., *Educators' Grade Guide to Free Teaching Aids*. 27th ed. Randolph, Wisc.: Educators' Progress Service, 1981.

Spencer, D. D. *Introduction to Information Processing*. 3rd ed. Columbus, Ohio: Charles E. Merrill, 1981.

Tests in Microfiche. Princeton, N.J.: Educational Testing Service, 1975.

Quotations

Bartlett, J. *Bartlett's Familiar Quotations*. 15th and 125th anniv. ed. Boston: Little, Brown, 1980.

Evans, B. *Dictionary of Quotations*. New York: Delacorte Press, 1968.

Kenin, R., & J. Wintle, eds. *The Dictionary of Biographical Quotation of British and American Subjects*. New York: Alfred A. Knopf, 1978.

Magill, F. N., ed. *Magill's Quotations in Context*. New York: Harper and Row, 1965.

Partnow, E., ed. *The Quotable Woman: An Encyclopedia of Useful Quotations Indexed by Subject and Author, 1800–on*, Garden City, N.Y.: Anchor Books, 1978.

References

Carruth, G., ed. *The Encyclopedia of American Facts and Dates*. 6th ed. New York: Thomas Y. Crowell, 1972.

Ethridge, J. M., ed. *The Directory of Directories*. 1st ed. Detroit, Mich.: Information Enterprises, 1980.

Harzfeld, L. A. *Periodical Indexes in the Social Sciences and Humanities: A Subject Guide*. Metuchen, N.J.: The Scarecrow Press, 1978.

Information Please: Almanac, Atlas, and Yearbook 1982. 36th ed. New York: Simon and Schuster, 1981.

Library of Congress: Subject Headings. 9th ed. 2 vols. Washington, D.C.: Library of Congress, 1980.

McGraw-Hill Yearbook of Science and Technology, 1962––. New York: McGraw-Hill.

Monthly Catalog of United States Government Publications. Washington, D.C.: U.S. Government Printing Office. (12 issues annually, serials supplement, semiannual index and cumulative index in addition to the catalog).

Moore, P. *The Rand McNally New Concise Atlas of the Universe*. New York: Rand McNally, 1978.

Office of the Federal Register. *The United States Government Manual: 1981/82*. Washington, D.C.: U.S. Government Printing Office, 1981.

Scull, R. A. *A Bibliography of United States Government Bibliographies: 1974–1976*. Ann Arbor, Mich.: Pierian Press, 1979.

Sheehy, E. P., R. G. Keckeissen, & E. McIlvaine. *Guide to Reference Books*. Chicago: American Library Association, 1976.

The World Almanac & Book of Facts 1982. New York: Newspaper Enterprise Association, 1982.

Walsh, S. P. *Anglo-American General Encyclopedias: A Historical Bibliography: 1703–1967*. New York: R. R. Bowker, 1968.

Writing for Publication

A Manual of Style. 12th ed., rev. Chicago: The University of Chicago Press, 1969.

American Psychological Association. *Publication Manual*. 2nd ed. Washington, D.C.: American Psychological Association, 1974.

Strunk, W., Jr., & E. B. White. *The Elements of Style*. 3rd ed. New York: Macmillan, 1979.

Van Til, W. *Writing for Professional Publication*. Boston: Allyn and Bacon, 1981.

Appendix B

Journals for Parents and Professionals

G/C/T[1]. P.O. Box 66654, Mobile, AL   36660. Five issues per year.

Gifted Child Quarterly[2]. National Association for Gifted Children. 217 Gregory Drive, Hot Springs, AZ   71901. Published quarterly.

Gifted Children Newsletter[1]. Gifted and Talented Publications, Inc. RD1, Box 128–A, Egg Harbor Road, Sewell, NJ. Twelve issues per year.

Journal for the Education of the Gifted[2]. The Association for the Gifted, The Council for Exceptional Children. 1920 Association Drive, Reston, VA   22091. Published quarterly.

News for Parents from IRA[1]. International Reading Association. 800 Barksdale Road, P.O. Box 8139, Newark, DE   19711. Published three times per year; available only from IRA members, such as reading specialists, school librarians, reading instructors.

Parents Choice[1]. Parents Choice Foundation. P.O. Box 185, Waban, MA   02168. Published quarterly.

Roeper Review[2]. Roeper City and Country School. 2190 N. Woodward, Bloomfield Hills, MI   48013. Published quarterly.

---

[1]Contains information and activities for home and school.

---

[2]Somewhat research-oriented.

Index

DATE DUE			
FEB 22 1988			
OCT 4 1988			
FEB 28 1987			
APR 11 1987			
MAY 02 1987			